MY ESCAPE TO TERRA AUSTRALIS

AND MY PART IN THE NEAR DEATH OF THE AUSTRALIAN WOOL INDUSTRY

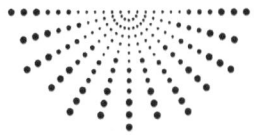

GERRY DUBBIN

Copyright 2017 © Gerry Dubbin. All rights reserved.

No part of this book may be copied, reproduced, adapted, stored in a retrieval system, communicated or transmitted in any form or by any means without prior written permission from the author. All inquiries should be made to the author via the web address below.

Contact the author: gerrydub@gmail.com

ISBNs
978-0-9945986-2-2 (pbk)
978-0-9945986-3-9 (e-book)

ALSO BY GERRY DUBBIN

Smoke and Mirrors, Egos and Illusions: The World of Real Estate

Conversations with a Small Boy: A Lad of Leeds

Liner Cruising: Your Guide to Travels Afloat

Why Should I Learn to Speak Italian? The Strugglers' Guide to "La Bella Lingua"

*This book is dedicated to my wife and fellow escapee from Britain in
1959, Rochelle Mavis,
my children, Simon, Philip, Erica and Léon,
my grandchildren to date, Chelsea, Emma, Jack, Joshua and Zara,
and my great-grandchildren to date, Harley, Ava and Ellie.*

To my children

In spite of all I'm here arrived,
With skills but few, have still survived.
But joy, that's different, I have so much,
With you my life's gained the Midas touch.
I've watched you grow, I've watched you thrive,
I've watched you stumble when tears they arrived.
I've watched when you slept, though you tried to persist,
My heart was full as I watched you trying to resist.
When sometimes I look back trying to understand,
What brought me to this beautiful land.
I know one thing and that is so true,
I'm glad that I arrived here,
and became part of you.
Love always
Dad

CONTENTS

Prologue	1
1. Introduction to a dream	33
2. Defender of the realm	59
3. Back to Leeds and seeking work	125
4. £10 Pommie migrant	141
5. Terra Australis	201
6. Hello, Melbourne	231
7. A challenging new role	283
8. Australian wool	321
9. Appointment to New York	383
10. Return to Melbourne – 1978	435
11. Transitions	453
Epilogue	489
References	513

PROLOGUE

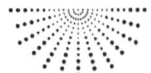

The history of modern Australia is a relatively short one, particularly that part which emerged following the 1788 landing of British sailors, a group of convicted felons and their guards on what then was then regarded by Europeans as an unexplored, virgin landmass located to the south of the equator.

That landing at the latter end of the 18th century and the 200-odd years since has been written about and analysed extensively by a whole host of learned historians and scholars. What most managed to provide, however, was a record covering but the blinking of an eye regarding Australia's complete history of settlement.

The account that follows spans an even narrower time slot, a period that commenced during the days of my boyhood; a time when I first learned of a distant and mysterious land, located somewhere to the south of the equator. Those first glimpses of Australia created in that then young boy the desire one day to follow in the footsteps of early European explorers about whom he had read about and learned of in school.

That interest in the land known also as 'Down Under', ultimately resulted not many years later in my arrival there and later experiences as a citizen – a young man who arrived midway through the 20th century as a British migrant.

The nigh-on 60 years since then have formed a relatively short part of Australia's history. Those years have since proved to be a period during which Australia's population, status, and fortunes have expanded and diversified in ways few among its earlier native-born[1] sons and daughters could have dreamed.

That period also represents the greater part of a more personal story, one that traces the years from my boyhood during the Second World War, through to the early decades of the 21st century.

During my boyhood, I recall having the desire to know more about a then distant, mysterious and fascinating continent. My fascination was for a land located on what at the time appeared to be the underside of the world. Australia during my youth at least appeared to be so, particularly as it was described on our school maps and globes of the world. That early learning continued to grow until it developed into a force that led me away from my home in the northern English city of Leeds, to seek a new life in the land that had stimulated my boyish dreams.

A substantial part of my business life in Australia was spent working within and among three of Australia's then major industries – wool growing, wool textiles and apparel manufacturing. Each of these industries at the time of my arrival in Australia had formed an important pillar of the country's economy, each employing large numbers among its working population.

I was then what some had been known to refer to as a 'new chum'[2] – an immigrant from Britain, just arrived in Sydney during May 1959. Alongside the need to meld into a different kind of life in a new, very different country, my business life became deeply involved with two of the three industries noted earlier, both soon to experience drastic government imposed changes.

Australia's earlier predominantly British population, which for many years had remained much the same regarding its composition and nature, was not only changing at the time but also diversifying rapidly. Changes, many of them profound, were occurring as the result of an influx of continental European, British and Irish immigrants. In later years, they would be followed by many more arrivals from South East Asia, Africa and the Middle East.

Notes

1. Native-born: belonging by birth

2. New Chum: A colloquial title, in use earlier particularly in Queensland to describe a recent immigrant arrival in Australia, especially from the British Isles. Source: Merriam-Webster dictionary.

A PERIOD OF CHANGE, 1960–2000

One of Australia's more notable industrial challenges arrived in the form of a crippling financial jolt that overtook the Australian wool industry in 1991.

It is fair to suggest that wool's long and chequered history, followed by the industry's devastating collapse in 1991, may well be regarded by some Australians today, as past history, something that occurred a long time ago of little enduring interest or having much meaning to the Australia of today. That line of thinking is understandable, as time and events have moved on since, and a much-changed country now finds itself facing a very different set of issues and challenges affecting its political, social and economic future.

Parallel to the wool industry's woes during the early 1990s, apparel and textile production were at the time also about to experience similar emerging challenges. Different to those confronting wool, these came about in the form of earlier import tariff protections that were being withdrawn from Australia's textile, clothing and footwear (TCF) industries.

These changes had a profound effect on Australia's future as a manufacturer, as they precipitated the rapid loss of a hitherto broadly based manufacturing sector of the country's economy, as the federal government continued to pursue the unrealistic ideal of what it continued to refer to as a 'level playing field'. Whatever was expected to occur on this idealistic and imaginary field proved to be something of an illusion, more so whenever the term was used by a procession of Australia's trade ministers when trying to explain issues relating to international trade negotiations with which they were at the time involved.

The changes here were the lowering of import tariffs and increases to quotas on textiles, apparel, and footwear imports that the then government promised, "These changes will have the effect of lowering costs to Australian consumers at retail level."

The promise of lower costs, like so many other similar promises made by governments over the years since, failed to eventuate. Australian consumers found little difference in the prices they were still having to pay at the retail level for goods now being imported – consumer goods that earlier were being manufactured in Australia.

What in fact occurred following an overly rapid reduction of protection for the local textile and apparel industries was that most of the savings realised as a result of the now reduced tariff regime and increased textile and apparel imports, were being retained by importers and local retailers. Its other effect – local jobs being exported overseas on a massive scale.

The loss of protection for Australia's TCF industries during the late 20th and early 21st centuries heralded similar losses coupled to some lost opportunities just over two decades later. In the latter case, this came about as the result of the recent Australian government decision to remove financial support for the continuation of motor vehicle production in Australia.

In the case of textiles and apparel, instead of opting for a narrower range of tariff adjustments to be phased in over a longer period, a strategy that would have enabled some form of equilibrium to be maintained, the reductions made were overly rapid, too widespread and too deep. This offered little hope for local manufacturers to be able to gradually adjust their activities, product selection and range, thus enabling them to retain at least a reasonably significant level of economically viable local production, and skills gained over many years.

Not much thought was given before the drastic series of changes that followed. What for instance was going to replace the many thousands of lost jobs and many decades of experience, specialised expertise and product differentiation that became lost, as these once major industries fell all too rapidly into decline?

The subsequent loss of local textile and apparel production has its echoes today with the recent decision to close down the last of Australia's three remaining manufacturers of motor vehicles: Ford, General Motors and Toyota. The now closure of all three manufacturing plants, preceded much earlier by the closure of Mitsubishi's Adelaide production plant, is once again being accompanied by a currently reported 40,000 direct job losses, plus much more when it came to losses of jobs from among component manufacturers supplying them. These losses were due in no small part to the earlier and overly abrupt Abbott federal government's decision to withdraw its financial and underlying policy support for the continuation of at least some form of vehicle construction being maintained in Australia.

This poorly thought-through, politically expedient option, as with that which had applied to the earlier TCF industries, while failing to plan more effectively much earlier and prior to the event, is already resulting in hardship for many of those unable to find worthwhile alternative work options.

The point to be made here is that with more considered, creative thinking and planning on the part of successive government ministers and their advisers, there was no reason why Australian textile, apparel, and vehicle manufacturing industries should have been placed in the position of being consigned to the industrial scrapheap!

All three industries could have continued to operate, thus maintaining a strategic and useful component of Australia's industrial base, perhaps in moderated form. All three industries should have been retained as a part of the country's changing industrial mix.

All three of the vehicle production plant closures noted above had been discussed earlier. Ford, General Motors and Toyota had provided notices of their plans to quit Australia. The final die was cast however, once the then Abbott government had indicated, through its then-treasurer, Joe Hockey, that there would be no further financial support forthcoming. Since then, there continues to be little evidence of an Australian federal government plan designed to cope effectively with or at the very least deflect such a massive hit to vehicle manufacturing and related employment in the two states mainly affected – Victoria and South Australia.

While on the subject of industry choices, the recent government decision to build 12 new submarines in South Australia, to be delivered sometime during the next 20 years, requires further explanation – at the very least! Why 12 submarines, and why the French proposal that apparently involves the total redesign of an atomic powered submarine model, to one using diesel propulsion? On what basis was that decision and the precise number of submarines projected, made? The question as to what the political situation will be like in ten years' time, let alone 20 or 30 years hence, bears much deeper analysis and questioning, much more than was apparent prior to the Australian government coming to its questionable decision.

A further question relating to the proposed submarine project came to light with the revelation that the highly specialised technical skills and equipment required to build high-tech submarines are currently non-existent within Australia. It also appears that the government, in making what can only be described as a political decision to build the planned submarines in Adelaide, refused to accept expert engineering advice that a better proposition would be to opt for a current diesel powered German or Japanese model? Either of the latter two options was expected to result in providing more flexibility and savings in cost and time.

The Australian government was reported recently as claiming that their plans to build submarines and ships locally would involve a permanent workforce of around 5,000 and the use about 10,000 tonnes of Australian steel each year. Some choice it would appear, as it is also relevant to point out that the vehicle manufacturing industry they so recently chose to abandon, employed more than 25,000 directly and used in the region of 50,000 tonnes of steel. In addition, the industry had managed to export around A$3 billion worth of cars and engines.

Even accepting the limitation of maintaining three plants manufacturing vehicles in Australia, it surely would have been in the country's long-term strategic interests to maintain the level of skills and vehicle building expertise built up over a generation, while maintaining an important part of its industrial base.

Like earlier losses in textile and clothing production, there is as yet little to be seen of an innovative replacement or retraining programme being implemented, following such a massive shock to now unemployed workers, suppliers of components and other services to the now demised motor vehicle building industry.

The story surrounding the Australian wool industry is different to textiles, apparel, shipbuilding and motor vehicle manufacturing, in that its near demise was the result of self-inflicted wounds – in other words, its collapse came about as a result of a poorly executed form of suicide!

The same may also be included here when discussing the case of Australian coal-based power generation – yet another industry, a long-used method of base-power generation, regarded by many as obsolescent and in need of replacement by a preponderance of renewable energy generating and storage systems.

With growing worldwide emphasis moving in search of more efficient ways to transition from fossil-based energy production entering a new era, how best to organise a smooth transition to less polluting ways of generating base-load power has become a contentious and divisive national issue. The impasse thus created, threatens to hold back Australia's ongoing development, if what appears to be the current federal government's ambivalence toward renewable sources of energy results in Australia missing out on potential business development opportunities.

The subject of global warming is currently being debated with less in the way of scientific and economics-based objectivity to be observed on the ultra-right side of an increasingly divided national parliament. The same may also be said about how the subject is affecting discussion across the country on issues surrounding forecasts of the expected rate of global warming, and projections of its effects across a future world.

Things change with time. Witness the apparently unbridled desire and enthusiasm shown recently by both the current federal and Queensland governments in support of a proposed loan or grant of close to A$1 billion in support of the Adani (Indian) mining company, in support of its projected export-oriented coal mine in Queensland's Galilee Basin. No bank, local or international at the time of writing, seems to be falling over itself to offer Adani the funding required?

Just a few years back the Abbott government declined to provide funds in the region of $200 million to keep either of General Motors, Ford or Toyota operating in Australia. The funds proposed in support of the Adani mine proposal, referred to earlier, are apparently needed to build a railway line to service their proposed but questionably viable mine, a project that at no time would employ more workers, short- or long-term, than would a vehicle manufacturer. Such a development, if allowed to go ahead, is also projected to add to the threat of increased pollution and that of long-term damage to Australia's Great Barrier Reef.

The question here: Why the eagerness to provide taxpayer funded financial support to yet another, much larger coal mining project, one more of many already operating, particularly one that appears unable to obtain financial support from any other supplier of finance?

Little has emerged to date to indicate that a creative and well-thought-through plan for the country's ongoing development and prosperity has managed to fight its way through the fog of verbal abuse and emotionally charged argument currently being thrown back and forth across Australia's federal parliament.

The government, Opposition, and cross-bench political parties these days all appear more intent on protecting their futures and less of those of the country and constituents they have been placed there to serve. It seems that federal politicians these days are more interested in trading blows and wedging each other in a fight that has more to do with their gaining, wielding or holding onto power, than long-term planning aimed at meeting the many future challenges facing Australia and its increasingly politically disengaged citizens.

Recent governments of all persuasions have succeeded in frittering away most of the less than adequate financial and social benefits that should have accrued to the nation as a result of the recent minerals boom. What benefits did accrue, failed to be thoughtfully used and invested in a long-term programme aimed at creating the wealth and financial security that could have been made to work better for its citizens and the country's future?

As a result, following the end of what has been referred to by some as a golden era for Australian mining, the country is now in danger of being left with a large number of large, ugly holes in the ground, growing pollution, a growing annual budget deficit and a host of other issues that threaten to undermine any hopes for bringing the country's books back into equilibrium, anytime soon.

Despite the oft-lauded creativity of Australia's universities, business and financial sector, the country, now having arrived in 2017, is less able to plan its future much further ahead than the relatively short 36-month span currently allotted to the rotation of our federal governments.

But that is now…

Back in the years following the ending of the Second World War in August 1945, Australia's vision was then being directed well into the future with regard to its long-term plans for new infrastructure projects, industrial development and the need for rapid population growth. The then Australian federal government, looking into its crystal ball at the time, saw the need to populate or perish – in an economic sense at least. And populate the country did.

As a result, the period 1946 to 1960 saw a 39.8% increase in Australia's population, from under 7.5 million following the ending of the Second World War.[1] Most was due to immigration, mainly from Great Britain and continental Europe. The influx of many thousands of migrants each year over the period, despite some opposition from Australia's more conservative, backward-looking politicians and some older, native-born citizens, served to boost and assist in the expansion of Australia's human resources, manufacturing industries and commerce.

Just two young people among those on-board one of the regular shiploads of immigrants to arrive in Australia from Britain in 1959, were my wife and I, aged just 24 and 22 at the time.

Notes

1. Australia's Population at the end of the period 1939–45 was 7,430.2 million. It had increased at end-period 1946–60 to 10,391.9 million. Source: Australian Bureau of Statistics 24/06/1996, 4102.0 Australian Social Trends.

£10 POMMIE MIGRANTS

The arrival of a young 24-year-old to Sydney during May 1959, was not an occasion to be remembered or recorded – at least by other than my wife, our parents, families and friends back in England. We were just two of many thousands of other hopeful British immigrants who, some 171 years following the landing in Botany Bay on January 24th 1788 of the so-named 'First Fleet', had decided to undertake the long journey to the other side of the world, in search of a better life.

In the vernacular of the time, we were a couple of '10 quid Pommie migrants', a very small part of a much larger group of people, many who saw themselves more in terms of 'escapees' –people in search of a better life, far away from a then uncertain and austerity cloaked post-war Britain.

The Britain we were leaving was locked in the midst of a period of enforced austerity, following a debilitating war. Britain was also experiencing the gradual loss of its status as a leading world power.

The country's economy was continuing to stagnate, with many basic foods and consumer goods still being rationed or subjected to an earlier post-war-time supply regime. The general mood of many of its citizens, particularly among Britain's working classes at the time, was one of gloom. The mood of the nation was bordering on discontent, critical both of the government and power elites seen to be running it.

The term 'latecomers' is perhaps a more accurate description to use here when referring to the many new arrivals in Australia at the time. Bear in mind that the original inhabitants of the vast continent on which we had decided to make our home had already been living there continuously for well in excess of 50,000 years!

A SMALL SLICE OF HISTORY

The story behind our decision to leave Britain in favour of a future in a relatively unknown country on the other side of the world, and the way of life that we found following our arrival there, provides an interesting comparison, particularly when comparing today's Australia with how it was just 60 years ago.

Sixty years doesn't sound much in terms of Earth's history, even when contrasted with the relatively short period that has passed since 1788. The 60-odd years involved however, still serve to highlight a period of massive and far-reaching changes that have affected every aspect of Australian life.

Our experiences as new Australians contrasts even more when measured against the experiences of today's indigenous inheritors of the lands of their forebears. People that for many thousands of years and countless continuing generations had successfully found ways to live on the world's driest, and in some locations, harshest continent. Those earlier ancient arrivals to the Australian continent had long ago found ways to live in concert with the land, its flora, fauna and natural resources. They had also learned to live in relative harmony – prior that is to the eventual invasion and takeover of their homelands, by pale-coloured strangers, who arrived uninvited (illegally many would argue) from across the world.

1788 was the year that saw the start of that invasion by aggressive white intruders. Britons, Scots, Irish and other foreign nationals, who for some time following their arrival and having once successfully established their presence on the land, precariously at first, a few years following James Cook's first landing on the continent a few years earlier in 1770.

Subsequent years saw the launching of brutal, often murderous attacks – land grabs and still later attempts to Christianise the native people that the early European settlers found living there.

History records that the British government at the time had seized the opportunity provided by Cook's landing on what they chose to regard as a newly discovered and empty continent, to establish settlements at various locations on its south-eastern and western fringes, and the island later named as Tasmania. The British saw the 'discovery' of Terra Australis as an opportunity to establish these locations as a repository for numbers of what, during the early process of colonisation, were regarded as the dregs of British society.

The wretched human cargos carried to Australia on-board subsequent ships were mainly criminals, outcasts and political troublemakers – in other words, most were unfortunates, defined as such through the filter of 18th century British justice.

Since that time, Australia's history has served mainly to present a lopsided and inadequate picture, a record written almost exclusively from the perspective of the white settlers who arrived and settled, over the two and a half centuries since.

The official history of Australia represents but a very small part of a much longer story, a factor that has served to distort a largely unwritten portion of the continent's full story of settlement.[1]

Before progressing further, a couple of important points regarding the history of Australia need stating – the record set straight:

Captain James Cook did not discover Australia. The continent had already been discovered and settled many thousands of years earlier. He did, however, locate and chart the east coast in 1770, along which he navigated and surveyed with a degree of accuracy few navigators since have been capable of achieving.

The history of Australia and the sequence of events from which modern Australia emerged, can be divided into three distinct stages:

- The initial discovery and settlement by indigenous people to whom we now refer under the general title of Aboriginal and Torres Strait Islanders. Local groups of these people were the ones first encountered by James Cook in 1770, Arthur Phillip in 1788, in addition to an assortment of other recorded visitors prior to that time.
- The second phase of Australia's history can be traced from the time of Phillip's landing in 1788 through the

subsequent centuries of British settlement, up to the time of the Second World War years, 1939–1945. During this phase, the British established the Westminster system of government, the country's laws and set up the social structures that formed the basis from which modern-day Australia developed and the process and rules by which the country is governed today evolved.

- The third phase of Australia's history can be said to have commenced with the mass migration of British, Continental European and an almost continuous stream of other immigrants from the four corners of the world, the bulk of whom arrived and settled following the ending of the 1939–1945 war. Those who came during this final phase provided the catalyst that served to accelerate the massive changes that resulted in the emergence of the Australia of today – a democratic country at peace with itself – the most diversified multi-ethnic society in the modern world.

The country the world has come to know, resulted following white settlement and dominance of land that later became known as New South Wales, a colony among others that followed, all later brought together in the form of the Commonwealth of Australia.

The land, its subsequent development and settlement continued to be governed, administered and subsequently written about mainly by white reporters and white historians.[2] Most early writings traced an initially long, drawn-out series of skirmishes with, and in some cases the regular massacre of scattered bands of native residents. All this took place alongside the continuing early development, white domination and continued settlement of the country.

That battle continues, thankfully not in the sense of a one-sided conflict of arms. Rather, the battles these days are being waged in Australia's courts, legislatures and more recently – in the hearts and minds of a growing number of non-Aboriginal Australian citizens, some working in direct support of the descendants of the continent's original owners. The fight today has become one in support of a current indigenous generation's continuing struggle for recognition of their ancestors' original ownership, and through that fact – recognition of them as the legitimate descendants of the 'first people' of the land we know today as Australia.

As we approach the third decade of the 21st century, there is a growing trend developing among non-Aboriginal Australians, for today's Aboriginal descendants to be regarded and treated by Australia's federal, state and territory governments in a way more respectful, than hitherto has been the case.

The original inhabitants of the Australian continent since the enforced possession of their lands by the invading British were regularly denied possession of nearly all the lands on which both they and their ancestors had lived and husbanded for thousands of years. Their descendants today continue to be denied full recognition of that fact and that of their ancestors' rightful claim to being Australia's original owners.

Notes

1. For further information on the 'discovery', settlement and subsequent history of Australia, see the writings of a number of different historians. Add to this list the recent book by George Megalogenis title "Australia's Second Chance", published in 2015 by Penguin Books.

2. See also "Talking to My Country" a book by Stan Grant, a Wiradjuri man. The book is published by HarperCollins. Stan Grant was the winner of a Walkley award for his coverage of Aboriginal affairs.

TERRA NULLIUS

Since the Australian continent was first settled by Europeans, the history and politics of a country that since has become known as one of the world's most desirable places in which to live has been chronicled, discussed and argued over by many.

The first landing by James Cook was followed later by a ceremony claiming the land for the British Crown, at the time under the rule of

King George III. It was enacted by a small group of alien visitors, upon a small beach in the south of a landmass that in January 1788 was then regarded by the British government as '*terra nullius*'.[1]

That landing and subsequent claim by Britain to the rest of what was later found to be a great island continent was made without much concern for, discussion with or reference to the land's prior occupants.

These were people, themselves regarded by the small contingent of white sailors who first landed there, as ignorant prehistoric savages. Their way of life did not conform to the way European communities functioned, they were also regarded as lesser forms of humanity and thus unworthy of any legal claim to the land's prior ownership.

On January 1st 1901, the British parliament enacted legislation that resulted in the binding together of the then six Australian Crown colonies into a Commonwealth of Australia. The country emerged from this federation as a constitutional monarchy under the British Crown, the bringing together of six states and two territories that has now become a modern, thriving and diversified population in the region of 24 million.[2]

Notes

1. Terra Nullius – This Latin phrase describes territory/land that belongs to no one.

2. Australia's population 2016: 24,348.6 million. Source ABS.

A SLEEPING GIANT

Meanwhile, back in early world history, that then sleeping continent had remained officially undiscovered and unclaimed, at least by Europeans.

European thinkers dating as far back as the 5th century had conjectured that the then well-known landmasses covering planet Earth's northern hemisphere, had to be balanced in some way by equivalent lands to the south. It followed, therefore, in the thinking of the time, that somewhere among the then vast uncharted regions lying to the south of the equator, a large tract of land or group of islands must also exist—lands yet to be discovered, 'antipodes' to which they gave the title 'Terra Australis Incognita' (unknown southern land).

That large, then unknown tract of land turned out to be a continent. In fact, it eventually became apparent when fully explored, that it was an unbroken expanse of land, greater in size than the whole of Europe! To use the terminology of the eighteenth century, perhaps it could also be acceptable today to refer to Australia as a modern-day 'Terra Australis Cognitus' – in other words a 'well-known southern land', as such it has been included as part of the title of this book.

Travelling to Terra Australis by sea serves also to define me, the central character of what follows, as a mid-20th-century-style boat person.

LIKE TRAVELLING TO THE MOON

Britain at the time of my leaving during 1959 was a country still struggling to come to grips with vastly diminished wealth, global power and prestige. Australia, on the other hand, was still a country that my ageing grandmother, herself a migrant to Britain in her younger days, described getting there as being like travelling to the Moon.

To folk of her generation, such a way of thinking was understandable. The thought in those days of even travelling the 190-odd miles south from their home in Leeds to the British capital London was far enough to dissuade all but a few, affluent and outward-looking citizens from undertaking such a long, then arduous trip.

To most living in and around the industrial suburbs of Leeds and other northern British cities during the 1950s, one of the few occasions on which most had attempted to travel in any direction far away from their homes, was during the first (so-called 'Great') war and recently ended Second World War.

The latter of these two major conflicts was a six-year-long period of chaos and death. A period that saw the British population fighting for its very life both at home and in some far-flung overseas land-war theatres. Many were also being called to the sea, to serve in Britain's fighting Royal and Merchant Navies.

While Australians had also suffered during the war years, the country was yet to acquire the baggage and established practices that usually come with a long, turbulent history. Britain on the other hand, then regarded by many native-born Australians at the time as the Mother Country, continued to suffer from the results of a long, debilitating war, the loss of a large part of its treasury and earlier world standing as a dominant, globe-spanning power.

Australia too had suffered human losses and injury to many among its then relatively small population. These were men and women who had been called to arms, to defend its existence, as well as that of Britain's.

The Australia of the late 1940s and 1950s, not so very long since a part of Britain's globe-circling colonial empire, was at the time feeling the urgent need to increase its population. To do so, with preference given to white British and European immigrants, the then Australian federal government was offering an attractive financial package to new arrivals, people who were able to meet what at the time were reasonably simple requirements. To the financial incentives offered at the time, one must also add the attractive vision of a new, potentially fulfilling life in a distant but reasonably secure part of the world.

Australia, to compare my grandmothers' analogy, was a place on Earth much closer than the Moon – just a mere 12,000 odd sea miles from this young migrant's Yorkshire home.

A YORKSHIRE LAD

This Yorkshire lad and many other British migrants, once having decided to take a chance by voyaging across the world in search of adventure or a new, hopefully better life – could not have picked a better country for our destination.

Few of the Britons among us could claim to have been treated like foreigners once having landed in Australia, certainly not in the sense of terms like 'refugees' or the foreshortened Australian version, 'refos'. This was a description, among others, often used by many native-born Australians at the time when referring to the many thousands of Europeans and other nationalities then flooding into their relatively empty country. Most of these newcomers were people intent on moving as far away as possible from the shattered remnants, post-war chaos and still lingering dangers and other difficulties still to be found in their European homelands.

We British immigrants were not to be compared with today's intending seekers of sanctuary in Australia, many today continuing to be branded by successive federal governments as 'illegal boat people'. Many of these people are still today being treated like criminals while being brutally imprisoned on islands to the country's north.

At the time of writing, the term 'illegal boat people' is still being used by the current federal government as a reason for denying the most basic of human rights to a whole group of current day refugees seeking sanctuary and a new life in Australia. Such a denial it seems is mainly due to their arrival at or near our shores in small boats and other precarious conveyances, usually as a result of them having become involved with people smugglers to facilitate their hoped-for entry to Australia.

The majority of those continuing to seek sanctuary in Australia are known to have left peril and danger in their own homelands. They take their chances wherever they can, arriving with hope in small boats on or near Australia's shores, mainly on islands and reefs to the north of the continent. Many subsequently have been turned away, or interned for long periods in detention camps located on tropical islands to Australia's north – New Guinea's Manus Island and Nauru in particular.

Many of these people and their children are at the time of writing still being treated appallingly in conditions that some observers have described as being comparable to those found in some of Germany's internment (concentration) camps during the Second World War. While such a stark description may well be somewhat over-stated, the manner in which refugees confined in New Guinea and Nauru continue to be handled and treated by the Australian government is well below the international standards agreed to by Australia many years earlier.

In contrast, it is also true to say that most migrants that came from Britain during the 1950s were not primarily seeking to escape from the devastation and still rampant chaos of a terrible war, a situation that continued to affect most of those still living in continental Europe during the late 1940s and early 1950s.

Unlike many of the immigrants arriving in Australia from post-war Europe, we British migrants were to find ourselves being welcomed with open arms by a government that referred to us in more kindly terms like 'Assisted British migrants'. We were regarded as people from the Mother Country, now seeking to join the happy few former British native-born colonials already resident in Australia.

Following our arrival in Australia, we British immigrants received little in the way of preferential treatment or ongoing financial support once having arrived. While our travel was being subsidised by the Australian government, so was that of other non-British immigrants.

Having settled in Melbourne, an important part of my life's work in Australia, the thread around which much of this record is provided, found me working in two then creative, virile and expanding industries – wool-based textiles and apparel manufacturing. These were closely followed by a near-decade working on behalf of the Australian wool industry during eight years that found me embroiled within Australian wool's fight against the inroads being carved into its traditional markets by competing synthetic fibres.

The worldwide market for apparel fibres was changing, at a time when both the wool and local textile and apparel manufacturing industries, together with many thousands of workers employed by them in centres far and wide across the country, were beginning to experience the trauma of federal government policy-induced decline. The part I played during a critical stage of that decline, and the disaster that overtook the Australian wool industry, forms an important and informative part of this account of the times.

My involvement with Australian wool during what turned out to be the most critical and tragic period of its long history is described in detail, commencing in Part 8.

Important note:
What follows is not intended to be a dry, academic thesis discussing the rise and fall of three, then key Australian industries.

While their story and near loss to Australia was and remains important from a historical and economic standpoint, those events will appear only to illustrate various events and side issues, in support of the book's main narrative.

Some people today may question the relevance of a period of Australian commercial history that has already been documented and analysed many times over. The question as to why, after nearly 30 years since it happened, will the views of just one employee of the then Australian Wool Corporation be of any interest, let alone assist in resurrecting a now vastly reduced former key Australian industry that came close to self-destruction during the last decade of the 20th century?

While some may question the dedication of three parts of this book to a period of Australia's contemporary industrial history that few today will even remember or have read about, there are at least three strong reasons for doing so:

For one thing, the period forms an important and detailed part of contemporary Australian history – and for another, I had a front seat to most of what occurred at the time.

A third reason could well be that what happened then has relevance to some of the more pressing problems Australia continues to face today.

Having worked on behalf of the wool, textile and apparel manufacturing industries throughout the latter part of the 20th century, I experienced it as being a period during which questionable leadership and poor decision-making on the part of some among Australia's then political and wool industry leaders prevailed, the latter group being mainly responsible for the wool industry's near demise.

The disaster that eventually hit Australian woolgrowers in 1991 was followed by the near decimation of textiles and apparel manufacturing across Australia. Both these happenings and their dire consequences for manufacturing across the whole country provided lessons that should have been well noted by later federal and state governments.

What occurred during the last decades of the 20th century and the early years of the current one has, unfortunately, failed to be learned by Australia's national leaders.

Painful lessons that should have been learned during the latter end of the last century ought to have led to better longer-term planning and creative, outward-looking policies being developed. They weren't, with the result that opportunities that could have ensured the ongoing financial health and economic future of the country, were lost.

It is therefore unfortunate, that since then and into the 2nd decade of the 21st century, Australian federal governments of all persuasions have failed to plan for much more than the three-year period of their reign in government. Three recent federal governments have failed even to run their full three-year time span!

Myopic and overly politicised policy-making has become the new norm, a situation that has many among today's increasingly exasperated Australian voting public wringing their hands in despair of the country ever getting back to financial equilibrium. Unfortunately, this trend looks like continuing for some time yet.

Few occupying the federal government's front bench in the current federal parliament have shown the leadership qualities or capacity to come to some form of mutual accommodation with other parties represented there. They seem to have little time in which to think about much of real consequence to the future of the country, other perhaps than how to retain, exert or get themselves back into power at the next election.

A LACK OF LEADERSHIP

The lack of foresight that resulted in the tragedy that befell wool, and later the textile and apparel industries during the late 1990s and early 2000s, has continued to be repeated in some other industries, if not directly, then in a similar or related way, detrimental to Australia and Australians. Just to note a few examples:

- Successive federal governments' inability to gain the maximum benefits that should have accrued to the people of Australia, as a result of the recent boom in iron ore and coal mining and gas extraction.

- Mega billions of dollars were and are still being accrued by individuals and companies, most majority foreign- owned, involved with the mining and sale of Australia's non-renewable resources. But where did all the income generated go? And what has the country got to show for all the millions of tonnes of coal, iron ore and cubic metres of gas that have been dug up or pumped, nearly all of which continue to be exported, irrespective of the country's ongoing needs?

- Why didn't the federal government act promptly, more innovatively and creatively, before the loss of the range of skills and expertise already gained over the years, well before the recent closing down of not one, but all three automobile manufacturing operations? And why is Australia now left without a well-thought-through alternative, longer-term action plan, initiated toward the possibility of retaining at least something from the wreckage left in the wake of these major closedowns, with which to set up replacement projects aimed at the continuation of an innovative manufacturing base into the future?

- Why couldn't Australia use the vehicle manufacturing facilities still in place as the basis for a new era of automobile construction by encouraging and supporting the design and manufacture of a new breed of electric vehicles, less dependent of the use of fossil fuels? Surely from within our people, we can find the vision, drive and technical expertise with which to design and produce such vehicles, together with their supporting energy storage battery systems?

- Why, in a mineral and solar-energy rich country like Australia, have we witnessed the loss of so many opportunities to turn Australia into one of the world's leading developers and innovators in the fields of solar and

related low-carbon-based industries and storage battery development?
- And on another currently important issue – Why didn't the then government think to reserve sufficient of Australia's natural gas for local industrial and domestic users' needs, prior to allowing the companies involved to satisfy overseas customers' needs as their first priority – at reported prices much lower than those being charged for local gas users? This was an oversight that has resulted in Australian domestic and industrial consumers of Australian produced gas having to pay considerably more for their gas than foreign domestic importers and users of the same gas. How could this happen?

The lack of any form of government acumen, at the start of the then so-called minerals boom, now has the current prime minister scrambling to devise a policy restricting the export of gas. Such action is now being proposed, belatedly, in the vain hope of ensuring sufficient Australian gas continues to be available, at a price lower than the 'gouged' prices Australian consumers are currently finding themselves having to pay.

There are other examples that could be included here, but the foregoing should suffice to illustrate the point. Australian governments have consistently let slip too many opportunities over the past three decades, during which they should have learned better, more innovative and forward-looking ways to defend Australia's economic interests.

Our current prime minister has often spoken of the need for Australia to become an innovative and creative country. Unfortunately, his words have proved to be just that – nice sounding words but empty rhetoric! As a result, creativity and innovation, at least when applied to creating and manufacturing, has faltered. Apart from digging out and shipping tonnes and tonnes of minerals, liquefied gas, some beef, wheat, wool and a steadily reducing list of manufactures overseas, successive federal governments have lacked a quality often described locally as 'nous' – the creative use of which could have resulted in Australia regaining and holding onto the position it once held – a successful, forward-looking society, with a financial position well in the black.

Just taking the case of minerals and gas exploitation: Following the mega-billions of dollars in profits being made by a few local individuals and their connections with foreign entities, Australia has failed dismally, to learn something from other countries, for example Norway and its carefully planned policies relating to the extraction and sale of its natural resources.

The Norwegian government earlier recognised and was able to shrewdly and successfully negotiate the best return for its people from oil search and the mining of its non-replaceable mineral assets. Norway, in contrast to Australia over the years, also managed to put in place and maintain, policies that have resulted in the setting aside of sufficient of its energy and other resources to cover its own future needs. Also, its government has been able, over the years, to plan and manage the careful investment of income from the exploitation of all the country's natural and other resources.

Norway, as a result, has become the envy of the world, at least in terms of its capacity to fund education, social and other community services, pensions etc., from royalties received and other income via a sovereign fund currently being reported by various sources to be in the region of US$800 billion.[1] The returns thus achieved have been used to set Norway up in a strong financial position.

Australia in contrast, while endowed with an abundance of natural and mineral resources, including dairy, livestock and a strong sector of agricultural-based production, continues to stagger along with increasing budget deficits, together with an inefficient and inequitable taxation system, while lacking an adequate range of social services, infrastructure and other national services needed to keep pace with an increasing population.

Australia's much larger size places it in a situation somewhat different and more challenging to that of a smaller country like Norway, particularly when it comes to issues of transportation and infrastructure development requirements. Even accepting the difference between Australia and Norway, years of indifferent preparation and creative forward planning have resulted in a country that continues to struggle in its efforts to cope with the long-term needs and aspirations of its people.

The current Australian government and opposition parties all the while continue to bicker and quibble at the edges about the best way to bring the country's accounts back into balance, while at the same time the country's economy continues to descend further and further into the red.

Notes

1. Norway Economy 2017. Source: 2017 CIA World Factbook and other sources.

RISE OF THE SHOCK JOCKS

Another element that continues to infect Australia's body politic is the growth of a group of unelected, often loud, raucous, mainly ultra-right-wing television, radio and press-based 'shock jocks'. These people, having emerged from their ideological caves over some recent years, are a group of highly vocal and opinionated individuals who seek to define themselves as being the only true owners of wisdom, ethics and political judgment.

This relatively recent rising of sometimes-extreme foghorn- like commentary and calls for their unelected but loud and demanding voices to be heard and acted upon, is occurring with increasing regularity. They seem to emerge from their caves whenever anything not meeting their narrowly based view of the world happens to be debated, or arises from various discussions taking place among the community. Usually this means anything currently being discussed or debated in the federal parliament or reported/discussed on what they usually term as 'lefty' media – meaning media different to that owned by their fellow travellers – sponsors, media owners and one or two politicians preferred, supported and endorsed by them.

A usually favourite shock jock target is the ABC, Australia's independent national broadcaster.

This trend has added an often-toxic element to the policy debate, its development and implementation across Australia, making it increasingly difficult to progress the cause of clear thinking and considered decision-making among the national parliament's elected representatives. Too often some of those among the federal government's ministers constantly feel the need to be looking over their shoulders, often defensive and too ready at times to acquiesce with some of those shouting the loudest.

It has also become a sometimes distressing and disturbing sight to witness the current political scene wherein one or two members of Australia's national parliament, perhaps as a result of them having earlier fallen from grace or ousted from leadership positions by their political party. They appear more than happy to lead and encourage the shock jock chorus, as they push their own far right views onto a population that has become tired of hearing their constant bleating against nearly everything the elected government of the day is endeavouring to deliver.

AUSTRALIA AND WOOL

History will show that the rapid and disastrous collapse suffered by the Australian wool growing industry during the 1990s, did not come about solely as a result of competition from synthetic fibres. The disaster that occurred in 1991 was self-inflicted, the result of a number of years of poor, unrealistic decision- making among its leaders – and a procession of irresponsible federal government ministers.

The industry's ultimate collapse came about as a result of a succession of failures of judgment by its own leaders – not forgetting the continued costly maintenance of two top-heavy, inefficient, and overly expensive organisations: the Australian Wool Corporation and the International Wool Secretariat.

Those running the industry were highly respected and honoured industry leaders. They included national politicians and others having some involvement with wool growing or an industry having a close connection to wool. These were people who continued, in spite of all the compelling evidence around them, to operate with their heads embedded (metaphorically) in the sand. They were people who, to use an analogy, drove ever onward with their foot firmly pushing the accelerator to the floor. The ultimate act of their stewardship, unfortunately, was to drive the industry over a cliff!

The tragic and abrupt decline of the Australian wool industry occurred at a time when it should have been still possible to maintain wool's position as a major apparel fibre. What occurred as a result proved equally disastrous for many others who in the past had relied on wool.

Following the arrival of synthetics onto the textile fibre market, Australian wool's share of a rapidly expanding world market for apparel fibres was never expected to be able to maintain the same level of market dominance it had enjoyed since the earlier days of a fledgling nation. There was no real reason however, why wool could not have continued to compete much more effectively than eventuated.

AN INTERESTING STORY

The story of Australian wool is a long and interesting one, worthy of repeating a little of it here.

Apart from the fact that wool had played a major role in the growth of Australia, also for much of my business life, its unique story traced the growth of a nation and its people, as both expanded and prospered from small beginnings during the last decade of the 18th century.

As the woolgrowing industry grew, so did the growth and advance of Australia's national economy. As such, it is considered worthy of more than just a cursory reference here. It is also interesting to note that despite the failures of the past, wool growing in Australia has since managed to stagger on into the 21st century, although in a much-diminished state.

The fact that this is occurring, in spite of years during which the sale of wool has languished, tells us that even today there continues to be a continuing consumer liking and preference for apparel and other products made from, or containing Australian wool. Demand that is, provided the right products could continue to be developed, presented and creatively promoted, at the right time and in the right places.

Australia's growth and development during its early years came about following the success of two industries. Both were based on working the land. They were oceans apart when it came to their respective activities – gold mining one, wool growing the other. The latter was based on the back of a small animal, the Merino sheep, the wool shorn from its back and the extensive range of down-the-line industries that later developed, based upon the sublime fibre it produced.

The Australian wool growing industry flourished for well over 150 years. It then declined to a point during the 1990s when it virtually collapsed in upon itself. The ensuing disaster cost the Australian economy, its citizens, individual farmers and Australian wool's international customers dearly. It was also an event that reverberated around the world's textile and apparel markets, as the market for wool collapsed.[1]

The story of Australian wool, like the settlement of Australia by white newcomers to the country, can be accurately traced nearly all the way back to the early 1790s, not many years following the landing of the so-called 'First Fleet' in 1788 under the command of Captain Arthur Phillip.

Uniquely, a large part of Australia's growth for many years following the 1788 landing became built around the Merino sheep. A four-legged legend upon whose back the prosperity of a still maturing nation was said to ride – even as late as the 1940s and early years of the 1950s.

In 1794, John Macarthur was said to have begun his first experiments aimed at improving the growth and quality of wool on the few sheep he had imported to his property at Elizabeth Farm, Parramatta, in the then-nascent colony of New South Wales. By crossing hair-bearing Bengal ewes sourced from India, with Irish wool rams, a few of which he had imported, he had hoped to produce fine wool on his farm in that fledgling new territory.

Later, Macarthur acquired further breeding stock, some in the form of Merino ewes and rams, the precursors of which he had sourced from Spain. Macarthur and another local farmer, Samuel Marsden, both later purchased more Merino rams and ewes, the feedstock from which many of Australia's fine wool flocks of today eventually emerged.

During the 1940s, as a schoolboy growing up some 12,000 miles away across the globe to the northwest, in the Yorkshire city of Leeds, I learned at an early age of the close connection between Australian wool and the English county of Yorkshire. Another indication of the close association with wool in that part of the world was the inclusion of what could be described as the form of a Merino sheep in the Leeds city coat of arms.

Leeds, Bradford, Huddersfield and other northern British cities were among Britain's major industrial centres, the emphasis in Yorkshire, in particular, centring on wool textile production, and in the case of Leeds a burgeoning apparel manufacturing industry based mainly on wool textiles.

The growth of apparel manufacturing in Britain, in particular around Leeds, had expanded dramatically following the influx of many thousands of immigrants, a large proportion of them being Jewish refugees. These in the main were people who had fled Russia and its Czarist dominated Baltic States during the early years of the 20th century.

Grandparents on both sides of my family were but a few of many thousands of people who, around the turn of the 20th century had made their perilous escape to sanctuary in Britain and other Western democracies. Most of those arriving on Britain's east coast did so with little or nothing in the way of personal possessions. They travelled onboard trading or animal transporting ships of all shapes and sizes, from various ports along the Baltic's eastern coast.

Desperate refugees all, they also could be described as 'boat people', as they made good their escapes from deadly, violent pogroms and other religious and government motivated attacks that they had been constantly subjected to in their then Russian dominated homelands.

This kind of treatment had occurred during most of the 18th and 19th centuries, in and among the many shtetls (small villages) and townships spread across Czarist Russia and its then western territories. In my grandparents' case on both sides of my family, their birthplaces had been in the Baltic state of Lithuania.

It can be said, therefore, that even as a young boy, my life and that of most of my extended family and many of my friends, had been closely related to Australian wool and the industries that wool supported downstream. In my family's case, most of the only work available to them at the time was on the fringes of an industry then known in Britain as the 'tailoring trade'.

On leaving school in 1950 at the age of 15, I found myself employed as a tailor's improver – a role best described as a young learner of the tailor's craft. This was a trade in which past members of my family had been involved for generations back in Lithuania.

Attitudes of the day during the 1940s and 1950s Britain had virtually predetermined my entry into the tailoring trade. It is noteworthy here to record, that at the time opportunities to try myself in a number of other trades and professions were virtually barred, even though my desire from being a young boy was to become a writer of some kind, perhaps working as a cadet on one or other of the local daily newspapers.

This unofficial barring from work in commercial establishments like banks, major newspapers some retailers and similar organisations, was due to my family's religious beliefs. Strange that it may seem today, the situation facing me on leaving school in the Britain of the 1950s was, for my family and many others like us, an everyday reality. There existed at the time an active yet unstated and unofficial bar to followers of the Jewish faith entering certain professions and trades. A bar to Jews even applied at one or two of the more upmarket tailoring establishments in Leeds. This I found to be the case, when at the age of 16, following my application for a position with what referred to itself as a firm of Gentleman's Outfitters, a company trading as Messrs Charles C. Whitelock.

Following an extensive interview and having passed a required hand and machine sewing test, my mother and I were both turned away by the manager, along with the bald assertion: "We do not employ people of the Jewish faith at this establishment!" The then trauma, later anger and resentment at being treated like a less than second rate citizen aside, this was the first and I am pleased to say, only time, that I have personally experienced such treatment.

Although that example of religious bias occurred many years ago, I still clearly recall the exact words of that callous rejection, and the anger I felt at the time having to stand there and listen to such a confidence-shattering rejection. Worse still for a sixteen- year-old, I had to witness my mother's tears on being dealt with and spoken to in such a brutal fashion.

Many years since that early rejection and following over 200 years of development since the first arrivals of British convicts, early settlers and many thousands of other immigrants and sanctuary seekers to Australia, I find myself recoiling, angry, disillusioned and shocked at the kind of rhetoric and treatment being directed by Australian government ministers, toward many of today's genuine refugees trying to enter Australia. Those trying to reach Australia's shores are also desperate people, much the same as my grandparents were – each having similar needs and hopes as my own grandparents over a century earlier.

It is worth repeating here the example of my grandparents. They too were once foreign, non-English speaking, uneducated village dwellers, people who followed a different religion to Christianity when they first arrived on the shores of Britain pleading for sanctuary. Britain during the early years of the 20th century was certainly a very foreign country to them – as they were to the British people. To the Britain that accepted them, most arrived there with all that they could carry at the time, together with what were found to be strange customs, different ideas, a strange language and religion, experiences and ways that were alien to the British way of life.

All those that made the journey to Britain's shores in the hope for a more peaceful and productive future, arrived in the hope of finding sanctuary and a peaceful and happy life for themselves and their children. Most settled down and adapted to life in Britain, where they continued to add to the richness and diversity of British life, arts, industry and commerce.

It is a credit to those immigrants that arrived in Britain, and the majority of the many thousands of migrants who arrived in Australia since the Second World War, that they and their descendants have managed to become fully contributing citizens, abiding by their adopted country's laws and values.

In a number of remarkable cases, some migrants who came to Australia during earlier years also managed to rise to the status of becoming instrumental in the making of and administering those laws. A number were also sufficiently motivated to take up leading roles in the country's local, state and federal governments – and the nation's courts.

I am the product of just one of the thousands of immigrant families who arrived in Britain from Lithuania during the first decades of the 20th century, where they eventually settled in the Yorkshire city of Leeds.

It was from Leeds, just a generation or so later when newly married, that my wife and I travelled across the world, seeking to land and settle in Terra Australis – a new country on the other side of the world.

Notes

1. The Rise and fall of Australian Wool: See Charles Massy's book "Breaking the Sheep's Back" discussed in a later chapter. Also, see the references section for suggested further reading.

1
INTRODUCTION TO A DREAM

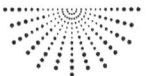

My part in Australia's story had its beginnings during a cold, miserable Wednesday in March 1935, at the Hyde Terrace Maternity Hospital in Leeds, the capital city of Yorkshire, 'Broad Acres' as the shire is known throughout England.

The entry of this particular baby into the world of the mid- 1930s wasn't what one would call really brilliant timing on the part of my parents, being just four short years before the outbreak of the Second World War. I wasn't to know this, of course, so had to put up with the inconveniences and dangers that the war brought to my early childhood, just four years later.

I was the firstborn of working-class parents, themselves first-generation British-born children of Lithuanian Ashkenazi Jews. My grandparents had been refugees, four among the many who fled to Britain around the turn of the 20th century. Grandparents on both sides of my family were among many thousands of other Lithuanian, Estonian, Latvian, Polish and Russian Jews desperately seeking to make good their escape from lives of poverty, fear and constant brutal attacks in the places of their birth.

Their circumstances, my family history and much more detail

relating to the history of the Jews of Lithuania, was described in my earlier book "Conversations with a Small Boy", published in 2012.

THE SECOND WORLD WAR

My early years, between the ages of four and ten, were happy ones, in spite of Britain being locked in a deadly struggle for its existence with Germany, Italy and a more distant but equally brutal Japan.

While some of the mayhem, death and injuries that were being inflicted by Nazi Germany across both Britain and Europe between 1939 and 1945 came close to my home, neither I nor any I knew of among my school and street pals were destined to be physically or mentally damaged as a result. In fact, to us young schoolkids at the time, our lives could best be described as something we knew to be normal. Let's face it – we had no way of knowing anything different.

I managed to grow through my boyhood years knowing nothing other than the war, German air raids, food rationing and shortages of everything, plus of course the need to attend Harehills County Primary school. I also learned to live with and dread the almost nightly bombing raids of the earlier 1940s. These were times during which we lived under the shadow of the German war machine and an inhuman, almost comically moustachioed Austrian born tyrant named Adolf Hitler.

Unlike many thousands of children living in other parts of Britain, and others facing danger among the ruins of their families and homes across a devastated Europe, Russia, the middle and far east, most of my young street pals were able to attend school and play our way through the greater part of our childhoods in relative safety. We were thankfully oblivious to the danger being felt every day by our parents, particularly during the early 1940s.

My parents, like most other Britons at the time, feared the real possibility of a German invasion of our island home and the Nazi-inspired terror that would surely follow, should that occur. My family, being followers of the Jewish faith, had even more to fear – that for our very lives, should Hitler's armies ever gain a foothold on British soil.

In reality, the six years between 1939 and 1945 were not normal. Many of my nights as a boy during the early 1940s were filled with dread, fear and fervent prayers that the German bombers would leave our house and my little family alone. Those prayers were usually at their loudest and most often repeated, as bombs fell not very far from my home in the working-class suburb of Harehills.

During regular nightly raids, the local battery of anti-aircraft guns would thunder, shaking the very foundations of ours and nearby houses each time they loosed off a salvo of shells upward into an ominous and threatening night sky. Each moonless night seemed to bring German bombers with it, all bent on our destruction.

I still retain many good memories of the war years in spite of all that happened. These included evacuation from Leeds in 1940, to the quaint and ancient village of Rufforth in North Yorkshire, along with my mam and baby sister Maureen Ruth, born in 1938. The post-war years followed, my dad and a couple of uncles finally returning home from the war for good. Their return at last allowed our lives to get started again, only to once more find the world moving once again into an uneasy period of peace – a few years that preceded what became known as a 'cold war'.

I grew up proud to be a Yorkshire 'Tyke',[1] a lad-of-Leeds born and bred. It is interesting though that even at a relatively early age, I was at the same time also beginning to realise that I was a little different in at least one aspect of my daydreaming, to most of my street pals.

I was a boy who from an early age had the ever-present thought in mind that one day I would venture forth and leave the land of my birth – the broad acres county of Yorkshire, and that part of Britain so poignantly described in the ballad "Jerusalem". Those stirring lines of William Blake's powerful verse, adapted so strikingly to music… "And did those feet in ancient times, walk upon England's mountains green…"

Notes

1. 'Tyke': The word *tyke* (from Old Norse *tík*, 'bitch') was first a term for a dog, especially a mongrel. It quickly became used to describe a

rough man and then a *Yorkshire tyke*, 'a person from *Yorkshire*', before being used as an affectionate term for a cheeky child.

AUSTRALIA

Another land, a very different place on Earth altogether from my native Yorkshire, located on the far side of the world, gradually took hold of my boyhood and youthful dreaming. A continent known as Australia was beginning to occupy a growing place in my mind, more so as I emerged into my teens.

The only real physical connection with Australia that I had experienced during my boyhood was through my beloved Leeds Rugby League Football Club, these days known as the Leeds Rhinos. The connection then was through the club's imported antipodeans – players regularly recruited during the post-war years, each an icon of the then rugby league code that came to Leeds from Australia and New Zealand. These men had names like Arthur Clues, Australian 2nd rower, and the first Australian player recruited. Keith McLellan, centre, who became captain of the club. Ted Verrenkamp, Bob MacMaster, not forgetting Ken 'killer' Kearney, hooker, and also that prodigious kicker of the ball, Bert Cook, fullback – a short, rotund player who hailed from New Zealand.

These players brought to Leeds my first impressions of the land 'Down Under', and people who later became my fellow citizens. They were young men, who spoke with a lazy, confident drawl, first heard when Arthur Clues addressed our school rugby team. All were champion athletes who played the rugby league code. Their home country, although I couldn't know it at the time, was destined sooner rather than later to become that part of the world that would play a central role throughout the greater part of my adult life. Australia, in particular, was the country in which I would put down roots and raise the family that now includes four children, five grandchildren and, at last counting, three great-grandchildren.

I have many times pondered the question as to why so early in my life, surrounded as I was by a reasonably secure, supportive and loving family, that I began even then to think of leaving the land of my birth for some as yet unknown land on the far side of the planet?

I can't remember just when such thoughts began to take root. I can only assume that my thinking evolved as a result of a keen interest in geography at school, and the books I enjoyed reading the most.

Always an avid reader of anything I could get my hands on, books in particular which, like the lyrics of an old song, described "Faraway places with strange sounding names" and the early explorers and sailors. I can only conclude that the desire to travel most probably developed as a result. Explorers, particularly the sailors among them, and the lives of adventurers who dared to explore and fight their ships on seas well beyond their then familiar world. These were men who held me in their thrall from as far back as I can remember.

In particular, my interest always seemed to revolve around the history and stories surrounding the adventures of swashbuckling captains of Britain's Royal Navy. Larger than life sailors like Sir Walter Raleigh, Sir Francis Drake, Horatio Nelson and others of their calling, who for well over 200 years had continued to savage the fighting galleons and gold ships of imperial Spain, and later the fleets of France.

Even today, my most visited bookshelf at home contains the well-thumbed and regularly re-read pages of fiction writers like Julian Stockwin, Richard Woodman, Dudley Pope, C.S. Forrester – and others who wrote along similar themes. My all-time favourite fiction writer, a man who brilliantly described the way of life and living across Britain's most successful period of naval dominance, has always been Patrick O'Brian, through his series of stories in which he described navy and political life in 18th century Britain. O'Brian's books were woven around the long and illustrious career of his colourful Royal Navy hero, 'lucky' Jack Aubrey.

My real-life childhood hero was Captain James Cook,[1] the Yorkshire bred navigator, whose amazing skills, drive and determination resulted in the discovery and charting of lands far remote from his birthplace in the North Yorkshire village of Marton. Cook's now famous voyage to the South Seas in 1770 has some distant relevance to this book, as it led eventually to the successful colonisation of what previously had been known only as 'Terra Australis Incognita'.

Terra Australis was the early description given to an originally hypothetical and then as yet then undefined southern landmass. That yet to be explored land, parts of which had only been briefly visited earlier from time to time by a few Dutch, French and Portuguese mariners, had remained an enduring mystery.

That mysterious and as yet uncharted land, still unclaimed by Europeans, first made its appearance on their early maps, depicting a then still vague area of the South Seas, between the 15th and 18th centuries. One then theory at the time had developed from earlier calculations which hypothesised that there must exist to the south of the equator a large counterbalancing landmass to Europe and other lands to the equator's north. A continent or group of islands they expected to be located south of the East Indies, a group of islands today known as the Indonesian archipelago.

Having myself sailed to the very same but much later version of Terra Australis and settled there for over a half-a-century, I believe it appropriate to look back through the mists of time to offer this short history. In doing so it is accepted that a far less illustrious voyager than James Cook and others of his time is offering this record. It is offered, nevertheless, as my contribution to the continuing story of that diverse, rugged and wonderful southern land we know today as Australia.

It eventually came to pass, 171 years following the arrival of Arthur Phillip and the so-named 'First Fleet', that on April 15th 1959 my new wife and I started out on our travels to follow in Captain Phillip's footsteps. Back in 1788 Phillip, along with a fleet of 11 ships, one thousand assorted convicts, marines and seamen sought to stake out Britain's claim to Terra Australis with the establishment of a penal colony on land in and around what became known as Botany Bay.

Our travel to Australia in 1959 was made very much quicker and in much more comfort than captain Phillip, his ship's crews and their prisoner passengers experienced in 1788. Unlike captain Phillip, my wife and I travelled to Australia in an altogether different kind of ship – the then ageing but still elegant and comfortable Orient Liner, Orion.

I recognise that any comparison of my coming to the fabled land down under, with the dangerous and overly long voyages of Cook, Phillip, Flinders and other earlier French, Dutch and Portuguese mariners, doesn't come even close in comparison. I just thought to include a short reference to the history of the land I came to call my home and raise a family, having arrived there much later, along with thousands of other 1950s-style European and British boat people.

Australia's relatively short history, a young nation relative to others across the modern world, has its critics – many having reason for being so to be found among its indigenous residents. Many 'first Australians' to this day continue to regard that fateful landing by Captain Phillip in 1788, as an invasion of lands upon which their ancestors had lived and successfully husbanded for more than 50,000 years. Be that as it may, the Australia I had the good fortune to migrate to in 1959 and in which I live today has developed and grown out of sight from those earlier times.

My presence here now at least provides me, the character scribbling this brief history of his journey to Australia and the way of life and living experienced since that time, a firm historical basis from which I can now proceed to record my small part in Australia's continuing story.

Notes

1. See Captain Cook's journal detailing his first voyage round the world made in H.M. Bark "Endeavour" 1768–1771. Published free as an e-book at www.gutenberg.net.

A SMALL BOY AND HIS DREAMS

As a boy and later teenager, I recall regularly wandering far and wide, at least in my mind, during the many hours I used to spend daydreaming.

This tendency to lapse into a form of daydreaming is something I have come to know as creating 'clouds in the sky'. The clouds sometimes become real, or they may just disappear into the ether. This peculiar way of conjuring up all kinds of possibilities is a way of thinking that has followed me throughout my life. Even four score years later I still sometimes find myself mentally wandering off into another world – one usually running parallel with reality, given over to possibilities to make-believe, often too obscure to be real.

To those with a belief in astrology, being what I am told is a Piscean, my birthday occurring on the last day of the northern winter, I am supposed to have dreaming among my particular characteristics. In my case that certainly was so.

My many and colourful mental wanderings often led me far away from my home in the northern industrial city of Leeds. My dreams in those days usually carried me along the routes and to many of the places discovered by the early explorers and sailors about whom I had learned, read and mused about as a young student.

What originally started out as an unusual line of thinking for a young boy, (my parents at the time would often scold me for gazing off into space when I should have been doing my homework), alongside the vivid imagination that regularly fired up my hopes and dreams I cannot say. The desire to travel far away from my home in Yorkshire though was a constant element in those dreams.

Perhaps this desire to travel to the more exotic places on planet Earth started out as being my only way of being able to break out, in a mental sense at least, from a relatively closed-in boyhood and sometimes confusing, often confronting early teenage years. One could never describe the streets of 1940s Leeds as being exotic!

My world as a boy was physically limited to the clustered and cluttered working-class district of the Harehills suburb of Leeds, among which I spent the first 18 years of my life. The reality of my life as a boy was that my earlier years were confined within the few square miles bounded by narrow streets and seemingly endless rows of back-to-back houses that filled the suburb in which I lived.

I recall that I loved to read a lot, mainly books that told stories of adventure, discovery, sailing and sailors. Those books included magical names like Ferdinand Magellan, Vasco da Gama, Bartolomeu Diaz, Christopher Columbus, Thor Amundsen, Robert Falcon Scott. These were men whose names and exploits became imprinted in my mind, as they and others like them, both historical and fictional, chipped their way into my boyish hopes and dreams.

My family situation, with its limited wealth and connections, when added to the history of my forebears and the relatively recent arrival in England of my grandparents, might well have served to diminish any chance that I then thought I would ever have of emulating my boyhood heroes.

Regardless, the daring, navigational skills and deeds of the early explorers, in particular, James Cook, always served to fire up my imagination and dreams that one day I too might find myself able to follow in his footsteps. At the very least, I regularly dreamed that one day I would visit and travel across the lands and sail the oceans that he had discovered and navigated across.

I still can recall one occasion of note. I must have been around nine or ten at the time, during an afternoon that found me digging a deep hole in grey semi-lifeless dirt at the centre of my parents' handkerchief-sized garden. My digging had followed a lesson in geography at my local junior school, during which while intent on my digging I found myself having to answer the inquiry of an inquisitive next-door neighbour, Howard Abrahams, a boy a few years younger than I. On witnessing my efforts for some time, Howard ventured, "What are you digging that hole for?" The answer he received must have surprised even him… "Can't you see?" came what must have seemed a strange retort, "I'm digging my way through the centre of the Earth to Australia!"

I vaguely recall that this patently futile project had followed a lecture at school during which we students had learned that Australia was located on the opposite side of the planet from Leeds. To my then fertile mind, this may well have opened up the possibility of perhaps digging one's way through to the other side of the planet? Who knows?

That highly unlikely excavating project was brought to an abrupt close with the arrival home of my mam from her work as a trouser machinist at a local factory. As usual, she was most likely to have been weighed down following a long, hard day at work, followed by the regular necessity to complete the family's food shopping at the local co-operative retail outlet in nearby Elford Grove.

She was not very impressed to see her young son digging an ever-deepening hole among her carefully nurtured bed of dahlias and geraniums, struggling plants that she and my dad patiently tended, along with doses of rotted horse manure previously shovelled up from the street, a usually pungent mix regularly augmented with used tea leaves and other stuff.

Every year my dad would plant a few sunflowers, that on reaching maturity, their seeds ripened, would be fed to 'Pretty Polly', the Perkins next doors' parrot. This was a large, aggressive and noisy bird that spent most of his days in a large domed wire cage in their bay window. My parents' plants each summer would shoot out a usually reasonable show of blooms, even as they sometimes struggled to thrive in the thin grey soil of our handkerchief-sized garden.

As you can imagine from this brief background, it can be said that even as a boy I was dreaming that someday into the future I would seek to travel to the land of kangaroos, koalas, sunshine and surf.

Ultimately, that dream did come true, in my case around 14 years later when, as an unworldly and inexperienced 24-year-old – and recently married, I did get to make that dreamed of journey to the far side of the planet. Not quite in the footsteps of James Cook, but an adventurer no less, though in a different sense, during a very different era and, for very different reasons.

HAREHILLS

The suburb in which I grew to adulthood was typical of most other working-class districts scattered across the north of England. It was a suburb of industrial Leeds grossly misnamed as Harehills. That name unfortunately failed dismally as a description of the place. While my suburb contained some hills, neither I nor anyone else I knew at the time could recall ever seeing anything resembling a freely running hare, or a rabbit hopping around its tarmacadam and cobbled streets, or among the handful of handkerchief-sized gardens and churchyards that dotted the local streets. There were plenty of rats and other vermin though, particularly in and among the local middens[1] and rubbish-choked waters of the nearby Bankside Street beck.

That local rivulet, not far from the bottom of my street, which during some long past time had meandered and burbled its crystal-clear way through an ancient grass banked, wildflower and tree-studded landscape, in my day had become an often turgid, vermin and rubbish filled stream. It continued to wander as well as regularly flooding, particularly when swollen with winter rains and melting snow.

Harehills Terrace and the small, pokey back-to-back house, among street upon street of the same kind of houses in which I grew into my teen years were located just three miles north of the centre of Leeds. Harehills was an old suburb, inhabited almost exclusively by working-class families, factories of all shapes and sizes dotted here and there – and local shops located on nearly every street corner.

Notes

1. Midden: A *midden* (also *kitchen midden* or shell heap; from early Scandinavian; Danish: *mødding*, Swedish regional: *mödding*) is an early term used to describe a dump for domestic waste which may consist of animal bone, human excrement, botanical material, vermin shells, shards, and other forms of house refuse.

THE WORLD OUTSIDE

The world outside the city of Leeds during my growing years, at least as it appeared to me before the age of 18, was experienced only as the muffled throb of a very distant drum. It was a world well outside the scope of my limited daily view as it then was. I grew into my teens in a small house, among many others that filled the Harehills district of Leeds.

My daily physical view of the world was via the long, narrow oblong strip of sky that formed the visible roof above my street. The occasional silver aircraft passing high above my street during the 1940s and early 1950s always seemed to me that it would forever remain beyond the grasp of the small boy gazing up at it from the narrow, often rain-swept street below.

Such distant hopes, however, were never capable of dimming this boy's dreams of eventually being able to travel beyond Leeds.

Harehills during the 1940s. Roundhay Road is at bottom left, the writer's street and home is one of the row of houses, just to the left of St. Aiden's church, itself located near the top left of the photo.

The one real exception to the limits of life among the narrow and crowded back-to-back housing and narrow streets of Harehills was that provided by our family valve radio. This was a piece of hi-tech gadgetry that during the 1930s and 1940s opened up a different, mostly distant and then remote world. It was a world intriguingly described by the names of places with strange names embossed on the tuning dial and knobs along the front of our ornate radio set. Our family radio also had a green coloured flowerlike tuning symbol that became focused on finding a foreign radio station on shortwave. Listening to our family radio served to open up a world far away. It was also an all too often distant world that spoke in strange sounding, foreign languages.

Our valve radio was a wonderful invention. It allowed the family, and occasionally me, physically confined as we were for most of the time within our little house in the north-east of Leeds, to tap into and listen to the as yet to be discovered world beyond Harehills – a world well beyond the shores of our island home.

The back of our radio's large, ornate timber veneered cabinet contained a glowing bank of valves, wire looms and other electronic parts that hummed away in the heat being generated by all the different sized valves that powered it.

This was still some time prior to the arrival of transistors and later electronic discoveries like black and white television. It was to be some time yet before the dreamed of luxury of owning a 'Telly' (television set) would become a reality. Since its invention in 1936 and later appearance in black and white during the late 1940s on the domestic appliance market, television would eventually become affordable to most Harehills folk – mainly in the form of a rental during the early 1950s.

Travel during nearly all of my early years was restricted to the local web of narrow streets, the shops servicing them and a couple of small local parks that offered a few trees and a patch of grass here and there.

My weeks were broken only by an occasional weekend tramcar ride, if the weather was good, to nearby Roundhay Park or Adel woods, or perhaps even an often looked forward to a bus trip to the Yorkshire Moors at Otley, or Ilkley. Occasionally the family would venture to other nearby picnic spots around Leeds and the closer Yorkshire Dales.

None of the families in our street or nearby that I knew of owned a motor car so it was travel either by bicycle, tramcar, bus or 'shank's pony' (walking) for us.

On one or two occasions following the end of the Second World War, our little family, comprising Mam, Dad, younger sister Maureen and me, would travel to and spend a week of the August summer bank holidays in a cheap bed-and-breakfast residence in Dickson Road, central Blackpool. A then favoured working-class holiday resort on the Lancashire coast, Blackpool always seemed so clean and fresh to us kids. For many years Blackpool remained a popular seaside resort, a place free from factory smoke and coal-fired fireplaces – the houses and other buildings there retaining their original red or cream brick colourings.

The colour of most things in Blackpool would stand out in stark contrast to the grey facades of practically every building in central Leeds, them having been ingrained with centuries of soot, smoke and grime, corrosive stuff that poured every day from coal-fired domestic house fires, and the unfiltered chimneys of local factories.

While on holiday in Blackpool, my sister and I would get to paddle in the grey, usually cold Irish Sea. We would also look forward to building paper flag crowned castles out of the wet beach sand, and the luxurious treat of slurping on an occasional ice-cream sandwich on Blackpool's famous North Pier. Another delight looked forward to by we kids was being able to suck our way through a personal stick of Blackpool's famous sugary sweet 'Rock'.[1]

Back in Leeds, often on a weekly basis during most of the year, we kids could also look forward to the regular Saturday afternoon shopping visit to the city centre.

Along with most of our local pals, we kids would be scrubbed until shiny, spruced up in our best clothes then taken out on a trip into the city centre. Along with our parents, the family would catch a local double-decker No.3 tram at the bottom of our street and ride it to the city's centre. On arrival, our little family, along with other locals would promenade along Leeds' ancient central street, Briggate.

During that weekly visit, usually spoken of by the locals as "gowin t'tarn" (going into town), we would wander wide-eyed through the small shops and larger stores that lined both sides of the streets radiating outward from Briggate. Some of these streets led toward Leeds' venerable Kirkgate Market, the imposing council flats at nearby Quarry Hill and the edifice of Leeds' Parish Church to the east. Other streets led to the west, in the general direction of the ancient Kirkstall Abbey, the site of one of England's earliest commercial iron forges, and further west still to Leeds' neighbouring and internationally known wool city, Bradford.

My own street was one among hundreds of other narrow and mainly cobble-stoned thoroughfares, some with their ancient and unsavoury outside, unsewered toilet blocks, others with open middens amid street upon street of pokey back-to-back houses. Some families like mine were lucky enough to lay claim to a tiny front garden, a bay window, two cellars, plus an inside bathroom and lavatory. A relative luxury was an inside 'lav' in those days!

None of my relatives in our wider family could afford to purchase their own house. Like most others of the local population, my parents could only afford to rent our back-to-back house, which they did from the time of their marriage in 1934, until the late 1950s, when they could finally afford to purchase it.

Similar streets to ours were spread, much like the closely interlocking threads of an immense web-like grid, a network of working-class residences that crisscrossed other crowded industrial cities throughout the north of England.

Notes

1. Rock: Often known by its place of origin, for example Blackpool rock or Brighton rock. A type of hard stick-shaped boiled sugar confectionery, usually flavoured with peppermint or spearmint.

THE LAND ACROSS THE DITCH

Another part of the world that sometimes used to excite my mind as a boy was located much closer to Yorkshire than Australia, just across the so-called ditch. The Atlantic Ocean, often known by that title, is big as ditch's go, the United States of America (US) on the other side of it, also playing its small part in my early life.

The US featured much lower in my musings and daydreams than those of that faraway continent and islands scattered around the South Seas. Tropical islands, swaying palm trees and coral beaches would always win in my mind, over the country on the other side of the Atlantic. Talking about tropical islands – I will never forget the riveting story surrounding the lives of a shipwrecked Swiss family and their animals. This was a story of the South Seas detailed so vividly in Johann Wyss's book, "Swiss Family Robinson" – another of my favourite boyhood reads.

Australia was a country that always conjured up images in my mind of a vast, relatively uninhabited land over which kangaroos, wallabies, wombats, venomous snakes, massive lizards, fearsome crocodiles and exotic birds roamed. Kangaroos, Emus and Wombats were intriguing, strange looking animals, particularly to us young British schoolkids.

The kangaroo, an animal that truly symbolised Australia, together with its smaller cousin the wallaby, were universally known and recognisable, due mainly to their unique mode of travel as they hopped at great speed across Australia's desert-like regions and wooded, low mountain ranges. Also, strangely, they carried their young in a pouch attached to their bellies and were animals hunted by what we were told in school were stone-age people. Primitive savages who lived off the land and did their hunting with boomerangs, spears and other ancient weaponry like the strange sounding nulla-nulla. These were ancient people, who we learned at the time were prehistoric, lacking any resemblance to modernity – continuing to be described thus, even during the 1940s.

My interest in the US, in direct contrast, was due more to our regular weekly injection of American cowboy movies, Mickey Mouse cartoons and similar, that we kids used to look forward to gorging on at each Saturday afternoon's matinee showing at the Gaiety Kinema – our local movie theatre. The Gaiety was located just a few hundred yards down Roundhay Road from the bottom of my street.

It was at the Gaiety that we kids would pay our silver sixpences and be ready to be enthralled. It was also at the Gaiety and via the comic books that visiting American soldiers introduced us English youngsters to during the Second World War that heroes like Superman, Batman, the Lone Ranger and his sidekick Tonto would flash across the Gaiety's silver screen, along with Walt Disney cartoons. We kids would sit through each Saturday afternoon matinee, chewing through our two-pennyworth of Rowntree's Fruit Gums or Basset's Liquorice Allsorts – as we sat transfixed by the daring do of fast riding, gun-slinging cowboys.

There were the 'baddies', usually dressed in black, who always lost out to a tall, handsome white-hatted hero – the cowboy who always got to win the pretty girl as we watched, cringed, cheered and booed as appropriate.

We also found time, having been successful in prising another penny or two from our mothers, to buy and suck down on a liquorice-tubed Ka-Li Sucker and its fizzy lemon sherbet powder contents, or purchase a small bottle of sweet tasting Tizer. Sometimes too, if I had been a good boy that is, my mam would include an extra few pennies, to enable me to buy a Whipped Cream Walnut chocolate treat to munch on, while I and my street pals gorged on each Saturday afternoon's programme of movies and cartoons.

OF GODS AND RELIGION

Growing into my teens, I began to find it more and more difficult to accept the beliefs and religious practices of my forebears in my case this meant Judaism. The religious teachings and dogma relating to the Jewish faith, with which we kids were being indoctrinated at the time, comprised stuff we were expected to learn, retain and believe. Our instruction by rabbis and lay teachers at a local Hebrew School was handed down, usually without any explanation or discussion being encouraged or allowed, other than the usual declaration that what was being taught was the only universal truth.

As I grew older, I gradually came to the view that those preaching to us young impressionable pre-teenagers were not capable, or perhaps not even interested in providing acceptable, unambiguous explanations of the biblical stories and assertions of ancient, learned rabbis and the faith's ancient commentators' writings in Aramaic. The reality, or that which our religious mentors saw as such, was instead being imprinted onto impressionable minds via stories, vividly illustrated religious publications and the requirement to learn the Hebrew language.

As a young child, the rules and principles surrounding Jewish life and living had always seemed real, the inviolable and only truth governing life and all living things. As I grew older however, I was gradually finding that the various rules, laws and supposedly unquestionable beliefs, biblical stories, fables and historical accounts supporting them, were becoming less acceptable – at least they were to me.

Alongside my gradually growing doubts and questions surrounding many of these so-called 'truths', when it came to religious dogma and the relatively restricted way of living that was expected of the more earnest adherents to the Jewish religion, I was also having similar doubts surrounding the claimed virgin birth of an ancient Jew called Jesus, as claimed by the Christian faith.

There is little, if anything actually known or recorded of Jesus's actual birth and early life. He seems to have arrived (perhaps discovered) as an adult? The story of him also being the Son of God, was also hard to believe, particularly when he has been reported as having performed a variety of highly unlikely miracles, including the raising of the dead. Details of these supposed miracles have been vividly described, and continually updated later, in stories attributed to his followers and assorted chroniclers since. To me, particularly during my teen years, a young mind seeking answers, most of the ancient biblical stories and those surrounding the man called Jesus posed far more questions than answers.

In my part of Leeds at the time, religions other than Christianity and Judaism, for example, Hinduism Buddhism and Islam were virtually unknown, not spoken of, experienced, reported on or practiced. This was probably a good thing, as both the teachings of Christianity and Judaism, as presented to me during my youth, left me with more than just a few questions and issues needing to be coped with at the time.

In my case, being the only 'Jewish' boy in my street also saw me coming under regularly painful physical attacks and equally painful verbal and written taunts. These I regularly suffered at the hands of one or other of the gangs of local adherents to either of the Roman Catholic or other versions of the Protestant faith – groups of youths that roamed the local streets.

As I grew older and able to think in a more objective way about religion related issues that surrounded me, my thinking was becoming more agnostic. Not that I was even aware at the time of the use or meaning of the word agnostic. It was, however, becoming clearer to me, as I grew into my teens, that the concept of an all-seeing entity called God – any god for that matter variously stated to reside in heaven or wherever else he, she or it was supposed to exist, was at best a questionably plausible theory and at worst a highly improbable and potentially dangerous myth.

Being older and better able to reason more clearly about what was going on in the world around me, I began to find myself leaning more and more toward the view that the concept of an all-seeing, all-powerful god could only have emerged from the imagined world and minds of ancient, desert living tribes.

It seemed reasonable, that the original source of the imaginative stories of gods, sons of gods and other superior beings that had emerged in ancient times, were sheep or goat herders, traders, thinkers and highly imaginative visionaries – early messengers and scribes from whom the Old Testament, ancient Jewish, early Christian and later Islamic writings originated.

Each religion I came up against (at that stage limited to Judaism and Christianity) presented as if they were non- contestable truths. At Hebrew School these were emphasised by means of a swish with a bamboo cane by one or other of our teachers. The need for such treatment usually followed any questioning of a passage or other from the Old Testament or other ancient Hebrew texts. Such treatment eventually left me with the firm conviction that the stories of god, angels and the virginal quality of the birth of Christianity's version of their god's son, Jesus, were much-embellished stories and little more. The various stories themselves had become more enhanced as each new generation of scholars, thinkers and religious leaders sought to add to and explain the original theories and reported visions of the ancients and later self-declared visionaries.

I saw them as powerful, evocative but highly improbable stories, questionable information that was being crammed into the heads of we children, Christian and Jewish – designed to create mind pictures not dissimilar but often less plausible and much less interesting than my reading of the tales of the brothers Grimm!

I continued to grow into my teens with more questions than answers, particularly around the required unquestioning acceptance of the teachings of ancient Hebrew texts and stories handed down over generations. I finally emerged into my mid-teens, the result of years of religious teachings endured, an individual that wouldn't have pleased my rabbis and lay teachers, filled with fundamental and seemingly unanswerable questions – at least to all but those who truly believe, or have themselves become successfully indoctrinated.

I do not intend boring you any further with my views on religion, religious beliefs and practices. It is sufficient to state here for the record, that I, religious faith, gods of any variety, angels and other deities, including both heaven and hell, parted company many years ago, well before I had reached my late teens.

A WORLD STILL IN CONFLICT

Growing up during the late 1940s and early 1950s, the latter end of my teenage years – particularly the three years following the ending of my formal school education at the age of 15, were being looked forward to with more than just a few pangs of real foreboding. Two years of what then was referred to as 'national service' were looming as an increasingly dark shadow over my young life.

I completed the formal years of my primary and Secondary Modern-style schooling at the age of 15, 1950 being the end of formal school education. That now meant swapping my schoolbooks for the rudiments of the tailoring trade and evening attendance at the Leeds College of Technology, before having to face the inevitable prospect of a soon to be two-year commitment in Britain's armed forces.

The Second World War may well have ended a few years earlier, but there remained a number of other more localised and often bloody conflicts still occurring across the globe.

In order to protect British interests and its citizens' safety at home and in a number of countries overseas, young men of my generation were being conscripted, expected to fight and if need be die, for a cause few of us had even the vaguest interest, or felt any commitment.

Little of real consequence to those of us just emerging into our late teenage years had changed since the ending of the Second World War. Add to this the lack of any kind of inspiring vision of what the British government saw as being the future direction of the country. Now that the war was finally over, there was a view growing among a large part of the population, that few among the country's politicians had any idea as to how to improve Britain's economic position and its lessening status among the world's nations.

Successive governments, whether of a conservative or socialist nature, continued to be tied down by the country's parlous financial state. At the same time, the British government was also feeling obliged to commit elements of its regular army and air force, heavily augmented by young national service conscripts, to locations abroad to put down local insurgencies among the remnants of Britain's fast-disappearing empire. Conscription was also said to be necessary, to bolster the ranks of Britain's fighting forces providing a bastion against what was also seen at the time to be a growing threat of world communism.

In terms of its power in the post-war world, any adult at the time with a basic understanding of history and recent affairs, would have been capable, of recognising that Britain's time was up when it came to its capacity to continue wielding control over all its far-flung pre-war colonies. Most of those illusions had already been smashed during the Second World War, following the loss of the Malay Peninsula and the then strategic island of Singapore on February 15th 1942, to what until then had been regarded by Britain's wartime leadership, as a poorly led and inferior Japanese fighting force.

The Japanese, it was also said at the time before their capture of Singapore, were unable to fight at night, due to the mistaken belief that they had inferior eyesight!

That supposedly inferior army, however, as a result of their successful earlier invasion of China, Korea, the Philippines and the Malaysian peninsula, demonstrated in the most dramatic and devastating terms Britain's incapacity to defend its main Southeast Asian outpost against a determined, well-equipped, well-trained and well-commanded army.

As the Japanese approached, most of the British administration, its managers and the majority of those families that could escape from Singapore by sea, did so. Their abrupt and ignominious retreat to safety in Australia left the local people and 130,000 British, Indian and Australian troops, (15,000 of which were Australian troops just recently landed), to despairingly surrender to the invading Japanese.

The loss of India in 1947 to that country's long sought independence, was also an indication that time and circumstances had ended any hopes that Britain could continue to hold onto some, if not all of the red-coloured countries that had featured on our wall maps at school. States that for well over a century had made up Britain's colonial empire. That famed and romanticised entity, of which it was once said, "The sun never sets."

In the face of an escalating series of revolts by people, who had felt oppressed following a century or two of British colonial rule and exploitation, the British government was eventually forced to relinquish control over most of the vast territories over which its forces and colonial administration had controlled millions of lives.

Looking back from the vantage of time, successive British governments had probably felt they had no option other than to keep on fighting against what they regarded as 'gangs of murderous insurgents' and terrorists – armed groups considered by Britain to be resisting the legitimate continuation of British rule. The choice to stay and fight for control of what remained of its colonial empire, while suffering decline back home amid dwindling financial resources, ultimately created a situation in which Britain's superior armed forces proved incapable of continuing indefinitely to exert control over local populations. These were people determined to overthrow what they had for years regarded as hated colonial occupiers.

The same was happening to other emerging nations on the African continent and across South East Asia. In these cases, they were countries and people that before the Second World War had been held under the colonial rule of Germany, France, Belgium, Portugal and Holland. These were people now rebelling against their former European overlords.

WHY NOT MIGRATE TO AUSTRALIA?

Such then was the atmosphere during the late 1940s and early 1950s across the British Isles, from where a growing number of families, many believing that they had lost the capacity to maintain a reasonable standard of living, or they saw Britain's future as a leading world power moving rapidly into a non-reversible decline, had decided to take advantage of Australia's recently introduced programme of assisted migration.

The Australian government, following the country's emergence from a brutal war, the latter part of which had been fought under extreme jungle conditions, not many miles to its north in New Guinea and the nearby Pacific Ocean, was at the time seeing an urgent need to increase its population. The initial need seen here was the replacement of citizens that had been either killed or injured during the course of the war. The government had also realised that for the country to compete on an international basis during the post-war world, there was a need to rapidly increase Australia's working population, its industrial output and thus its economic strength.

The urgent need to increase Australia's population, at a time when there were many thousands of refugees and others seeking a new and safer life far away from ruined homes and cities across Europe resulted in the development of an innovative assisted migration programme. The sole intent of this programme was to attract as many fit and variously skilled new people to its shores to bolster the country's ongoing development. This resulted in financially attractive assisted passages and settlement assistance being offered to British citizens wishing to migrate to a still young, relatively underdeveloped and underpopulated country.

Passage to Australia was being promoted to white citizens, at the cost per adult accepted under the Australian government programme, of £10 sterling! Just think of it – the Australian government, for the nominal cost of the now equivalent to around ten times that amount in A$ per adult individual, was offering healthy, law-abiding British citizens the opportunity of a near fully funded transfer to a new life in Australia.

Interesting turnaround that – the only qualification needed to become one of Britain's original migrants to Australia during the 18th century, had been a conviction! Most arrivals in Australia from Britain during the 18th and 19th centuries had resulted from mostly unwilling dissidents and felons, who had been arrested and convicted, often for very minor offences, then forcibly shipped off to a then remote Australia – whether they liked it or not!

Even members of Britain's upper and middle classes, many well-educated citizens but considered to be too radical or were voicing opposition to the then-current class system, also found themselves on the wrong side of British law courts. Many of these, a large proportion of whom were intellectuals and reformers, were being summarily convicted and shipped off to the far side of the world – hopefully out of sight of the then British ruling class.

The Australian government's post-war offering to provide passage to Australia during the 1940s, 1950s and 1960s proved to be a powerful incentive.

It was against this background that Mavis, my wife of six months and I, followed in the footsteps of thousands of earlier British citizens, who had already left the country in search of a new life under the stars of the Southern Cross.

Boyhood dreams of following in the steps of my hero Captain James Cook were soon to be realised.

2
DEFENDER OF THE REALM

FOR KING AND COUNTRY

Before delving deeper into the events that led to my departure from Britain to Australia, two years of compulsory national service in either of the British army or Royal Air Force, was looming ominously over my horizon. The imposition of national service promised to inflict some profound life changes on me that were beyond my control. These would be drastic changes soon to be imposed on my young life – a life that along with many thousands of other young men had barely got started.

The requirement to undergo two years of what was described by the government as 'service in defence of the nation' heralded the possibility of an East Asian, African or Irish Republican Army (IRA) bullet or bomb being the cause of a premature end to this young life.

We recently emerged schoolboys were soon to become subject to the British government's policy of conscripting as many fit young men as possible, to bolster the country's armed forces.

The imposition of national service in one or other of the nation's military services was presumably aimed at boosting Britain's rapidly weakening capacity to maintain a military presence in the world. A last gasp attempt to hold onto some of the British Crown's remaining colonies for as long as possible.

The situation that was to decide my fate was something altogether and questionably different to what could otherwise be described as the actual defence of the country. The reasons being used by the government to justify the imposition of national service did little to improve the mood among a greater part of the population, particularly how the word 'defence' was understood by most of Britain's war-weary citizens. Think also of just how the British government's urgently felt need for reinforcements came across to a group of young men? We were still youths, just newly arrived into our late teens. We had already spent the greater part of our lives growing up during a bloody war, the memories of which still remained in the nation's psyche.

At the time Britain was also still living with some of the last vestiges of food rationing. Some families throughout the country were also continuing to mourn the loss of loved members as a result of German bombing and missile attacks, and the deaths of near and dear who had been fighting both at home and abroad. Too many Britons had lost their lives or had returned home injured, physically or mentally, from the various far-flung theatres of conflict.

The Second World War may well have officially ended seven years earlier, but its effects still resonated across a country and among a people, most of whom were still desperately trying to come to grips with an as yet uneasy peace and a still- sluggish economy.

The British government was still struggling to recover from the almost complete depletion of the country's wealth, much of which had been handed over to the US in return for the supply of military equipment under America's wartime 'Lend Lease' scheme. All this in addition to many lives lost or permanently damaged.

Other than the occasional confrontation with the IRA, to me and most other late teenagers there seemed little or no apparent reason for us to be shoved into uniform, just like our fathers before us.

This time, though much different to the situation that had confronted Britain in 1939, there was the distinct possibility of being sent off overseas, to oppose an insurgency of unhappy locals, somewhere on the African continent, the Middle East or South East Asia.

Troops were also needed to assist in maintaining the fragile peace in a defeated, devastated and still divided Germany. Any fighting, however, particularly when it came to groups of rebellious colonials, was not the same as had been the reason to fight against a marauding army of German Nazis, Italian fascists or the Japanese. This fighting, if there were to be any, would be against native populations, in their own countries and against people who were determined to rid themselves of their overlords – us!

National service had also applied to recruiting for the army during the local war that raged between June 25th 1950 and July 27th 1953, up and down the Korean Peninsula. This thankfully was a war that by the time I had turned 18 was in the process of running down to an ongoing stalemate along Korea's 38th parallel.

This uneasy peace remains a stalemate even into the 21st century, with a pariah North Korean state well-entrenched and increasingly belligerent north of the border, as its leadership continues to rail against the West while exhibiting the capability of literally exploding into violence at any time!

Back in 1953, coming so close to the ending of a worldwide conflict, just the thought of having to emulate our fathers by being 'called up' to attend what essentially were other, perhaps smaller, more isolated, but potentially bloody affrays, was surreal. Add to this, the potential threat to our still young lives for no apparently sound reason.

The whole international scene and the need to maintain an armed force that was instantly ready for combat represented a form of deception by a government and its ruling elite, people who in reality were more afraid of facing the prospect of Britain's loss of control over its former colonies. Britain also found itself facing the prospect of losing face among its peer nations and former fighting allies from the Second World War.

Millions of Britons did not necessarily share those concerns. In the main, the population following the recent war's ending were more concerned with issues of a more immediate nature – like a reduced standard of living, a stagnant economy and concern for their children's health, education and future job prospects.

Who were the ones destined to bear the results of such fears and concerns? To which history usually answers:

> *A non-complaining, long-suffering civilian population, which in the past had always risen to the urgent beat of the military drum and the rousing call of an army bugle, whenever the monarch, dictator or government of the day deemed their sacrifice to be necessary.*

National service, therefore, when I became caught up in its net during 1953, meant that every fit eighteen-year-old male Briton was to be conscripted into either of the khaki-clad Army or blue-clad Royal Air Force for two years. National service was to be supplementary, a boost to the regular volunteer members of those services. The Royal Navy was a little different. In the case of the navy it seems that the 'Senior Service' was happy enough to rely on recruiting sufficient personnel to man and fight its ships. I don't believe many if any, national servicemen were in fact allocated to a Royal Navy ship?

What did it mean to we young men you may well ask? And why was it that very few among us, unlike at the time of the later war in Vietnam, were refusing to undergo compulsory national service?

At the time, there was a residual fear that some, if not every Western democracy were in danger of being attacked or overrun by a threatening social system known as communism. This was a system that earlier in the 20th century had overtaken Russia (USSR) and later Mainland China, the latter becoming known as the Peoples Republic of China (PRC).

Added to an overt threat from the USSR, there also existed in the minds of many military analysts of the time, the possibility of what became known as the 'falling domino' effect applying. At the time, this was seen as a distinct threat to every Western-style democracy, should a combination of the USSR and PRC link together in an aggressive sweep through continental Europe, the Balkans and Asia, potentially gobbling up emerging nations and even one or two Western allies in the process.

The late 1940s and early 1950s were indeed troubling, as well as confusing times.

Whichever service we were to be allocated to, presented every eighteen-year-old with the same distinct and unwanted possibility of being dispatched, rifle in hand to any one of the then potential trouble spots overseas.

The only means of avoiding or deferring national service at the time was if an individual was undertaking an apprenticeship or some other kind of trade training or tertiary study recognised by the government. At the time, I was attending the then Leeds College of Technology (LCT), where I was in the early stages of studies in apparel design, production and textile technology.

I could have applied for a deferment until my course had completed. In considering the prospect of still having to serve in one or other of the armed services at or around the age of 22, however, I decided instead to get my national service commitment over and done with as soon as possible. This meant deferring my studies in favour of completing my stint in defence of King George VI and his government by the time I was 20.

A SHORT DIVERSION

It would be useful at this point, if I were to leave this rather depressing view of life in the then not so 'Great' Britain of the 1950s, to those historians better qualified to define and argue around whatever academic points remain to be discussed and chewed over.

From here on, I will concentrate on the events and thinking that formed and later influenced me and many fellow Britons, to leave the land of our birth during the 1950s, to migrate to a relatively empty and relatively unknown former British colony on the far side of the world.

Thought processes and other issues that eventually led to my departure from Britain in April 1959, began to take shape in the mind of this eighteen-year-old national serviceman, at the time serving in the Royal Air Force (RAF). Experiences and skills gained while a member of the RAF during the period 1953–1955, and later following my return home to Leeds were crucial to my later decision to leave Britain.

NATIONAL SERVICEMAN, 1953–1955

Sometime during early March 1953, the local postman pushed an official looking letter containing a formal invitation on behalf of the then British monarch, George VI, through the letterbox at 25 Harehills Terrace, Leeds 8. That not very welcome letter politely but firmly invited my participation, with others, to provide services deemed by His Majesty's Government to be necessary for the defence both of the realm and government interests at home and abroad.

At the time, this did not include the occupation of countries, which much earlier had also been colonies under the rule of London. Australia, New Zealand, South Africa and Canada were four former colonies that had, during various periods in the past, already successfully loosened the strings binding them as British colonies, thankfully without much, if anything in the way of armed conflict.

No matter how hard one looked around the world at that time, there did not appear to be a recognisable militant group or country, other perhaps than the IRA or Russian communists, perched as the latter was, on the other side of what Winston Churchill once referred to as the "Iron Curtain". Few others at the time were realistically considered to represent a direct threat to the lives of those of us then residing in relative peace across the British Isles.

There was the regular occurrence of often bloody and thankfully irregular shootings and bombings by some of the more militant elements of the IRA in various parts of Great Britain and Northern Ireland. Rather, the government's national service programme seemed to be based on their desire to delay what many outside Britain saw as the predictable loss of what remained of the country's overseas possessions. Most, if not all of those at the time were intent on breaking away from the not too gentle embrace of Mother England.

It is understandable that the possibility of later conflict with Britain's former ally in the war with Germany, the USSR, was also a distinct possibility in the minds of British intelligence analysts and political commentators at the time. Such an occurrence, had it eventuated, would almost certainly have required a great deal more treasure, fighting personnel and the possible commencement of a devastating third world war.

As 1953 rolled around, most of Britain's military attention for the past three years continued to be concentrated on the uneasy standoff that had followed a particularly bloody war that had been raging up and down the Korean Peninsula. Forces, other than those required to maintain the tentative peace between the north and south along the neutral zone near the town of Panmunjom in central Korea, were also considered vital to the task of keeping a growing number of local dissidents in check among trouble spots in Britain's far-flung, fast disappearing colonies.

Britain was also required at the time to maintain elements of its army as part of the BAOR (British Army Over the Rhine), in western Germany alongside American and French troops. All three allies were there keeping a wary eye on and confronting the USSR's armies in Eastern Europe and East Germany.

Berlin, the German capital, was at the time surrounded by Communist USSR and East German forces. The city had earlier been divided into two zones – the so-called 'allied zone' co-ordinated three ways between the US, France and Britain, and the Russian/East German zone.

Britain's commitments, being mainly of a military nature, meant that most national service entrants were being channelled into one or other of the various khaki-clad army regiments. Other national service personnel were being inducted into the RAF Regiment, a quasi-defence force designed along army lines, whose main role was the defence of RAF installations and aerodromes, within Great Britain and overseas. At the time, relatively few national servicemen were being allocated to the Royal Air Force.

'BRYLCREEM BOY'

Now faced with the inevitable prospect of being inducted into Britain's armed forces, it became clear that there was less chance of a loaded .303 Lee Enfield rifle, 'Bren' or 'Sten' machinegun being thrust into my soft, young unenthusiastic hands, if I were to be allocated to the RAF.

The RAF certainly seemed a preferable option to being sent to assist in quelling IRA violence in Northern Ireland or insurgents elsewhere overseas. Should I have the bad luck to find myself allocated into an army regiment, there existed the distinct possibility also of being sent to some supposedly exotic, but usually malarial infested destination like Malaya or Kenya or similar location.

Given this, the obvious and preferred option open to me was to become a member of the RAF, and it's so-called Brylcreem Boys.[1] Thus, there was sufficient incentive to do all possible toward achieving the more desirable end of being allocated to the RAF.

Being the kind of lad always keen to grab any opportunity that came his way, mine came during the preliminary medical and interview process that took place as we future national service draftees neared our 18th birthdays. The objective here, if at all possible, was to become a Brylcreem Boy.

During the preliminary exploratory interview in Leeds with a recruiting officer, inductees seeking to be considered for the RAF were being tested as to their knowledge of things militarily aeronautical, in addition to their physical fitness. It also became apparent that those able to claim that they had completed a stint in their school's air cadet corps, a usual occurrence at most private schools and colleges across Britain, gave them a distinct advantage, being preferred by the RAF over others with no history of involvement with an air cadet programme.

Noting this piece of information, gleaned earlier from a discussion with one or two earlier subjects of the medical examination and its following interview, I added 'yes' in the column requesting information on earlier membership of a cadet group. Suffice to say, any claim on my part along those lines was a long way distant from the truth.

On being interviewed, I followed an extensively rehearsed line designed to explain how the school cadets system had operated at my school. I should add here that this required the application of a vivid imagination on my part. I also sought to expand further on my knowledge regarding the various aircraft in use by the RAF, and the history of air warfare – a subject in which I did have a genuine interest.

My explanations and knowledge of things aeronautical, particularly the possibility of me signing on for a longer term with the RAF, seems to have resulted positively with my allocation to that august service, as I eventually found myself on April 15th 1953 nervously entering the gates of the Padgate induction centre. RAF Padgate was located 16 miles west of the Lancashire city of Manchester, east of the town of Warrington.

I recall entering the base, a youthful eighteen-year-old, not long out of school, clutching a cheap fibro attaché case containing a change of underclothes, bathroom requisites and a packet of sandwiches provided by my mother in one hand, and the government's thoughtfully provided travel warrant in the other.

I was answering the call to duty issued by my then seriously ill monarch George and what was left of his terminally ill British Empire.

Notes

1. Brylcreem Boys: The *Brylcreem Boys* was a 1998 romantic comedy film set in the Republic of Ireland during the Second World War. The title derives from a popular nickname for RAF personnel during that war as a result of a then popular and widely advertised men's hairdressing product that featured an RAF pilot.

A SPROG'S LIFE[1]

Apart from two short periods during my childhood, spent in one or other of what was known throughout Britain as a convalescent home, RAF Padgate was the first adult experience of my being located far away from the comforts of family and home. A place for convalescents RAF Padgate certainly was not, being more accurately described by its temporarily resident national service inmates at the time as the RAF's version of a sentence of hard labour and deprivation of any form of care or comfort.

The convalescent home concept incidentally, both before and following the Second World War, comprised nursing institutions that over many years had been established in various parts of the country. Specifically designed and staffed establishments, not unlike that of a hospital, they were mainly intended to operate as a retreat where sick, usually, elderly patients were accommodated to recover from a hospital stay or some other ailment that required them being away from their family home.

Some convalescent homes were turned over during the summer school holidays to children from working-class families, whose parents could prove a financial need to have their children looked after during a week or so of the holiday period, while they continued to work. Such a change may well have been some kind of trip for the children, but more likely it was a way the parents could enjoy a childfree couple of weeks. I recall while still a small boy, being shipped off to one such establishment located in the Lancashire resort town of Southport. My memories of that place were not very pleasant.

My short stay at Padgate was certainly no holiday. The days there were long and hard, at times difficult even to comprehend what was happening to me. They were days filled with an aggressive shouting, swearing and threatening breed of people, in the form of Air Force blue-clad corporals and sergeants. One or other of those immaculately uniformed alien beings seemed intent on having we confused and mostly unfit and disoriented conscripts, literally running from place to place and always in a state of frenzy. I recall wondering at the time if anyone in the RAF had ever thought of slowing down to walking pace?

As individuals, we new conscripts first found ourselves entered into the RAF's records as aircraftmen 2nd class (AC2) and divided into groups of around 30. From there each group was allocated to one or other of the rows of Second World War vintage 'Nissen'-style huts located around the base's central parade ground. These huts were semi-circular wooden framed and rounded corrugated iron structures, remnants from the recent war, in which we were to be housed until our allocation to one or other of the various RAF recruit training facilities.

Along with my confused and anxious colleagues, still hanging on grimly to my attaché case – my last connection with my past life, we were marched over to one of these miserable looking huts and told to stand in a line outside one such gloomy structure. Following a long cold wait in intermittently drizzling rain, attended by much haranguing on the subject of what the RAF expected from its recruits, most of which flew off over our confused heads, we were then allowed to enter the dank smelling, near freezing cold hut and told to select an army-style stretcher bed, on which was located a straw-filled paillasse.

Those of us with the thought of claiming a bunk as far away from the doorway as possible made a dive for one located near the centre of the hut, close to the wood burning stove. The weather was still quite cold, being early spring. The choice of a bunk near the wood stove, however, proved to be a pointless exercise, as, for the duration of our relatively short stay at Padgate, there was to be no wood or coals provided with which to light the stove.

Later, paraded in front of our designated hut, the shivering group of lads allocated to my group, were introduced to the first elements of our induction into the RAF.

This first day as a national serviceman was a complete shock to the system, comprised as it was with quick marching, and eardrums aching from the barking of orders from various blue-clad aliens. Their uniforms were enhanced with shining boot-caps, shiny brass buttons and belt brasses, nearly every one adorned with impressive looking stripes on their sleeves, chests sometimes also enhanced by a row of coloured ribbons.

Following this, we were then quick-marched over to one of the large corrugated iron stores scattered around the base. There we were fitted out with a kitbag and side-pack, onto which we had to stencil our earlier allocated RAF number (mine was and probably remains 2588475). All this together with the frenzied grabbing of uniform parts and other gear as it was issued (more like thrown) to us – one lot following on from another. We were then marched to and paraded at one after the other of the various equipment stores located around the base.

The rest of the day followed with a medical examination, during which it appeared that special attention, once the doctor conducting it had satisfied himself that the individual being examined was alive and kicking, was then concentrated on a minute examination of our sex tackle. Possibly they were seeking out anyone exhibiting some form of genital disease, or perhaps even an attempt at weeding out a potential female imposter? Yes, a highly unlikely event – but an interesting proposition non-the-less.

Phew ... it had become a day of transition from an earlier comfortable life as a civilian, to one filled with the strange accoutrements and language of a service life.

"Ah well, it's only for two years after all" were mine, and probably the innermost thoughts of most other of my confused fellow inductees at the time – definitely a case of having to resign oneself to getting used to life in the military! At the same time, I well recall the feeling of desperation and utter resignation to the overpowering and unyielding force that had taken complete control over my life.

Having dumped our gear back on the bunks in our designated Nissen hut, we were then quick-marched back to another store to make our final pickup of the day, in the form of a pair of cotton bed sheets and pillow cover, a lumpy pillow and a rough wool blanket which, having lugged them back to our hut we were then instructed how to set up and 'square' our bunks preparatory for each morning's inspection. This seemingly pointless exercise, pointless that is to anyone other than a member of the armed forces, involved what at first appeared to be an unusual structure that we were expected to build at the head of our bunks every morning, on top of the smoothed down paillasse.

This strange activity, like everything else in the service, was precisely defined. It required the blanket, sheets and pillow to be assembled, folded and squared away with such precision that the inspecting corporal, sergeant or officer was able to check its integrity and squared perfection – using a right-angled device! The various layers required to be formed by the folding of blanket and sheets into a form that reminded me of one of the alternating liquorice and soft-coloured and sugary layers of the famously tasty 'Basset's Liquorice Allsorts' confectionery.

As the day passed it soon became clear, even to us untrained and unmilitary-minded young men, that the armed forces depended on a pattern of precise disciplines, the ritual of morning blanket and sheet squaring being just one.

As we later got used to how the RAF operated, even the ritual of squaring off one's bunk each morning became just another part of the background to our lives, easily accepted as a part of living and existing within the military.

Following folding and squaring off our blankets for the first time, with varying degrees of success, all traces of our former existence were then permanently erased, with our being instructed to disrobe down to the skin, take a shower, a near cold one at that – the final act in divesting ourselves of our civilian identities.

Notes

1. Sprog – RAF vernacular used to describe a new member of the service – one usually occupying the lowliest ranking – Aircraftsman 2nd class (AC2).

I'LL NEVER GET USED TO THIS!

Donning the rough, scratchy and uncomfortable blue-grey wool trousers and work tunic for the first time and struggling with the studs with which we were supposed to attach the stiffly starched detachable collar to the top of our shirts, was nigh impossible to do at first. I for one had never been so uncomfortable in my young life, as the sharp-edged starched collar kept digging itself into my neck. After only a day, the bloody thing managed to leave me with a sore neck, leaving an angry red mark in its wake each evening where the sharp edge of the collar fold had come in contact with my soft skin!

Worse was to come though when it came to trying to walk for the first time after pulling on the hard, thick and greasy leather boots.

My feet for the first few days ached and became very sore, even raw in places, as my tender ankles and toes came in contact with the hard, coarse and unyielding leather. The coarse, grey wool socks, thick as they were, didn't help much either.

Help was at hand though, in the form of the tall, immaculately turned out and unusually sympathetic corporal in charge of our hut. After standing and gloating for a while in front of his group of weary, sore, uncomfortable and confused young lads, most who were probably wishing they could be spirited many miles away from this hellish place, he proceeded to provide some highly technical advice as to the techniques to be followed in the preparation of our new boots.

SPIT AND POLISH

Anyone having spent a period of service in the military would be familiar with what we sprogs found ourselves having to learn very early in our stay as guests of His Majesty's Royal Air Force.

On returning to our nominated flight hut with our new boots and the rest of our kit, one of the first lessons to be learned related to the required preparation of the toecap of our service boots. The objective here, as explained by our instructing corporal, was first to remove the layer of grease covering the entire boot, something that proved to be a lengthy task. This process was then followed by applying many hours of work in preparing and later creating a mirror-like finish to the still greasy and knobbly surface of each boot's toecap.

Interesting here that appearance was considered well before anything in the way of comfort!

The actual practice of boot preparation involved the handle of a toothbrush, spoon handle or similar, which was used to rub over the initially rough and knobbly surface of the new boot cap, the process lubricated regularly with dabs of black boot polish, liberally laced with gobs of spittle. This process, 'Boning' being its technical name in the RAF, we learned was primarily aimed at reducing the uneven and knobbly surface of the boot's toecap down to a flat smooth finish. This then allowed the proud, by now dry-mouthed owner, who, having once achieved a clear base to work on, to then continue the 'spit and polish' routine, until a mirror-like shine began to appear, following many hours of work.

We also learned more regarding the value of stuffing wads of wet newspaper or toilet paper into the body of our boots each night on retiring. This, we learned, would assist in softening the hard, stiff leather slightly, while the warmth of our feet during the day would combine with the moisture from the paper to soften up the leather upper. What went unsaid however was that this treatment required the wearer to march with damp boots the next morning, always in the hope that he would avoid getting chilblains while enduring this decidedly unhealthy process.

The assurance that perseverance would serve to mould the by then semi-pliable leather until the boots would eventually get to fit 'like a slipper' was a little hard to take at the time. This blandly offered assurance took days and many applications of sticking plaster and antiseptic ointment being applied to bruised, swollen feet and raw toes, until the hard leather eventually began to yield to the treatment. Thankfully, in my case, the threat of chilblains failed to eventuate.

My boots did eventually get to fit, not quite like a pair of slippers, but comfortable, just like our instructor had forecast. Getting there though involved a couple of weeks of sore, sometimes raw toes, aching feet and ankles from all the marching and running. Add to that hours and hours of boning, spitting and polishing.

We also learned more regarding the advised practice of shaving the inside of our working trousers. This was supposed to cut down and smooth out most of the rough wool fibres sticking out into the inside of our trouser legs, particularly where they lay against the insides of our thighs and the more soft and sensitive parts adjacent to our sex gear.

Some of the more artistic among us took to soaking their wool work berets in warm water then moulding them, while wet, onto their heads and into a variety of shapes. This practice was considered to be 'slightly' illegal in the RAF, while at the same time also threatening to inflict a severe cranial chill on the victim. The treatment was condoned though, with individual berets being moulded by their owners into some creative forms.

"Dear god!" (Whoever he, she or it was) Intoned I on looking into the mirror in the ablutions area of our hut for the first time on donning my new and very uncomfortable uniform, "So this is what they have done to the newly minted 2588475 AC2 Dubbin". What a hellish place I had landed in!

FIRST NIGHT IN HOTEL PADGATE

That first night in camp followed a march to the mess hall for a largely unpalatable but hot dinner, followed by a plate of lukewarm and lumpy custard, swilled down with a pint mug full of tea. My new uniform was hellishly uncomfortable. I recall having feelings of depression, misery and loneliness in the extreme. I would suspect that this applied to every other one of my suffering companions, all in dread of what our first night and tomorrow would bring.

In addition to being cold and draughty, as a cold wind whistled constantly through the cracks in the walls of the old Nissen hut, through nearly every window frame and down the ill-fitting rusty chimney, the forthcoming night trying to sleep in a strange, uncomfortable looking straw-filled bunk, loomed ominously.

To make matters even worse, if that was possible? There was no wood or any kindling anywhere to be found to at least enable us to start a small fire in the stove. The hut seemed at least as cold and bleak as the windy and rain-filled Lancashire night outside its cold, depressing interior and its distressed occupants, as we wearily readied ourselves for the night ahead. We all were almost too stressed and tired even to want to sit around and discuss our predicament. Instead, each seemed more intent on withdrawing into their thoughts and anxiety for what was yet to come. Our future seemed hopeless.

My thoughts that first night, as I tried to find a reasonably comfortable place for my body, somewhere under the coarse wool blanket and rough paillasse beneath me, were of my mam, dad and sister Maureen, not forgetting my warm and comfy bed, so unwillingly left behind in faraway Leeds.

Unfortunately, Leeds was 50-odd miles away across the Pennine Hills to the east. That night it felt like my family and bed were more like a thousand times the distance!

A STRANGE, NEW WORLD

I had been cast into a cold, strange and threatening world. It was a world inhabited by equally strange beings. Insular and uncaring non-commissioned officers (NCOs), all of them clad in immaculately presented uniforms, with 'blancoed' belts, shining brasses and boot toecaps that possessed a mirror-like shine. These strange beings, controllers in every respect, had ultimate power over every minute of our day and night. They seemed to enjoy the sport of beating any remaining resistance out of their barely comprehending charges, as they quick-marched us everywhere while barking out orders in a language that most of us found difficult, if not frustratingly impossible to understand, let alone obey…

It was a case of "Eft, eft, eft arrht eft, keep those puny bloody arms swinging until they feel like they'll drop orf, Rrright wheel, eft wheel…" We were wheeled and marched until we were dizzy. Our feet bled and ached, while our new, uncomfortable and razor-edged starched collars bit into our necks, and the coarse wool of our new uniforms had us itching uncomfortably as our bodies grew hotter with all the unaccustomed physical activity.

When it came to getting into an uncomfortable, straw- stuffed bunk that first night in the RAF and during the nights that followed, most were so exhausted, both physically and mentally, that it was a release just to lay flat on one's back, pull the rough wool blanket and bed-sheet over pyjama clad aching limbs and sore toes, and fall off, absolutely exhausted, into a deep abyss of dreamless sleep.

On that first night, while I still lay huddled in my uncomfortable bunk desperately trying to get warm, I could feel what seemed to be every piece of straw pushing with grim intent toward working itself upward through the fabric of the paillasse, thence through my comfortingly thick cotton RAF issue pyjamas and into my body. That also got me thinking as to what kind of bugs and other nasty's might be lurking among the straw packed into my particular paillasse?

Following a day during which we recruits had barely a minute or two to ourselves, sleep eventually and inevitably invaded this sprog's jaded brain, and I managed eventually to drop off, over the edge of consciousness and into a deep dreamless sleep.

The day had been hectic and stressful as well as tiring, and it wasn't long before I succumbed, in spite of the lumpy, straw- filled paillasse.

Sleep didn't last very long on that first night, and it was perhaps an hour or so later that I awoke with a start to the sounds of abject sobbing and wailing. I had arrived back into consciousness to sounds of anguish emanating in waves from the depths of the bunk next to mine. Its occupier, a lad from Wales as I recall, was taking the wrenching away from his comfortable home in one or other of the Welsh valleys and the loss of his civilian bed to heart.

I was awakened by the continuous and loud wailing of my next-door neighbour, who was crying like a lost wraith and, to make matters even worse than they were, he kept on calling out for his Mummy! The wailing got to be such that I and a couple of other tired sprogs, following our inability to get the guy to shut up by shouting at him, took more drastic action. Dragging ourselves out of our own barely warm bunks and physically yanking the covers off him, we demanded that he, like the rest of us, try to get some sleep and forget about his mother, much as we had to do!

Our shouting and my neighbour's moaning resulted in the corporal in charge of our flight, presumably having just emerged from a dreamy tryst with some voluptuous maiden or other of his acquaintance and also being abruptly awakened by our shouting – erupted from his room.

With a roar that awakened more of my exhausted fellow sprogs, he demanded that the noise stop, otherwise he threatened to "Get each of yous noisy little bastards out onto the square and march yous around in the rain for a couple of hours!"

That eventually did the trick. The crying in the next bunk did eventually stop, and sleep once again overtook a now very tired Yorkshire lad. Not for very long, as the whole hut was suddenly shocked into instant awareness by the now fully dressed and resplendent corporal, walking up and down the hut and banging on a dustbin lid with his baton.

Dear god! It was 5am on a dark, cold morning – my first real day in the RAF, uggggh! With nigh-on 24 months of this shit life still to endure. I was sure that if this is what RAF life was all about, I for one would never make it to the end of what on that day felt more like a two-year prison sentence with hard labour, sore feet, a sore neck and an itchy uniform thrown in for good measure!

Following our first morning parade on the cold drizzle and windswept parade ground in front of our hut, we were quick-marched to the mess hall for our first breakfast.

The RAF's version of breakfast that morning comprised a dish of lumpy porridge followed by a strip or two of streaky bacon and a dollop of baked beans, accompanied by a greasy fried egg that had been cooked until it had a constitution similar to vulcanised rubber. This was followed by white sliced bread, together with a couple of pats of margarine and jam, to be washed down by a pint-pot full of hot tea.

It was then off, later again marching at double-time to another questionable practitioner – a person who the RAF referred to as the base 'hair stylist', in other words, Padgate's sheep shearer.

The hair stylist on this particular base knew of only one style – short back and sides! So short, in fact, that in my case, my then beautifully kept mop of long black hair and lovingly set and very fashionable 'DA' (Duck's Arse) hairstyle quickly disintegrated into stubble, so close-cropped that it was almost on the verge of baldness! Ugh! This time I really did feel depressed and near naked, when I eventually emerged into an early spring day, accompanied by a cold wind blowing from the north.

A few days followed, during which we raw sprogs were started along the hard road to learning the rudiments of saluting, marching, counter-marching, slow marching, quick marching and other of the basic skills that the RAF considered necessary to successfully achieve our metamorphosis from 'slack-arsed' civilians to ordinary aircraftman. In RAF speak, we were ranked and henceforth to be known as an aircraftman second class (AC2), the lowest form of life in the RAF.

On the other hand, I well remember thinking to myself at the time, that it would probably have been a hell of a lot worse, had I been allocated into one or other of the regular army regiments?

4 S OF RT – WILMSLOW

After a few decidedly uncomfortable days and nights trying without much in the way of success to find a comfortable spot on my prickly paillasse at Hotel Padgate, I was eventually allocated, along with a group of my shorn headed colleagues, to no. 4 School of Recruit Training at RAF Wilmslow.

This centre of basic training was located just south of Manchester, near the then small township of Wilmslow, just over the Lancashire border, in the county of Cheshire.

One of the most memorable images I still retain of the place, following our transportation there in the back of a draughty RAF truck and following weeks of what was known as 'square bashing' in early 1953, was its original, Second World War Spitfire fighter that proudly guarded the entrance to the base. Later, during the 1960s or perhaps later, RAF Wilmslow was decommissioned. I believe eventually the whole area was later turned into a housing estate.

Weeks of marching, with and without my issued Second World War vintage .303 Lee Enfield rifle, from which I was allowed to fire a few clips of live ammunition toward a distant target, passed by with little to excite my earlier mentioned possibility of signing on for a further period in the RAF. That thought had disappeared – long before I had entered the gates of RAF Wilmslow.

I finally emerged from No. 4 S of RT a much fitter eighteen- year-old than the one that had originally arrived there six weeks earlier. Also, by the end of recruit training, I possessed a pair of boots that eventually did get to fit like a comfortable pair of well-worn shoes. Both toecaps eventually got to gleam in close to a 'snot-on-the-wall-on-a frosty-night' like state from my constant boning, following the application of pints of spit, a couple of tins of black polish and a deal of 'elbow grease'.

The amount of physical effort and spit expended to maintain a pair of boot toecaps that actually got reasonably close to the appearance of a steel mirror needed to be incessant. To maintain a shine, however, became difficult following training days that found me and my boots often having to slog our way through thick mud and rain, thus requiring a couple of hours cleaning and more spit and polish each evening, to be ready for next morning's kit inspection.

The accommodation at RAF Wilmslow, while still well down toward the more Spartan end of a night's accommodation and comfort, at least provided this recruit with a sprung bed frame, upon which were located three reasonably thick and flexible 'biscuits', in lieu of a civilian-style mattress.

By the time a couple of weeks had passed by during our initial training, I was so tired following a day of marching, climbing over obstacles, rifle drills and having to submit myself to a couple of minutes in the camp 'gas chamber' – just to illustrate what a dose of tear gas felt like – I would be happy just to collapse into my bunk and sleep the proverbial 'sleep of the dead'.

As the weeks passed, a few colleagues and I had slowly developed into a loose group of mates. The reality of being a lowly and thus powerless member of the armed forces, an occupant on the lowest rung of the RAF's rankings, quickly passed into the realm of complete indifference.

THE VALUABLE ART OF SKIVING

To the uninitiated, skiving is the carefully honed practice, more likened to a fine art. It is a required skill that anyone intent on avoiding some, or even better, most or all the more onerous duties that will, with the certainty of the sun rising tomorrow, come one's way at some time or other during a stint in the armed forces.

It was always too easy to get caught out for all manner of onerous tasks – If you were not careful or alert enough to grab every opportunity on offer to an ever-alert sprog. To be capable of skiving with at least some degree of success was an important skill to acquire, alongside having to learn to march, salute, square one's bunk, bone one's boots etc. It was at least one way that any aspiring individual on entering the armed services, could seek to make life a little more comfortable while in the clutches and at the mercy of the military.

There were many advantages to be gained by making a concerted effort to learn and practice with diligence, the means of worming oneself out of any kind of duty that could with the speed of lightning, be sprung upon any unprepared sprog, at any hour of the day or night.

Among the early duties to be avoided at all costs, was being included in the detail having to stand overnight guard at the station's gate, a thankless duty that invariably meant standing for two hours on and four hours off throughout the length of a usually cold, wet and windy night. Avoiding as much marching as possible came a close second, particularly having to front up to what were regular weekly Saturday morning 'bullshit' parades.

The pinnacle of skiving (degree 1st class in skivology) could be enhanced by the acquisition of various kinds of 'chits'. These were official forms or signed notes, endorsed by someone in authority like the base doctor, or obtained from the Station Warrant Officer's office (SWO) – upon which the lucky owner was deemed exempt from a specified duty.

How one went about achieving such a valuable slip of paper depended to a large extent on the acting or other skills, physical or medical attributes of the student skiver. Such useful, official pieces of indemnity were considered by most to be well worth any hardship endured on the road to their acquisition.

The most valuable aspects of the art of skiving relied more often than not on an individual sprog's capacity when it came to their ability to think quickly – under any and all circumstances. For example, training oneself in the art of being what was termed as 'being unavoidably absent' during the issuing of verbal orders by anyone in authority, and that meant anyone other than an AC2.

Skiving was just one of the few ways in which those sprogs so inclined to do so, found ways and means by which to slip out from beneath the various layers of commissioned and non-commissioned officers' attention, whenever the opportunity to do so presented itself.

As the early days at No. 4 S of R T got to roll on a little, we raw newcomers also got to learn how to live in harmony with the rest of the lads in our particular flight. We also learned to look out for each other, and by so doing coalesced into smaller groups – more or less becoming what were generally known as 'mates'.

JANKERS!

One of the more memorable and bizarre incidents of my stay at RAF Wilmslow occurred during a stint of what was universally known as jankers[1] – a few days of which that I was summarily sentenced to undertake, following being charged with some petty transgression of the RAF's rules, the precise nature of which continues to elude me.

Being caught out in this way came about during my earlier days of recruit training, filled as it was with from before dawn 'til dark of 'square bashing' (marching and rifle drills). Being caught out in this way was understandable, occurring as it did well before I had managed to move up slowly, but with concentration and intent, toward becoming a practiced exponent of the skiver's art.

The particular infraction of the rules in question, more than likely something related to my failure to follow an order or something similar, which in the normal scheme of things would have seemed petty. The misdemeanour in question eventually found me standing stiffly at attention, paraded in front of the Commanding Officer (CO), on what was commonly known in the services as a 'charge'.

At this short hearing I, among a few other transgressors that day, was quick-marched into the CO's office by one of the attending base military policemen (SPs). Once brought to a halt in front of the CO's desk and stood to attention with my beret dragged off my closely cropped head by the attending corporal SP, I was confronted with the gory details of the issue that had landed me there.

The CO, having spent what seemed an inordinately long period during which he appeared to be perusing all the intimate details of the charge, written in triplicate by the accusatory NCO, then proceeded to appraise me of the need to obey each and every order given by any superior. That of course meant everyone other than a lowly AC2 in the whole RAF.

The CO then went on to sentence me to a week of jankers. This meant five days of extra and usually dirty or heavy work, all of which were to be spent in the base cookhouse.

Cookhouse duty was a decidedly onerous task which usually involved the tedious, but useful task of potato peeling, vegetable washing, cleaning out the massive steel vats in which the base's meals had been cooked, scraping out pans and other, usually greasy utensils. All the above, in addition to doing every other lowly job that was on offer in the vicinity of the cookhouse.

Being sentenced to a week of jankers didn't free we jankees from having to front up for the regular morning parade, and a full day of marching and rifle drill, following which the current crop of jankees were required to parade outside the base police (SP) station after the evening meal. We were then inspected minutely by the sergeant SP, for what I never got to know, then quick-marched off to the cookhouse to carry out our daily stint of extra duties there.

The incident referred to earlier occurred during one very special day, at least I suppose it was for Britain, and an evening during which I had been delegated to clean out one of a long row of large cooking vats that lined one side of the base cookhouse. This was a distinctly hot, greasy and tedious job. Coincidentally, that day just happened to be the very same, during which the earlier Princess Elizabeth, following the recent death of her father King George VI, was to be crowned Queen Elizabeth II of Britain.

Notes

1. Jankers – Having been subjected to military law and being 'sentenced' to a period of extra duties (often hard and dirty).

JUNE 2ND 1953

On that memorable day, all regular square-bashing activities had been curtailed earlier to prepare and organise the various training groups (flights)[1] for a parade on the base parade ground. This was yet another opportunity for the base's 'brass' to organise a 'special' bullshit parade to acknowledge the ascent of our new monarch to the British throne. The current crop of jankees, including me, was told off to report to the cookhouse.

The whole country was being held in thrall as the young princess was soon to be made a queen.

As the shimmering diamond and other precious stone encrusted crown was being placed upon the royal head of Queen Elizabeth II by the Archbishop of Canterbury, I had my closely cropped head and shoulders buried deep inside a smelly, fat-streaked vat that had recently been full of some foul smelling something or other soup-like stew. In my hand was a stiff wire brush with which I was trying to loosen some of the smelly and stickier stuff that was still adhering to the sides of the vat.

At the moment of the crowning, the cookhouse tannoy (loudspeaker) was blaring out a commentary of the solemn crowning ceremony, directly from Westminster Abbey in London.

Overcome with a bad case of nationalistic zeal, the sergeant cook, a fat overbearing regular who seemed to take great delight in giving us jankees the shittiest jobs going, took it upon himself to order all the cookhouse staff and jankees in the vicinity, to come smartly to attention in salute to our newly crowned monarch.

All he got from the depths of my particular vat was an echoing, heartfelt cry of "Bollocks to the f*****g Queen", plus my refusal to spring to attention.

The attitude of this even then republican inclined sprog, was more to do with his firm belief that British royalty already enjoyed excessive and unearned privileges, due solely to their privileged mother having been bedded by some inbred, 'chinless wonder' prince or some other underemployed so-called 'royals'. At the very least, I had felt at that moment that my expression of disinterest in anything about the British royal family and its crowd of hangers-on, to be appropriate and just.

Not so the sergeant cook. My outburst resulted in an extended stay in the cookhouse through to that evening. I recall feeling at the time that whatever the result and consequences, my feelings regarding what was going on at the time in Westminster Abbey was well worth any additional duties I had to undergo. Had we been on the parade ground, well things would have been different when it came to giving our new monarch a well meant, properly constituted general salute. In the hot and smelly cookhouse, covered in grease, muck and slush? No sir, not this lad.

The event and loudly echoing result of my admittedly not very respectful comment and refusal to leap to attention, spread rapidly among the sprogs in both mine, and nearby flights. The extra work in the cookhouse that my 'statement from the cooking pot' and refusal to stand to attention in salute, had attracted was also added to, even later, on my sweaty return to my buddies by the NCO in charge of our flight, an Irishman – Corporal Delaney.

On learning of my transgression, Delany, normally one of the more reasonable of the base NCO's, took it upon himself to award me further with two circuits jogging around the perimeter of the parade ground. And him a real Irishman at that! What the hell – it was bloody well worth it!

The weeks of recruit training passed quickly, during which each graduating recruit was later interviewed for a second time, before him being allocated to a trade on being subsequently posted to a permanent base.

Some sprogs considered to be more worth to the RAF Regiment, mainly those excelling in army-like traits like marching, saluting, polishing boot-caps and brasses, bullshit parades, rifle drill and shooting at targets, were subsequently winkled out for their trouble and posted off to undergo further, intense training. Eventually, following more square bashing, those poor misguided souls usually ended up being allocated to airfields thought to be in danger of being attacked by the IRA, or based at some strategic airfield or other RAF installation in far-off East Asia or Germany, the latter still operating under BAOR arrangements.

My eventual RAF trade designation in the role of 'base tailor' was probably assisted as a result of me having cultivated some satisfied customers among the interviewing NCOs for whom I, being the only tailor among our particular intake, had been both willing and able to provide a skilled uniform or civilian clothing alteration service.

This service, earlier provided to one or two of my fellow sprog mates, had expanded somewhat over the weeks. The fact that I could sew and cut professionally had spread among other flights, ultimately also coming to the attention of one or two of the NCO's. In the case of the latter, a sergeant specialist involved with interviewing personnel for their future roles within the RAF, I had the good sense to refuse payment for a number of sewing services performed for him, suggesting instead that the RAF would do well to recognise my professional skills as a qualified tailor.

My tailoring skills, learned and improved upon since leaving school at the age of 15, had proved to be valuable in many ways at RAF Wilmslow. Most of my work here related to trousers shortening, or to a lesser extent some minor refitting of ill-fitting, badly designed and cheaply made working tunics. At times, my evenings would see my bed space taking on the role of fitting room and workshop.

While limited at the time to hand sewing, I blessed the day that my dad had suggested that I also pack my tailor's shears and personal sewing kit on entering the RAF. His comment at the time along the lines, "You'll find your tailoring skills useful in the RAF," proved to be right on the button.

Whatever had prompted those in authority to allocate me to the trade in which I had trained as a civilian, I will be forever in their debt. I also noted at the time that my sewing and tailoring skills should prove to be of immense skiving value during the rest of my enforced two yearlong stay as a reluctant small cog in the massive RAF machine.

Notes

1. Flight – Term given to a group of trainees, also used to describe a group of aircraft.

NO. 3 FLYING TRAINING SCHOOL – FELTWELL

From RAF Wilmslow, my first permanent posting as the base's resident tailor was to RAF Feltwell, a primary flying training school located in the eastern shire of Norfolk, not far from Thetford and the picturesque Norfolk Broads.

No. 3 FTS had operated as a primary flying training facility since its establishment during the war in Europe. The base's location was in the midst of some of the prettiest country in Britain's eastern counties, among what remained of a some other, now derelict wartime bomber and fighter bases, most of which were abandoned following the war's ending.

RAF Feltwell's location under the flight path leading to the United States Air Force's (USAF) strategic bomber base at Lakenheath just a few miles to the south, afforded anyone living nearby in the local villages a regular view of the US's latest fighter aircraft and strategic bombers, as they came and went on training or deployment assignments.

You could stand anywhere in the vicinity of Feltwell village or the base proper, and watch B47 Stratojet bombers and behemoth B36 bombers with their six piston and four jet engines roaring and thundering across the local skies, spewing black exhaust trails as they came and went.

Compared to the small propeller-driven Percival Provost and Chipmunk training aircraft that were being used at RAF Feltwell, the sight of these American behemoths was an awesome reminder of the power being projected across the world by the USAF.

On occasions, one could also sight one or other of the US's U2 high-altitude spy aircraft, as they took off from Lakenheath on a training flight. Perhaps they were instead on their way to a spying mission over Eastern Europe or even the USSR? This type of mission, regarded as being dangerous at the time, brings back memories of the later story of a USAF U2 spy plane, piloted by Gary Powers that the Russians shot down while it was flying on a reconnaissance mission over their territory on May 1st 1960.

MIGRATION – FIRST SEEDS

It was on one or two occasions early during my two years' service in the RAF, that a lively discussion on the relative qualities of life, following our eventual return to civilian life was being canvassed, usually during any spare time during which all other interesting areas of discussion had been exhausted. These usually were conversations during which the possible alternatives of continuing in the service, returning to our civilian lives or migration to either of Canada or Australia, were being explored by some of my companion sprogs. Both countries were thought to be popular destinations, although Australia almost always seemed to capture more imaginations than the reputedly colder cities and countryside of Canada.

It was during one or two such discussions with fellow national service personnel, that the seeds of my later departure from England gradually developed and blossomed. The period during which I was coming to the reality that my future, beyond national service, could well lie well beyond the hallowed hills and William Blake's "Dark satanic mills" of Britain.

To be more precise, my thinking in those days was already leaning toward Australia. The swaggering words of 'Banjo' Patterson's unique poetic style, his famous ballad "Waltzing Matilda", and thoughts of sun-drenched beaches, kangaroos and wide-open spaces – far, far away from the rain and regularly smog shrouded north of England!

Canada for me always came a distant second to Australia – due mainly to its location even further north than the British Isles – and apparently much colder.

Apart from considerations of climate, my childhood hero being that redoubtable Yorkshire bred sailor and navigator Captain James Cook, it had always seemed natural that at least one of the countries to which this young Yorkshire lad would eventually venture, should the opportunity ever present itself, was more than likely to be Australia. Migration anywhere at that stage however only represented an item for general discussion. It is interesting though that even among a number of my colleague national servicemen, discussion on possible alternative directions in which we could go, once our national service commitments had ended, were actively being canvassed.

Some time yet was to elapse until the possibility to emigrate would eventually come to pass. In the meantime, I had some months yet to spend at the pleasure of my new monarch, Queen Elizabeth, whom I hoped had not received a report on my disparaging comments uttered in the RAF Wilmslow cookhouse on the occasion of her recent elevation to the British throne!

BASE TAILOR

The position of RAF Feltwell's base tailor offered its new incumbent a number of very real advantages, one being always sure of possessing a smartly turned out uniform.

Of even greater value, however, was regularly finding my sewing and cutting skills in demand from everyone – from the base's senior brass down to other ranks, both male and female. Calls for my tailoring expertise regularly came, particularly on the many occasions when someone or other required alterations to be made to uniforms or newly purchased civilian clothes. Most of my 'official' work involved alterations to the uniforms of lower ranked colleagues and WAAFs (female RAF types). Out of hours I often also found myself being requested to alter or remodel civilian skirts and dresses for one or two of the local WAAFs, in addition to various other sewing jobs from anyone else on base, including some of the officers and a few civilian day workers.

Being the base tailor also meant that it became possible to establish an enclosed area of personal territory within the base stores section. Equipped with sewing machines, a hand iron and a large table upon which to work, the tailor's shop became a place in which none, NCO or Officer alike, other of course than the officer in charge of the stores group, saw any need or occasion to impose their authority.

Once having settled down into my new posting, life became relatively easy-going and acceptably accommodating. At the same time, finding myself in a position that allowed me to organise my workload, also provided the opportunity (not to be taken lightly) of being able to absent myself on most occasions from the tedium of guard duty, weekly Saturday morning bullshit parades and other less than interesting tasks and duties.

Saturday morning bullshit parades were a real bind requiring the application of a great deal of thought. The issue was solved by my offer to provide an additional 'after-hours' valet service to fellow base personnel involved with the preparation of their uniforms for either a Saturday morning or other form of 'special' parade, an offer accepted by my boss, the base stores chief.

This strategy achieved two objectives: Apart from the few extra pounds I was able to earn by the approved application of a small charge for pressing and valeting services rendered, a portion of which was to be donated to the RAF benevolent fund, my boss also awarded me the following morning (usually a Saturday) free of work or the need to parade – a reward no doubt for my conscientious dedication to duty?

CIRCUITS AND BUMPS

One duty that I did welcome and one I enjoyed during my time at RAF Feltwell, was an occasional overnight stay, which required three service personnel to act as guards, patrolling in and around the control tower of a nearby abandoned Second World War bomber base.

The tower and long-time abandoned concrete airstrip in question, located a few miles from Feltwell, was regularly being used to provide daytime and overnight flying training. Here was the sort of flying that involved trainee pilots learning the skills of taking off and landing on a hard airstrip. In other words, a sealed airstrip – a very different proposition to the grass version they were used to using more generally on the base at Feltwell.

For the uninitiated, 'circuits and bumps' refers to the practice whereby a trainee pilot lines the aircraft for a landing on the chosen runway. Instead of landing and taxiing away having once touched all the aircraft's wheels down onto the runway, the engine is then gunned and the aircraft returned to the air for another circuit and landing. Hence a circuit and a bump.

The degree of 'bump' occurring is directly in proportion to the angle and speed at which the pilot was able to put his or her aircraft safely down onto the runway.

Should the pilot come in at too steep an angle or too fast, it can be amusing to watch the aircraft bounce high into the air then descend back onto the runway with a definitely painful sounding 'whack' to its undercarriage. Amusing to watch yes, but not so for the pilot, particularly when they find themselves on the receiving end of a blast over the radio from one or other of the training officers.

Use of the runway required the control tower and its equipment to be manned and guarded during the training wing's daytime and night flying operations.

This kind of overnight duty started during the previous morning, with that night's guard, comprising a corporal and two other (usually lower) ranks being transferred to the old Second World War airstrip, together with a load of food enough at least for that day, night and the next morning.

The sole function of the guard was to patrol around the perimeter of the control tower and runway – keeping a sharp lookout for any potential looters. In reality, little if anything in the way of looting was ever known to have occurred, so that the duty came to be regarded as only a slightly inconvenient but very acceptable, well-fed diversion from one's normal daily routine – particularly if the weather was good. Not so during the winter months.

The old and near derelict airstrip had been an auxiliary bomber base during the recent war with Germany. What remained of its deteriorating wartime buildings were interesting, both to fossick through and just sit outside and muse upon what life there must have been like on the then active base during actual bombing operations during the 1940s.

The airstrip itself was isolated and well away from the nearest road, in those days virtually surrounded by hayfields and cow paddocks. The only real evidence of its wartime activities remaining was the control tower, itself getting somewhat dilapidated, and the concrete strip of its one remaining runway, plus a couple of serviceable taxiways. The rest of the old base had become overgrown with grass, brambles and low shrubs, much of which during the late spring and early summer months stood head high, alive with insects, wildflowers and birds.

When night flying was on, and it was my turn to be allocated for overnight duty, having put my name on the designated 'volunteers list', it was always interesting to listen-in to the flying instructors talking their trainees in onto the circuit, either flagging them off with a wave of their red hand- held torches, or providing a critique on the regular occasions a trainee fouled up their approach and landing. It was all very instructive, following which one could look forward to a feed of steak and vegetables, usually followed by fruit and ice cream, the main course usually cooked by one or other of the night's guard. Sleeping facilities though basic were comfortable.

I still recall one or two warm late spring nights, sitting on a grassy mound at the end of the runway. The various training aircraft, landing lights gleaming through the day and late evening mist, would join the circuit downwind, fly lower onto their base leg, approach glide and then land. Once all the aircraft's wheels were on the runway the pilot would gun the motor, accelerate and take off again.

At the time, I would just sit there trying to rekindle in my mind's eye the sight and sound of the roaring multiple exhausts of four massive engines, as back in the 1940s they propelled bomb-laden RAF Lancaster and Wellington or American B17 Flying Fortress or B25 Mitchell bombers into the darkening sky as they flew off to the east and into the darkness, on their way to bombing runs over Nazi Germany.

Those particular evenings also served to bring back personal memories of the swarms of bombers that during the latter stages of the war years would thunder over our house in Leeds toward the east, each on their way to bomb the German Reich and other strategic targets across northern Europe.

In those days, like many other young lads, I used to dream of a time when I too could fly one of those thundering Lancaster bombers, or perhaps better still to be able to fly the fabled Spitfire fighter.

On those late spring and early summer nights in Norfolk, now as a national serviceman sitting at the end of the runway watching trainers landing and taking off, it was great just to allow my mind to wander back to my boyhood days and dreams, now long gone but never forgotten.

LOVELORN

It was around this time that my world, at least the emotional side of it, came crashing down into a confused heap of emotions. To explain:

Just before my entry into the RAF I found myself teetering on the edge of strange new, disturbing emotions. During one of my earliest leaves back to Leeds, I had fallen in love for the first time. Yes, I had met and fallen in love with a cute little girl. To be more exact, at that age it was probably more accurate to describe the emotions I was feeling as being more akin to infatuation or even an early and healthy form of youthful lust.

Cynthia was her name, and although a couple of years older than me at the time, she came into my life during a Sunday night dance at the Leeds Jewish Institute.

The Jewish Institute, then located in the then predominantly Jewish suburb of Chapeltown, was an active social club – a meeting place that catered for Leeds' Jewish community. Both Alec, my long-time pal, and I had recently become members. Most of our close friends were also members, some joining the club's football section, while others played table tennis, billiards and snooker – or just attended the various social events and weekly dances.

I had often noticed Cynthia's saucy little figure across the ballroom floor during previous Sunday night dances. I finally plucked up sufficient courage one evening to ask her to dance, after we had eyed each other across the floor. My young life changed that night as we slow fox-trotted and waltzed our way, dance after dance, around the floor to the music of Johnny Addlestone and his locally based show band.

During the 'last waltz', the dance that usually ended a dance night in those days, my sweet-smelling partner snuggled up so close that I could hardly breathe. Her very closeness began to create feelings of disquieting discomfort, as my heart began to beat faster and I began to experience a growing sensation awakening in my lower abdominal region!

Following that dance, which I hoped would never end, and in answer to the perennial question usually asked by young men from time immemorial of the girl of their choice, usually during or following the last dance of the evening – "Can I walk you home luv?" she answered with what to my dazed ears and aching body sounded very much like a breathless, sexy, "Yes."

I didn't have to walk her to her real home that night, thank goodness, as I learned that she lived not in Leeds but over ten miles outside the city proper, in the outer suburb of Dewsbury, some distance to the south of Leeds. Luckily for me, she came up to Leeds each weekend, where she stayed with her uncle and aunt at their house in the St Martins, in those days a relatively upmarket residential area, just to the north of Chapeltown.

That first evening ended well after midnight with us kissing, cuddling and 'messing about' on the couch in her uncle and aunt's front room. Leaving her that night and walking the two or so miles back to my house in Harehills, my heart continued thumping long after we both had detached ourselves from each other. It had been a very steamy and passionate session, during which the nether regions of my body ended up with an ache that lasted for at least a couple of days.

I was in love – or was it lust? Don't really know, but I do know that I thought I was in love, and for the very first time in my young life.

The relationship blossomed over several weeks, following my entry into the RAF, with Cynthia writing to me, sending perfumed letters written on rose coloured paper, and me daydreaming of the next weekend leave back in Leeds and the chance to once again get my arms and everything else around her gorgeous little body.

Interestingly though, our passionate trysts never reached that ultimate climax, although often it got close on a couple of occasions – leaving my poor hormone charged body aching with unfinished business. This, of course, was happening during the days before the availability of the 'pill'. While condoms were readily available for such an occasion, the girl of my dreams always stopped short, stating that she was saving herself until she was married.

Ah well, so be it, at the very least I was beginning, in my always vivid and inexperienced imagination at least, to wonder what it would be like spending every night of one's life with this lovely creature.

Yes, I know dear reader – I still had a lot yet to learn about loving and living – but one had to start somewhere?

Inevitably perhaps, the road to enduring love never seems to run smoothly. In our case, my infatuation with Cynthia from Dewsbury should have seen the signs when she would sometimes say things like: "I wish you weren't just a tailor, Gerry," or "When I get married I want to have a large house and a car," and themes of a similar nature.

It is understandable I suppose, that being 18 years old and having had little prior interest in or experience with girls or young women, that I was more than a little naive when it came to stuff like love and loving. Other than my attendance at an occasional 'necking party' I had had little experience with girls. 'Necking' in my youth, I should explain, was best described as a party, where a group of teenagers would get together to play games like 'postman's knock' and swap partners. This usually ended up with a lot of innocent kissing, accompanied by a small amount of exploratory fondling.

Getting back to Cynthia, all I could then see was her face and cute, cuddly figure, and not what her words were saying. Of course, in answer to the comment on me being just a tailor, I would truthfully reply that I didn't plan on just being a tailor for the rest of my life. But, even that being so, the ending of my youthful love affair came about sooner than I had expected.

A SOUL IN TORMENT

The end to my dreams came during a telephone call I had made to the object of my youthful desire. This was before a weekend leave during which I was due to return to Leeds the following Friday. At the time, I was a little concerned that she hadn't written to me for over a week. On telephoning her at home, hoping for us to meet up as usual on the next Saturday, she made less than interested noises – before eventually breaking the news (and with it my heart) saying, "I have met someone else and won't be coming to meet you."

She went on to explain to her erstwhile and now devastated ex-love, that the new man in her life was older than she, and he had a nice car (very important) and: "His father owns a shop" – obviously even more important. My plea for us to talk fell on deaf ears and was met with the comment: "What really can you offer me, Gerry, you're only a tailor!"

It is interesting to note here that even so many years later, I can still recall the exact words that a young girl ended my first tentative love affair with and – how deeply those words had hurt and burned into my very soul at the time.

Rejection at any time can be a painful experience, but at that time and in those circumstances, the abruptness of her words came very hard. Yes, it certainly was the truth then that I was just a tailor, one who at the time seemed to have very few prospects – and, I wasn't even a qualified tailor at that.

For some weeks following my loss, I continued to feel intense hurt. As the weeks passed by though I was slowly able to come to grips with what had happened and accept that there was little I could or indeed should try to do, to try and win her back. I was eventually able to accept that she had articulated her feelings very openly to me – and the truth was that she was obviously on the lookout for something that I couldn't offer. In any case, at the tender age of 18, I very soon concluded that I was much too young to be thinking of getting myself involved in a permanent relationship, or even thinking to settle down.

The whole experience was my first awakening to that ancient male observation when it comes to dealing with the women in our lives, an all too often situation so eloquently defined in the famous aria from Giuseppe Verdi's Opera – "La donna e mobile" (the lady is fickle).

Following an understandably bleak few weeks mourning my loss, my mind was diverted relatively quickly toward the many other opportunities on offer for a young man. Although currently a mere tailor and not very far from being penniless and certainly car less, had his eyes and mind fixed firmly on a more interesting and hopefully successful career over the years yet to come.

I guess the attitude that emerged as a result of that first emotional setback was to make sure that in future I would seek to protect myself when it came to matters of the heart. Perhaps also, the experience and my determination never to allow myself to become too closely involved emotionally in the future, had some bearing on my later inability as an adult to allow myself to become wholly dependent on a relationship. Perhaps?

I think for this record, it will be best if I now move on – leaving any further analysis to those more adequately equipped or interested, to delve further. As for me, well I had a life to get on with and a long way yet to travel…

JAZZ AND GIRLS GALORE

While all this emotional stuff was going on, I had managed to become involved with two other lads on the base who, like me, were interested in what in the 1950s was known as modern jazz. One had studied classical guitar, and the other played bass guitar. I played piano reasonably well, following a number of years during which our parents had provided both my sister and me with the opportunity to study classical pianoforte.

Our coming together happened as a result of also becoming involved with the base's concert party, a group that included singers, a few actors and one comedian. The Feltwell concert party also had a WAAF group featuring four girls who specialised in songs recorded by the 1940s American female vocal group, the Andrews Sisters. They were also interested in presenting modern jazz ballads currently being featured on the local radio and vinyl records. Eventually, we all got together and formed the Feltwell Jazz Group. One of the drum players from the base's RAF band joined us later, which then turned our jazz trio into a quartet.

Playing with the group, in addition to playing the organ at the various Christian church services on a Sunday morning, made for a reasonably interesting and liveable life at Feltwell, particularly as I had by then put my recent loss of the lass from Dewsbury behind me. As a result, I had also begun to realise that the world around me was filled with an abundance of good-looking young women.

My attention, when it came to the opposite sex, latched eventually onto a singer in the concert party, in this case, one of the local WAAFs, a buxom lass, who also possessed a lovely voice and went by the name of Beryl. One of the NCO's, also a member of the concert party and a rather pushy guy who fancied himself as a crooner, apparently had also set his sights on Beryl, to the extent that a later strategic withdrawal was eventually called for. Not however before me having tasted the sweet lips and other interesting bits of Beryl's person to reasonable excess, having also visited her and a couple of her mates, after work and usually at night, via a back window into the base's WAAF residential block.

The WAAF residence for a host of good reasons was known to be well out of bounds to all male ranks. It was also well known that should any airman be unlucky enough to get caught in the vicinity of the WAAF quarters at any time, never mind during the night hours, their neck would surely be on the chopping block, with much more than a period of mere jankers being the threatened result.

Such threats, however, did little to present a challenge to those lads possessed of an adventurous spirit and driven onward and upward (in the words of the RAF motto "*Per ardua ad astra*") by the effects of increasingly rampant hormones and a fast-maturing sex drive.

What the hell – when it came to stealing a kiss or a cuddle, even the threat of being caught never got to be a real deterrent! Even if it meant being in danger of being caught out by the overseeing WAAF block NCO or patrolling SPs. Anyway, a kiss and a cuddle with, on or under a warm, loving WAAF always presented an attractive opportunity not to be passed up by any young airman, whose rapidly developing carnal desires at the tender age of 18 were starting to rage within his fast- maturing body.

The lure of the opposite sex was indeed even starting to interest this young lad who, up to the age of 18 and before his recent experiences back in Leeds, had exhibited little in the way of any real interest in the opposite sex.

Looking back over that period, those halcyon days at RAF Feltwell in truth represented my early, hitherto slow emergence into adulthood, in addition to the start of a keen and growing interest in attractive young women.

I guess most of the young WAAFs were also going through a similar physical process as we lads, although some were understandably more interested in dating the trainee pilots, NCO's and single officers. WAAFs on the base preferred the former to plain 'other ranks', which certainly included run-of-the-mill and lowly AC2s, most of whom were unable to flash the necessary cash around, when entertaining. We lads in the jazz group though usually were able to attract the attention of sufficient of the local WAAFs and even more from among the groups of local village girls who regularly flocked to the weekend dances in pubs and village halls around the local countryside, enough to satisfy any interests we had in that quarter. We often took good advantage of the many opportunities on offer.

Our jazz group's attendance at local dances sometimes resulted in a standoff between us and a few of the local lads, who seemed to regard any usurping of what they saw as their province and ownership of the local female company. A few of the local young men often felt particularly threatened by boys from the RAF, an excuse for sometimes threatened violent disputation.

One or two such disputes occasionally did descend into a scrap, but these were usually brief with not too much in the way of injuries resulting on either side.

Unfortunately, just as I was becoming well settled into the RAF Feltwell routine, Queen Elizabeth, in consultation with her ministers on the question of the deployment of her forces, had obviously come to the decision that 2588475 AC2 Dubbin's services were now required elsewhere.

Perhaps news of my outburst in the cookhouse at RAF Wilmslow on the state occasion of her coronation had finally filtered through to her – who knows? At any rate, whatever reason had prompted my move from RAF Feltwell, my sweet sojourn and nightly escapades in and around the WAAF block and surrounding fields, pubs and village halls, both in and near the base and villages in the vicinity across Norfolk, was soon to come to a close.

I was about to be posted to my third, and final RAF base for the remainder of my quota of national service.

CFS – LITTLE RISSINGTON

My last posting was to Little Rissington, the RAF's renowned Central Flying School (CFS). That famous wartime airbase was located among the rolling hills, quaint villages and townships, pubs and, as I later found, both the base and local towns across rural Gloucestershire were home to a whole host of lovely, lively and usually loving young ladies.

RAF Little Rissington was affectionately known to those of us posted there as 'Rissi'. During my time based there, it was a bustling operational airbase, its primary function being the RAF's Central Flying School – an advanced training school for the RAF's instructor pilots.

Adjacent to the base was No. 8 Maintenance Unit RAF, a research and testing facility. Here aircraft and various control systems were being tested and developed as part of the RAF's strategic planning and operations during the 1950s. Both installations, not far from the quaint village of Little Rissington, were located on the crest of one of the higher Cotswold Hills.

The Little Rissington airfield was established in 1938, at the time comprising just one grass airstrip. During 1942, three asphalt runways were laid down. During 1944 the main runway was strengthened and extended to enable it eventually to take the later development of jet fighters and heavy strategic bombers that had started to enter service during the 1950s. In 1946, the RAF's Central Flying School moved to Little Rissington, the base there later becoming home to the RAFs famous aerobatics team. The base was extended over later years with additional hangars and technical facilities.

By the time I arrived at Rissi, now as a fully-fledged tradesman, also sporting an upgrade from AC2 to LAC (leading aircraftman), I had become comfortably established in my role with the RAF. I still had 14 more months to serve before completion of my national service commitment.

Once having adjusted to service life, everything about it had by now become familiar and comfortable. I nevertheless was yet to get used to being required to salute and take orders from some of the younger officers and more officious ranks among the NCOs. Most of those officers around my age had only recently emerged from officer training school. There were still some ex-Second World War pilots and other officers, who had remained active since the end of the war and now headed up various sections of base operations. The older and more experienced officers proved to be much easier to get along with and included a couple of famous ex-Battle of Britain and Bomber Command pilots.

I got to meet and speak with some of the latter as part of my role on the base – also during a number of informal education sessions at which they discussed subjects related to the recent war in the air and their part in it. These discussions sometimes extended to include some of the then-current developments and forward thinking that was being developed among the RAF's hierarchy.

One memorable session I attended was during a visit to Rissi by the Second World War Spitfire ace group captain Douglas Bader CBE, DSO & Bar, DFC & Bar. Bader was an amazing man who, even though he had lost both legs during an earlier flying accident, later became a fighter ace, prior to being shot down and captured by the Germans. Even as a captive, Bader tried to escape on a couple of occasions on his 'tin legs', only to be re-captured.

One part of my RAF service I really enjoyed was the capacity to study and discuss subjects related to strategic planning. These included details of the newer aircraft types that were entering duty with bomber and fighter command. This aspect of on-base activities took the form of a series of sessions specifically designed for ground staff interested in learning more about RAF operations. Prototypes of a number of the newer types of operational RAF aircraft regularly landed at Rissi, while doing the rounds of testing. All such discussions, while covering subjects low in the area of strategic planning, were interesting, as they allowed even we national service personnel the opportunity to learn more about the RAF and the service's view of the future.

I'm not sure what difference my presence in the RAF made to the defence of the realm, probably very little in my role as base tailor. Here I was, very comfortable working at my civilian trade while based at the RAF's leading pilot training establishment. This was a role that enabled me to get along well with all levels of the base command structure.

On reflection, the two years between 18 and 20 spent knuckling down to what was probably a gentler form of military discipline that would have been the case had I instead found myself in an infantry division in the army, served to add to my personal confidence and capacity to work among a diverse group of colleagues and superiors. An additional benefit was being able to add to my range of trade skills.

I am sure the relatively mild form of RAF discipline did my fellow national servicemen and me very little harm. On the contrary, finding oneself having to learn to live among and deal with the broad range of air-force personnel on base, in particular also needing to learn how to deal with and handle NCO's and the various levels of officers in authority over us proved of immense value on moving back to civilian life. Any ideas of signing on for more years as a longer-term regular, however, had disappeared into the ether many months earlier.

Once the initial enforced and painful detachment from my close family had receded since leaving Padgate and Wilmslow, I had found that life in the armed forces could provide a number of opportunities for an enterprising individual.

Life in the RAF was a healthy one, and that also tended, in my case at least, to assist in the transition from callow youth to young adult – and with it an accompanying advance in self-confidence and more than a little regarding how to deal with new situations, new people and moving to new places.

WHO GOES THERE?

During the first weeks of my sojourn at Rissi, before I had been able to organise myself, I had the bad luck to be drafted as an overnight guard.

On that night we guard, a highly unlikely bunch I might add, were paraded outside the base armoury following our evening meal, and issued with Second World War type.303 Lee Enfield rifles and six rounds of live ammunition. The ammunition strangely enough, we were instructed to keep outside our rifle – perhaps to avoid a potential accidentally released shot occurring as a result of an overly nervous guard? This strange arrangement negated any idea of having a capable, alert and well-armed guard in place in the first place. God only knows what bright spark officer or service committee had decided on such a useless set of rules of engagement? Perhaps the reasoning here was to ensure that none of we totally unprepared guards that night, got too excited and while being so, got to shoot himself or a fellow guard?

What we were expected to do in the unlikely event of being confronted by an IRA assault team I never really got to know. Our first action, in the event of an attack, we were told, was to flick a switch in the guardhouse to raise the alarm! Alarm? But to whom I wondered? Not that it really mattered in my mind – I had already decided to run in the opposite direction if the IRA came to call.

During our earlier weeks of 'square bashing', I been schooled in the rudimentary skills of firing an.303 Lee Enfield rifle and the reliable 'Bren' machine gun as part of our initial training. Firing a rifle or machine gun on the firing range, of course, did not equip any of we

RAF national servicemen to be effective – in the unlikely event of being confronted by a desperate member of the IRA.

The guard situation at Rissi, like a number of other similar circumstances and occasions met up with during my two-year stint as a national serviceman, could accurately be described by the use of that well-known military term SNAFU – meaning: Situation normal – all fucked up!

In the role of overnight guard, I spent a cold night, high up in the Cotswold Hills at this caper, vowing that I would never let it happen to me again. There we all were a group of four AC2's, plus one SP, who played the role of guard commander.

Throughout the long dark hours of that night, we guards were required to stand on guard for two hours, followed by four hours relaxing in the warmth of the guardhouse – from sunset to dawn the next day, throughout an incessantly wet, cold and windy night.

It was inevitable, particularly with the potential threat posed by the IRA at the time, for any one individual among we reluctant guards to jump at every shadow and even the slightest noise that broke through the stillness of the night. Even the distant cough of a passing fox, or the hoot of an owl, any noise in fact, however small, even the howl of the wind as it whipped at speed through the branches of trees nearby would serve to raise the hairs on the back of one's neck.

Thankfully the dawn arrived at last and with it a welcome and long-awaited hot dinner-plate overflowing with crunchy bacon, fried eggs and a mug of hot tea in the base canteen – plus the day on reduced duties in lieu of 'dangerous' overnight duty.

Looking back, I don't think the IRA would have been very interested in trying to steal a few elderly .303 rifles and whatever else was being stored in the Rissi armoury. There would surely have been much more useful pickings from the army base at nearby Aldershot – if they were after modern weaponry and explosives.

TAILOR TO ALL RANKS

At RAF Little Rissington, the base tailor's shop, located as it was within the store's group, was well provided for by a good-sized workshop. I also had a designated WAAF assistant, a couple of different types of sewing machines and other assorted equipment, including a large cutting table and a commercial sized hand operated steam iron.

As the only recognised clothing and textile savvy individual on the base, it soon became possible to generate much-needed extra funds by providing additional design and tailoring services to all levels of base personnel. These services, mainly involved alterations to RAF and WAAF uniforms that the owners desired to have remodelled, so that they fitted better or more stylishly. Most of my non-uniform work occurred outside normal working hours, with permission happily granted by the base stores officer, whose wife also became an occasional private client, particularly when on the hunt for replacement curtains and alterations to recently bought clothing, both for her and her children.

I eventually became involved with orders from one or two of the ranked officers on the base, for the actual tailoring of uniforms. This kind of private work required much more attention than most of the usual requests for repairs and minor alterations. Becoming involved with alterations and remakes for some officers required the drawing of required yardage of RAF specified fabrics and trimmings from the base stores. This and similar services outside my everyday work, gradually developed into a useful sideline, and one that eventually extended into designing and making up civilian-style skirts, slacks, blouses and other kinds of fashion tops for some of the WAAF personnel.

This extracurricular activity even included the making of a wedding dress for the WAAF who had been working with me and was soon to leave the service to be married.

The wide variety of work I found myself regularly becoming involved with, certainly assisted in my transition from learner tailor to the point where I found myself capable of handling most kinds of tailoring work, even the more technical aspects of design and machine work. This particularly when working on some of the more intricate or 'way-out' designs of skirts and tailored tops that were being ordered by one or two of my on-base WAAF clientele.

THE GAME

The sequence of events that later resulted in my leaving Britain for Australia became further consolidated when I and a few fellow residents of our accommodation block decided to establish a regular game of cards. The initial motivation here was to enable us, bored residents, to pass the time over a non-working weekend, while still being confined to remain on base.

The Game, as it eventually and covertly became known among many of the lower ranks throughout Rissi, started out as an exclusive arrangement being held each weekend in one of the larger rooms of our residential block.

This particular residential installation was a modern-style prefabricated structure. It was an arrangement that provided each of its inhabitants their own, private room. On the upper of the two floors was located a lounge room, a convenient location in which we could relax during our spare time and weekends.

Located as it was outside the perimeter of the base, our home on the base offered its usually disinterested occupants some of the choicest views of the landscape – hills and dales that rolled away across western Gloucestershire.

These were rolling hills that during the springtime were clothed in clouds of yellow daffodils, crocuses and a whole host of other wildflowers, shrubs and other woodland species. It was also strategically located a relatively safe distance away from the prying eyes of the station police (SPs). In other words, a prime location that provided a position from which any movement that looked like a possible raid being launched on the weekly card game, could be quickly and easily observed, while its participants and any cash could be quickly dispersed.

The game expanded over the months, usually continuing non-stop through nearly every weekend its resident members were not away from the base. Our absence from the game meant that we were either in the process of wooing some local lady, attending some form of weekend training or duty or, more preferable, many miles away from Rissi on home leave.

The weekly game, usually with a packed house of lads all looking to pass a boring weekend on base, involved gambling, often with substantial amounts of money changing hands. This was a highly illegal activity in the RAF.

One of the lads, a Scot by birth and known inevitably to all and sundry as Jock, ran a regular book as a sideline, on which he accepted wagers on horses running at some of the better-known horse races currently being held around the country.

With our humble residential block changing its role into a well-frequented den of iniquity nearly every weekend, the need to maintain a regular lookout for SP's was critical. Rain, snow, hail, wind or shine, it never mattered, the game went on regardless. In fact, we once found ourselves snowed in during one bitterly-cold, blustery winter weekend, with those of us present at the time having to dig ourselves out of the front doorway of our block, then fight our way across deep snowdrifts to reach the base canteen, a necessary trip if any of us were to obtain some sorely needed nourishment.

Inevitably, when the need to fill an empty stomach with food or drink drove the players over to the questionable delights of the base canteen, either for a meal, a brittle tooth- rattling Eccles cake, or feeling the need for a sandwich and mug of tea at the nearby motorised 'NAAFI'[1] wagon, some of us present at the time would get to discussing subjects, other than the state of the game.

The lads resident in our block were a diverse lot. About half were national servicemen, having little enthusiasm for our enforced two-year stay at Her Majesty's pleasure. We represented many different walks of life, most having different accents and diverse ways of thinking, drawn as we were from all corners of the British Isles, levels of society and culture.

Discussion, other than on the game in progress, usually commenced around the subject of football, or perhaps the various horse racing meetings in progress across the country, particularly if Jock was running a book that weekend. Conversations during a 'char' (tea) break would also inevitably drift toward an exchange of views concerning the base's WAAFs. This naturally would include discussion around the local country girls – in particular, their agreeability, or otherwise, when it came to the subject of casual sex.

Casual sex in those pre-'the pill' days often proved to be more than a little restrained. Many of the base WAAFs and young unmarried local ladies and even some of the married ones living in one or other of the nearby villages and small towns, were understandably reticent when it came to jumping into bed for a sexual romp with any Tom, Dick or Gerry. At the very least most usually wouldn't consider sex, without first ensuring that a fully intact and correctly installed condom had been correctly installed between them and the lad in question.

Things of a sexual nature changed considerably with the later availability of the pill, a development that was quickly followed by a period of what became known as the 'sexual revolution' among single women, all now able to access a safer, more certain means by which they could be in control of their own fertility. Perhaps more importantly and immediate – their being able to avoid the possibility of incurring an unwanted pregnancy as a result of recent sexual congress.

Some of the more erudite, or perhaps more questioning among those present during our weekend card game, even at various other times during a working week or twice daily NAAFI tea break, would get to discussing deeper and more meaningful subjects. Subjects broader than just limiting ourselves to rating the known range of potential sexual partners among the locally available, usually enthusiastic and co-operative young women. Life issues like religion, politics and in particular, what we intended doing following that sublime moment when our commitment to Her Majesty, Queen Elizabeth II and her government came to its long-awaited end.

Notes

1. NAAFI – An organisation created by the British government in 1921 to run recreational establishments for the Navy, Army and Air Force.

THOUGHTS OF AUSTRALIA

Our personal futures, when viewed by more than a few of we national servicemen at the time, tended to centre on the question of what possibilities beckoned, following our eventual return to civilian life?

At the time, it was well known that the British economy continued to be depressed. What with the continuing potential threat that the USSR represented to Europe and possibly Britain at some indistinct time into the future, to some it also seemed worthy of consideration that a move to either of New Zealand, Australia, North America or Canada presented an attractive option, well worthy of consideration.

Australia and New Zealand always seemed to be in favour, in particular due to their being the countries more distant from any expected future international unrest.

I was also lucky in my role, being the base tailor, to have the opportunity of meeting up with a few Australian flying officers, pilots who at the time were in Britain on secondment to the RAF. One pilot in particular was from New South Wales. Both he and I had found a subject in the form of the rugby league code that interested us both. During the course of our chats, I also got to learn more about the way of life 'Down Under'. Life in Australia as he and a couple of his 'Aussie' colleagues described it, served to tweak a chord in my mind, particularly when it came to the officers' description of Australia's need to expand its population and the potential opportunities, both work and leisure, that their young country offered. A gift to me of a couple of Australian newspapers and magazines greatly assisted my knowledge about Australia and the way life was lived there.

Occasions, during which either he or one of his fellow members of the RAAF (Royal Australian Air Force), required repairs or adjustments to their uniforms or civilian clothing, provided further opportunities for me to delve further into the subject of my growing appetite to learn more about life and living in their country down under.

THE LITTLE RED MG

Meanwhile, life jogged along comfortably at Rissi. By that time thoughts of my lost love, Cynthia had all but disappeared from my mind. Leeds, while always occupying a central place in my life was also tending to fade a little into the background. Life in the RAF had gradually taken over. While on the occasions that I was home on leave in Leeds, it was nice to catch up with some of my earlier friends, I was beginning to realise that I was becoming a little different in my attitude to life. I was no longer a stranger to service life.

My direct and more personal interests, particularly when it came to the opposite sex, had moved rapidly and at times successfully, in the direction of the many opportunities for progressing my interest, in and around the beautiful Cotswold Hills, and the nearby villages and towns, Cheltenham in particular. I was at the time also enjoying the lifestyle that presented, living as I then was among one of the most beautiful parts of the English countryside to be seen each day outside the window of my room. The Cotswold Hills, rolling and picturesque as they were, presented very differently in so many ways from that of my home county of Yorkshire – its Dale country and more severe, heather clad Moorlands.

On the base, among the general store's section and vehicle maintenance group, there was a quartet of lads who, sometime before my arrival at Rissi, had bought and refurbished an old MG roadster. I'm not sure what vintage the vehicle was, but it was an old car even then, and constantly in need of regular servicing, plus a high degree of tender loving care from its owners. The manner in which continuing ownership had been organised was that anyone of the group being posted away from Rissi, or about to leave the service, would sell their share to another interested party. Thus, as personnel came and went, the MG continued to service the needs of its current group of four owners.

Now as a new part owner, I even got to acquire the skills of driving the old roadster, and in doing so managed to run up many happy miles along the winding roads around the base and local villages. I even got to learn the rudimentary skills of double-declutching when changing down to a lower gear.

The MG, driven almost exclusively by non-licence holding lads, was used mainly as a convenient means of getting the proud owners to one or other of the local dances or watering holes (country pubs) in and around the Cotswolds. Local towns like Evesham, Broadway, Upper Slaughter, Lower Slaughter, Bourton-on-the-Water, Upper Swell, Lower Swell and Banbury among them.

Sometimes four of us would pile into the two-seater, weighing its ancient structure down and adding to the strain on its already ageing engine and undercarriage. The hills in many parts of the Cotswolds, being quite steep, usually necessitated at least one or even two of the passengers to jump off a third or so of the way up from the base of a particularly steep hill. They then were required to bend their backs to assist the straining little MG to get up and over the summit.

During the time I was a part owner, none of the local constabulary members seemed very interested to try and detain our affectionately named 'Red Flash' as it roared its noisy way down their high street. The fact that the local 'copper' usually had the somewhat limited services of a pushbike with which to chase us, should he be so motivated, possibly had something to do with the car and its unlicensed owners being regularly successful in avoiding apprehension.

One of the lads, an engine mechanic who conveniently worked in the base's motor workshop, later managed to modify the carburation and other parts of the engine. This enabled us to then use a mixture of aviation grade 'AVGAS' aircraft fuel (illegally 'scrounged')[1] with normal petrol in the tank. Whatever he did while I was around, it certainly put much more life into the ageing engine, although I don't know how long it lasted following my leaving the RAF and selling my share to the next proud part owner.

Notes

1. Scrounge – To beg, borrow (or steal) with no intention of reparation.

A STRATEGIC RETREAT

Our little red MG also provided its owners with many opportunities to interest one or other of the local ladies in a romantic night out, drinks or dinner in one or other of the local country pubs. On one memorable occasion, I came close to getting more than I bargained for, following a boozy night well away from her hometown of Evesham in the Cotswold Hills, along with my date for the night, the ex-wife of a local village resident.

On returning my date home late that evening and being invited in 'for a good night drink', I had parked the car, at her suggestion, a little away from her house. Accepting with alacrity the offer of a drink or three, we both ended the evening in one of the upstairs bedrooms, getting 'better and more closely acquainted'. The evening looked to be set for a long, steamy session.

I hadn't even bothered to find out who else lived in the house, empty at the time of our silent and late arrival, my mind at the time understandably fully occupied with other thoughts for the night ahead.

It was well after midnight and into the early hours, that the door downstairs slammed, instantly electrifying my date, who shook me violently, along with a smothered yelp, closely followed by the suggestion: "You'd better get out of here quick like, or there will be hell to pay – my ex will kill us both!" This was a demand which prompted me into a state of instant wakefulness, at the same time hastily pulling on my pants and shirt, to the accompanying advice: "Quick, climb out of the window and get down, as quick as you can!"

"Shit, her ex-husband!" Realising my potential dilemma and,

without any desire to stay a moment longer than necessary, I made a beeline for the thankfully low window and down what appeared to be some kind of wooden trellising which unfortunately for me had some thorn clad roses curled around it. In my haste, I dropped nearly all the way down to the garden below and hot-footed it to where I had left the car, dragging on my jacket, which she had thoughtfully thrown out of the window following my hasty departure, before shutting the window.

Back in the MG, the car refused to start at first, eventually doing so to the accompaniment of a rain shower that threatened to grow later into a storm.

Driving back over the hills toward Rissi toward the safety of my room and comfy bed, the shower became steadily heavier. With the car's hood leaking at the time, all I could do was to drive on, gradually getting wetter and wetter. As if that wasn't enough, a mile or so still from my bed and safety from a full-blooded storm, the car gave up with a few wheezy coughs and a splutter, then stopped abruptly, leaving me standing on a deserted road, now slowly being soaked to the skin.

Just able to push the MG closer under a thick hedgerow and away from the roadway, I then started out at a brisk, waterlogged jog for the rest of the way back to the base. All the way back to Rissi I kept a sharp lookout, just in case an irate ex-husband had taken up the chase – luckily not as it turned out, which left me thanking my lucky stars that I had avoided a confrontation with her ex-husband, or whatever else he turned out to be.

With lightning flashing all around and thunder overhead I finally made it back to Rissi. Now safely in my room I peeled off my by now thoroughly wet clothes and crept into my bunk. At first, unable to sleep I kept thinking along the possibility that I had been seen by what in my mind's eye I was imagining to be a massive, broad-shouldered country farmer, intent on screwing my neck round, if he ever got the chance.

I learned later that the lady in question was in fact in the process of separating from her husband. They both were still living in the same house, which was owned by his family until she could find elsewhere to live. I did see her later and was glad to hear that nothing further had eventuated following that night, although he had accused her of "playing fast and loose behind my back", and later kicked her out.

And the by now waterlogged MG? The next evening, along with a couple of the other owners, one of whom was the mechanical genius who kept the car going, we managed to get it started, then drove its waterlogged body safely back to its shed on base.

So ended a close shave, a scene reminiscent of a third-rate movie, but one that taught me to make sure that when undertaking any future similar kinds of romantic trysts, to keep clear of married or semi-married women. If impossible to escape the temptation, however, the message learned that night was that one should always aim to avoid 'pooping on one's own doorstep'. A little crude perhaps – but apt and good advice in the circumstances I think.

PER ARDUA AD ASTRA

Like nearly every young boy living through the Second World War, the sight and distinctive sound of an RAF Spitfire and the unmistakable roar of its Rolls Royce Merlin engine used to (still does) send shivers up and down my spine. During the wartime years of my boyhood, I would often dream of one day flying in one against the then hated German Luftwaffe.

Being keen on the latest RAF fighter and bomber types, I would often seek out flying magazines, so that by the time I had arrived at Rissi, I had been able to build up a comprehensive knowledge around the RAF's current range of front-line fighters and bombers.

The 1950s were at the height of the cold war period, with both the US and Britain rapidly developing, testing and introducing faster and more efficient offensive air combat systems – aircraft designed to counter the then dreaded threat of world communism.

The USSR's version of that demi-religion, communism, dominated much of the Western allies' strategic thinking during those times, its members, including Britain and its Commonwealth, the United States and France, always on the lookout for an opportunity to gain any strategic advantage. Regarding strategic weapons, the 1950s saw the introduction of Britain's newest developments in long-range heavy jet bombers, with the Vulcan, Victor and Valiant versions coming into service. It was, however, to be the last hurrah for Britain as the builder and maintainer of squadrons of state-of-the-art strategic heavy bombers.

While still posted at Rissi, I was keen to fly in as many of the aircraft being used there from time to time. Opportunities to do so were usually available and actively encouraged by our senior officers, should there be vacant seats or places available on any one of the base's regular flying schedules. The opportunity to fly as a passenger was open to any non-flying personnel wishing to apply to the air-wing for a spare seat in one or other of the base's aircraft, flying either on a training mission or some other general duty.

I was lucky enough at the time to see many of the RAF's then front-line jet fighters and bombers as they were being used to provide advanced flying training to some of the RAF's more experienced pilots. These were senior flying personnel selected for training as advanced flight instructors on the various new aircraft types.

We even had a few Second World War aircraft, one notable in the form of an ancient Avro Anson twin-engine light bomber. This was a type that just before that war had been one of the RAF's strategic bomber types – not very successful against what the Luftwaffe was using at the time. The base also had a Lincoln bomber, a few North American Harvard single-engine fighters, and a Mosquito medium fighter/bomber, which used to come and go occasionally. In addition, the current crop of Meteor, Venom and Vampire jet fighter types were in use every day for training purposes.

One memorable flight I was able to experience as a passenger was in one of the few remaining Seafire fighter aircraft, a two-seater development of the famous Spitfire, which was used mainly by the fleet air arm during the war, particularly during its latter stages. Soaring into the sky in the modified Seafire was an experience I will never forget. It also brought back the memory of a young boy, as my schoolmates and I back in Leeds watched on from the questionable safety of our schoolyard, as an RAF Spitfire chased a German Heinkel across the sky above our primary school during the middle stages of the war.

To be seated in such a close relative of the indomitable Spitfire, climbing and steeply banking over the Gloucestershire countryside was the culmination of most young boy's dreams during the long war years between 1939 and 1945.

FORCED LANDING

A much slower flying machine than the Seafire, the relatively ancient but reliable pre-war Avro Anson, was the form of air transport that was regularly used when it became necessary for me and others to travel to one or other of the RAF's variously located stores. In my case trips such as these were to pick up replacement bolts of fabric, trimmings and accessories, bed sheeting, replacement uniforms and other replacement gear like flying equipment, gloves and flying overalls.

This meant a long, slow flight in the Avro Anson, usually flown by Flight Sergeant 'Chiefy' Hill. Hill was an ex-Battle of Britain pilot, whose wartime stories, which he enjoyed relating over and over again as the old plane noisily rattled its way across southern England, assisted in passing the time in that slow, noisy and draughty old aircraft.

One flight of note in the Avro Anson occurred on a trip to pick up replacement uniforms and basic uniform fabric from an RAF store group somewhere near London. It proved to be a trip that was to be interrupted when the aircraft was passing near the USAF base at Brize Norton, on our way home to Rissi.

Finding ourselves running toward an unexpected bank of fog on our way home to Rissi, the Anson, being restricted to VFR (visual flight rules) flying, our trusty pilot called Brize Norton for permission to land, at least until the fog had cleared.

Being a strictly limited bomber base, the requested landing of our diminutive Anson resulted in two US police jeeps full of pistol-toting guards positioning themselves on either side of our little aircraft, as we were waved over to a parking bay just off the main runway. There, just me and our Avro Anson had to wait for three hours, under armed guard, while our pilot wandered off toward the US canteen. Unable to leave the aircraft the prospect of a long stay there appeared inevitable.

So, there I sat in a cold, draughty cockpit, huddled up in my leather jerkin, with hood up and a thick scarf wrapped around my neck.

Time passed by with me getting colder and colder, having visions of being restricted to the aircraft overnight.

Thankfully the fog, at last, began to clear heralding the welcome return of the pilot, who presumably had been enjoying US hospitality. He arrived back, together with a couple of paper cups full of steaming hot coffee, a box of Hershey chocolate bars and a few packets of American chewing gum that he had bought at the base PX store.

The fog bank, a usual temporary weather event which sometimes occurred without warning during the autumn in that part of southern England, eventually cleared, allowing us once more to head down the seemingly never- ending runway, take off with a flourish, waggle our stubby little wings in thanks and trundle off to our nearby home base. We arrived home with time to unload and just make it for a late dinner in the base canteen.

INTERESTING INTERLUDES

My position of base tailor proved to be valuable again and again when it came to being able to get myself onto a number of varied flying opportunities in different aircraft.

During my stay at Rissi as a result of doing tailoring jobs for some of the squadron commanders on the base, including my own boss, also an ex-Second World War type, to get myself on-board a range of front-line and training aircraft. Most of these were flights scheduled either for testing purposes or aircraft being based at Rissi from time to time.

One notable flight I managed to snare on more than one occasion was on-board one of the last Lincoln bombers to be actively flying with the RAF. The Lincoln was also the last piston-engine powered heavy-bomber type to enter service with the RAF.

The Lincoln model was essentially a scaled-up version of the famous 'Dam Busting' Lancaster. The first Lincoln of the series was known as the Lancaster Mk IV, the prototype flying in June 1944. It was intended for use in the continuing war in the Pacific, but appeared too late to see any real action in that theatre.

Even though the Lincoln was not one of the famous dam busting bombers, Lancaster or not, to me, a Second World War Spitfire and Lancaster aficionado, the opportunity to fly as a passenger in the front turret of the Lincoln was an experience I had also often dreamed of as a boy. On those occasions, I was able to recall the regular evenings when many other local Leeds folk and I would stand in the street in front of our little houses, just to watch the multiple bomber raids going out across the Yorkshire sky toward the east, all engaged on their deadly missions to targets in Germany, during the latter stages of the war.

At Rissi I got to fly a few times in the Lincoln bomber currently being used by the base navigation school for training purposes or similar.

One could never forget the unmistakable sound of the Lincoln's four engines, as they started up one by one, and once going were slowly spooled up to full power on the ground, the wheels of that beautiful, but deadly aircraft locked in preparation, before rolling onto the base's main runway. The full four-engine roar, as the pilot pushed her throttles to the limit, made the whole aircraft vibrate. It felt as if she was straining at her leash, snarling to be let go toward the enemy.

Being 1954, there were no Luftwaffe Messerschmitt fighters awaiting us on the then relatively peaceful European continent, only the soft contours of the English coast and part of the North Sea that the aircraft usually transited during that kind of training or testing mission.

On take-off, being seated in the bomb aimer's post in the Perspex covered front turret could be scary, potentially giving a nervous passenger the feeling that they were in some danger of being deposited into the tarmac as the Lincoln started its take-off roll down the runway. This sensation was known to occur, as the great plane gradually lifted her tail up from her original parked and rolling position. With only a thin Perspex dome between the bomb aimer position and the rapidly accelerating runway beneath, the take-off process commenced with the aircraft's nose pointing up at an angle to the runway.

As the Lincoln gathered speed, its tail would then rise until it was level with the nose. This was a position that gave an unfamiliar passenger seated and securely strapped within the Perspex bubble, the strange and worrying feeling that the nose was actually in danger of dropping lower and lower, toward the runway. Thankfully it didn't and, as the aircraft levelled itself out into its take-off attitude, we were finally off the ground and rising majestically into the air, the four Rolls Royce Merlin engines calibrated and roaring in unison.

In contrast to the Lincoln bomber, I also managed to fly a few times as the passenger in a Meteor NF 14 jet night fighter. This late version Meteor for a number of years, was, one of Britain's front-line fighters, just prior to the entry of the Hawker Hunter, Supermarine Swift and the North American F-86 Sabrejet fighter. The latter of these fighters were also flown by the RAAF, particularly during the Korean War 1950–1953. All three jet fighters were much faster and more deadly than the earlier fighter types, having just started to replace the then ageing and slower Venom, Vampire and Meteors.

On one particular flight, the Meteor NF14 took off and we soared to well over 34,000 feet over the Gloucestershire countryside, an altitude at which you really do get the first view of the curvature of the horizon. The speed at which the Meteor flew would have left the Lincoln bomber well in its wake, as the pilot turned toward the east. We then flew up to the North Yorkshire coast, turned back across country to the Lancashire coast then veered back to return toward home base at Rissi.

I also managed to fly in a propeller-driven Harvard Trainer, a Vampire jet fighter as well as a few flights on one of the Douglas Dakota 3 (DC3) transport planes, a most reliable aircraft used extensively both during and for many years following the ending of the Second World War. There are still DC3 aircraft flying today, such is its sturdy and functional design and the carrying capacity of that unique airplane.

MORAL LEADERSHIP – AN INTERESTING DIVERSION

It was during the latter stages of my stay at Rissi that I learned, via the base's RAF chaplain, of the existence of an RAF authorised course that offered a welcome opportunity to be able to spend some free time in the British capital London – a city which I had yet to visit.

At the time, the various religious denominations had established courses designed with the object of providing members of their particular faith serving in the armed forces with a week-long 'live-in' study course. While a resident at such a course, the personnel involved were to be instructed and guided, as a means of improving their adherence to the principles and moral posture of their declared faith.

Being the only one on base designated as Jewish, agnostic at the time not being an acceptable religious denomination in the RAF, it followed that I would eventually get to be sorted out as a potential attendee at such a course. This course was being run by the Jewish version of similar other religious councils of education. Not that it mattered to me either way as to who was the organiser of such a convenient means of getting away from the RAF for a whole week in London, with accommodation and sustenance being supplied by the religious organisation involved.

The accommodation provided in London was at a house owned by an elderly lady who I believe to have been either of the wife, sister or some other close relative of the then famous international film actor Conrad Veidt. I recall that the house was one of a fashionable terrace, located somewhere in the vicinity of Hammersmith and not very far from where the moral leadership course in question was being held.

Suffice to say that I and the other ten or so lads attending that particular course, were more interested in checking out the local young ladies at the Hammersmith Palais dancehall, local pubs and other local hangouts, as opposed to any interest in what the people running our particular moral leadership course had intended for us.

I returned to Rissi, following a week or so of hard drinking, dancing and other memorable events, with little to show, I must confess when it came to any improvement or indeed increased interest in any form of religiously oriented study or participation.

Moral leadership or whatever the course had been intended to achieve in a week, proved to be a welcome diversion, as well as my very first visit to London. It was also another week closer to the ending of my national service commitments, still faithfully being recorded on my personal 'demob chart'.[1]

Notes

1. Demob Chart: A record regularly kept by most national servicemen, charting the weeks and months still to be served prior to the ending of their service commitment.

BACK TO CIVVY STREET

Life at CFS Little Rissington continued apace for the rest of my service in the RAF, with many happy days spent in and around Cheltenham and the rolling farming country and villages tucked in among the surrounding Cotswold Hills. I even later got to find my feet, so to speak, as a member of the base running team, proving to be a reasonably fast middle distance runner – competing against other RAF stations, the USAF and a French team.

In direct contrast to those early, traumatic days and weeks spent as a raw sprog recruit at Padgate and Wilmslow, life in the RAF actually got to be quite agreeable and relatively easy to manage, particularly once I became established in my trade role.

My role as base tailor also managed to provide a regular supply of additional funds over the 18 months spent at Rissi, most of which usually managed to get spent on wine, women and song. Apart from the pittance paid to us lowly ranked RAF types, any spare cash that came my way was mainly from the design and making up of civilian clothes for some of the base's WAAFs and male ranks. During periods of my spare time, I sporadically continued to study textile design and used any opportunity to increase my design, hand tailoring and machining skills, so that by the time my two years of service came to an end, I felt that I had improved considerably when it came to my trade skills.

As to extracurricular activities, there were many. On the more darker side, having unlimited access to officers' and other ranks uniforms also presented an interesting possibility on a few occasions for some play-acting, an activity fraught with potentially dire consequences. This involved myself and a close mate borrowing and donning flying officers' uniforms complete with wings and stripes of rank, then waltzing off to a dance or pub strategically located some distance and well away from the base. It was interesting and useful to find how the uniforms attracted hordes of local young women, all of which added to the thrill of doing something really crazy.

What we were doing was, of course, illegal and subject to dire consequences, should we be sprung or confronted by officers from the base, the RAF or civil police. But what the hell, we were young, still silly young kids at heart, more than a little foolish at that age and not averse to embarking on anything that offered an opportunity to engage in activities requiring some creativity, potential enjoyment, maybe a little in the way of sexual activity, and a degree of risk into the bargain.

That particular jaunt was just one of many happy and not always legal events entered into from time to time, often just to break up a boring weekend, or some other time with not much happening.

As with everything in life though, even the most enjoyable holidays and other happy periods of one's life must come to an end at some time or other. So then did my contract with Her Majesty's Government on reaching my 20th year.

My personal demob chart at long last began to trace down to the last days of my two years of service in the RAF, and my role in defending HM Queen Elizabeth II and her ancient realm.

I don't believe that my role had much to offer in the way of the actual defence of Britain. It was however a role that managed to keep the officers and all ranks at CFS smartly dressed, in addition to a two-year period during which I did manage to bridge the gap without too much trouble, between arriving into the RAF, a callow and totally inexperienced youth, who two years later, ended up being closer to becoming a reasonably confident young man. I was still young and a little stupid at times, but on the whole, I would like to think that I was well on the way to becoming a reasonably responsible young adult.

April 1955, when at the still tender age of 20, saw me emerging unscathed from battling with the enemies of Queen Elizabeth II. Whatever the truth, I had completed my apprenticeship and had graduated to become a reasonably skilled exponent in the art of skiving, not an inconsiderable feat I might add. In fact, over my two years' service, I had become quite adept at disengaging myself on many memorable occasions, from the more onerous duties and less-loved bullshit parades and guard duties regularly imposed upon the backs of we young and relatively powerless lower ranks. I had also ascended to the not so dizzying height and rank of LAC (leading aircraftman), itself a still low ranking but at the very least two ranks above the lowly AC2 status in which I had entered national service.

It was my position however within the Rissi community that had served me well. My two years of national service had assisted me to create, within my role as base tailor, something more positive in terms both of my ability professionally, and perhaps more importantly – my becoming a little more mature. Being so, even though it was sad to be leaving a lot of friends and valued colleagues in and around the base, I was now also looking forward to the next phase of my life, in whatever form that life was to be.

In terms of coping with service life, I had found that most of the difficulties we ground-based RAF staff found ourselves having to face on base, came mainly in the form of some of the younger, more officious and pushy commissioned officers who, unlike the older and longer serving ex-Second World War types, often sought to be overly precious, once having donned their tailor- made uniforms displaying their insignia of rank as a pilot officer (the lowest commissioned officer ranking).

Most of we 'other ranks', particularly some of us older and more experienced national servicemen, usually found it relatively easy to deflect much of some officers' often overzealous orders or demands. It all got to be a sometimes tense but challenging game at times.

My position as base tailor had served to provide me with a regular supply of extra funds, all too often dissipated on local WAAFs or civilian ladies living within a reasonable distance of Rissi. On-base and finding oneself in the relatively unique position of the base tailor, placed me in a position from which I was able to exert at least some power in the maintenance of my personal well-being. My position also made it possible for me to escape from time to time from under the often overbearing and cloying weight of the many layers of authority above my still lowly station in the cumbersome RAF machine.

My position was a unique one and of some value, particularly regarding my ongoing life and trade skills. As part of my job, I was also able to attire myself in one of the smartest tailored uniforms, in which to make my way along the paths, among the white painted stones and green painted patches of earth where no grass would grow, at CFS's venerable airbase at Little Rissington.

I had also managed to fumble and change my sexual status from virgin sprog airman to one of having 'been there and done a little of that' – with more than one happy to oblige, usually helpful and enthusiastic member of the local female population.

I had even entertained thoughts once or twice, but only on rare occasions I might add, usually following a drinking or hot and steamy session with one or other of the local WAAFs, around the possibility of 'signing on' for a further four years with the RAF, as a regular. Such a possibility did offer the promise of promotion to a position involving much more responsibility in the future and was stated as such by my then boss of stores, who suggested that there could be a bright future ahead in the RAF, for an enterprising and inventive young man.

Good sense prevailed however, the day finally arriving for me to bid a fond farewell to male and female friends on the base and among the local villages. For the last time in my short career with Her Majesty's Armed Forces, I was able to pack my bag and pass in my kit – at least that which I was not required to hold onto in case of being re-called up into reserve service at some unspecified future date.

Leaving Little Rissington for the final time, it was a case of being transported by RAF truck down to Cheltenham and finally, onto the 'Devonian', the daily express train that steamed its way from Cheltenham toward the north-east and Leeds. Also for the last time in a number of years, I also found myself bidding a sad farewell to the beautiful, rolling, Cotswold Hills.

The RAF and two full, eminently instructive years had turned out to be happy, healthy and comfortable. Now it was back to Leeds for me, hopefully soon to a good position with one or other of the local 'shmatti' (clothing) factories.

For the foreseeable future, it was to be civilian clothes from here on and back to my cosy little bedroom at 25 Harehills Terrace Leeds 8, my bed clad in smooth white and blue edged bed sheets – compliments of the RAF.

3

BACK TO LEEDS AND SEEKING WORK

My immediate reactions on returning home to Leeds were a little different to what I had expected or had imagined they would be, the change from national serviceman to civilian proving to be a challenge, but thankfully nowhere close to that which I had faced on entering national service two years before. Like many others, I emerged after spending the latter part of my teenage years in the RAF a much-changed individual from the youth whom, just 24 short months earlier had unwillingly left my boyhood and youth behind.

At 18 I was then still very young and inexperienced, particularly when it came to being on my own, having to fend for myself while trying to cope with a very different way of life. For the first time in my life, I had then found myself needing to adapt to an existence totally beyond anything that I could have contemplated, even in a bad dream! The reality of my then new situation was difficult enough to contemplate, but the additional thought of two long years of military discipline ahead had found me both overwhelmed and threatened.

It had been a shock to the system at first just trying to adapt to the alien military environment, plus having layer upon layer of superior military rankings, all holding near-absolute power over one's everyday life. In short, it was a real shock to now find myself deposited into a strange new world of saluting and discipline. I might well have landed on another planet at the time, the people I found myself having to deal with, including my fellow sufferers, being worlds apart from my family and those I had grown up with and among from childhood.

In some important ways, now returning to my parent's small home in Leeds and the miles of narrow, smoke and smog- stained streets that surrounded it, also felt strange. To make things worse, my boyhood pal Alec was himself now in the army. He had decided to defer his national service commitment to pursue studies as an electrical engineer. I also found myself missing the comradeship of my former RAF buddies and a girl I had been dating in Stroud, in addition to the relatively comfortable existence I had managed to carve out for myself at RAF Little Rissington.

At first and within a few days of arriving back in Leeds, I even began to seriously think of applying on the spot to migrate to Australia. Already having an aunt, uncle and cousin living in Melbourne did offer the possibility of being sponsored as an assisted migrant. The reality however gradually kicked in, as it seemed preferable to first knuckle down to readjustment back in Leeds, then hopefully being able to find me a job with some sort of future with one or other of the local apparel manufacturers.

The need to return to and progress my tertiary studies in textiles and apparel production also took on importance. Once qualified, I should then be better able to decide where to go from there.

While I was still thinking to migrate to Australia sometime in the future, it soon became clear that now back in civilian life, there were a few other things that needed to be set in place first, before even contemplating such a drastic move.

On a more personal level, it was good just to be out of uniform, more particularly, to be far away from the rule-bound military service lifestyle. Returning to a position in which I needed to re-establish myself into the group of friends and acquaintances left behind two years earlier, however, I found more than a little difficult.

It was all so strange; old friends seemed to have remained much as they were when I left, while I was now seeing them and the way they all appeared to have matured little since then. It seemed as if most of my earlier friends had remained in a kind of time warp, with attitudes and interests similar to those that had seemed so natural, prior to my entering the RAF.

I, on the other hand, felt that I had changed a great deal and moved on, but to what I wasn't sure? One thing was sure, I didn't feel as comfortable as I used to, now that I was back in and among my old haunts and re-establishing contact with childhood friends and acquaintances. That felt very strange, much as if I had awakened from a two-year dream, only to find on awakening that I no longer related.

These strange and often negative emotions sometimes got to be extreme, particularly when they began to dominate my thinking, which then tended to push me toward more introspection and more than a little in the way of brooding. It was in such circumstances that I found myself thinking more and more about the possibilities of eventually leaving Britain, certainly Harehills and Leeds.

Even meeting up occasionally with the object of my first love – the girl, who for want of a car and a few thousand pounds in the bank and a father with a shop had spurned me for someone else. Bumping into her once or twice now left me wondering what I had ever seen in her and why I had grieved so much at losing her? A stranger is a good description I think, of how I then saw myself.

It was also interesting to realise just how much I had changed over just two years, both in outlook and the way I was now seeing the world around me. My world since the age of 18 had become a world well outside the old limitations of Harehills, my street, the local shops and all the other familiar places of my boyhood. The past two years in the RAF had certainly been the catalyst through which my life had now changed in a way that left me uncertain in ways that I had not expected. Even more worrying at the time were my more personal relationships, particularly those concerning my immediate family and what remained of my few earlier close friends.

It also seemed like I was now looking at life through different eyes and from the outside, having arrived back into a world that seemed smaller and itself was now feeling restricted. This was also strange, as in reality what I had left behind in the RAF was certainly more restricting and controlling with all the saluting and the inevitable requirement to acknowledge those senior with a "Yes sir, no sir," according to their ranking. Add to that the constant need to observe a whole host of rules and regulations, much narrower than those to be found in a civilian environment.

Perhaps, I recall thinking, the times during the past two years during which I had thought more and more about the possibility of leaving England for somewhere else, is catching up with me? Was such thinking realistic? Whatever was happening in my mind, it was slowly becoming clear that I had no desire to drop back into a lifestyle similar to that which most of my old friends seemed happy and contented.

Some of my earlier group of male friends had already paired up with girlfriends – one or two had somehow managed to avoid national service. They, for the most part, seemed to have regular jobs and one or two were even beginning to talk about getting engaged and settling down.

The enforced move from civilian life into the RAF had represented a leap into the unwanted and unknown outside my ability to control. My return to life back in Leeds now seemed not unlike that of a chicken trying to climb back into its egg and finding the task difficult, if not near impossible.

On the positive side, I was now feeling that I had gained a deal of experience on the practical side of my chosen trade. I was also confident of being able to become a fully skilled tailor and eventually progressing further to becoming a proficient pattern-cutter/designer, given half a chance. Maybe things would improve once I had been able to secure the kind of position that would provide the opportunity I needed?

On the latter score, my hopes were based on knowing that my main driving intention on returning to Leeds, was not to spend the rest of my working life sitting, sewing cross-legged upon a tailor's 'board' like most tailors before me. Nor was I interested in the prospect of sitting crouched over a sewing machine all day, year in and year out. The thought of having nothing better to look forward to other than waiting for retirement to crawl along, with the usual presentation perhaps of an inscribed watch or clock, to be followed by a paltry pension or similar being the real result of many years of hard, uninteresting work, was not what I had in mind.

If I was to progress anywhere while being employed in the apparel industry, I had somehow first to find a way of moving toward a more prestigious position somewhere within the local industry. Eventually, perhaps I could then aspire to become a company's head designer, or take up a senior position in factory management. Later, was also the possibility of eventually moving into product marketing and ultimately, who knows? Maybe a senior management position or my own business would come my way? The task now was to find the best way to get started.

My mam, now the manageress of the trouser manufacturing section in one of Leeds' wholesale apparel manufacturers played a valuable role here providing, as she always had in the past, some down-to-earth advice for me to add to my thinking.

She had always offered encouragement, advising me to continue with my technical studies, with the ultimate aim of augmenting the value that I would then be able to represent to a future employer, perhaps even advancing to become my own boss? Achieving such a status, she always pointed out, whenever we got to discuss such issues, was higher than both she and my dad had been able to achieve during their working lives.

Both my mam and dad were skilled operators in their respective fields, successful as such in terms of what they had been able to achieve, considering the few real opportunities that had come their way. My mam was a highly regarded trouser machinist, her skills as an organiser of staff were also now being recognised by her employer. My dad was a skilled maker of beautiful furniture.

While even at the tender age of 20, I needed even now to begin to think more and more about what it was that I wanted to achieve in life. I was even then coming to realise that it was now time for me to set some personal goals and, wherever possible to strive to exceed even my own expectations.

Is it not a universal truth in life that not everyone can – or even desires to – become their country's prime minister, a multi-millionaire tycoon, media mogul, a rich entrepreneur, an accomplished artist, film star or best-selling writer, no matter how much they may dream?

In my eyes, both my mam and dad were successful. As parents they certainly were successful, managing to produce two healthy, well-educated children, both of us they loved deeply and provided everything within their power, from limited financial resources and a basic level of academic achievements. Their desire was for my sister and I to eventually be able to aim higher in our lives than they had been able to achieve in theirs.

My mam and her six brothers and sisters had spent most of their adult lives working in either of a large clothing factory or one or other of the myriad small tailoring establishments, similar to those in which I had served my earlier working years,[1] between leaving school and commencing national service.

As subsequent events turned out, quite soon in fact and much earlier than I had expected, the universe or whatever form of a god or other deity exists out there in the cosmos, must have been looking over my shoulder. Having delved into my dreams, something or someone, somewhere, decided to come to my aid.

The aid did in fact arrive much sooner than I had expected. It appeared in the form of an opportunity that emerged out of the cloying, foggy gloom that had been swirling around me since arriving back in Leeds. As a result, I was lucky enough to secure the very position that eventually provided the momentum to start me along the path to Melbourne, Australia, four years later.

Notes

1. My family history and details of those years are contained in an earlier book "Conversations with a Small Boy", published September 2010, soon to be reissued as an e-book.

BACK TO THE RAG TRADE

Soon after my return to Leeds, I applied for and, was able to secure a position as an alteration tailor with the second company I had approached – a mid-sized manufacturer of high- quality men's outerwear. My casual factory door inquiry had been assisted when surprisingly, the factory manager who unbeknown to me at the time turned out to be a distant relative of my dad's.

On hearing my surname from the doorman, he came out to meet me, obviously thinking I was my dad's brother, my uncle Wolfe – himself a highly respected local tailor. Following a brief chat on my RAF background, and what I thought were my capabilities I was offered a trial starting position with the company as an alteration tailor. The role – a fairly minor one involved the making of required alterations to garments during the process of them being 'made up' as private orders for individual customers. This was a relatively simple position, in which I was to work, initially as the assistant to the tailor who ran that small section of the factory.

Another lesson in life this highlighted, "It's not necessarily only a question of what you know, but sometimes one of whom you know in this life." In this case, it luckily proved to be someone who knew my dad and Uncle Wolfe. Whatever, I had secured a position at £8 for a 44-hour working week.

That was a start at least – and at only my second attempt. The company, Benjamin Simon and Sons Ltd, was one of a number of medium-sized family-owned apparel manufacturers involved in the wholesale production of high-quality men's outerwear.

On commencing work with the company, I also returned to my earlier studies in Apparel and Textiles design and technology, attending classes on three evenings a week at the Leeds College of Technology (LCT) – later the college was to become known as Leeds Polytechnic.

After eight months, having proved myself competent at handling the various kinds of alterations and adjustments from the bespoke side of the company's business, I was offered the opportunity of filling a recent vacancy in the company's design office. This was a promotion that took me off the factory floor and into a new role as assistant to the company's head designer.

My new position allowed me to shed the need to clock-on-and-clock-off each day. Also, I was required to exchange my tailor's apron for a jacket. Now appointed to the company's permanent staff, meant that I now moved onto a weekly salary, instead of being paid at an hourly rate. The change in status, however, made little real difference, other than the fact that I was from here on to be paid on a weekly basis, I continued to receive the same £8 per week.

A few months later the company, in recognition of excellent annual exam results achieved at LCT, in addition also having taken on more responsibility at work, decided to release both me and another staff member for a full day of study leave each week. With this extension, I was able to augment my studies toward achieving Full Technological Certification in men's wholesale clothing, and textile design and technology. This one-day release to the LCT was in addition to the earlier three evening classes a week that I was required to continue with at my own expense, as part of the deal. An additional perk (as some of my former factory workmate tailors regarded it) the change in the job also provided my own key to the supervisor's toilet.

Wow! Here then I now found myself, still 20 years of age and the newly appointed assistant to Tom Barker, the company's designer. Not only that but also now I was authorised to sit newly appointed bum on an upholstered chair in the executive dining room for lunch, a perk that enabled me to mingle with others occupying various management and supervisory roles within the company. I can't say that I got paid more per week than what I had been earning working as an alteration tailor on the factory floor – but what the hell? The move proved at the very least to be a rung upward on the management ladder.

Over the next two years, I knuckled down and worked hard at my job, gradually taking on more responsibility. I continued to attend LCT, studying there for a full day each week on release from work, in addition to attending three evening classes each week, together with a great deal more in terms of hours of study, work at home and research on my own account over the weekends and during other spare time.

My day/night studies over two full years and the extra experience gained at work, eventually proved successful when I emerged in 1958 with first-class honours in both men's apparel design and advanced textile technology.

I was also pleasantly surprised to be honoured in my final year of study by the national award of the prestigious English Silver Medal.

This medal was a highly coveted award – the highest possible to achieve throughout Great Britain, one being awarded each year to the leading national apparel technology student. The Silver Medal was an award issued by the Worshipful Company of Taylors, a venerable and ancient guild, whose guild history stretched back over four centuries.

In addition to the Full Technological 1st and Silver medal, also that year I received various cups and book prizes, in addition to being awarded the highly prized Associateship of the Clothing Institute (ACI London). I was now authorised to append that industry-wide recognised letters after my name.

The levels achieved at LCT now placed me in a position from where I should now be able to apply for a senior position with a future company later on in my career. While still young, I now needed to build on my current level of expertise, a situation assisted as I gradually took over some of the technical assignments in the design department. A junior was later employed as my assistant.

Now having reached my third year with the company, the real highlight of 1958 was my marriage, at the tender age of 23, to my beautiful fiancée, Rochelle Mavis Brown. With not much in the way of funds between us, Mavis and I started our married life sharing my in-laws' council flat at its location adjacent to the Cranmer Bank Hotel (the local pub), on the Leeds City Council housing estate located in the outer suburb of Moortown.

Apart from our week-long honeymoon, spent at Redmans Hotel on the north shore at Blackpool, the first part-year of our married life was somewhat less than exciting, living as we were, as tenants with my in-laws.

At the time, we were also without much real hope of being able to finance the purchase of a home of our own for some time to come. Mavis was also working in the local apparel industry, in her case as the wages officer with a local women's wear manufacturer.

TICKET TO THE LAND OF OZ

During my 23rd year, and the final year of advanced studies in textile design at LCT, in addition to the City and Guilds Silver Medal, I also received an award from an overseas apparel manufacturer. This award proved to be the means by which the lives of my new wife and I would change forever.

The precursor of that change came in the form of a cup and a monetary prize awarded by an Australian men's apparel manufacturer Ernest Hiller Apparel Pty Ltd. Ernest Hiller, the company's owner, had also written to me offering his congratulations on winning his annually awarded prize.

Not being one to sit back and wait for things to happen in their own good-time I wrote back to Mr Hiller, thanking him for the award, also requesting his advice as to the possible future opportunities in Australia for what I described as a 'talented young menswear designer'. I soon received his return letter, also via airmail, which contained an invitation to join his company – should I ever consider migrating to Australia.

Without a great deal in the way of long and deep consideration, his offer was accepted. Following an exchange of air letters over a few months (no computers, emails or World Wide Web in those days), Mr Hiller offered me the position of designer with his company – at a starting salary of A£26 per week. More important than the attractive salary, he arranged to sponsor my wife and I under the then Australian government's 'assisted immigration' programme. This on the basis of me holding internationally recognised qualifications, of value to the Australian textile and apparel manufacturing industries.

A quick calculation also showed that the salary I was being offered was well in excess of the £8 sterling per week that I was earning in Leeds. Even taking into consideration the exchange rate between pounds sterling and pounds Australian at the time, the salary was well beyond my wildest expectations. Almost a fortune!

Mr Hiller's offer also included the provision of a fully furnished house, which he advised was located a short distance from the factory, itself located close to Guildford, a small township located on Sydney's western fringe.

While Mavis and I were understandably excited by the opportunity being offered by the Australian company, not everyone among our close relatives and friends were in agreement with our decision to take up the offer. Few supported our decision to travel as far as one can go on-board planet Earth, without the possibility of actually falling off! Some even considered that I was too young to be thinking of taking on such a prestigious and potentially difficult position.

It is also interesting to note here that most people living in and around Leeds and the north of England at the time regarded Australia and New Zealand as being remote from what was seen by them as 'the real world'. Both countries represented the 'ends of the Earth' in many people's minds, populated more by sheep, cattle and kangaroos in Australia's case, than people. Australia was also known to be a country inhabited by all kinds of weird animals, poisonous snakes, crocodiles, poisonous spiders and tribes of belligerent, near naked, wandering natives from prehistory.

Remote in this context was certainly a word that accurately described the general view of what was also known as 'the Antipodes', at least as those lands were seen, from the streets of many a northern British city, even as late as the 1950s.

Little else was known about the country that was also a continent, other perhaps than the vast distances that separated Australia's few major cities – population centres mainly established around the continent's eastern and southern coastal fringe. The greater part of Australia, in particular, its central regions were known to comprise many thousands of square miles of desert areas and low, ancient worn-down mountain ranges and hills. It also appeared from the outside that most of the country was incapable of supporting much more than kangaroos, sheep, cattle, wild horses and camels – most of which roamed far and wide across rural properties – some much greater in area than the British Isles!

Our announcement that Mavis and I intended to migrate to that distant continent was regarded by most of my friends and workmates as bordering on foolhardy. My newly acquired mother-in-law was most decidedly opposed to our move. She certainly didn't wish to see her only daughter being whisked off to the far side of the world by her impetuous new husband. My parents, on the other hand, particularly my mam, were supportive. Others among my friends and workmates also expressed the view that my future in and around the then busy and widespread apparel industry then operating profitably in Britain and across post-war Europe, was assured. I now possessed the highest technical qualifications – and had a good, seemingly secure position.

Thus went the argument: "Why even think of going off to the ends of the Earth and a place full of snakes, spiders and other dangerous nasties, so far away from home, family and friends?"

My mam in particular, although not wishing to see her firstborn take off for the other side of the world, was the most positive. I was even surprised to learn that she, at the age of 21, back in 1929, while then working as a trouser machinist, had been offered a trainee management position with a company then located in Rhodesia (now Zimbabwe), by a former manager of her then employers. He was a man who, along with his young family had left England a couple of years earlier, in favour of life in a then prosperous British Rhodesia. On a visit back to Leeds, he had offered her the opportunity to migrate to Salisbury, the capital, to take up a position assisting him in the setting up of a modern trouser factory, of which he was now a co-owner.

Unfortunately, though she had wanted to make the change, her father, my maternal grandfather Tani Wolfovitch, a devout and very traditional Lithuanian Jew, forbade her from even thinking of moving away from the family home in Leeds. His was an understandable attitude at the time, being a relatively recently arrived refugee from Lithuania, particularly when it came to one of his unmarried daughter's ongoing life plans. He was one of many thousands of Ashkenazi Jews, people who but a few years earlier had themselves barely escaped from the clutches of the Russian Czar and his harsh, murderous religion-based pogroms.

Ultimately, my then-single Mam had to decline the job offer in deference to the wishes of her father. Luckily for me, I guess, as had she left Leeds for a new life in Rhodesia in 1929, I would perhaps have not seen the light of day and be sitting here, writing this?

Back in Leeds, several weeks dragged slowly by, during which both Mavis and I found ourselves having to undergo X rays, blood tests and a medical examination, all carried out in Leeds by a medical examiner commissioned by Australia House in London. Also, there were a number of official forms, plus an agreement that the Australian government required to be signed, this to start the process for us to be accepted, under Australia's assisted immigration programme.

Travel from Leeds to our intended destination in Australia was to be funded by the Australian government at the total cost to us of £10 each, the full amount we would be required to pay toward the total cost of travel to our destination, near Sydney Australia.

AUSTRALIA'S IMMIGRATION PROGRAMME

If travelling under the 1959 version of the Australian assisted immigration scheme, the agreement that all intending migrants were required to sign, bound them to remain in Australia for at least two years.

The Australian government for its part undertook to fund and organise passage to Australia from an approved migrant's home in Britain to either the city of their sponsor or the location of the Australian government's migrant hostel to which they were being allocated. The latter applied in the case of those intending migrants who, while not being sponsored by either an Australian resident family member or prospective Australian employer, were able to meet the government's minimum requirements and pass a medical test. In either event, should the migrant or family thus funded decide to leave Australia before the two-year minimum period had expired, they would be required to repay the total cost of their travel, before being allowed to depart.

The thought of travelling to the far side of the world, away from our families and friends, eventually began to catch up on both Mavis and I, particularly during the final weeks that we were in Leeds.

While on the one hand, the exciting prospect of travel to a new country, far away from the continuing austerity and relatively confined lives we were then leading in Leeds, proved to be a much more attractive option to a couple of youngsters in their early twenties. The thought of leaving our close family behind us, weighed down heavily.

Mavis had given notice of her leaving to her employers at a local apparel factory where she handled wages and other administrative duties. Pay-wise, she was receiving the same salary level as me. In the climate current throughout the north of England at the time, there seemed little hope of us being able to build up enough capital to be able to put down a deposit on a house or apartment of our own for some considerable time into the future. Our Australian sponsor's offer of a furnished house as part of my salary package had certainly added a large plus here. We were both looking forward to being able to move into a home of our own.

The prospect of having to remain as guests of Mavis's parents in their small council flat for some time into the future offered little incentive for us to stay. Not that I even wished to stay living in Leeds or any other part of Britain for that matter. My mind on that score had been made long ago.

At the same time, it was also true that while the opportunity to migrate to Australia had presented itself, arriving virtually 'out of the blue' via the Ernest Hiller offer, the opportunity had appeared much sooner than I had planned for or had expected.

At the time, some of the negative opinions and suggestions from various acquaintances continued to echo in my ears. These, while mainly along the lines that I was still very young to be taking on such a senior role so far away from home. Another suggestion was that Australia offered little that couldn't be obtained still in Britain – and, I knew hardly anything about the company and the man who had offered me the position. The latter was certainly true, I knew next to nothing about the company in Australia, nor did I know anyone in Sydney who I felt I could turn to for an objective opinion on the offer I had received.

While I had thought long and hard about the offer, and the need to travel to the far side of the planet to take it up, I had concluded that the offer was just too good to pass up. Even if I eventually found that the job was too big for me to handle, surely I would always have the fallback option of taking on another position somewhere else as a pattern-cutter, or even as a tailor, should that become necessary.

What was the best course to take? When it came down to basics, it was a case of nothing ventured – nothing gained, and in any case, in my heart, I had already crossed that Rubicon, having decided long ago to grab hold of any real opportunity that came my way.

As to continuing to remain in my present job in Leeds, that prospect alone of continuing to live as guests in my parents-in-law' small council flat was itself an added incentive to move. Australia, particularly Sydney, seemed at the very least to offer access to its famous harbour and its many beaches, plus the promise of a warmer, healthier climate – in addition to a well-paid job, confirmed in writing, and a house near the Hiller factory. What more was there to think about?

The salary level offered by Ernest Hiller was attractive. It should enable us to maintain a reasonably comfortable lifestyle, according to the cost-of-living information being provided by Australia House in London. In any case, what did we have to lose? If things didn't work out after two years, we could always return to Britain?

One other factor was the local economy. It had continued to remain sluggish, even 14 years since the ending of the Second World War. More important perhaps, not having anything tangible in the way of property, financial commitments, dependent children or any other impediments sufficient to dissuade us from migrating, we could see few reasons to doubt our decision to make a move.

From the standpoint of my qualifications and experience to date, having now achieved technical qualifications recognised worldwide, the fact that I had been so quickly offered the opportunity to take up a senior position in Australia seemed to be a 'message from the universe' that beckoned – nay it demanded to be grasped!

The promise of being able to open a new life in a new country was itself an exciting prospect. Why not? Australians spoke the same language as us, while Australia's British heritage, its laws, legal and legislative practices, also its currency were much the same as those with which we were familiar. These factors alone seemed good enough reasons to give the job a try, overpoweringly represented in the plus column.

On fronting up to my employer to provide the company with adequate notice of my intention to leave, I surprisingly found myself in a position I had not expected. The company's managing director, on hearing my reasons for migrating to Australia, stated that should I decide not to leave the company; my position would be guaranteed (whatever that meant?). Not only that but when the time came for my boss, Tom Barker, the company's designer, to retire at the expected retirement age, which I was to assume was in the region of him reaching 65 or thereabouts, his position would be mine.

I nearly laughed on hearing that statement, seated as I was on the other side of his massive and ornate timber desk from Danny Simon, the company's MD, as I contemplated having to wait for years and years, for an offer that could well disappear before that time.

Bearing in mind that Tom Barker was only 42 years of age at the time, would mean me having to wait for at least 23 years for his position to become vacant! Even then, there was no guarantee that it would be me who got the job, even if the company was still in business 23 years hence, which it wasn't. The company, like many others in later years, was eventually taken over, ceasing to exist long before that!

When I pointed this out, my boss, perched majestically behind his ponderous, exquisitely carved executive desk, offered to immediately raise my current salary by a princely 40%, to around £11 pounds/week, should I decide to stay with the company. He even offered to consider a loan, should I wish to purchase a motor vehicle.

While the offer of an increase in salary was a not inconsiderable amount at the time – it was too late. My Boss's offer had come too late and as such fell on deaf ears, prompting me to point out: "Why is it that you can only now offer me a raise? Why didn't you even consider my request for a salary review when I last requested one just six months ago, based as it was on the number of additional responsibilities I had undertaken over the past year?"

No, my mind was made up and Australia it was for me. Goodbye, it was to Britain, Leeds and the three venerable brother bosses at Benjamin Simon and Sons Ltd.

4
£10 POMMIE MIGRANT

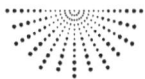

April 15th 1959 saw Mavis, my wife of just over six months, and I setting sail from London's Tilbury Docks. We, along with hundreds of other intending British emigrants, were about to embark on the aging but still elegant 24,000-ton Orient Line ship Orion for the month-long voyage to Australia. Interestingly, our departure to Australia was exactly six years to the date since my last big change – entry into national service with the RAF in 1953.

One way or another, everyone due to sail that day was embarking on the journey of a lifetime, the decision to do so taking all far away from our loved ones and homes throughout the British Isles. In our case, our destination was to be Sydney or to be more exact, the nearby small town of Guildford, situated as far as I could discern on Sydney's outer western fringe.

Every one of those among the passenger list leaving Britain that day knew that we were sailing toward an unknown city or town, and an uncertain, potentially promising and possibly exciting future.

Mavis and I saw the occasion as the way to our future. It was yet to really register in our minds that Australia, far away and well down below the equator in the South Pacific, was about as far as one could travel away from the British Isles. We also knew that it would probably be some years before we could afford to return to Leeds for a visit.

The 1950s and 60s saw many thousands of families, couples and individuals from all walks of life leaving the British Isles, on the first stage of their migration to Australia, all more than likely having similar thoughts to us in mind. We all were taking our chances and 'throwing the dice' while being unsure as to the eventual outcome of the voyage upon which we were about to embark. At the same time, all had accepted the Australian government's promise of a reasonably paid job and the potential of finding better living conditions and prospects for those with children, on their arrival in Australia, than most were then seeing ahead for themselves in Britain.

Publicity and information on the kind of living standards prospective immigrants should expect in our new country were at the time being aggressively promoted in advertising, pamphlets and advertorial news bulletins, regularly screened in movie theatres across Britain.

Other Western countries were also trying to attract migrants wherever possible. Canada and New Zealand were each vying with Australia for their share. Each country was on the lookout for potential settlers, preferably skilled ones. All were intent on replacing people lost during the recently ended six years of war, and were mindful of the need to boost their national economies over coming decades.

There was a downside to our decision to leave Britain – a powerful one at that! We all were about to leave our homes, families and close friends for a distant southern continent that very few of us knew anything, other than the little we had learned about in school. What information we possessed about our new country, was that being provided in pamphlets and statistics distributed from Australia House in London. Even this information helped little, as none among us had access to any other reliable sources with which to compare that being received from Australia House. For all we knew, the information being received could well have emerged from the imaginations of creative writers then being employed by the Australian government? To counter this, a number of reports had been filtering back to Britain from earlier British emigrants. Most of these reports had been positive, at least providing something of value for this latest batch of voyagers to take in and consider.

Contrast our situation with that of someone contemplating a move to another country or location on the opposite side of the planet today? Today's traveller is in a position to access an unlimited amount of relevant information on just about anything and about anywhere upon the surface of the planet – simply by switching on his or her laptop computer and surfing the Internet!

Back in 1959 few of us possessed little more than a limited concept of the size of our new country, or had even read much more than the relatively limited range of information that was being provided by Australia House.

We did know that Australia was big, more like immense when compared to the size of Britain! Most were also of the view that the country had more than its fair share of sunshine, warm seas and surf. We knew about Australia's beaches and that the rest of the country was very far away from anywhere else in the Western world – except perhaps for an even more distant New Zealand and the then still sleeping Asian countries to the north.

Most of us leaving that day had learned in school that the coastal fringes and large portions of the so-called Australian 'outback' and more arid regions of the country, had been inhabited for well over 50,000 years by what, even then were still being described as a race of prehistoric, backward wanderers. These were said to be people that comprised many different tribes, that over millennia had spread out across the continent following their earlier migration across an ancient land bridge and shallow seas, then thought to have existed between a then vast, uninhabited continent and the lands of an ancient Southern Asia. Descendants of the group of Australia's original inhabitants still living in various parts of the country were called 'Aborigines'.

THE ORIGINAL AUSTRALIANS

At school, I had learned much about James Cook's earlier charting of Canada's Newfoundland and the entrance to the Saint Lawrence River, followed later by his charting of New Zealand and the eastern coastline of the Australian continent. During Cook's later voyage to Australia, he wrote about his brief encounter with a few of the people then living on Terra Australis. Apart from Cook's notes, little else was then known about the continent's inhabitants.

During geography lessons at school, I had learned briefly of the ancient people that had populated Australia for millennia. As far as I knew in 1959, they probably continued to wander their way across the vast outback, deserts and hilly regions of modern Australia?

I was aware that a local tribe of Australian Aborigines had been among those who had confronted the first small force of British sailors to set foot on the continent, on their arrival in 1770 at a place that was later named Sydney Cove.

On April 23rd 1770 Captain James Cook made his first recorded direct observation of a meeting with indigenous Australians at Brush Island near Bawley Point, noting in his journal: "and were so near the Shore as to distinguish several people upon the Sea beach they appear'd to be of a very dark or black Colour but whether this was the real colour of their skins or the Clothes they might have on I know not."

On April 29th, Cook and his crew made their first landfall on the mainland of the continent at a place now known as the Kurnell Peninsula. Cook originally named the area Stingray Bay, but he later crossed it out and renamed it Botany Bay, after the unique specimens retrieved by the botanists Joseph Banks and Daniel Solander. It is here that James Cook made the first contact with an Aboriginal tribe known then as the 'Gweagal'.[1]

Little about the earlier history of Australia's original inhabitants had even been considered important enough during my student days in England, to avoid them being described as little more than "ignorant, primeval savages".

Those supposedly ignorant savages had in fact found a sustainable way by which to live, hunt, move around and generally prosper – according to their spiritual beliefs, unique culture and social/tribal arrangements, across one of the driest and perhaps most inhospitable continent on the face of the Earth.

Notes

1. The 'Gweagal' people: earlier references to the 23/29th April 1770 landings in Australia by Captain Cook. Source: Wikipedia.

MY SCHOOL GEOGRAPHY BOOK

How earlier Western eyes and generations of historians and politicians have viewed Australia's Aboriginal culture is illuminating, particularly the way in which at least one writer described them.

I still have in my possession an official school textbook, copies of which had been provided to we British students during geography classes throughout my school days during the 1940s. This geography book from that period made some reference to Australia's first inhabitants. Apart from being capable of making and throwing boomerangs and roughly made spears with which to kill kangaroos and other animals for food, little else was said about them, other than them being a backward stone-age race, not unlike some of the stone-age tribes of Europe – people often described as 'wanderers from prehistory'.

Looking back to the time of my departure from Britain in 1959, I had little else in the way of information as to what to expect, other than a generalised description of Australia's indigenous people, other than as my school textbook described them as, "one of the lowest of all savage races". This had me wondering just what I should do, say or even perhaps fear, if I actually got to meet an Australian Aborigine, preferably one without a spear or 'nulla-nulla' with which to club me!

Were there Aborigines living in Sydney and Guildford where I expected to live and be working? Would any Aborigines be employed in the clothing factory to which I was destined? I knew little, other than the accounts I had read about the tribes of prehistoric people who, we had learned of in school, who were said to spend their entire lives wandering semi-naked around the Australian hinterland, living off the land, its animals, fish, birds, berries and roots. These we learned were 'ancients' who didn't build permanent houses like the ones in which we lived. Instead, they were said to have sheltered in caves or under portable bark and branch screens, the latter some carried with them on their constant wanderings. Is that the way Australia's Aborigines still lived?

It is instructive, living as we are, hopefully in more enlightened times in the year 2017, to recall just how British school publications of the 1930s and 1940s referred to the ancient people who had populated the continent of Australia, since the dawn of history.

In words more familiar to us today in modern Australia, the recorded first landing by the British upon Australia's shores in 1788 should have been reported by historians as: "The country was invaded by a horde of aggressive, pale skinned illegal boat people flying a tricoloured flag which they referred to as the Union Jack"!

In my schoolbook titled "The World", its author Lewis Marshall wrote of the Aboriginal race in clearly pejorative terms in a chapter titled "Black, White and Yellow Men". The words used by the author bear repeating:

> The black fellows of Australia belong to one of the lowest of all savage races. Cut off from contact with the inhabitants of the Old World, without animals to provide milk, or grasses from whose seeds bread could be made, they were far too busy struggling to find food to be able to raise them much above the animals they hunted.
>
> As their lives were entirely devoted to the chase, these men developed remarkable powers of imitation, observation and endurance. They have imitated the shape and movement of the Acacia leaf as it flies through the air blown by the wind, and have invented the flat, curved, wooden weapon called the boomerang, which can be hurled so as to return to the thrower.
>
> These ignorant savages have no knowledge of the arts of life, and they travel about from one place to another searching for food. It has been found impossible to teach them to do anything useful, or to make them understand even the simplest forms of agriculture. Disease, especially lung-complaint, is rife amongst them, and they are rapidly dying out.
>
> These aborigines are not what we now call the "natives", which is a term invariably applied to those whites (who have been) born on

Australian soil. The possibilities of Australia as a stock raising country and above all the discovery of gold, attracted to the continent a large number of white men, most of whom are to be found in the eastern, south-eastern, and south-western coastal districts, where the climate is sufficiently cool and moist for Europeans. Many settled down as farmers, artisans, and tradesmen, and some made their home in the bush, where their descendants are still known as Bushmen.

This section goes on to include a brief description of another kind of settler in early Australia, continuing along the following lines:

In the wake of the white men, another race came out to Australia, much to the disgust of the settlers. This was the Chinese, most of who originally came from California, whence they followed the American miners who rushed to the Australian gold diggings on the discovery of gold. By heavy taxes the states have tried to keep John Chinaman out of Australia, but without success. He is industrious, economical, and especially successful as a market gardener, laundry-man and furniture maker.

Reading through the foregoing paragraphs on pages 263–265 of my schoolbook, leads one to understand how the early history of Australia's settlement by Europeans has regularly been misrepresented. This has continued even up to relatively modern times. During the first two centuries of European settlement, those governing the country, and its later states and territories, together with the various Christian churches, set in train attitudes, policies and actions designed to perpetuate such ignorant and prejudicial views.

It is also to the enduring shame of every newcomer who settled in Australia during subsequent centuries, that the original inhabitants of the land, prior to a referendum in May 1967 changed their official status, were not even counted as citizens in the nation's periodic national census.

It has often been said that until that May 1967 referendum, Australia's Aborigines had been regarded as part of the country's flora and fauna. Attempting to balance this, a 2014 SBS article described the notion that indigenous people had been classed as fauna as being a myth, listing it as one of: "Four key misunderstandings persisting about indigenous history and the referendum".[1]

Whatever the truth, the treatment of Australia's first people since the 1788 landing, remains a mute but damning accusation against many of Australia's early and even later British settlers.

We current day Australians still struggle to come to grips with the irrefutable fact that the people first encountered late in the 18th century by James Cook, Arthur Phillip and others, were the continent's first residents. As such they were Australia's legitimate first owners. It follows therefore, that they and their descendants, at the very least, have the right to be recognised as such.

For over 200 years since 1788, settlement of the continent has occurred as a result of people, much like my wife and I, foreigners who migrated here and decided to settle. Other than those subsequently born in Australia, most who continue to refer to themselves as 'native Australians', nearly everyone else arrived here by sea, in small boats or, as in the case of many recent arrivals, my wife and I included, onboard a large ship. Later arrivals came via one or other of the world's international airlines, or were born here.

None leaving the British Isles throughout the 1950s were contemplating migration to Australia as a result of experiencing some form of racial oppression or a physical attack in Britain. Most had been attracted by the possibilities Australia offered, together with the promise of a more relaxed lifestyle, coupled to much better working and pay conditions and a healthier future, both for them and their children. Many had been attracted no doubt by the glowing advertisements and brochures being issued by Australia House in London. These came in the form of images and messages that depicted a relaxed and potentially prosperous lifestyle as being the norm in Australia.

Notes

1. The Australian referendum of 27 May 1967, called by the Holt government, approved two amendments to the Australian constitution

relating to Indigenous Australians. Technically it was a vote on the Constitution Alteration (Aboriginals) 1967, which became law on 10 August 1967 following the results of the referendum. The amendments were overwhelmingly endorsed, winning 90.77% of votes cast and carrying in all six states. These amendments altered sections 51(xxvi) and 127 having the immediate effect of including Aboriginal Australians in determinations of population, and also empowered the federal parliament to legislate specifically for this racial group. Ref: Wikipedia.

FAREWELL TO LEEDS

Saying our last goodbyes to parents on the platform of Leeds' City railway station as the time of our leaving arrived had been heartbreaking. As it was, the excitement and anticipation of the long sea voyage and what lay beyond four weeks of travel on a beautiful ship across the world and into our future had already robbed me of the ability to fall into any semblance of restful sleep during the week before our departure. Now, standing on the platform of the station, the time had finally arrived to say our goodbyes to both sets of parents. That moment also brought with it the realisation that our leaving was now final. The emotional impact of the project that we were about to embark upon, now struck home with force.

Wow! We were today at the start of a trip of a lifetime, a voyage to the far side of the world! The picture that such a trip had already implanted in both our minds was beyond belief, a vivid and unreal dream, one that continued to hold us in its thrall, as we were now about to embark into its midst.

Our impending departure, particularly during the last few remaining days before leaving Leeds, was a disturbing mixture of excitement, plus a variety of other, more negative emotions. Our excitement was tempered with a deep sadness at the prospect of leaving our loved ones, for what possibly could be the last time. Both Mavis and I had come to think of our leaving as being more or less permanent, perhaps even for a lifetime? We were planning to settle 12,000 miles distant from those we had known and loved all our young lives. Those at the railway station that day were well aware that the cost of international travel and our financial position at the time, offered little hope of being able to return to Leeds for a short visit for some years to come.

Standing and saying our goodbyes on the station platform, I will never forget the look in my mam's eyes. I loved her deeply and knew that I was going to miss her. I was thankful for having such a loving, helpful and supportive parent and felt pain just seeing her tears flowing as she said goodbye and wished us both a successful and happy future. To her, it must have felt like she was saying her last farewell to her only son and his wife – not knowing if she would ever see us both again. Her sadness, standing close to me on the platform, just before we had to board our train to London tore at my heart. I also knew that even though my dad had always found it hard to show his emotions, even at the most tender of times, that he too was feeling the same kind of sadness. My dad, unlike my mam, had never been able to express his love and deeper feelings, even though I knew deep down that he too was going to miss us both.

We kissed for the last time, my mam holding onto me tightly. Mavis's parents too held onto her until the very last moment, before the guard blew his whistle and the time had come for us to board our train to London. Once on-board, tears welling on all sides, the carriage window rolled down and our handkerchiefs waving, the train started forward with a jerk. We were finally starting out on the journey of our young lives.

Were we doing the right thing? What would life be like in

Australia? Please let the job and life we were going to in Australia prove to be a success. Hopefully, we will be happy in our adopted country?

Preparatory to Mavis and I departing from Britain, Australia House in London had sent travel warrants that provided both with pre-paid transit via train from Leeds to London, then on to Tilbury Docks the next day. We had also been issued with temporary passports in readiness for our entry into Australia. Regarding our luggage – what we were physically carrying represented nearly all our worldly possessions and a couple of changes of clothing. We had no furniture, furnishings or other domestic equipment to take with us in any case. Unlike other families who had much more to ship, we had little – with the possible exception of wedding presents and other personal stuff. Most of what we possessed was packed into a blue brass bound cabin trunk. The trunk had previously been freighted down to the docks as cargo, and all we had other than that we planned to carry on-board as hand luggage. Our day-to-day needs like toiletries and a change of casual clothing was contained in an additional carry-on bag each.

TWO INNOCENTS IN LONDON

On arrival at London's bustling Kings Cross railway station, our priority was to search around for a hotel in which to stay the night before meeting the train that was to carry us down to Tilbury Docks early next morning.

Where to stay overnight in London was the immediate question. We had neglected to pre-book accommodation for the night before boarding the train for Tilbury. In any event, neither our parents nor we had any idea which hotels we should contact in London. The decision, therefore, had been left until we arrived at Kings Cross.

Two 'lost souls', our arrival found us standing outside Kings Cross station as we considered our next move, finally deciding to stop a passing cabbie, requesting him to convey us to a reasonably priced, family hotel. Big mistake! The cabbie happily took us to an establishment not very far from the station that claimed via its sign above the door, to be a 'family hotel'. Had we been experienced travellers at the time, just one look at the place would have told us to look elsewhere.

The building from memory was in dire need of refurbishment and a coat of paint – cheap looking it certainly was, very cheap! The carpet in the reception area had also seen better days. The receptionist, a scruffy-looking woman, cigarette dangling from the corner of her mouth, looked like she had herself just emerged from her bed. Welcoming we two bright-eyed 'yokels' from the north, she hardly paused to extract the glowing cigarette from the side of her mouth, as she led us to a room located on the first floor, up a flight of badly lit, creaky stairs. The door she opened led into a small room that reeked of cigarette smoke – obvious signs of recent habitation. This was confirmed when my wife stooped to examine the bed, which still appeared to be warm – also retaining signs of recently being vacated, together with what appeared to be hair, pubic or otherwise, that was still adhering to one of the sheets.

Luckily, we hadn't parted with any of our limited supply of cash so it was a quick about turn, back down the rickety stairs as fast as our legs could carry us and out into the street and fresh air, post haste.

Considering our position again, we decided that it called for a case of, "Hang the expense! Let's book into a real hotel and live it up on our first and probably last night in London." Having made that momentous decision, we once again waved down a passing taxi that returned us back to Kings Cross where we checked into the Great Northern Hotel, located close by the station. Our earlier search for accommodation had been unnecessary, when we thought more of it, as earlier we could have strolled just a few yards from Kings Cross station and booked into the Great Northern Hotel on the spot.

Checking in now, we soon found ourselves entering a really nice room, where we settled ourselves into our new 'swish' surroundings. Now, this was more like it! The evening was now drawing in and, by now also feeling the need for some sustenance, we located the hotel dining room where we both tucked into a grand meal.

By the time we had finished dining and had relaxed a little, the earlier emotional partings from Leeds, followed by the rail journey and earlier attempt to find a room for the night had served to leave us both feeling emotionally drained and ready to turn in. It had been a full, sad and trying day.

Now with full stomachs and still empty hearts, neither of us felt any further interest to explore more than the little we had already seen of London.

Climbing into our big, comfortable bed and feeling the luxury of clean, crisp sheets, following closely on a hot bath, saw us both drifting off quickly into a deep sleep.

Next morning, following breakfast, it was onto the train for Tilbury Docks and our appointment with the good ship Orion, now awaiting our arrival and ready to bear her two young adventurers to the South Seas and Australia.

TILBURY DOCKS

On boarding the train to Tilbury, along with a crowd of other expectant passengers, it didn't take long for us to strike up a conversation with another couple sitting on the other side of our carriage, as our train puffed and jerked its way toward Tilbury. Like many friendships, this one started out in the form of guarded smiles and glances across the railway carriage. The ice was eventually broken as a result of a tentative greeting, and it didn't take long until we really got into the swing of things, following Mavis and I being invited to select from a proffered bag of boiled sweets. This tentative first meeting was followed by introductions that launched a friendship that, having started on such a casual basis, lasted for many years, even to the present. Well before the train had arrived and deposited us at Tilbury, we had become well acquainted with Norma and Frank Brown, both also travelling as assisted migrants from their home in Manchester.

By the time we had arrived at Tilbury Docks we were already good friends. During the short journey to Tilbury, we learned that neither Norma nor Frank had a job to go to, being destined initially to stay at a migrant hostel in Melbourne. For Norma and Frank, as with many other migrants, it was a case of on arrival in Melbourne, or some other city designated by the Australian immigration authorities, and a hopefully short stay in a government hostel there. In their case, both were looking forward to being able to obtain work relatively soon after their arrival. Once having managed to find suitable jobs would then enable them to move out of the hostel and into a rented place of their own.

On arrival at Tilbury Docks on the morning of April 15th, Mavis and I boarded Orion, after first being required to identify our blue, brass bound cabin trunk, prior to it then loaded on-board along with many other cabin trunks and heavy luggage, boxes, cases and crates, all packed with the possessions of other passengers boarding the ship. The best surprise, following completion of all the necessary boarding arrangements at the dockside, was being collected by one of the ship's stewards and shown to our cabin – also delighted to find it located in the after (rear) part of the ship, one level above the promenade deck.

Most of the people boarding the ship had been assigned to cabins below the main promenade deck. Some were housed one or possibly two decks lower down, with others located even lower down in the ship – closer to the waterline. Those lucky enough to be allocated an outside cabin below did at least possess an opening porthole. Most others finding themselves allocated to inside cabins had no view outside the ship, not even a porthole that opened out into a mid-deck well. Hopefully, anyone placed in one of these cabins didn't suffer too much from being confined in a windowless space or were sufferers from claustrophobia.

On making ourselves comfortable in our month-long home, further inspection of our cabin by my eagle-eyed wife discovered a small hole drilled through the bulkhead dividing our cabin from one adjacent to ours. The hole had obviously been intended as a means whereby one or more of the cabin stewards, who we later learned were bunked in the cabin next to ours, could spend some of their boring off-duty time on the ship, by checking out the form of a female occupant?

We soon put a stop to that caper by the simple means of hanging something over the hole after filling it up with screwed up toilet paper. A minor diversion this turned out to be – probably robbing one or two randy seamen of a raunchy viewing platform, a diversion to be looked forward to during their off-duty hours. Perhaps they also saw it as a substitute for the lack of TV on-board the ship?

A SAD GOODBYE

Just before our ship was due to pull away from Tilbury Docks, a brass band on the dock started to play "Auld Lang Syne", that well-known song of goodbye.

As the time neared for Orion to leave, many lines of hand-held coloured streamers began to festoon the dockside, forming a colourful but fragile final link connecting departing passengers with their relatives and friends bidding them a fond but sad farewell from the dockside. The scene was at times joyful but mainly sad, as the latest group of hopeful emigrants were about to commence their voyage to the far side of the world.

Farewell to old England forever

Farewell to old England forever
Farewell to our family and friends
Farewell to Leeds city and Harehills
and a county that's set so many trends.

We're tired of austerity and rationing
We're sick of the rain and the smog
Impatient just waiting for nothing
And promises politicians do flog.

There's a country down under we're making for
There's a job there been offered – that's swell,
There's good weather and beaches we've heard about
life's supposed to be easier they tell.

Taint leaving old England we cares about,
Taint leaving our past lives behind.
But because were still young and we're looking for
something better – we hope we can find.
It's been twenty odd years we've been living here
but the future's not looking so good,

> For the rest of our lives there has got to be
> Something better to look forward to.
>
> Oh, if we had the wisdom of Socrates
> We'd know what to look forward to,
> But being two young 'uns from Yorkshire
> We think thinking too much is not good.
>
> So, to all our young pals and acquaintances,
> Take notice from what we've to say,
> If yourselves leave old England in future
> You'll find us near Port Phillip Bay.[1]

As our ochre and white clad Orient Liner Orion fired up her engines and slowly began to move away from the dockside, the lines of streamers that were connecting those departing with friends and relatives seeing them off, gradually stretched out and ultimately began to drift apart, becoming broken coloured strips of paper that fluttered and drifted away forlornly on the wind. The ultimate parting of so many strips of coloured paper represented a final poignant reminder to us all that we were now about to leave our past lives and Britain behind us. It was a sobering moment.

Recalling the scene, even though Mavis and I had already bidden goodbye to our parents in Leeds the day prior, it was still emotional nevertheless for us to watch, as the distance from ship to shore slowly and inexorably widened. Britain, our home and all that it and our past lives had meant to us to date were now slowly drifting away into the misty, drizzle filled distance.

Many among those present on the departing ship were weeping openly, their tears being felt also by us, as people continued to wave handkerchiefs, scarves and hats, all of these fluttering in a mute expression of goodbye, as faces and figures faded away. The dockside gradually slipped astern, getting more and more indistinct – until it too finally disappeared into the distance.

It seemed as if we, particularly those leaving Britain without first securing a job, now were looking forward to the prospect of life for a few weeks or even months, in an unfamiliar migrant hostel, located somewhere or other in the various states to which they were bound. They more than any other passenger, some of whom were looking forward to joining relatives in Australia, were sailing toward a greater unknown. All those migrants had to look forward to at this stage was the reality of being temporarily accommodated on their arrival in Australia. This would mean them living in a state-run migrant hostel, located within one or other of the capital cities in the state to which they were destined, or another location near one or other of Australia's inland population centres, similar to Bonegilla,[2] a small settlement located near Wodonga in north-eastern Victoria.

I, on the other hand, had a job to look forward to. My wife and I were feeling lucky in comparison to those having few expectations regarding work and accommodation on their arrival in Australia. At the tender age of 24, I at the very least could look forward to taking up a senior position as company designer, along with a healthy salary, plus the provision of furnished accommodation. Was this almost too good to be true?

Regardless of our ultimate destination and fate, nearly everyone on-board Orion had by now irrevocably committed themselves to a month-long voyage into the unknown. It was already too late now to even be having second thoughts. We were now at sea, bound south down the English Channel and North Atlantic, east across the Mediterranean Sea, through the Suez Canal, then across the Indian and Southern Oceans – our final destination Australia, in a month's time.

April 1959 was many years before the advent of the Internet, the development and universal availability and use of cellular phones, colour television and satellite navigation systems – not forgetting today's world of instant communications like email, Twitter, Facebook, Messenger, Skype and instantly reported TV and radio news.

The late 1950s were also before the phenomenal growth and emergence of transnational conglomerates. Business groups that gradually began to straddle and finally dominate the world's financial systems. Many of these organisations eventually honed their operations to such an extent, that in many cases they began to exert more political power than the governments of countries across and through which they chose to operate.

In the late 1950s, the world was yet to experience the current pace and ease of international communications and low- cost air travel coming within the capability of practically everyone. For us then leaving for Australia during 1959, the only affordable and readily available means of communication with family and friends back in Britain was via a written letter.

This form of communication could, if using surface mail, take some weeks to travel the distance from Australia to Britain. In the case of our announcement to both sides of the family back in Leeds of the birth of our first son Andrew Simon in August 1961, the news of his eagerly awaited arrival was sent home via a few words on a telegram. Even that took many hours to transmit and deliver to both sets of grandparents on the other side of the world.

Contemplating the making of a transcontinental telephone call from Australia during the late 1950s and 1960s also meant going through a fairly involved and often costly process. Making a call from Australia to Britain in those early days involved first booking the intended call to the phone number in Britain via the local Australian telephone operator. The process could be painfully slow, with the local telephone operator calling back to the person ordering the call, once the connection requested had been made with a telephone exchange serving the person being contacted in Britain.

Even having once obtained the desired connection and, depending on the sometimes solar-induced phenomena outside the control of the telephone companies in both countries, the party making the call could never be sure that the link would not fall out and have to be reconnected, sometimes resulting in a considerable extra delay. Transcontinental, or as it was in Australia's case, trans-world conversations in the 1950s were also often difficult to conduct, due to tentative connections, which could and often did vary in strength and clarity.

So, when it later came to communicating with our families back in Britain, living on the other side of the world in Australia may well have been compared, at least in some people's minds, as us having relocated to the Moon!

Notes

1. With apologies to whoever was responsible for the original version of the ditty 'Botany Bay'.

2. The Migrant Reception and Training Centre in Bonegilla, northern Victoria, was the first home in Australia for some 300,000 migrants from over 50 countries who arrived between 1947 and 1971. The site of a former military camp, the Commonwealth Immigration Centre at Bonegilla opened in December 1947 following a decision by Arthur Calwell, minister for immigration, to reuse military camps to house the huge wave of migrants coming from war-torn Europe, known as displaced persons.

UNDERWAY TO THE LAND DOWN UNDER

As Orion settled down to her cruising speed and steamed out into the English Channel, most of her new passengers began to wander around the various decks. The initial aim of most on-board was to find our way around the ship, while also trying to locate which of the dining rooms to which we had been allocated. Mavis and I found us seated at a table in the ship's first-class dining room, hosted by the ship's first officer/navigator.

As I wandered around the ship, the realisation that Mavis and I were travelling on-board a great liner that was to take us across the world to our new country only began to dawn on me for the first time. It was the first time that either of us had even been in the vicinity of a luxury liner, let alone actually to find ourselves on-board one. The immensity of our decision to leave Leeds was also just starting to sink in.

The sheer excitement of finding ourselves on-board a seagoing luxury liner for the very first time in our lives persisted throughout our first day on-board Orion. Underneath that excitement, however, also lurked a number of unanswered questions, now that we were on our way to Australia? One theme in particular that would continue to push its way into my consciousness, as our voyage of a lifetime progressed: "Are we doing the right thing?" "Will everything turn out as we were hoping?"

As to the ship – it seemed so big at first. In addition to the various bars and dining rooms it also had a shop where passengers could purchase all manner of things, ranging from pharmaceuticals, leisure clothing, perfumes, cigarettes, confectionery, films, etc.

Over subsequent weeks the main 'promenade' deck became the most visited part of the ship where eventually it became a case of first come first served, especially when it came to the availability of deck and lounge chairs, once having arrived in the Mediterranean and able to take advantage of warmer weather. There was also an accommodation deck above the main promenade deck, most of which was reserved accommodation and additional facilities for the use of Orion's private, paying passengers.

The weather, bearing in mind that we were travelling in the early northern hemisphere spring, was at first cool but rather pleasant, even sunny, as we turned to starboard (right) and steamed to the southwest and out into the English Channel proper. The weather began to change as Orion steamed closer to the infamous Bay of Biscay, a section of the nearby French coast that had the dubious reputation of regularly being stormy. Perhaps even now it was waiting patiently for us landlubber £10 migrants?

As Orion steamed south, the seas progressively getting more boisterous, the wind started to get stronger, eventually beginning to howl and, in the best traditions of a potential storm at sea, the sky began to take on a dark, ominous and threatening look, the further south we proceeded. The weather, to this then non-seafaring passenger, very soon began to take on the look that it was about to unleash a storm upon we unwary landlubbers. And so it did on the second day of our cruise away from Tilbury.

INTO THE BAY OF BISCAY

As if trying to emphasise the fact that they could, whichever gods controlled such events, in particular, the making of the lives of the people on-board Orion a living hell, they certainly got down to their task with a will that day, as we and our ship entered their salty kingdom.

"With her sharpened bows and rounded hull lines, she will breast the seas like a yacht." This was a statement made to me by of the ship's officers with whom I had raised the question of the reputation of that infamous stretch of water, soon after boarding Orion. Well, so much for the advice of experts, as our experience was to demonstrate as we steamed into the Bay of Biscay that April day.

Orion breasted the seas ahead alright – but when confronted with cross seas, massive swells and increasingly strong winds blowing across our course south-south-west that we met on entry into that infamous bay, there were plenty of other, more frightening motions that Orion found herself and her increasingly scared passengers, having to cope. This worsening situation included our futile efforts to stay upright, while at the same time as we were trying to keep down a recently eaten meal!

In addition to the ship's earlier regular and relatively gentle fore and aft motion Orion began to roll in the most alarming manner. Added to all that, one minute the ship seemed to be sitting on top of a large swell and rolling to the left, when in the next, she was leaning over to the right. At the same time, we apprehensive passengers appeared destined to be carried downward toward the bottom of what appeared to be a lowering dark cavern amid towering waves.

The high seas rolling toward the ship tended to make the waves thus created look even more frighteningly ominous – as though they would come crashing down from a height above us and surely engulf the ship and all its passengers in a maelstrom of wild, slashing water. The storm was seemingly intent on driving the ship and all on-board down into the depths of the ocean!

Thankfully, Orion always managed to climb back out of the abyss, rolling all the time as she went. Of course, to us poor landlubbers, the waves that reared up behind and all around looked much higher and more threatening than they probably were in reality. Unlike modern liners, Orion did not possess stabilisers – underwater plates that on modern ships are used to dampen down the worst effects of a storm at sea. In our situation, therefore, it was a case of trying to stay upright on what felt like a riding atop a bobbing cork, at the mercy of an angry sea.

The crew, at least those still on duty on the main deck, in anticipation of stormy weather in the offing had already stowed all the deck and lounge chairs safely. Everything else that could be tied down or safely stowed away had also been secured.

It wasn't long before many of the passengers began to succumb to what any sailor will tell you can be the most debilitating reaction to the motion of a ship in heavy weather. Even in light weather with a small sea running, the motion of a ship or yacht in a seaway can and often will serve to reduce even veteran seafarers to distress and sickness.

A close neighbour in Australia, Captain Richard Williams, some years later confided that even he, following many years at sea as a boy apprentice, officer and later a ship's captain, found himself succumbing to a bout of seasickness during the first few days he was at sea following shore leave.

On-board Orion for the duration of our passage through the Bay of Biscay, it became almost impossible to keep on one's feet when trying to walk along the ship's companionways. Most people attempting to walk anywhere at the time were mainly intent on making for the closest vacant head (toilet).

To even venture out onto the promenade deck became a task few, even those of us able to cope better with the effects of motion sickness, dared to attempt. As for ascending or descending the flights of carpeted stairs up or down to the dining rooms or bars, if you were feeling peckish or in need of a drink, was fraught with the potential danger of falling or being thrown as if by a giant force, from one side of the staircase to the other. Even those brave enough to try and hang onto the handrails alongside the staircase while negotiating their way either up or down found themselves in danger of being thrown off from whichever handrail they were clinging. It was that bad – the forces at play so powerful, particularly at the height of the storm!

At night when trying to sleep, the ship's motion at the height of the storm caused the weight of one's body to sink, rise and roll in an alarming manner – a situation which allowed even fewer of we mere mortals and non-sailors to get a full night's sleep. On the contrary, until you got used to the motion or were at the very least dead tired by that time and were beyond even caring whether you lived or died, it became almost impossible to find a comfortable position in your bunk in which to hold yourself in one place. Being on the top bunk also seemed to heighten the motion – possibly an illusion brought on by a tired mind?

It was a case of staying put in most people's minds, with many of our fellow passengers choosing to seek solace in their cabins and bunks. Unfortunately, staying in one's cabin could prove to be one of the worst things to do in the circumstances. Being enclosed in what for many was a shared and windowless cabin, served only to augment further the sudden shuddering and other contrary motions of the ship. This together with a lack of fresh air and what gradually became an overpowering stench of regurgitated food that began to permeate the more enclosed areas of the lower passenger decks, made life on-board even more excruciating.

Prior to Mavis and I leaving Leeds, and in the knowledge that neither of us had ever been even in proximity to a seagoing ship, her father who, during the 1939–1945 war had served in the Royal Navy, gave us both advice on how he used to cope with the onset of seasickness.

My new father-in-law, Gerry Brown, had spent most of his service in the navy as a sick bay attendant. A large part of his time at sea had also been spent on the very same ship that his daughter and son-in-law were travelling on to Australia. He advised us both thus:

"Once you get on-board any ship and have settled into your cabin, the next and best thing to do once you set sail is to get up as high on the ship as you can and face the bows (front of the ship).

"Try to get yourself familiar with the normal movement of the ship on the sea and its fore and aft dipping and lifting motion as it breasts the swells in the open sea." The trick (he said) was to watch the horizon, while at the same time trying to relax and let yourself go with the movements of the ship and in the process getting the feel of the ship's motion."

He went on to say that in a rough sea, the worst part of sailing usually occurs when experiencing the combination of motions as the ship lifts and falls in a fore and aft direction, while at the same time rolling from side to side, with the visible horizon gyrating wildly. Tell me about it!

My only previous experience on water up to that time had been at the oars of a wooden rowing boat on the placid waters of the Waterloo Lake in Leeds' Roundhay Park. What we were now experiencing could only be described as feeling totally out of control and in constant danger of being thrown sideways from every which way. In addition to being thrown from side to side, hoisted up and thrown up and down, it also felt as if we poor migrant passengers were in constant danger of being dropped into the very jaws of hell!

During the recently ended Second World War, cinemagoers in Britain had seen movies of allied warships and struggling freighters, as they fought their way past the packs of German U-boats, during the battle to secure the North Atlantic. Never could the watching of such a movie come even close to paralleling how every passenger on-board Orion must have been feeling in our current predicament. It was probable that on each occasion that Orion lurched or reared, every one of my fellow passengers, like me, would find themselves uttering the same appeal to the local sea gods: "Please can you calm the raging seas down, make the wind drop and the sun re-appear?"

I did take my father-in-law's advice though, once the ship got underway from Tilbury. Climbing as high as I could and leaning into the rail facing forward, I tried to focus on the horizon as advised and stayed that way for some time. Upon seeing one of his young guests staring forward with a fixed expression as he gazed at the then gently undulating, watery sun-lit horizon, a passing deck officer was probably wondering if he had come across some religious nut engaged in a prayer to the sea gods for a safe passage? He stopped and asked if I was ok and when I told him of my father-in-law's advice he laughed and suggested that I should try to relax more and instead of staring transfixed to a point on the horizon, to allow my eyes to wander across it.

He also comfortingly confided that he too spent time early in every cruise doing something similar – but, he advised: "The secret is to keep yourself relaxed as much as possible and try to roll with the ship's motion". He went on to add at the same time that the advice offered should help anyone going to sea for the first time to cope with the ship's motion, and reduce the possibility of them actually losing their breakfast!

This proved good advice, because in the midst of all the sickness that my poor, suffering wife and most of the other ship's passengers were experiencing, I found that standing on one of the upper decks and hanging on for dear life to the rails, as the ship dipped and swayed wildly beneath me, actually seemed to work. Even while trying to follow his advice, I developed a persistent headache and alternated between an empty and decidedly queasy feeling in my stomach. I don't recall losing a meal during the whole voyage though!

My poor wife spent most of the first few days of the voyage alternating between her bunk bed (the bottom one in our cabin) and the nearest untenanted toilet.

Trying to eat meals in our designated dining room meant clutching onto every possible support while negotiating the rolling motion of the ship on my way to breakfast, lunch and dinner. I usually found myself alone in the dining room, except for a few other hardy souls, all like me determined not to miss too many meals. Even trying to eat while seated as we transited the Bay of Biscay, required a conjuring act, just trying to stop the accompanying slice of bread and whichever meal I was eating from jumping off its plate and sliding across the table.

I finally resorted to taking meals that could be handled more easily. This meant limiting myself to dry toasted bread, or soup served in a cup instead of a soup dish. Occasionally I would attempt to eat a sausage or two, meat or chips – all of which could be safely impaled on the end of a fork, my spare arm crooked around the plate in a desperate effort to keep it and all it contained in one place.

I would also try to get my suffering wife to down a slice or two of dry toasted bread, but even that suggestion was usually met with a firm, muttered refusal, sometimes combined with a lurch past me and a hasty retreat to the nearest vacant toilet. Even to venture down to one or other of the lower decks in the ship was itself likely to invite a bout of sickness. The motion seemed to be more pronounced when lower down in the ship, particularly having no visible horizon.

In the circumstances, it was wise to avoid moving too far away from the fresh, salt-laden air that was battering the ship. This meant locating myself on a higher deck, within sight of the horizon – when you could actually see the horizon through constant impenetrable spray, low clouds and the towering swells that continued to roll our ship up and down and from side to side.

In addition to seasickness, a few of the ship's passengers suffered accidents. These were sustained either from a fall or having slipped down one or other of the staircases. Injuries were mainly heavy bruises and cuts. One or two unfortunate passengers also managed to break bones.

I am sure that at least half the passengers going through the torment of our stormy Bay of Biscay passage would have gladly got off the madly gyrating Orion and onto dry land – if they had the chance.

Hope was at last in sight though as we passed Spain's Cape Trafalgar, a few sea miles from where Admiral Lord Nelson fought his most famous and final battle on October 21st 1805. From Cape Trafalgar it was south, then southeast and finally east through the strait of Gibraltar, with its towering rock and tales of tall ships and Arab dhows of the past. We were at last steaming through the narrow gap between Spain and the North African coast, Orion's bows now at last pointing to the east and the Mediterranean Sea.

The weather moderated even before we arrived at the straits of Gibraltar as we, the bashed, bruised and debilitated migrants on our way to the far side of the world had our first glimpse of an intensely blue Mediterranean. At last, we began to feel the caresses of a soft following breeze, together with a now steadily dipping, non-gyrating ship beneath us! What luxury! What a feeling of redemption and escape from the violence of the storm that had beset us during past days.

The sun's appearance also served to raise the spirits of those of us who had suffered the most during the storm. People began to emerge from their cabins, their sick, bruised and in one or two cases, battered bodies, slowly starting to heal.

The smelly mess that had littered some of the companionways and cabins gradually got cleaned up. The faces, of many of my fellow passengers, some ghostly white, others sickly green, gradually changed to a more normal colour. Some of these quickly started to glow and all too soon to turn into badly sunburned noses, cheeks, heads and bodies, as passengers once again began to crowd the promenade deck. People now started to compete for a deck or sun lounge chair on which to flop and bask in the welcome sunshine. The now welcome change in the weather was more like that we had hoped for at the start of our long voyage.

THE MEDITERRANEAN SEA

The blue Mediterranean, the 'Middle Sea' of ancient times, where Roman, Greek, and even earlier fleets had fought and traded throughout history was now spread out ahead of us to the east. It was a sea that had been dominated throughout the ages by kings, countries, religions and despots alike, even up to the recently ended Second World War. Now the Mediterranean was thankfully serene – and so blue.

Under a hot sun, skin ointments and other balms began to emerge, as some of our fellow passengers found themselves now having to pay a visit to the ship's doctor and dispensary. More than a few, now having gone from one extreme to the other, seasick to sunburn, had been too intent on over-exposing their previously pale English skins and still green tinged facial pallor to the rays of a hot Mediterranean sun. Some as a result now found themselves suffering a different kind of pain to the one they had succumbed to earlier as a result of seasickness.

The crew began pumping seawater into the small swimming pool located on the ship's stern deck, allowing people to at least splash around. While the small size of the pool provided little space in which to allow for lap swimming, it did at least offer some respite from the rapidly increasing heat of the sun.

Since passing Gibraltar, the voyage, at last, was leaning more toward the Idyllic. This was starting to become the kind of cruise that most of us had imagined it would be. The main competition during the now balmy days was for deck lounges, as opposed to earlier endeavours, which only a few days past had seen most of Orion's passengers competing for a session in one or other of the ship's toilets.

Everyone was by now beginning to relax, starting to chat and establish new friendships.

It was during this time our friendship with Norma and Frank Brown, our newly found friends from Manchester, became closer. Our little quartet expanded a little later, to include Harry and Celia Silverman, a couple from Leeds who were travelling to stay with relatives in Melbourne, along with two young children. Interestingly, they also turned out to be a couple whose children Mavis had baby-sat some years earlier. It really is a small world!

We also became friendly with a Christian priest and his wife, who I remember as having the surname Hillier and Bill his Christian name. Both he and his wife were heading for Albany in Western Australia.

Bill Hillier was an interesting man. He later recounted how, during wartime service in the RAF, he had received his calling to serve what he saw as his God. We talked quite a lot about how Bill's calling had manifested itself, a subject, which even I, a rank non-believer found interesting, particularly when he went on to explain how such a radical change could occur in a previously non-religious person.

There was also another family from Leeds on-board, but not long following their arrival in Melbourne, they decided that the climate or some other issue there did not suit them. They eventually chose, as had a number of others following their arrival in Australia, to make an early return to live back in Britain.

It seems strange looking back, how some folk failed even to attempt to allow themselves sufficient time in which to settle, following their arrival in Australia. I met the husband of the latter family many years later while on a business trip to Britain. It was interesting to learn that looking back he felt that they had made a mistake in returning to Leeds so soon. Apparently, his wife had found that she was missing her friends and family too much – I guess it takes all sorts to make a world?

The cruise through the Mediterranean passed day-by-day under cloudless skies, an azure blue sea and plenty of time in which we passengers were able to take advantage of the constant sunshine, and indulge our Bay of Biscay beaten bodies.

Most passengers were intent on getting a lifetime of English pallor out of their skins. Of course, as is usually the case, some tended to overdo the sunbathing. The sun at this latitude was much higher and hotter than was ever possible to experience in the regularly cloudy and rain beset skies of Britain.

Games like deck quoits, shuffleboard and other distractions were enthusiastically entered into by many of our fellow passengers. As a result of the warmer weather, the various ship's bars began to make a roaring trade. Many of us also crowded into the swimming pool and splashed around in the warm seawater.

A number of different games were initiated by the ship's crew, including one in the form of a pole set across the pool upon which two combatants armed with bags filled with Kapok, attempted to knock each other off the pole and into the water beneath. Lots of fun but I can't say that I fancied my chances at such a 'sport'. That was understandable as at the time I weighed in at around a skinny 140lbs and considered that I had little chance of belting the heavier lads who were entering the contest.

As the voyage progressed, most families and couples tended to gather in groups along the promenade and other accessible decks, lounges and bars, where both they and their children played games or just chatted. People would seek to meet and spend the time getting to know as many of the other passengers as they could. Most of our fellow passengers also seemed intent on exchanging their personal stories, being happy to discuss the circumstances that had led to their decision to leave Britain.

The dominant theme of most of the adult conversations at the time, once initial introductions had been made, tended to centre on the subject uppermost in most people's minds – the question around what they could expect, once Orion had deposited them at their port of disembarkation? It also became clear from the tone of most conversations, that many of the people on-board were going out to Australia with little or nothing in the form of plans as to what kind of job and living conditions they would be able to find once having arrived there.

One reasonably large group among those due to leave the ship in Adelaide had been employed in one or other of Britain's vehicle manufacturing plants in the Midlands. Most of these were planning to settle in and around the South Australian town of Elizabeth. This apparently was a relatively new city, located close to the General Motors Company.[1] This was a US organisation – one among other Australian-based vehicle manufacturers in the process of being established as part of Australia's relatively new vehicle manufacturing industry. Other vehicle related manufacturing facilities of various kinds were being established in other parts of South Australia and Victoria.

While at sea, a pastime I enjoyed whenever I got the chance, was gaining entrance to the bridge deck and watching the navigating and other deck officers going through their duties.

Ship navigation during the 1950s lacked the variety and range of accurate communication and tracking equipment available universally today. While radar and depth sounding equipment was in general use and had been for some years, even more accurate digital seagoing satellite navigation systems were still four or five decades away into the future.

During the late 1950s, shipping still relied predominantly on visual means – assisted by depth soundings and printed charts, alongside radar and radio direction assistance on approaching other sea traffic or closing with the coast, when the need arose to establish their positions as accurately as possible. On occasions, I watched as sextants were being used to shoot the sun, this method traditionally carried out to accurately establish the ship's latitude at noon, probably also as a check on what his other calculations were telling the ship's navigator.

"This is the life," was probably the thought going through the minds of most of our recently recovered fellow passengers, following our harrowing passage through the Bay of Biscay, the memory of which was now rapidly disappearing.

I was beginning to feel that special kind of exhilaration that one can only really experience when doing something so radically different from the usual. This trip was something out of the ordinary and well beyond anything that Mavis and I could have afforded, or would have thought of doing, even if we could afford the fare. Add to that, the realisation that we were sailing on a luxurious ocean liner toward a distant and to date unfamiliar destination that continued to remain a mystery. It was to be some time into the future that we would actually get to discover Australia.

The possibility of a new and exciting future ahead of us once we arrived there, served for a time to lessen the variously occurring questions and doubts that remained. These were thoughts that occasionally bubbled through to the top of my mind, particularly when I found myself occasionally dropping into a more reflective mood.

Such thoughts would have also been true, I think, if one could have delved into the minds of most of my fellow travellers. Australia was still many thousands of miles and nearly a month away from us. Between our port of arrival in Australia and the beautiful Mediterranean, surely there was much more yet to be experienced and enjoyed. Anything remotely negative surely could wait until later in the voyage?

Exotic, soon to be experienced arrivals like Port Said in Egypt, Aden in the Yemen and Colombo in Ceylon to name new experiences yet to come, were awaiting us.

On-board Orion, activities were plenty. Should you desire it there were a card and other games in the various lounges, music for dancing every evening, as well as the promenade deck for jogging. If so inclined, you could walk around the promenade deck, or spend time leaning over the ships side rail gazing into the distance at nothing in particular. Alternatively, you could lounge or snooze in a deck chair, read a book – or an outdated British newspaper that someone had either retained, or found squirrelled away somewhere on the ship.

One thing was for sure – life on-board ship was so much more preferable than having to turn up to my late employers' factory back in smoke shrouded Leeds every working day!

Each Sunday the various religious services were held. Other than that, the shipboard routine quickly settled down to a regular call on the gong for breakfast (these days attended by nearly all on-board), lunch and the evening dinner. This was regularly interspersed with coffee, tea, fresh cakes, nibbles and biscuits, served twice daily at one end of the promenade deck ballroom. Alongside all this, the ship's bars always could be relied upon to be doing increasingly brisk business, particularly now that the weather had become so much warmer.

This certainly was the life and all at the relatively low cost to us migrants of an affordable £10 for each adult! Luxury indeed! At least it would continue to be our way of life for a few weeks yet, until the reality of our arrival in Australia and what was to come next needed to be faced.

Following our arrival, we would from then on be busy having to cope with settling into a strange new environment, meeting new people and hopefully for most on-board – being able to find a good, well-paying job.

In the meantime, the usual saga of blossoming shipboard friendships and one or two budding romances began to flourish. Everywhere on-board, folk who just a week or so prior had been complete strangers began to meet and become new friends, while others were more content with just 'letting it all hang out', virtually enjoying the moment.

I often wondered during later years, what had happened to some of the shipboard romances that had started to blossom on-board. Did most of them peter out? Or perhaps, there were others that might have developed into long-term relationships?

For Mavis and me, the sea voyage was to us just like being on a second honeymoon. We had married not quite a year before leaving the grey clouded, and usually soot and the smog-laden city of Leeds. What more could a skinny 24-year-old and his wife desire?

Looming up ahead at last after nearly a week cruising was our approach to the coast of Egypt and Port Said.

Notes

1. General Motors: This company, along with Ford and Toyota announced during 2014, that they would be closing down their vehicle manufacturing operations in Australia during 2016/2017.

PORT SAID – EGYPT

At last, emerging from a hot, humid and hazy horizon, Port Said began to loom ahead of us. Land, at first in the form of a low-lying tan coloured strip, began slowly to emerge. Almost it seemed, and as if by magic, the land began to rise before our eyes, out of an azure blue sea.

As our ship slowly drew closer, the low outlines of land became clearer, its various features gradually forming themselves into the approaches to Port Said and the northern entrance to the Suez Canal, adjacent to the port.

As the land drew even closer, it became possible to make out the shapes of buildings, the spires of prayer towers that soared above mosques, and the outlines of what looked to be a relatively large number of low-lying shapes, which eventually took the shape of ships. These appeared from a distance to be anchored in a cluster across the harbour and toward the entrance to the Suez Canal.

There were already a couple of large ships anchored outside the harbour. As our approach took us closer in toward the port it became clear that what had appeared to be ships, scattered at different angles across the approaches to the outer harbour, were the superstructures of ships that had earlier been sunk!

What we had been observing as we drew closer, were the upperworks of all kinds of ships, some that had listed onto their sides. Others appeared to be sitting upright on their keels on the bottom of the shallower waters closer in toward the harbour proper. Not only that but as we progressed nearer and steamed slowly toward the inner harbour itself, the ship finally dropping anchor, we could clearly see people along the docksides waving toward us.

At first, the general view among those of us crowding the ship's rails and waving back was that the people on the dock waving their arms in our direction were offering a friendly welcome. Not so! When I was finally able to view them through a pair of borrowed binoculars, those waving at us from the dockside were shaking their fists at us, seemingly in anger! They also appeared to be shouting in a non-friendly way toward what was clearly a British ship, the passengers crowding along her side waving back to them in all innocence.

It didn't take too long for everything to become clear. Recalling that our entry into Port Said was but a few years following the ignominious withdrawal of French, Israeli and British forces from the Suez Canal Zone that they had earlier invaded and occupied for the briefest time.

That hasty withdrawal of British and French troops from the canal zone had occurred at the behest of Dwight Eisenhower, the then US president. General Eisenhower had demanded the withdrawal of British, French and Israeli forces, following their earlier three-pronged invasion of the Suez Canal Zone. Eisenhower's demand and their humiliating retreat had been the result, following an earlier orchestrated move by all three countries, designed to wrest back control of that strategic waterway from Gamal Abdel Nasser, the then Egyptian president. Their assault on the canal zone had followed the Egyptian president's earlier decision to nationalise the canal.

Following President Nasser's action, both the French and British governments, assisted by the Israelis, the British, led at the time by

Anthony Eden as prime minister, unilaterally attacked Egypt and seized control of the canal, claiming Nasser's action to be illegal. Eden's position as Britain's prime minister eventually became untenable as a result of the forced withdrawal. His health deteriorated soon after, leading to his later resignation.

The British, French and Israeli armies had been told to get out of the Suez Canal Zone by the then US president and finally did so, literally with their tails between their legs, their then international reputations in free-fall. Having found them in a position with no option other than to withdraw, resulted in British morale sinking, and the joint reputations of Britain and France as a consequence, also falling to an all-time low on the world's diplomatic stage.

This incident was just another step downward with regard to Britain's world standing, sealing her retreat from what was left of her once world-encircling empire, international power, wealth and prestige.

What had happened to Britain's world leadership status – a lofty position that had taken over 200 years to build up to its peak during its Victorian heyday? That reputation took but a decade or so to completely unravel most of Britain's earlier glory, together with the loss of nearly all her former colonial possessions. What possessions remained under some form of British control, were soon also to become free and independent.

It was learned later that the Egyptians had deliberately scuttled most of the sunken ships we had observed earlier, in an attempt to deny access to the canal and Port Said to the invading forces.

GULLY GULLY MEN

While anchored at Port Said, the ship's public decks soon became thronged by a group of Egyptian traders, some of whom we got to know as 'Gully Gully' men. Apparently, the title Gully Gully was an Egyptian term given to roving actors, artists and traders. The traders that began to throng the promenade deck of Orion that day were obviously those favoured by the ship's owners, all seeking to relieve this new shipload of intrigued passengers, of as many of our hard-earned British pounds as possible, in the short time at their disposal.

All manner of goods, including woven baskets, assorted fruits, stuffed toys, (some of which were found later to be stuffed with dirty rags and medical waste) and anything else that they thought they could unload onto their unwelcome guests in exchange for very welcome English pounds. All these offerings were laid out on brightly coloured rugs on the ship's promenade deck. There were also Gully Gully men intent on entertaining their English guests with magical tricks, one or two aided and abetted by a tame monkey.

While all the entertainment was going on around the ship, it was clear that we British passengers were not welcome in Egypt. The Egyptians, as a nation, were still cursing the British government for having the effrontery, in addition to earlier decades during which Britain had exercised a form of colonial control over the country, so recently also to have unilaterally invaded sovereign Egyptian territory. The Egyptians had always regarded the canal as being Egyptian territory, hence most Egyptians' support for their president's action in nationalising that strategic waterway.

Designed and built by the Frenchman Ferdinand de Lesseps between 1859 and 1869, the Suez Canal had first been part-owned by Egypt. It later auctioned off its holding, which was bought by Britain.

Like most traders, while the bunch that swarmed on-board Orion at the time may have come to hate anything British as a result of many years of losing out to British interests, they seemed happy enough to welcome British pounds being poured into their outstretched hands.

The scene in Port Said was colourful, sometimes a little angry but on the whole entertaining. Most of we passengers were intrigued by the persistence of the Egyptian traders' attempts to sell what usually proved to be poor quality products like handbags, stuffed toys, bangles, beads and suchlike.

Mavis and I, and a couple of other brave souls, eventually decided to purchase some fresh dates from an on-deck trader, which proved to be delicious – after taking the precaution of thoroughly checking and washing the fruit carefully before proceeding to eat it.

Following our short stay in Port Said, with none of us passengers being allowed ashore for obvious reasons, it was goodbye to the Gully Gully men and off into the Suez Canal proper, leaving behind another new experience. Having upped anchor, Orion then proceeded cautiously to steam slowly toward the entrance of the canal via a snake-like course that had been cleared through most of the wrecks, sunk at and near its mouth, a number still in the process of being salvaged.

THE SUEZ CANAL

Traversing the canal in 1959, a narrow one-way street for ships passing along its length to the north and south was an experience to remember. It had been cut, painfully slow at times, through low sandy desert country. At the time we passed through, its sides were occasionally lined by a few settlements, many different kinds of plantations, in addition to one or two obviously military camps and their associated works dotted along its length. Our ship, in convoy with others – nearly all freighters carrying goods to Indian, Southeast Asian, Chinese and Australian ports, steamed slowly along until we entered the Great Bitter Lake. Here we waited overnight, as a Europe bound convoy made its way past us, steaming north to the Mediterranean and northern ports. The rest of our journey then took us through the southern portion of the canal, finally emerging at the port of Suez.

For someone having only recently learned about the famed Suez Canal in school, just the thought that I was actually sailing along that famous stretch of water, a canal that had been dug out mostly by simple machinery and hordes of human labourers, was a task difficult to imagine. Eventually, the canal was completed and as a result, here we were, a thousand or so British migrants, all blithely steaming along its length nearly 100 years later. Few of us at the time gave little more than a passing thought to the hardships, technical difficulties and deaths that had been involved with its construction – at the time regarded as an engineering masterpiece.

THE RED SEA AND THE PORT OF ADEN

Our exit from the canal at its southern end and the port of its name, Suez, heralded Orion's entry into the Red Sea, a famous stretch of water that had often appeared in many ancient biblical writings.

The ship's next port of call was to be Aden, in those days still a British Crown colony – at least it was until 1967 when it became the Peoples Republic of South Yemen.

The country later descending into civil war, a war later to be complicated by the involvement of a local branch of Islamic extremists and other assorted groups opposing the national government. This situation continues to this day, along with a bloody and dirty war that recently also resulted in many among the civilian population succumbing to injury, death and dispersal, including the reported recent arrival of widespread famine and cholera.

The town of Aden at the time of our arrival was and had for many years prior been a major stopover port for British traders and the Royal Navy, a strategic base positioned at its location on the eastern coast of the Red Sea.

While watching the passing sea as we steamed through the Red Sea toward Aden, it became apparent, particularly with the wind blowing from the east, that the sea had possibly got its name from the swathes of reddish coloured dust and sand blown onto its surface. In parts this gave the sea the red appearance for which it had perhaps originally been named?

As we steamed further south, the weather became hotter and more humid. Thankfully, by this time most of the sunbathers on-board Orion had by now recovered from the discomforts earlier experienced with their newly sunburned faces and bodies. Most of us were, in fact, beginning to look decidedly healthier than when we had embarked at Tilbury.

Our arrival at Aden was without the overt antagonism that our earlier arrival had encouraged at Port Said. Some Arab traders managed to row or motor their way out to the ship, which was anchored some distance outside the actual port proper, all with the intention no doubt of trading with anyone remaining on-board. As for most of we passengers, we were impatiently waiting to be allowed to go ashore, to stretch our legs on dry land and explore the shops and bazars that lined what appeared to be the main commercial section of the busy port. This was a broad, dusty strip that ran along the shoreline adjacent to the port's inner wharf area.

Prior to leaving Orion on one or other of the ship's motor launches, all we passengers were advised to be careful while on shore and to watch out for pickpockets. We were specifically warned not to venture into any of the numerous side streets and alleyways that radiated out from the main shopping area. With dire warnings like this in mind, womenfolk tightly clutched handbags and purses close to their chests and we menfolk transferred wallets and other valuables from our hip pockets to a pocket in front. After having done so and now feeling the need to maintain a watchful eye on everything we held dear, it was off into what for all of us promised to be our first opportunity to visit a genuine Arab bazaar.

Arriving on shore, most were just happy to watch, as others tried their hands at bargaining with the Arab traders who were offering everything imaginable in the way of trinkets, pots and pans, rugs, fruit, gold and silver jewellery.

Aden was a revelation, a cacophony of strange sounds, heady wafts of windblown dust, human odours, both of these mixed with the aroma of exotic spices and strong Arabian coffee. All these sensations seemed to mingle together in noses unaccustomed to the intense, dusty and dry heat, now that we had arrived on shore.

Everything we were about to experience in the port of Aden was in complete contrast to the more familiar wafts of smoke and dirt that constantly emanated from factory and domestic coal fires back in Britain, and the soot and smog most had been used to breathing in on a daily basis during previous lives in industrial cities throughout Britain. Not to forget here that peculiarly English aroma regularly to be found wafting down nearly every high street from one or other of the local pubs and fish and chip shops.

In contrast to the environments from which most of us had come, everything that we saw, smelled and felt here in this exotic but decidedly (to us at least) smelly Middle-Eastern port was a new revelation.

The assault on our British senses did nothing to stop the sheer delight of just being able to get away from the confines of the ship – at least for a few hours, and enjoy a stroll along the Aden shopping strip, soaking up the atmosphere. Many of us were also on the keen lookout for an opportunity to buy a few trinkets, jewellery or fruit at the same time.

One or two of the more adventurous passengers had bought cameras while in Aden, and I did hear later that at least one found that the fixed lens of his purchase had a flaw in it. That lens fault, of course, didn't make its unwelcome presence felt until well after its purchase, following the exposed film being developed on its arrival in Australia. The lesson here, unfortunately a little late for some: Always be wary when purchasing a highly technical piece of equipment like a camera or similar from a fez capped 'expert' in an Arab souk.[1]

We passengers had earlier been warned to be careful when negotiating for or purchasing gold or silver jewellery, in particular, technical equipment from shops claiming to be the 'official' representative of a well-known British, European or US brand.

When the time came for us to leave exotic Aden, Orion's officers and crew eventually rounded up all their charges and deposited us into the ship's tenders patiently waiting to convey us back to our floating home. All seemed to have been accounted for, with none kidnapped for ransom, or spirited off to some distant Arabian slave market.

Our transportation loaded once again with a group of sweaty, dusty but mostly happy passengers, it was back on-board Orion, a quick shower to wash off the dust and clinging sand that seemed to have got into everything we were wearing and carrying, then down to the dining room for a slap-up evening meal.

From Aden later that evening, and with the sun lowering into an intensive deepening red sunset below the rim of the western horizon, Orion once again started up her engines, hauled up her anchor and steamed back out into the southern fringes of the Red Sea. We then proceeded southeast across the Indian Ocean, around the southernmost tip of the Indian subcontinent, turning north toward the fabled spice island of Ceylon.

Notes

1. Note: 1959 was many years prior to the commercial availability of digital still and movie cameras. That being the case it was extremely difficult to immediately check the integrity of an intended camera purchase – especially in a shop in Aden.

COLOMBO – CEYLON (SRI LANKA)

Talk about exotic, in 1959 Ceylon certainly lived up to its reputation as an ancient and fabled spice island, where tea and spices had been grown and exported across the then known world throughout centuries past.

While our ship waited at anchor in the port of Colombo, Mavis and I, along with a group of other inquisitive travellers, went ashore and took a taxi trip up to the town of Kandy, located in the north of the island. On arrival, we took tea and munched our way through a platter full of delicious cakes. While gorging on cake and scented tea, we watched as local boys climbed up and down coconut palms on request, provided you paid them for the pleasure of photographing what was to us at least, seemed to be an almost impossible feat.

While in Kandy some of the women bought colourful Saris but other than that, for me it was just the opportunity to observe life in what to us appeared to be a colourful and exotic paradise.

What we were now witnessing having arrived in Ceylon seemed to be an exotic paradise to the eyes of a thousand or so expatriate British folk. This was particularly so when trying to compare what we were seeing in Ceylon with the narrow streets of Leeds and its soot and smog blackened back-to-back houses, and similar streetscapes up and down Britain.

Here on this ancient island, at least, the people seemed happy; the women wore bright and colourful clothes, there was plenty of sunshine and seeming good cheer – at least that's the way things looked to be on the surface to us short-term visitors.

I don't recall in 1959 that there was any sign or evidence of the terrible interracial fighting which finally came to a head across Sri

Lanka in 1983 and continued until the defeat of the Tamil Tigers, some 26 years later. That civil war's reports of terrible, genocidal attacks on the beaten Tamil forces and the civilian population that followed, flashing across the world's news broadcasts at the time. The defeat of the Tamil forces in Sri Lanka later precipitated an exodus of displaced Tamils seeking refuge as far away possible from their war-torn country. Many of them sought sanctuary in Australia.

If there had been any trouble in 1959, there certainly appeared to be none of the reports of mass killings that were known to have occurred, following the later defeat of the Tamils forces by the Sri Lankan government's army in May 2009. The results of that terrible civil war continued to affect relationships between the various religious groups across that troubled island, even as late as 2015.

Colombo was to be the last of our scheduled stops on the way to Australia, so it was with regret that we had all too soon to return to Orion, anchored in Colombo Harbour. From there we proceeded to steam our way across the equator, southeast toward the tropic of Capricorn and the still distant coastline of Western Australia, a long way south and still to be discovered, under the rim of a seemingly never-ending horizon.

ACROSS THE INDIAN OCEAN

The voyage across the Indian Ocean was relatively uneventful. There were many sightings of dolphins, flying fish, one or two of which amazingly even managed to land on the ship's promenade deck. We were also able to observe that amazing seafaring bird, the Albatross. Lone specimens of those magnificent creatures were forever winging their seemingly effortless solo way along and over the ocean's waves, often and without an apparent beat of their massive wings as they soared and dipped on high. From on high, and at a point in the sky where they were difficult to see from the deck of Orion, they would then glide down faster and faster, until becoming lost temporarily from view in and among the valleys that were constantly being formed between the long oceanic swells that rolled before the wind.

By the time we began to close with the latitude of the Australian continent, most of our fellow passengers were starting to get bored with the endless sea-days that had been passing by, each day following on from the previous one. Shipboard life had also by now become routine, its regular calls to breakfast lunch and dinner operating like clockwork. While some forms of entertainment were still being provided and attended, these too, following three weeks of cruising from Tilbury, were getting to be repetitive.

The closer Orion came to the Australian coast, the more our thoughts began to turn toward the vast continent that continued to loom – as yet unseen. While it was known to be there, to those of us on-board Orion it was as yet invisible under the eastern horizon, even as we drew ever closer and closer.

As Australia neared, it was interesting to observe that a number of our fellow passengers had returned to discussing and questioning whether the rhetoric and advertisements of the Australian government concerning our soon to be new homes, and our hopes and impressions, as a result, would be realised?

Orion steamed steadily onward totally unaware of the people crowding her decks, some who by now were becoming anxious and apprehensive, particularly those getting closer to their future homes in Western Australia.

On and on Orion steamed on her south-easterly course, oblivious to the hopes, fears and uncertainties that were increasingly being felt among the expectant passengers she was carrying, across a seemingly endless ocean, upon and over which there appeared less and less of anything interesting to see. By now, most on-board failed to make any comment when sighting the occasional seabird, some floating debris or a squad of flying fish, as they skipped over the surface and away from Orion's advancing bows.

Not knowing much when it came to really valuable information about how life was being lived in Australia, made it difficult for any of us at the time even to begin to think clearly about what to expect once finally arrived on the rapidly approaching continent. Everything that was being discussed at that late stage could only be conjecture; what eventually faced us on our eventual arrival in Australia would only become real once we had disembarked from the sanctuary of the ship carrying us there.

Already having an aunt, uncle and cousin living in Melbourne, I was looking forward to re-establishing contact with them, particularly my cousin Terry. Terry was a few weeks older than me and had been more like a brother during our pre-teen years. He was also someone with whom I had spent many happy days during our boyhood and early teens, rambling and cycling along the hedgerows and byways around Leeds and the surrounding countryside.

Terry had migrated to Australia some year's prior along with his mam and dad, the family settling in the Melbourne suburb of Bentleigh. They were currently living in a nearby suburb called Elsternwick. Terry's wife Brenda, also a Leeds girl, was expecting their first child in a few weeks, so both Mavis and I were looking forward to renewing our earlier close relationship.

As the coast of Western Australia drew closer, many on-board possessing binoculars began looking forward to our first sighting of the Australian coastline. Those of our new-found friends destined to disembark at the port of Fremantle were by now girding themselves for their eventual departure in Fremantle. Most of we migrants had become part of a relatively close-knit group. Some for the first time were beginning to express feelings of uncertainty, while others, in contrast, were more openly excited at the prospect of arriving in a new country.

In a few cases, people were becoming openly apprehensive, particularly when it came to what they might expect following their arrival on the now fast approaching, as yet unseen continent. Australia continued to remain hidden under the rim of a still unbroken horizon to our east.

When it really came down to the reality of our situation, as opposed to some of the perhaps distorted feelings around our being newcomers to a strange land, it needed to be recognised that none onboard our ship would actually be arriving in a foreign country. That thought at the very least should have given most some feelings of confidence, particularly when it came to the question of their capacity to eventually mix and meld with the general population, wherever we landed in Australia.

Australia had until relatively recent times been a British colony, its laws and running controlled by the Colonial Office in London. Its people continued to be officially regarded as British. Earlier in 1901, the country had begun its modern incarnation as a parliamentary democracy, the 'Commonwealth of Australia'. Even then, the country was still subject to the British Crown. Constitutionally, on federation, the country began to operate under a statute that had transferred power to the new Australian parliament, with internal arrangements that brought the interests of the then six self-governing colonies together, all now operating under the Australian Federal, various state and territory governments. From 1901, with the power to govern being delegated to the Australian parliament, the British Crown, Australia's head of state, continued to be represented in the form of a governor general.

Australia, following its formal federation in 1901, continued to maintain its inherited British traditions. Its government continued to be organised on the 'Westminster'-style parliamentary system. Australia continued to inherit British laws, the English language, the infuriatingly difficult British monetary system of pounds, shillings and pence – and often difficult to understand systems of distance, weights and measures.

In reality and for all practical purposes, what we all were about to experience on landing in our new country, shouldn't affect the lives of most of us too deeply – other than finding ourselves far away from our homes, families and friends in Britain. In a practical sense, we understood the monetary system and were used to using the same denominations of currency as those used by all Australians.

We all spoke and could read and write English, a significant advantage, while also being well aware that in Australia the people and presumably businesses and shops there operated along similar lines to those we had been familiar with in Britain. That being the case, the situation we were soon to experience in Australia should at least prove to be less of a problem to we British newcomers, particularly when it came to dealing with the suppliers of products and services in the towns and cities that we would soon come to know as our own.

Thinking back, one could well imagine the feelings of migrants arriving from foreign, non-English speaking countries like Greece, Turkey, Italy, Germany, Poland and other European population centres. They, in contrast were about to step onto foreign soil. Life for most of them, particularly with most having to learn to converse in a strange language, would be much more difficult than it would ever be for us.

We were in fact about to enter a country that, although many thousands of miles away from the land of our birth, was to all intents and purposes British in every practical way possible.

On becoming registered in Australia as an arrived British immigrant, we had also been advised that in addition to having the privilege of paying income tax – once having found a job, we would also be eligible to vote in federal, state and local elections. As incoming new settlers, we would also become eligible to receive an aged pension, once having completed the minimum required years of residence in Australia.

Nevertheless, even I, excited though I was to at last be soon arriving in Australia, with the promise of a well-paid position that appeared to offer me good prospects, was beginning to feel the first pangs of uncertainty deep down in my 24-year-old entrails.

For the first time since leaving Britain, now that we were nearing Fremantle, it became so much easier to realise just how far away our close family and friends in Britain were. While not quite in isolation, we were about as far as could be travelled away from Britain on the planet.

Being young and as yet not having established a permanent home and family of our own, the excitement that accompanied the promise of a new beginning, including that generated by the great adventure we were now embarked upon, served to counter some of the still negative emotions Mavis, and I might still be experiencing. Our loss of parental and close family connections though had loomed larger the further we travelled away from Leeds and Britain.

On the positive side, we had each other, we were in love – at least I like to think we were – and, being newly married we were still in the process of adjusting to a relatively new relationship and way of living, now as a couple.

Mavis and I each had our personal, private dreams and were yet to experience becoming partners and parents in an established family unit. Already having an aunt, uncle and cousin and his wife currently living in Melbourne, even though I hadn't seen my aunt and cousin for some years, at the very least having them there tended to provide me with the feeling that a small part of my extended family would be relatively close by in Australia. On the other hand, we also were beginning to understand just how far apart (in the region of several hundred miles) we would still be from my cousin and his family once we settled near Sydney. The distance was close enough to the distance from Land's End to John O'Groats – the total length of the British mainland!

We kept reminding ourselves that our situation was unlike those of many of the other families on-board, including our new friends Norma and Frank. In addition to them being housed in a migrant hostel, not a very exciting prospect to be looking forward to at the best of times, others would also be faced with the task of getting their children settled into a nearby school. To be able to leave their migrant hostel, all those not expecting to be living with relatives already established in Australia would need to find a job and somewhere of a more permanent nature in which to live. In addition, they would also find themselves having to adjust to new relationships, new streets and the need to become familiar with the towns or cities in which they eventually decided to settle.

We both at least had time on our side as well as a youthful attitude to the world, coupled with the belief that anything and everything was possible.

FREMANTLE

The coast of Western Australia drew gradually closer, and with it many of us continued to strain our eyes, seeking to be among the first to sight the western shoreline of our new country.

When at last that day dawned, at first all that we could see was a thickening line to the east, an increasingly wide strip of land on the horizon that slowly emerged and became even more identifiable the closer we steamed toward it. Later, a few trees could be detected.

I well remember that on looking through a neighbour's binoculars I could make out a clump of what looked like palm trees on the land. These later turned out to be a stand of eucalypts on the by now clearly emerging shoreline. Passengers crowded against the ship's rails as the land drew closer and we were later able to make out more and more features of the landscape. Buildings began to appear as well as the cranes, a few smaller ships, fishing boats and other equipment at the port of Fremantle.

How exciting! At last, we had arrived in Australian waters. We were here, following our long sea voyage. Our future beckoned, welcoming us to the fabled land of Terra Australis – our future home and the focus of so many of my boyhood dreams.

Those of Orion's passengers who were bound for somewhere or other across the vast state of Western Australia bade farewell to newly found friends, some exchanging names, addresses and promising to keep in touch.

As the ship was to remain in the port of Fremantle for a full day, Mavis and I decided to take a stroll toward the town – in those days quite small, the town centre located reasonably close to the docks. On disembarking from the ship, however, Mavis became overcome with a dose of what we later learned was a condition well known to mariners as 'land sickness'.

What she was experiencing was similar in its symptoms to seasickness, but for the opposite reasons – she was apparently being affected by just being back on a surface that wasn't in constant motion. Strange? With my poor, suffering wife continuing to complain of dizziness and nausea as we tried to make our way toward the town, it was thought prudent to make a hurried return back on-board Orion. Once back on-board, we paid a visit to the ship's doctor, who prescribed a few pills, accompanied by the recommendation that she spend a couple of days in her bunk.

Mavis's discomfort put an end of our plan to take a look at our first port of call in Australia. Her bout of land sickness lasted for two days, subsiding only when Orion was well on her way from Fremantle, to Adelaide.

Now we were steaming in Australia's territorial waters, our course taking us into the Indian Ocean, south down coastal Western Australia, past Albany, then around to the east and across the Great Australian Bight toward the South Australian capital, Adelaide.

A large number of those migrants still on-board were due to disembark in Adelaide. Most were attracted by reports of the ready availability of work in and around the city of Elizabeth. This relatively new city was located close to General Motors Holden, one of Australia's new vehicle manufacturing plants.

The ship was scheduled to stay for a full day in Adelaide so, along with some other passengers travelling on to Melbourne and Sydney, Mavis and I together with our new friends from Manchester, Norma and Frank, decided to take the train that operated between the port and the city of Adelaide proper.

Thankfully Mavis had by now thrown off her mysterious bout of land sickness, so it was off into Adelaide to see what our first visit to an Australian capital city would bring.

IMPRESSIONS OF ADELAIDE

The light rail ride into the city proper, from the port of Adelaide, was a new experience. Interesting and different that is, our transport being similar and reminiscent of the American West in the design both of its carriages and engine – all very Wild West, just like in the movies! This day the train was filled with wide-eyed escapees from Britain, all excitedly straining to take in the sights, sounds, and senses of the country surrounding the sea entry to the capital city of the state of South Australia.

One thing was very sure – the country through which we were passing on our way into the city bore little resemblance to that which most of us had left behind on the other side of the world. Something else really noticeable here was the sky. It seemed so big, so open and so wide in every direction, in comparison to what we had been used to, in and among the streets of crowded British cities!

I still recall being impressed with the feeling of openness that the sky here seemed to bring to one's senses. Even as we neared the city proper, the same impression prevailed. How different the sky seemed here – an impression also being expressed among our travelling companions on either side of our carriage. Some compared the sky over Adelaide with that to be seen over the cities, towns and countryside that they had been familiar with in Britain. Cities and towns with their narrow streets and rows upon rows of small terraced, often back-to-back houses, shops and commercial buildings, all packed relatively close together.

The sky in the part of Leeds, in which I had grown, even during outings to the nearby Yorkshire Dales, seemed small compared with what we experienced that first day on the train taking us into Adelaide. Maybe it was an illusion? It was one however so noticeable that others travelling into Adelaide that day also voiced similar thoughts.

Our transport finally disgorged its cargo of newly arrived visitors from the Mother Country, all of us intent on checking out the centre of Adelaide.

The city of Adelaide in the late 1950s was still relatively small and compact. Little groups formed and wandered off in all directions, each seeking to explore our first state capital on the Australian mainland. Adelaide gave one an overpowering feeling of space, even at street level. It was an instant revelation. The streets were so wide and the sky, even when walking along an inner-city street, still seemed to go on forever. At least it appeared to do so when compared with our memories of lives lived back in Britain.

The shops selling food were indeed a revelation. For people recently emerged from austerity-bound Britain the city's shops provided us all with yet another eye-opener. Meat, butter, eggs and nearly every other form of staple food and most of the more exotic kinds of fruit – oranges, lemons, peaches and grapes, all were in abundance here. In Britain at the time, most of what we saw in Adelaide's shops still needed to be imported – much continuing to be in short supply.

It seemed that we had arrived into a veritable cornucopia. It was mouth-watering for we newcomers, so recently used to food rationing, just to see the range and what appeared to us to be the low cost of food products. These included every different cut of meat, a wide range of vegetables and fruit, all of which were on open display in the various shop windows that lined both sides of the city's streets.

Walking down Adelaide's Rundle Street and the streets radiating from it, (this was well before Rundle Street became a mall) you can imagine the looks on our faces. On passing a butcher shop and seeing meat of all descriptions on show without even the need to proffer coupons to obtain a meagre weekly ration was a strange experience!

And what prices! Everything seemed to be so plentiful as well as cheaper than we had expected, in comparison to the prices we were used to paying for meat, vegetables, butter, cheeses and other foods in England.

We newcomers must have looked like the two orphans that featured at the time in the series of 'Bisto' advertisements back in Britain. Our faces were constantly pressed against the various shop windows, certainly shops selling any kind of food. This was reminiscent of the two well-recognised figures of a young boy and girl that regularly appeared in the series of 'Ah! Bisto'[1] advertisements being used to promote that famous product across Britain.

Stopping at a local café for lunch, our senses, already filled to the brim with the range of foods that were often difficult to obtain during late 1950s Britain, were further assailed by the aroma of grilled hamburgers, fried bacon and eggs, in addition to some of the largest tomatoes I had ever seen. What a revelation it was that day in May 1959, to experience such a broad range of foods so readily available in Adelaide's shops.

I am sure you can picture the scene. There we were, Mavis and I, with our noses virtually pressed against the glass windows of butcher shops, fruit vendors and other shops along Adelaide's city streets. It was all so strange. It seemed to us at the time that the folk here in Australia had not suffered as much from the food shortages that we had experienced for the best part of a decade in Britain, certainly during the war years. This of course was not true. Australians during the war years had been subjected to the rationing of basic foods and other scarce domestic goods, caused in part by the then need for Australia to send shipments of food over to a then beleaguered Britain.

This thought also brought back memories of brown coloured grease proof packages of powdered eggs, powdered milk, butter, dried apple rings and apricots that we occasionally received in Leeds, having arrived from Canada New Zealand and Australia during the long war years. Such luxuries were received in Leeds on erratic occasions, whenever a convoy of ships had managed to get through unscathed from the marauding packs of German U-boats awaiting them in the south Atlantic and western approaches.

Here in Adelaide, there were also locally grown grapes, olives, bananas, oranges, peaches, apricots and surprise, surprise – even watermelons and pineapples galore for sale!

Mavis and I bought a few bananas, a large bag of grapes and oranges for later on in the voyage.

What a haven of produce we had come to and how different it seemed to be here when compared to the situation in Leeds, where some of the more exotic fruits like bananas grapes and oranges were still difficult to obtain.

Each of the limited shipments of foods arriving in Britain from overseas suppliers were then still having to be sought out by a shopper who had their antennae well tuned in. It didn't take long in Leeds to miss out on being able to purchase from a new shipment of imported foods and some of the more exotic fruits. People needed to be aware whenever choice fruits or other hard to obtain products were being snapped up by shoppers lucky enough to locate the inevitable queue that would form outside a shop having some stock of imported fruit. Queuing for food continued to be the norm in Leeds for nearly a decade following the ending of the war in 1945. This was a period during which frozen meat continued to be imported from Argentina and Australia.

Before returning to the ship we also paid a short visit to the Adelaide Zoo. From the zoo, on we wandered, happily munching on grapes and bananas, finally catching our 'Wild West'-style light rail transport back to the port and onto the ship, in time for our continuing voyage – ever onward to the east and the major capital cities of Melbourne and Sydney.

Notes

1. 'Bisto' was reputed to have been the very first meat flavoured gravy powder to be introduced onto the British market, initially in 1908, which over later years rapidly became a bestseller throughout the British Isles.

HELLO, MELBOURNE

Orion entered Port Phillip heads, the seaward entrance to the city of Melbourne, during the afternoon of May 17th 1959.

As our ship slowly steamed up the immense expanse of Port Phillip Bay toward the Port of Melbourne, we could see some of the early lights beginning to twinkle along the western shoreline of the Mornington Peninsula.

The final cruise up Port Phillip Bay toward Station Pier at Port Melbourne took a couple of hours. During our approach to the capital of Victoria, ship's passengers due to disembark in Melbourne, our new-found friends Norma and Frank among them, crowded along the starboard rails, seeking to identify points of interest along the shore.

The day had been sunny and remained so as Orion made her final approach to the Station Pier terminal at the Port of Melbourne. It was exciting to think that I would at long last be able to meet up once again with my Auntie Rachel, Uncle Barney, cousin Terry and his wife Brenda.

Once alongside Station Pier, more of our fellow passengers began to depart for destinations within Melbourne or elsewhere within the state of Victoria. Knowing the name of the migrant hostel where Norma and Frank would be staying, we promised to eventually re-establish contact, once Mavis and I had settled down and had a permanent address in New South Wales.

It was also a great relief to meet, at last, with my aunt, uncle and cousin as they rolled up to Station Pier in Uncle Barney's FJ Holden car. While not quite like we were coming home, it was at least comforting to at last be greeted by my mother's younger sister, my uncle and cousin. Just to meet our only relatives on this vast continent on the far side of the world was reassuring. How lucky we both were to have at least some family here in Australia.

Following initial greetings and the exchange of snatches of news from the rest of the family in Leeds, it was unfortunate that they couldn't stay long with us at the dockside as Terry's wife Brenda, who had been unwell during her pregnancy, needed to return home. Nevertheless, in the short time we were together that evening, just being able to embrace my aunt and cousin and exchange news of the rest of the family, provided both Mavis and me with good feelings for our future lives, now that we had nearly arrived at our ultimate destination.

I was also thinking at the time that at least we would have some family to go to, should the position in Sydney not turn out as expected.

Later, following our arrival at Station Pier, we received a message from an ex-boyfriend of Mavis's. Stan Moss, also from Leeds, had been living in Melbourne for a few years. Stan arranged to pick us up for a spin around Melbourne the next day. As the ship was due to stay in the Port of Melbourne until the following evening, we agreed to meet Stan at the ship early the next day.

Following a short evening walk along the Port of Melbourne waterfront, Port Phillip Bay and an early night on-board, Stan and his FJ Holden picked us up early the next morning for a promised tour around Melbourne.

We drove up what then was to us the very strange sounding Dandenong Road to an outer lying suburb called Oakleigh, at which point – surprise, surprise – Stan's distinctly old, slightly battered and obviously infirm FJ Holden gasped and expired at the side of the road! After some time under the bonnet of his not so 'trusty' chariot, Stan, at last, got the car going and it was off to explore the outer areas of the city, which included a visit to another, strangely named place a little south of Melbourne proper. This turned out to be a small, outer seaside township on Port Phillip Bay, known to the locals by what we learned was its Aboriginal name, Mordialloc, the name meaning creek or stream in the Aborigine language.

In answer to a comment I made regarding not having sighted an Aborigine thus far during our visit to Melbourne, our guide for the day laughed and said that he had yet to encounter an Aborigine, at least one brandishing a nulla-nulla or spear, in or around the city of Melbourne. That at least was a comforting thought, bearing in mind my earlier impressions, gained as a result of reading about Australia's first people, in my school geography book.

We were later driven over to Stan's auntie's place for afternoon tea at her home in Baird Street Brighton.

Here again what a surprise it was to see a wooden bungalow-style house, complete with a large back garden in which Stan's auntie was growing oranges, lemons and grapes – in addition to vegetables, and this was in late autumn here in Melbourne!

To Mavis and I, coming as we were from a different environment in the northern hemisphere, a wooden house such as that we now entered was a rarity. Mavis later wrote home to her folks in Leeds about seeing an Australian-style house made entirely of wood, in which people seemed to have few problems living, the year round. This in spite of Melbourne's winters, which we were given to understand could get to be rather cool at times.

All too soon, though, it was time for Orion and what remained of her passengers to leave Melbourne, turn east through the Bass Strait, then north toward the port of Sydney, our final destination. Bidding goodbye to Stan and his decidedly unreliable motorcar, which had at the very least managed to get us both back to the ship on time, we rejoined Orion for the last stage of her long voyage to Sydney.

The good ship Orion had managed to bring yet another cargo of hopeful migrants from the 'old world', the British Isles, or 'Mother Country' – the title by which Britain was still affectionately known by many of Australia's native-born citizens during the late 1950s.

It would take only a further two days for us to make our way back into the Bass Strait, around Wilson's Promontory, past Point Hicks, then north into the Pacific Ocean and approaches to the fabled Sydney Harbour.

ARRIVAL IN SYDNEY

Wednesday May 20th 1959 dawned sunny and clear as Orion made her final approach, this time toward the city of Sydney. Entering through the high and impressive heads, the cliffs on either side of the entrance to that famous harbour, it was to us an exciting experience, for the first time to watch in awe as that famous harbour started to open up before us. And what a sight Sydney Harbour proved to be.

As we steamed past Watson's Bay and opened the inner part of Sydney Harbour proper, we were then able to take in the impressive sight of that famous coat hanger like shape in the distance – Sydney's famous Harbour Bridge. We had made it at last.

The late morning remained clear, the sun shining, as our home for the last month, our saviour during the terrible few days crossing the Bay of Biscay steamed her proud and stately way down Sydney Harbour.

What remained of we passengers lined the ship's rails and took in the sights and sounds of that great and busy harbour. Ferries ploughed their way to and fro across and along its length, with powerboats and one or two yachts scooting out of our way as we made our majestic entrance toward, then under, the Sydney Harbour Bridge and toward our final berth at Pyrmont. Our long and eventful voyage to the other side of the world was nearing its end.

The question now: "What to expect from our new country? How would we like it here, would the job I was going to turn out as we both hoped?"

These were just a few of the many thoughts that had started to wing their way once again through my brain, as the excitement at our actual arrival rose and fell, alongside growing uncertainty and the feeling that here in Sydney we were alone, without friends or family. Orion closed and finally touched the shore of Sydney Harbour for the final time this trip, tying up to her berth at Pyrmont.

Now having arrived in Sydney the usual doubts and yet to be answered questions began to push their way to the top of my consciousness. It was with feelings of nervousness deep down in my being, to now actually find us at the end of our journey and not knowing a single soul.

On the other side of the coin, it was equally true to say that we were both looking forward in anticipation to meeting up and greeting our sponsor. We were hoping that he might even personally come down to Pyrmont to meet and welcome us, once the immigration procedures had completed, our temporary entry papers given up, and we were officially allowed to enter Australia. If our sponsor couldn't meet us personally, then perhaps he would send someone to welcome and transport us to Guildford?

A STRANGE KIND OF WELCOME?

We waited for a long time in the dockside immigration area until practically all the other passengers had departed. We continued to wait until it seemed that we would be among the last of Orion's passengers to be claimed. Surely Mr Hiller, or at least his secretary, would have been aware of our expected date and time of arrival, both of which I had advised by air-letter well before our departure?

It was to be some time later when nearly everyone else had gone from the dockside that a driver eventually turned up to the immigration counter to claim us.

Without receiving so much as a word of greeting or welcome from the Hiller Company's driver who arrived to pick us up, we and our luggage were then loaded into a car. Nothing further in the way of a few words of explanation or conversation was offered as we were driven out of the city. Eventually we were speeding along the road toward Guildford, the location of the house that had been promised to us by Ernest Hiller.

Guildford in 1959 seemed to be a long way out from the city of Sydney proper. There was hardly anything recognisable, in terms of it even being able to be described as an outer suburb of Sydney at the time. Our driver, silent throughout the journey to Guildford, spoke up only to point out the location of what we expected to be our home in Australia, as we passed its location at 334 Woodville Road. Interestingly, he advised with what looked suspiciously like a smirk, that the property was still in the process of being renovated, we in the meantime being accommodated at the local hotel.

From there we were driven to what was to be our temporary accommodation – guests of the Guildford Hotel, a commercial hotel, which we later learned was mainly used as overnight accommodation for travelling business and salespeople. The hotel was also their daily 'watering hole' (pub), being used regularly by the town's residents.

Following a short drive around what appeared to us as seemingly endless paddocks sprinkled with houses and small farms, still being borne along by our uncommunicative driver, we were eventually deposited at the front of the hotel, again without a word. My question as to whether we would be meeting Mr Hiller later was replied to with a few mumbled words that sounded like, "I'll pick you up tomorrow." What a strange way to welcome us to our new country.

It got even stranger. On entering the hotel, I was handed a scribbled phone message from Mr Hiller, our sponsor, which baldly stated that I was to be ready to be picked up from the hotel at 07.30 the next morning!

The lack of an appearance by anyone to greet us, not even a simple, friendly phone call welcoming us to Australia, when added to the abruptness of the scribbled message, hit both Mavis and I, literally with a thud.

After travelling halfway around the world and been summarily deposited at the front door of a local hotel, some distance outside Sydney, not knowing anyone or having even had any time to drop our bags, settle into our temporary accommodation and lower our backsides onto a chair! We had not even received a welcoming phone call – only a not very welcoming scribbled message at the hotel reception desk telling me to be ready to start work early the next morning.

That cold message left us both more than a little flat. I was even more than a little bemused that we had not even been allowed a day or so to at least acclimatise ourselves, or perhaps provided with a brief tour around the local town and countryside, nor given the opportunity to visit the house that Mr Hiller had promised us?

It would also have been pleasant and just a little thoughtful, to have had at least a day or so grace, before me being expected to front up for work at the Ernest Hiller production plant.

It seemed such a strange way by which to greet someone who had just travelled halfway across the world to join his new company.

"Could this be an example of the laid-back way that Australians were said to operate?" I mused. But even this later gave way to the feeling that even if that were the case, one would have at least thought that the arrival of someone new, who was supposed to be joining the company in a senior position, would surely have been greeted with a little more interest? This was not the way in which we had hoped to start our lives in our new country.

5
TERRA AUSTRALIS

A NEW BEGINNING

Guildford, from what we had seen thus far, was a small town, separate and well outside the then built up suburbs of Sydney. Both it and the neighbouring town of Merrylands were located just off the main highway that exited northwest from the city. Both seemed to be more in the style of small country towns, well outside the hustle and bustle of Sydney's CBD and inner and outer suburbs. Was this what was known hereabouts as 'the Outback'?

Once settled into our room in the Guildford hotel during the late morning of our arrival, we still hoped for some form of communication from our sponsor. After waiting for some time, and hearing nothing, not even a phone call from anyone at the Ernest Hiller company, we decided to take a walk around the local streets. At least this should give us both a better feel for the location near which we were expecting to settle on a permanent basis.

How different the local streets were here, and in parts not having any properly concreted kerbing at their edges. Everything was so very different from the streets of Leeds. These were wide-open thoroughfares, country roads more like, with single storey 'bungalow'-style houses, many of which had roofed verandas surrounding them. Many of the houses outside the small shopping precinct, appeared to have been scattered randomly. Interestingly, also, some of the verandas were furnished with what appeared to be beds and lounge chairs, all positioned under what looked to be curved corrugated iron roofs.

"Do people actually sleep on their front verandas over here in Australia?" It certainly appeared so.

The weather at the time was decidedly cool, surely too cool for anyone to consider spending a night sleeping virtually out in the open? To us, on that first morning, it was so strange to see what appeared to be the manner in which some of the folk here apparently spent their nights – sleeping outside, surely only during the hotter months of the year?

Each house we walked past had a relatively large garden at both the front and back of the property. We also noticed a strange looking contraption in one or two of the back gardens. These had the appearance of a large galvanised steel umbrella, but without a fabric cover – the base set in concrete. We later learned about the Australian 'Hills' brand clothes hoist, which in those days was the more modern form of contraption used by many households on which to hang and dry the family's weekly laundry. Otherwise, some of the older houses appeared to hang their washing out to dry on a contraption comprising a couple of stout wooden poles, set wide apart into the ground, complete with boom-like timbers centre bolted across their tops. The horizontal booms were connected by thin rope lines, upon which washing could be 'pegged out' to dry.

Many of the houses appeared to be clad in cement or asbestos sheeting – remembering that asbestos in those days was not yet officially regarded as being dangerous to people's health and banned from use. Others were clad in stained or painted wooden siding, still others being clad in bricks of various shades. A number of the houses we saw were painted in a variety of colours. Nearly all had roofs made of corrugated iron or some other form of sheeting, with but a few, particularly the larger and more expensive looking houses having roofs capped with cement or terracotta tiles.

Another first experience was just walking around Guildford and contrasting the feeling of openness that we were once again experiencing as we walked around the township. This brought back to mind our visit to Adelaide. The streetscape in Guildford, like Adelaide, also gave one the impression of space – its openness together with most of the houses being of single storied construction added further to the impression of a seemingly vast, unending sky.

Also interesting, every house appeared to have a wide strip of grass set between its front fence and the roadway, many having been planted with shady trees. The individual properties that we were passing in and around Guildford certainly looked to possess far more space than we were used to, but there again, Australia being so much larger than little Britain – we supposed that larger blocks of land were usual out here, particularly in country towns like Guildford?

Most gardens had been planted with trees too. This contrasted with most of our local English streets, including my own in Leeds, which had been denuded of any earlier treelike vegetation over the years. In my street, most had succumbed eventually to years of trying to cope with dense winter smog, soot and other forms of corrosive pollution throughout the rest of the year. Most impressive of all – a large proportion of the gardens we were passing possessed large vegetable plots, in addition to a variety of fruit and nut-bearing trees. We counted the number of orange, lemon and some fig trees, the latter appearing to be still bearing fruit.

Finally, we wandered back to the centre of Guildford – not a difficult or a long way to go in the circumstances, where following the changing of the last of our English pound notes in what appeared to be a combined post office and bank, we bought our first late lunch in Australia. Our first lunch comprised a not very appetising ham and lettuce sandwich between slices of white bread, which we washed down with a cup of tea. Not a very happy arrival celebration in the circumstances.

We then made our way back to the hotel and our room over the main bar to discuss how we were feeling about where we now found ourselves.

The fact that my new employer had not even thought it important enough to, at the very least, call or arrange to meet up with and welcome his new designer, his factory presumably being located not very far from Guildford, began to create more than just a few negative feelings about our situation. Had it been a wise move to come all this way, to find not even a kind word of welcome to greet us? Were those who had advised me against moving across the world, right after all? What was it with these Australians? Were they all like that, seemingly not even interested to at least try to make a new arrival to their company and his wife feel just a little more welcome? The driver who had picked us up had uttered not more than a couple of words the whole time we had been in his car.

The whole afternoon of that day, our very first in Australia, passed by – still with nothing in the way of either a word or further message from my new employer. No one seemed even interested enough to visit or ask if our accommodation was satisfactory. Everything about our arrival in Guildford had been so unexpected. At the very least we had hoped to be contacted by someone from the company – if not Ernest Hiller himself.

Once again came the thought: "Perhaps they do things differently here in Australia?" That being the only explanation either of us could think of at the time.

FIRST DINNER IN AUSTRALIA

Following another short wander around the limited streets that made up the New South Wales town of Guildford in the late 1950s, we returned to the hotel (the only one in town). Making our way through a throng of local drinkers, we decided to order dinner in the nearby dining area, a part of the hotel apparently referred to as a 'bistro'.

It is important to remember here that coming from a couple of working-class families in the north of England, neither of us had been used to regularly dining out in restaurants or the larger hotels in the city, particularly during the working week. Later into our early twenties, young people would either pair off or go in a group to dine out in one or other of the restaurants in the city, before moving on to the cinema or one or other of the city's live-band dance venues.

It is well also to remember here that in austerity-bound Britain, the range and quality of restaurant food were often limited to relatively basic fare. What was served up, apart from the usual fish and chips, was generally speaking so basic in variety as to encourage anyone really interested in the culinary arts to turn their noses up at the usually over-cooked, often stringy meat or over-boiled, limp vegetables. The usual range of restaurant food presentation, in addition to its relatively high cost during the 1950s, made eating out in and around Leeds an expensive, often questionable luxury. Here, of course, we must exclude the broad range of fish and chip shops and at least some of the more professionally run restaurants and inns established for many years across the United Kingdom.

Here, in what we deemed to be semi-outback Guildford, we were in for a pleasant surprise – at least when it came to the quality, presentation and amount of food on offer.

On ordering our evening meals, mine being a T bone steak, and Mavis's lamb chops, what later arrived in front of us served to buck up our flagging spirits on this, the occasion of our first evening meal in our new country.

When my meal arrived, not only was it served on a large plate, the plate was crowned with the biggest, thickest and certainly the juiciest piece of steak that I had ever seen or tucked into. It was nearly an inch thick! Onto what remained of the rest of the plate, was piled an assortment of lightly steamed vegetables and new potatoes! Wow, these Australians seemed to live high off the hog – at least when it came to eating! And the price too seemed low for a main course, to be followed by a sweet yet to come. The whole meal was cheaper and far superior to would have ever been possible to expect in an equivalent dining establishment in Leeds.

I also ordered a beer, receiving what the locals termed a 'schooner'. My beer came in an overly large glass, inscribed with a statement that the very strong amber coloured liquid it contained had come from somewhere called Carlton. We both were pleasantly surprised with our meals.

On ordering a glass of sherry, Mavis had expected to receive a thimble-sized glass half-filled with the wine. Not at all! She was surprised when a near tumbler full of a really nice locally produced sherry wine was placed on the table in front of her. Her order of lamb chops also arrived on a large plate containing three humungous, juicy loin chops (the only way to describe their size), accompanied by plenty of crisp, steamed vegetables.

It is illuminating to recall our first impressions of our new country and comparing the way people in the outer regions of Sydney similarly lived and ate when compared with their counterparts in Leeds.

That first meal at least gave us both a full stomach each, also heavy heads from the effects of my schooner of strong beer and Mavis's large glassful of sherry wine. Our first evening meal did at least give rise to a slight lift to our spirits, as well as our feelings for our new country – at the very least we both felt good thus far regarding the food we had received.

My feelings about what to expect from my new employer the next morning were very different. Maybe I was reading too much into our first day in Australia? Perhaps things will turn out to be better, once I was able to meet face-to-face with Mr Hiller?

Amply filled and sated by our first real meal in our new country, we were tired and somewhat deflated in spirits following the ending of our long voyage from Britain and the feelings of disappointment when thinking further about the lack of even a friendly welcome from my new employer or a representative from his company.

Following a short walk in the gathering dusk we settled into our temporary home at the Guildford hotel, both filled with hopeful expectations for the next few days, although I must admit to having more than a few negative feelings about what to expect from the next morning at the Ernest Hiller factory.

Following a long, frustrating first day we slipped between the sheets of our bed in the Guildford Hotel. To the sounds of a local band banging out their version of the day's hit songs below us in the main bar, we both snuggled together and sank into our first night's sleep in our new country.

My last thoughts before sleep took over my mind that night were a recounting of the events of a day that had started out with us both looking forward so much to meeting a friendly welcome to our new country – hopes that as the day wore on gradually descended toward disappointment and growing uncertainty.

FIRST DAY AT WORK

With more than a few misgivings in my mind as to what to expect on my arrival at my new employer's factory, at 'sparrow's fart' on my first full day ashore in Australia, I awaited the ordered pickup at 07.30, my loins tight and suitably girded.

On arrival at the factory following a short car ride, instead of being greeted by Mr Hiller and briefed on the company and his expectations for me, I was led into a small room off to one side of the main factory floor. On entering, I was surprised to find the room already occupied by two other men. On introducing myself, I was somewhat taken aback to learn from one, who seemed to be the leader, that both had been recruited earlier by Ernest Hiller – as designers!

"Silly me," was the first thought that entered my confused brain. Here was I expecting to be the only designer, as nothing to the contrary had been said in Mr Hiller's letters to me. On later reflection though, for me to have even thought that there was not already someone fulfilling the role of designer before my arrival, was perhaps a case of me being a little naive?

On the other hand, it did appear to be more than a little strange to find that I was to be one of three designated designers! Ah well, it was early days yet, and it would seem a better plan to wait a while and give things time to sort themselves out. A, early face-to-face chat with Ernest Hiller was called for.

With the latter thought in mind, I was hoping to be able to meet with my new employer during the day, at which time I should be able to sort out just what kind of working arrangements I had landed in.

As the day wore on I continued to be disappointed, the hoped-for first meeting with my new employer failing to eventuate. Instead, I was given a short tour around the factory by one of the two guys with whom it seemed I was to share what looked to be the company's design office. During our tour, it was interesting to learn further, that he too had migrated from England along with his young family two years earlier. He went on to explain that he had already been appointed as the company designer. He also offered the pointed comment that he didn't think there was enough work to keep three designers busy. "Hmmmmm... what goes on here?"

I had a distinct feeling, even at that early stage, that all that had been offered to me, clearly in writing no less from Ernest Hiller himself, was perhaps not all 'kosher'. Still, it was probably best to await my first meeting with my new and as yet invisible employer, who should be able to clarify the situation. At any rate, the promised salary at A£26 per week was not to be sneezed at and, I had Hiller's offer set out clearly in writing. At least that was some consolation, should the situation get to be a little rough later.

So proceeded my first day of 'work' in Australia, during which I was provided with a tour through the various sections of what at first sight appeared to be a simple, inflexible style of production layout. This was in direct contrast to what Ernest Hiller had described to me earlier as being a modern production plant.

The day progressed with me being given the simple task of pasting pieces of soft card onto various parts of existing patterns. These presumably were later to be altered to make some change or other to the shape or fit of the garment, for which they were supposed to be the master templates. This kind of work, to say the least, was basic and not at all interesting. Nor from my experience, having worked in a relatively modern production plant in Leeds, did it appear to be a professional way to be running a design department.

The other two occupants of what I was assuming to be the design office, at least were reasonably helpful during my first day, but still no Ernest Hiller, who I understood to be in and around the factory at the time. I had cherished the hope that he would make his appearance, even possibly joining Mavis and me for lunch or even dinner that evening, at which time I could seek to try to unravel what at first sight appeared to be turning into a 'can of worms'! But no, the elusive Ernest Hiller didn't even bother to make an appearance during the remainder of the day.

On being driven back to the Guildford Hotel that evening, the day's frustrations worsened somewhat. On arriving back at our hotel, I was met by a tearful wife, who obviously had also been having a trying second day in Australia. In her case, we both had yet to become familiar with the way commercial hotels operated in Australia, circa 1959. Specifically, just how Australian men regarded the sanctity of the public bar in their local pub – a place where women were unwelcome.

When it came to the Australian males' well-known propensity to engage, along with their mates, in their reputedly cherished pastime of drinking copious amounts of strong, ice-cold beer, it seems that the public bar in most local pubs across Australia at the time were regarded as an exclusive males-only domain.

Apparently, also, the Guildford Hotel did not serve lunches, only breakfast and dinner being the only meals provided. This arrangement, we later learned, was designed to service the dining needs of travelling businesspeople. Unaware of this, when Mavis went down to the dining room in the hope of ordering some lunch, she was informed that there was no lunch to be had. Not even a cup of tea was forthcoming, or offered.

To make matters worse, on re-entering the hotel after stretching her legs in Guildford and obtaining yet another uninteresting sandwich for her lunch in what locally was referred to as a 'milk bar', she apparently had committed a gross act of daring as a mere woman by entering the Guilford Hotel via its main bar.

On stepping over the threshold of that male sanctuary, she had been confronted by one of the drinkers and told in no uncertain terms that women were not allowed in the public bar! To make matters worse, as the afternoon wore on no one from the company had called to inquire if they could assist her in becoming more familiar with her new surroundings. Mr Hiller, or at least someone in his office, must have known that she would be feeling the need for at least some form of communication during her first day, alone, in a strange country?

Thus far, the reception we both had experienced, or rather the lack of anything resembling even the minimum level of friendly greeting and the least level of assistance that a company would usually provide to a new arrival from abroad, was non-existent. Nothing! My antennae by then were beginning to twitch, rather rapidly too – my inner thoughts telling me that there was the possibility that the situation could get worse.

The next day, also 07.30, I was picked up from the hotel. The difference this time though, was on arrival at the factory I was ushered into Ernest Hiller's office. He smiled and extended his rather belated greetings, mumbling something along the lines that he hoped I would enjoy my new position with his company. My questions regarding his two other designers were brushed aside, his explanation being that the other guys would be involved with as yet unspecified production management work. He then stated that I alone was to concentrate on the pattern-making aspects of the company's technical design work.

My question as to when my position vis-a-vis the other two men would be clarified, preferably with them present, so that everyone was clear as to who was responsible for what, was met with the promise to organise a joint meeting later that week. This was the kind of answer that added further to my earlier doubts. I was also beginning to wonder if everything else that he had written about and promised would be forthcoming?

As there was little I could do at this stage, I decided to wait a while, keep my options open and wait to see what the future would bring.

THE PLOT THICKENS

The days that followed didn't provide much in the way of hope. It gradually became clear, though, that one of the other two guys I found myself working with was continuing to assume seniority. I was being given tasks like continuing to stick bits of soft cardboard onto patterns for him to subsequently alter. It was also becoming apparent during our general conversations throughout the day, that neither of the two guys I was working alongside, had any practical experience with garment design and pattern drafting. Neither of them had even the slightest knowledge when it came to any discussion on the subject of applying the technology necessary when it came to the 'grading' of a set of working patterns from a master template.

Experience with this aspect of pattern design was a primary

requirement in the production of a range of sizes from an original master template. From conversations and questions that I sought to put to my two 'learned' colleagues at various times during the day, it very soon became clear to me that neither had any previous practical experience working in the area.

I was constantly being asked if I knew how to prepare a 'grade'. This was a technique used at the time for the creation of a full size range, the process then used to produce of a full range of garment patterns. Patterns thus created would be used to 'mark out' and cut fabrics according to a client's order.

I decided not to be too forthcoming, declining their invitation to demonstrate how I would go about grading and setting up a working size chart. It later also became very clear that neither of my companions had even a basic idea of how to prepare a simple draft (design) for a standard sized pair of trousers. They were certainly not designers.

It also became apparent that while both may have had some experience as cloth cutters or trimmers, a function that involved the marking out and cutting out of cloth and lining trimmings, using patterns and templates provided to them by a designer, that that was about the full extent of their experience. Both, to date, had apparently been used by Hiller to do odd jobs around the production floor, in addition to sticking bits onto patterns or cutting bits off as required by him from time to time. Other than that, it was unclear where else they had been employed, certainly not when it came to the exacting task of pattern-making.

The patterns being used at the time in the factory's cutting room were in a dreadful state and quite old. They clearly had been altered and chopped about time after time, over a number of years. This was not a professional way to approach the design, production and long-term maintenance of a full and accurate size range of patterns, master patterns that were required to be used every working day by cloth cutters operating in a well-functioning apparel manufacturing facility. The work situation had by my second day at the Hiller plant become much clearer!

In the meantime, my poor wife, on a day when she had to return to the hotel following a sudden and heavy shower of rain that had descended over Guildford, had made the mistake again of trying to take a short cut into the hotel via the main bar. Once again she had been abused by some of the local 'barflies' drinking there.

On my return that evening, in addition to her frustrations at having to stay in a hotel that didn't provide lunch and having to kill a whole day alone until I returned to the hotel each evening, had been boring. The place and her situation were beginning to wear her down, there being nothing for her to even occupy herself with since her arrival.

We had not even received any word or information regarding the furnished house Hiller had promised me in his earlier correspondence. Nor did the meeting to "sort things out" he had promised me for later in the week eventuate, despite a second request, sent through his secretary. All that was being expected of me was the seemingly endless task of sticking bits of cardboard on patterns, under the direction of one or other of my two companion 'designers'. This was regularly being added to by a stream of questions from them both, mainly on the subject of how to grade.

The situation was getting to be more than a little weird. No – the situation was surreal!

Mavis and I had reasonably expected to be able to familiarise ourselves with the promised house, the address of which we had learned was 334 Woodville Road, but as yet nothing had been said as to the possibility of that happening.

On our first Saturday in Guildford, John Pardoe, an executive from the finance department of the company, offered to show Mavis and I around Sydney and the nearby Blue Mountains. John and his wife Ellie were our guides for the day. During our tour, John suggested that as Mavis was an experienced wages and general finance secretary and qualified to provide valuable assistance in the company offices, he would be very happy to find her a temporary position. This at least would provide her with a temporary position, until she had time to settle down to her new life in Australia.

At least someone from the company had taken the time, belatedly as the offer was, to show us around Sydney. Now at least Mavis could also look forward, starting the next week, to working and acclimatising herself for a time in the company's offices, in a position that she had managed as part of her previous employment. When asked about the house we had been promised, John did not appear to know of any progress. Nor, it seemed, was he apparently aware that the offer of accommodation had been offered to me?

The following day, being the first Sunday in our new country, with not much else interesting to do, we decided to take a longer exploratory stroll around our new surroundings.

Bearing in mind that Guildford during the 1950s was more like a rural town located well outside metropolitan Sydney, the way people were living in and around the town was, to us at least, more than a little different – just to note a couple of areas to illustrate this:

Being a Sunday, there was little road traffic around. Most people living in or around Guildford appeared to be spending most of the day at home. Most of the local shops were closed on Sunday, the local newsagent only operating for part of the morning. Apart from the local hotel, it was impossible to find somewhere different to eat or just drop in for a cup of tea or coffee. Apparently, there was a fish and chip shop somewhere in the vicinity, but we had as yet been unable to learn of its location.

The local churches appeared to be the only venues in and around town where more than a few people were gathering.

We did manage eventually to find the local sports ground where we were able to watch a couple of teams playing rugby league, a game very familiar to me. The ground had a small wooden grandstand and lean-to clubhouse, next to which someone had set up a barbeque, from which a couple of the local ladies were selling hot dogs, hamburgers and plastic cups of tea. Both Mavis and I were hungry, having missed out on lunch except for a couple of chocolate bars and a bottle of soft drink, bought earlier in the morning, we ordered a hot dog and a cup of tea each and engaged one of the ladies in conversation.

Not surprisingly, it didn't take her very long to recognise us both as being 'Pommie migrants', following which, after offering us a heartfelt welcome to Australia, confided that we had arrived in what she referred to as "God's own country". She then proceeded to advise us on some of the local delights that we should try during our stay in Guildford.

There weren't many delights, as she had described them. It did appear however from her soliloquy, that one feature of local life that was looked forward to each week, other than Sunday church and a weekend rugby league match that is, was the weekly social outing to the local picture (movie) show ... so, following the advice of our Sunday acquaintance, we were looking forward to our first visit to the local cinema.

THE LOCAL CINEMA – GUILDFORD 1959

One evening during the second week of our residence in Guildford, to get out of our hotel room where there was no TV provided, Mavis and I opted for a visit to the local theatre as recommended by the lady we had met at the previous Sunday afternoon's rugby ground sausage sizzle. With the promise of seeing a movie in the local theatre (wherever that was located), we consulted one of the locals en-route on what was already proving to be a boring evening stroll around town. Following enquiries around town it was learned that a movie would be showing at the local town hall the next evening – and, we were also informed, it wouldn't be necessary to pre-book seats.

At the appointed time, Mavis and I dressed up as well as was possible from the limited selection of changes we had been able to bring out to Australia. I should add here that our outfits for an evening at the cinema would have accorded with that worn when deciding to attend one of the local cinemas in Leeds.

On our arrival at the local Guildford hall, we were surprised to see that all the locals entering were variously attired in tracksuits overcoats or dressing gowns. Some were even carrying blankets and other cosying items. In some cases, couples were arriving with young children in tow.

I cannot recall what the film was about, but it soon became clear to us that dressing up to attend was not the recommended mode of dress for a Guildford film soiree, circa 1959.

The seating provided in the hall was in the form of rows of folding wooden chairs and, as the evening progressed and the temperature dropped alarmingly, we both began to regret that we hadn't inquired further as to the heating arrangements – of which there were none!

At a mid-film break, during which the projectionist struggled to change the film reels, most of the evening's patrons began opening bags containing thermos flasks and cakes. In a number of cases, others left the hall to pick up newspaper wrapped servings of fish and chips that earlier had been pre-ordered from the fish and chip shop, located somewhere in the vicinity of the town. No such thing as a cheekily clad, long-legged girl offering ice creams or soft drinks here – at the Guildford movies it was a case of serving yourself, or stay thirsty and hungry, in addition to enduring the cold!

In contrast to our bizarre cinematic experience in Guildford, I should also add here a further, and to us, an also weird experience encountered on a later weekend trip into the Sydney CBD, during which we decided to attend one of the cinemas there.

In the city, seating and other arrangements were similar to what we would have experienced when visiting a city cinema in Leeds. The main difference here though occurred at the beginning of the show:

As a picture of Queen Elizabeth II was projected onto the curtains covering the screen, they then dramatically drew aside as the National Anthem ("God save our gracious Queen" etc.) began playing. We were then absolutely astonished to observe that everyone in the theatre was rising to his or her feet, with most fervently singing along with the British National Anthem. We, of course, remained seated, watching the gathered audience with amusement, as they sang ardently along with the accompanying music. That is until I received a sharp tap on the shoulder along with a gruff and distinctly Australian accented admonishment from the row behind me that asserted in a tone that suggested that I should: "Get to your bloody feet dago and honour our queen!"

Now, I could easily understand being mistaken for an off-white and foreign looking southern European person, due mainly to my black hair, which I wore well below my collar line, and what could also have been taken for a distinctly southern European complexion, due to a recently completed month-long luxury cruise through the tropics.

But that aside, I had not the slightest intention of standing up in a movie theatre in Australia, just for a picture of the Queen. Nor did I appreciate the tenor of the man's tone.

Turning to the tapper on my shoulder and, in the best broadest Yorkshire accent I could muster, I stated: "Listen lad, I've just arrived in Australia after escaping from England – where we never stand to salute royalty at the start of a picture show and… I'm not about to start doing that here – not for you, your prime minister or anyone else around here for that matter!"

The sound of my broad Yorkshire accent and the vehemence with which my statement had been delivered, must have mollified him, as I then received a "Sorry mate, I thought you were a bloody wog!" after which by that time the music had died and everyone had sat themselves down once again to enjoy the film.

What had just ensued left me with the distinct impression that in Australia: "The people here are obviously more in awe of British royalty than most of us had been back in England?" Perhaps this was as a result of years living under the direct rule of successive British governments, following which they were all regarded as being British and the loyal, ardent citizens of one of Britain's far-flung, red-coloured colonies?

It is significant that in 1959, Australia's then governor general was Sir William Slim, a Bristol-born Englishman! It wasn't until later into the 1960s that every following Australian governor general henceforth was to be selected from the ranks of distinguished home-grown Australians. In Australia circa 1959, the country, in some very noticeable ways, seemed to be still operating as a far-flung British colony among the South Seas, way down below the equator.

DAGOS, WOPS AND WOGS

Our attendance in May 1959 at a cinema in Sydney was the first of many later occasions, on which I was to hear one or other of the terms 'dago', 'wop' and 'wog' being used to describe new arrivals in Australia. One or other of these distinctly derogatory terms, were then being regularly and openly used by many among some of the more red-necked variety of 'native-born' Australians. The terms were usually used when referring to immigrants recently arrived from countries like Italy, Greece, Turkey and others from southern European countries. Large numbers of immigrants from these and nearby countries in Europe and the Balkans, in addition to Britain, had regularly been arriving in Australia since the ending of the Second World War.

Being from the British Isles didn't stop some of the locals from referring to us by the use of the less hard-sounding term 'Pommie'. This was sometimes also extended to 'whingeing Pom', the latter being an adaptation of the expression often used to describe recently arrived British immigrants, many who were known to complain about anything they found was not to their liking.

All in all, the term Pommie, or the more expressive 'Pommie bastard', was sometimes applied in the more acceptable form of a relatively friendly greeting, as in "Ow yer goin' y' Pommie Bastard?" or some other form of Australian-style endearment or expression of well-acquainted friendliness.

This was very different from the way terms like wog, dago, wop or even 'spag' (spaghetti-eater) were used, often as a not very endearing reference to people from southern Europe. Interesting that as I rarely heard a migrant hailing from Germany or Austria being referred to as a 'kraut'.

I should include here a reference to one or two of my boyhood comic books. These were weekly issues, popular with us kids, during the Second World War. One or other of these, the 'Dandy' or perhaps the 'Beano', regularly referred to one character being featured as, "Musso the Wop, he's a big a da flop." This, of course, was a pejorative reference to Benito Mussolini, leader of the wartime Italian Fascist movement.

I must state here that the title 'whingeing Pom' was often a reasonably accurate expression to use when describing some of my acquaintances among recently arrived British migrants. Many of these people seemed to spend much of their time complaining about this and that, and how life in Australia didn't come close to that which they said they had enjoyed back in Britain. In reality, complaints being made by some British migrants were well wide of the mark. Complaints such as these failed to recognise that in the Australia of the 1950s and 1960s, living conditions were distinctly better than those which most 'working-class' people had left behind them in Britain.

The weather in Australia was far better and more predictable, the food superior as well as being more plentiful and cheaper. Opportunities to find reasonably well-paid work in most of the states across Australia were relatively easy to come by. Housing was reasonably affordable, and it was at the time still possible to maintain a family on the wages or salary of one breadwinner, a situation far more difficult, if not impossible to achieve today in 2017.

Looking back to 1959, when I arrived in Australia a young immigrant, the first few months of my arrival did much to open my eyes to the broad range of possibilities for all kinds of work that was on offer. During the later 1960s and 1970s Australia, while a relatively underpopulated country, was still capable of offering anyone wishing to work, the opportunity to do so, whether they were a Pommie, Kiwi, Yank, wog, kraut, wop, spag or dago!

Unfortunately, as a new arrival to the Ernest Hiller company in Guildford, even during the second week of my being there and continuing still to be picked up for work each morning, it remained impossible, as yet, to come to grips with what my role there was going to be.

Following my first week working for my remote new boss and his strange duo of pseudo-designers, it had continued impossible to arrange a meeting to define our responsibilities. I was by now getting closer to losing whatever patience had remained since our arrival, and what appeared to be a determined lack of interest on the part of my elusive employer to meet and clarify what was expected of me?

My first week with the company had not given me any confidence that the unsatisfactory situation we had found on our arrival would improve. The growing uncertainty of our situation also did little to assist Mavis toward the thought of spending the rest of her life in or around Guildford or even continuing to be connected with the Ernest Hiller company. In fact, even after our first week in Guildford, she had already expressed the desire to get on the next ship back to England!

I believe she would gladly have done so had I not expressed the conviction that we should persevere for a little longer.

334 WOODVILLE ROAD

During the second week since our arrival, during which neither Mavis or I had heard anything more regarding the furnished accommodation that Hiller had promised, I decided to 'take the bull by the horns'. Via Hiller's secretary, I requested details of the progress being made on the renovations – earlier referred to by the non-communicative, smirking driver who had picked us up from the docks.

Since settling into work at the Hiller organisation, both Mavis and I had received guarded and unsettling reports from various people around the company, most concerning the state and progress of the accommodation we had been promised in Hiller's letter. I should add here that following two weeks we still had not received anything in the form of a progress report. Nor had the promised meeting to define my responsibilities taken place.

My employer, strangely enough, was apparently still happy to continue providing us with accommodation and meals at the Guildford Hotel. This was not an arrangement that suited us. We both wished to get ourselves settled down in our own home as quickly as possible.

Our third request to view the property that Hiller had promised, finally resulted in him reluctantly arranging to pick Mavis up from the company offices where she had commenced part-time work in the finance department, and taking her on an inspection of the promised accommodation.

The result of this inspection of progress revealed that no progress had been made! The property, in fact, was described by Mavis as being unliveable in its present state. Much worse even than that, instead of us receiving the level of accommodation described by Hiller in his correspondence to me, Mavis's report on her return to the factory that afternoon left me, on the top of everything else that had occurred thus far, more than a little angry. Yes, a very angry Pommie!

In addition to her report on the state of the property on her return to the factory, she claimed amid tears that Hiller had been particularly aggressive and had threatened her. Hiller's threats had occurred following her questions and comments on what she described as being the deplorable and unliveable condition of the property. On their return to the factory I was called to Hiller's office where he began to harangue both Mavis and I while making number of uncomplimentary comments, included the assertion: "You arrogant English, what do you expect to live in here, a mansion?" This accusation had been thrown at us both after my wife had stated that in its present deplorable condition, she would not consider moving into it.

My answer to Hiller's comments was, "No Mr Hiller, all we expect from you is what you promised me and described in writing, should I decide to join your company."

The house as my wife and subsequently other people in the company who had inspected the property when Hiller had bought it earlier, could be described as:

Flooring and internal walls in the house suffered from rising damp. Doors were swelled, one or two warped and difficult to open or close properly. Internally, the working area floors that had been covered with linoleum were torn and cracked. Carpeted areas were mildewed in parts. Furniture that had been left uncovered in the building was damp and mildewed. In addition to all this, someone had recently erected a wooden partition across the centre of the main living area of the property, in an apparent attempt to divide it into two separate units!

The problem here was that only one of the halves of the property had access to the inside toilet, bathroom and cooking facilities. The partition dividing the house into two only extended to within two feet of the ceilings, thus leaving a wide opening at their top – an arrangement that prevented any form of privacy for anyone living on either side of the partition. The roof had been leaking in places, which had added to the dampness that pervaded the entire house.

In short, it was quite obvious that any self-respecting building inspector would condemn the condition in which the house had been offered to us.

In addition to the sad state of the house, which I also visited later, there was an outside toilet that had been broken and was unusable. The gardens were overgrown to such an extent that various forms of vermin, spiders and also a couple of snakes had been found among the rubbish, timber and other stuff that had been dumped there and left to rot, over a long period.

As this situation unfolded, I must admit to nearly blowing my top. After the promise of a furnished house in which to live, this latest finding was even worse than the already unacceptable situation regarding the position I had already found myself in professionally. But more was yet to come.

To cap all that had occurred thus far, earlier that same day I was also to learn that instead of the £26 per week salary that had been offered in his letter to me, Hiller had decided to start me on the lower weekly salary of £15. This without any previous discussion or explanation!

With that, I blew up – storming into his office, where within earshot of everyone in the vicinity of the company's offices, and beyond, I threatened Hiller with legal action. He subsequently upped his salary offer by a miserly couple of pounds. But for us that day the die had been cast as far as Hiller, his company, his mildewed house, empty promises and unreasonably aggressive attitude were concerned.

After all that had occurred during the short time since our arrival in Guildford, the absolute wreck of a house we had been expected to live in, plus Hiller's decision to renege on the salary which he had himself offered me in writing, was too much to stomach. Not only that – having to spend endless hours doing nothing more than sticking bits of cardboard onto old, worn out patterns was less than I was prepared to put up with professionally.

Bear in mind that Hiller already had two other people working for him, at least one that continued to regard himself as the designer in charge of whatever Hiller apparently saw as being the functions of a designer.

No thanks! As young and relatively inexperienced as I then was, I was not prepared to put up with that sort of crap from anyone, let alone a dishonest employer like Ernest Hiller.

Having decided to take legal action and leave Hiller, his company and Guildford, I phoned my aunt and uncle in Melbourne to explain the circumstances in which we now found ourselves. Both immediately invited us to stay with them, should we decide to move to Melbourne.

That decided, I demanded a further audience with my bloody-minded liar of an employer.

During a second session of loud and widely broadcast haggling, overheard by most of the office staff, I threatened to place the matter into the hands of a solicitor. I also threatened to report the state of his mouldy, damp and unliveable half-house in which he expected us to live, to the local building authorities. Following much argument, he reluctantly backed down and agreed to discuss terms.

The upshot of this conversation resulted in Hiller finally agreeing to cover our costs to date, including the trans-shipment of our trunk to Melbourne, plus compensation for having arrived in Australia to take up a promised position that had not existed in the way he had described it in his letter of offer.

Ultimately, we agreed to accept the sum of £450, plus both our wages to date, mine at the promised £26 per week.

Having first arranged to ship our still undelivered cabin trunk to storage in Melbourne, Mavis and I decided to extend our stay at the Guildford Hotel for a few more days, also at Hiller's expense.

I was now without a job, but we were both now looking forward to meeting up again with my cousin and his family in Melbourne, a move that hopefully would result in a happier and more productive period to that experienced to date.

Surely things could not get any worse than we had experienced so far? Hiller's misrepresentation of the position and salary was bad enough. His attitude was even worse when it came to his offer of a house, unfit for human habitation. Worse even than that, the way Hiller had threatened my wife was totally unacceptable.

A number of Hiller's employees later described earlier situations similar to those we had encountered. One leading section leader in the factory went even further – describing his and other colleagues' work situations that they were finding near impossible to put up with. My only comment here being: "Why stay working and trying to cope, if finding yourself in such an impossible situation?"

The unhappy period spent in Australia thus far had been so strange and so unnecessary that one needed to question the mental state of

Ernest Hiller and in my case at least, to ask why he invited me to join his company in the first place?

Whatever, we were both bound to stay here in Australia for at least a further two years. We now faced the need to regroup and decide where to from here?

It was also about this time that Mavis and I came to an agreement that in the event that the rest of the next two years turned out to be as difficult as the first few weeks had been, we would leave Australia and perhaps travel to Canada, before returning to Britain. Having made that decision, with little else to detain us in Guildford and having no interest to remain in Sydney looking around for accommodation and another position, we decided to try our luck in Melbourne. At least we were a healthy few hundred pounds to the good than when we had arrived in Sydney. We then prepared to leave Guildford with the view to taking a comfortable overnight railway trip down to Melbourne.

While I could have stayed longer in Sydney to seek other employment, the way things had turned out, in particular, the man who had so readily sponsored us and sounded so keen for me join his company, only to be arrogant and deceitful once we had arrived there, had turned things sour. I was lucky to be at least able to move to another city in which I did have three members of my extended family.

A RAIL JOURNEY TO REMEMBER

Having arranged for the trans-shipment and storage of our sole trunkful of worldly goods in Melbourne, we decided to stay a few days longer at the Guildford Hotel. As my former employer was paying the cost of our accommodation, we spent a couple of days getting to know a little more about Sydney, its magnificent harbour and the Harbour Bridge. It was a thrill also to take a ride on the Manly Ferry – not forgetting a visit to Sydney's famous Taronga Park Zoo.

Before leaving, we decided to splash out and book first-class tickets on the train to Melbourne. This was in the expectation of travelling in style, with comfortable seats on an overnight train.

Consulting the official departure timetable, we learned that our train was scheduled to leave Sydney's Central station in the evening, its connecting train from Albury due to arrive at Melbourne's Spencer Street Station reasonably early during the following morning.

In our innocence, we had expected that our journey would go something like the transcontinental rail journeys that one usually saw featured in Hollywood movies of the time. Scenes where passengers dressed in their best clothes boarded their train, to be seated comfortably in a well-appointed compartment with corridor access to a dining car able to cater to their dining needs.

Having first advised my uncle Barney in Melbourne of our scheduled arrival time in Melbourne, we were looking forward to a new experience on one of the Railways of New South Wales' express trains.

Unfortunately, the lesson we had learned regarding the laid-back way local Australians went about their weekly attendance to view a movie in Guildford's cold, bleak and uncomfortable hall had not sunk in. Nor had we inquired carefully enough as to just what a first-class booking on the Railways of New South Wales, 1959 version, meant in practice. Surely, we thought, the rail journey down to Melbourne would be speedy, comfortable and on time?

We had also failed to understand fully at the time that there was no such thing as a continuous rail line running between Sydney and Melbourne. We learned later that the disjointed travel arrangements that existed between Australia's two major capital cities were primarily due to the politics and separation that had operated between the previously self-governing Crown colonies, both before and following their federation in 1901 into the Commonwealth of Australia.

From a historical perspective, before and following federation, each of the various states and territories had considered it their sovereign right to continue with what they regarded as being the most appropriate gauge to adopt for their intrastate railway system. This attitude resulted in New South Wales and the state of Victoria opting for different rail track gauges. A similar situation was the case among the other individual states and territories.

Thus, in 1959, some 58 years following federation, it was still necessary, when undertaking a rail journey between Australia's two major cities, to change from one train to another. In our case this was scheduled to occur during the middle of the night at Albury, then a small town located on the border between the two states.

The establishment of a single 'standard gauge' rail system serving Victoria and New South Wales did eventually occur three years later in 1962. A nationwide standard gauge rail system took until 2004 to be completed, the final stage of that long-awaited national rail system being laid from Alice Springs to Darwin.

Meanwhile, back on a wintry June evening in 1959, Mavis and I arrived at Sydney's Central Railway Station, complete with hand luggage and dressed in what at the time were our best outfits. In our innocent ignorance, we were looking forward to a comfortable, well-serviced journey to Melbourne. On entering the station platform before boarding our train, however, we were taken aback to see that most of our fellow passengers had decided to travel dressed much as their fellow movie-goers back in Guildford had been – in a variety of tracksuits and other kinds of warm, relaxed clothing.

Also disconcerting, some appeared, as in Guildford, carrying blankets, baskets and handbags bristling with thermos flasks, food and drinks for the journey. Children travelling were also well wrapped up in 'snuggle' suits and baby blankets. Not only that but to our surprise and dismay, our vision of having a cosy evening meal in the train's dining car, while gazing out on the passing countryside whizzing past, was shattered further.

We only later got to realise, on entering our supposedly premium class compartment that while the seating appeared to be more comfortable than in most of the other carriages, there was little else differentiating the various classes of travel. There were to be no dining facilities anywhere on-board the train!

So there we both were, me smartly attired in my beautifully tailored 'Crombie' overcoat, trilby hat (every male wore a hat in those days) and gloves. Mavis was elegantly dressed in her three-quarter-length green wool Dolman sleeved coat with pearl buttons and wool green and white houndstooth skirt. This was an outfit that I had proudly designed and made for her prior to leaving England. We both were completely unprepared for the rail experience to come.

BROKEN DOWN NEAR WAGGA WAGGA

The train left Sydney at the appointed time, but the heating, if there ever was such a service installed in our supposedly first-class compartment, proved non-existent.

As we travelled southwest toward Albury and the night drew in, our would-be first-class compartment got progressively colder, a situation exacerbated by not being able to obtain a hot meal or a drink! To make things a lot worse, the engine pulling our train decided to break down not very far from two towns located somewhere among the backblocks of New South Wales – Yass and Wagga Wagga.

The latter, strange as it may seem, was a place-name that we had already heard of much earlier back in Britain –the supposed hometown of an Australian comedian of the time by the name of Bill Kerr. Kerr used to enter the stage, or appear on radio, commencing each of his performances with a slow Australian drawled soliloquy, preceded by the words… "I'm only here for four minutes!"

So, here we now found ourselves, stopped in the middle of god only knows where, in the dead of night – our supposed 'express' train having ground to a halt among the cold, windswept hills between Sydney and Albury, obviously for much longer than Bill Kerr's four minutes!

The stoppage resulted in a delay that lasted a number of hours, during which a forlorn string of railway carriages languished at a standstill in the middle of nowhere. It was a night with no lights or any other signs of life discernible in any direction, even when either of us tried to poke our heads outside the compartment into what had become a really cold night.

The temperature was near freezing – or so it felt. All we could hope for was that arrangements were being made to repair or find a replacement for our broken-down engine and attach it onto the front of the train. Hopefully, also, things might go right for the rest of the trip to Albury, with what we and presumably every other passenger that night, had come to regard as the 'Shambolic Railways of New South Wales'.

As we continued to wait, it became colder and colder. In the middle of that bleak, cold night it seemed that we had jumped out of the frying pan and into the fire – or rather into a refrigerator on wheels – metaphorically speaking. The only way Mavis and I could maintain any semblance of retaining some warmth in our bodies was to snuggle together, with both our coats wrapped around us. In normal circumstances, this would have been a desirable and romantic way in which to pass an evening in front of a roaring fire, but in our present predicament, we were more in need of keeping some warmth in our bodies as opposed to anything else.

As time and the cold night dragged on, we were also fast becoming desperate for something hot and wet to drink.

"Dear god – what an awful country this is, and what strange people," was the tenor of the not very kind thoughts running through my head that night. To think that in this day and age, these strange Australians couldn't even arrange to run a train from one capital city to another, without having it break down in the middle of nowhere, in the almost numbing cold of a Southern Highlands night!

Mavis by now was teetering on the edge of exasperation and tears, particularly when our current cold sojourn somewhere in the seemingly uninhabited centre of New South Wales was added to the disappointments we had already experienced since landing in Sydney not much more than a couple of weeks prior. She actually got to the stage of threatening: "I'm going to catch the next ship back to England, when – and if we ever get to Melbourne in one piece!" I must say that even I was getting much more than a little angry and frustrated, as the cold night wore on.

The train journey, like our stay in Guildford, had been a disaster so far, but I must say that in spite of all that had happened since arriving in Australia, I was even more determined to explore the job possibilities, once and if we ever got to Melbourne. At least there, I reasoned, we did have relatives and one or two old and new friends that should make a difference to life and living, so far away from home.

If I couldn't get work with an apparel manufacturer in Melbourne, I was prepared to look elsewhere. Surely there has to be someone interested in my skills, young as I am?

Finally, after what seemed hours, someone, somewhere at last had either located an engine that worked or had managed to fix the one attached to our train.

Following much banging, shouting and with lights flashing across the darkened countryside, we eventually got moving, this time quite slowly. We finally arrived at Albury on the New South Wales/Victorian border, to learn that due to the long delay on the Sydney to Albury leg of our journey, we had missed our scheduled connection to Melbourne.

Following the performance thus far since our arrival in Australia, what else could happen? Surely things couldn't get any worse?

THE 'SPIRIT OF PROGRESS'

Changing over trains from the New South Wales side of the border found a stream of cold, tired and frustrated passengers lugging cases, bags and in some cases children and near freezing bodies, to the Victorian end of the platform. At least on gaining the Victorian side and another long wait, we were able to purchase a cup of weak but steaming hot tea each and what appeared to have a distant resemblance to a chicken and salad sandwich. In addition to its limp and down-at-heel appearance, even the sandwich tasted like it had been hanging around on the counter of the station cafeteria for much more than a couple of days.

"At least the tea is hot, and the sun promises to make an appearance anytime soon" was the general feelings of we frustrated passengers. The sun did eventually appear, spilling its brilliant early dawn light over a frost-laden landscape that stretched as far as the eye could see in almost every direction. Australia certainly did have an endless vault of sky hanging over it. Today all Mavis and I wished for was to get to Melbourne, down a hot meal, have a long sleep and to hell with the bloody landscape, the endless Australian sky, New South Wales and its shitty railway. I couldn't also forget to include in my mental diatribe our former lying bastard of a sponsor, his crappy house and his two non-designers and often altered patterns back in semi-outback Guildford!

A very angry young Pommie you could have accurately described me as at the time, as my wife and I stood huddled together in a cold, bleak and unheated platform waiting room, in what felt like and probably was – the middle of nowhere!

We had yet to wait for the arrival of the daylight version of the train from Albury to Melbourne. I had also by that time morphed into the form of a very angry 'whingeing Pommie!'

I was, however, more angry with myself for having got us both into such a crappy situation. If things don't get any better in Melbourne, what would we do then? I was also beginning to regret having committed us both to two years in this strange country. It had been me after all that had jumped feet first at the first opportunity on offer to migrate here that had presented itself, although realistically who could have foreseen what was to eventuate at the Ernest Hiller company?

Hours passed, the air still cold and we hungry for a hot meal and a good night's sleep among people we knew and loved.

Eventually, a train heaved into sight from the south, the train in those days known as Spirit of Progress. It eventually appeared over the southern horizon, its semi- streamlined dark blue shape speeding toward its long-suffering passengers to Melbourne. Everyone on that cold platform was looking forward to a speedy transit to Melbourne, at the very least, all were hoping for a distinct improvement over what we had experienced on the New South Wales side of the border.

In due course, as the sun rose higher in the north-eastern sky, we were able to climb on-board the Spirit of Progress and eventually into what turned out to be a warm, comfortable compartment, on a train that did claim to have a dining car among its carriages. But for we two cold, hungry, unenthusiastic and dead-tired £10 Pommie migrants, all we wanted to do was snuggle together as best we could and, as patiently as possible await our eventual arrival in Melbourne.

At last and the best part of a day after leaving Sydney's Central Railway Station saw our train journey from hell thankfully ended, as the Spirit of Progress steamed into Melbourne's Spencer Street Station during the afternoon. Thankfully also without having to experience another breakdown or long stopover en-route from Albury.

We were welcomed into Melbourne by an aunt and uncle who,

after bundling two exhausted and angry young people into Uncle Barney's FJ Holden, said that they had nearly given up hope of seeing us again after such a long delay. We also learned that on the day of our arrival, my cousin's wife Brenda had just given birth to a beautiful baby daughter that they had named Sandra.

At least in one sense, our arrival in Melbourne had proved to be a source of joy. That good news served to crowd out some of the frustrations of the previous 20-odd hours – crawling along on a Third World-standard railway service that the New South Wales transport authorities had grossly over-described as being 'first-class'.

My aunt suggested that we should register a claim against Railways of New South Wales for the inconveniences experienced on our trip to Albury. At the time, all we were interested in was to get as far away as possible from the Railways of New South Wales, trains in general and the most frustrating and disappointing few weeks of my life to date. Surely, things must get better…?

6

HELLO, MELBOURNE

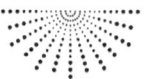

On arrival at my aunt and uncle's house on Glen Eira Road, Elsternwick, Mavis and I ate our first meal in over a day. After an evening during which we sleepily chatted while exchanging news of the family back in Leeds, we were then bundled into a single bed hastily set up in a corner of the dining room. Despite the lack of room in which to spread ourselves out, we cuddled together, as snug as two bugs in a rug, falling into what proved to be a long, dreamless sleep, until well into the next morning.

Following breakfast, Mavis by that time had calmed down a little, although I couldn't blame her in the circumstances for wanting to book herself onto the next ship back to England. She had reasonably expected to be at least provided with what we had been promised regarding my position, salary and our accommodation in Guildford. Not only that, but when she finally got to visit the mouldy near-hovel that our sponsor had expected us to live in, I believe anyone would have reacted the way she did.

That man Hiller had acted like an out-and-out moron, but he overstepped the mark when he started to abuse my wife. That finally did it for me, and even though slow to blow my top, it took most of my control not to lean over his executive desk and clock him one on his ugly, smirking dial.

Thankfully by now, Ernest Hiller, his factory and his false promises were now nearly 800 miles behind us. That being the case, we decided that after a day or so familiarising ourselves with the surrounding streets and shops around Elsternwick and St Kilda, we would seek suitable permanent accommodation. Perhaps we might now be able to settle down to a more comfortable and productive life?

Financially, we felt that we would be OK for a while, our supply of ready money having been boosted somewhat with both our wages added to the additional compensation we had wrung out of Hiller.

On the negative side, I now found myself in much the same situation as most of my fellow travellers on-board Orion. I was now without a job, but was assured by my uncle that there were plenty of positions available with one or other of the apparel manufacturing companies based in and around Melbourne. I learned that a number of these had been established along Flinders Lane, in central Melbourne. Other apparel manufacturers of varying sizes were apparently also spread around other suburbs around the city, mainly to the north of the CBD – Carlton, Fitzroy and Brunswick.

Over the following weekend, in addition to exploratory trips by tram down to the local beach and the Carlisle Street shops in nearby St Kilda, I spent most of the time studiously scanning the 'positions vacant' column in *The Age*, one of Melbourne's morning newspapers.

The host of classified advertisements in *The Age* appeared to confirm Uncle Barney's view on the local employment scene. There certainly were a large number of various kinds of positions being advertised. Unfortunately, looking through the main Saturday morning version of *The Age* newspaper, there didn't appear to be any of the local apparel manufacturers seeking the kind of services of real interest to me.

100 HOTHAM STREET, ST KILDA

Mavis and I had been successful during the weekend, in our search for accommodation reasonably close to my auntie's place. We were overjoyed following a quick inspection, to find a comfortable single-bedroom apartment that looked to meet our needs at its convenient location at 100 Hotham Street, St Kilda. The apartment was located close to the intersection of Hotham and Carlisle streets, a position that was also close to public transport and shopping. And, it was only a short tram ride from our new accommodation to St Kilda's beachfront onto Port Phillip Bay.

Our first, permanent home in Melbourne was simply but adequately furnished and, at the very reasonable eight pounds, ten shillings per week was one of three apartments earlier subdivided within what in earlier days had been a large rambling old house. The elderly owners of the property, Mr and Mrs Grey, had vacated the original house for a newly built modern home located on the Hotham Street frontage of the property, having later decided to divide the old house into three, good-sized apartments.

Our first home in Melbourne was located at the back of the house. It comprised a high-ceilinged lounge room, adjacent to which was a small kitchen. It also had a shower and toilet located outside the flat and across the back corridor. Our bedroom was located above the old house's laundry, accessed from the lounge room via a short flight of stairs. It was a quaint, comfortable and homely apartment, a simple layout that suited our needs perfectly. We later learned that our new home had served as accommodation for the original owners' live-in servants, sometime during a bygone era.

We secured our new accommodation on the Monday following our arrival in Melbourne.

ON THE LOOKOUT FOR WORK

Following Uncle Barney's assertion that there should be plenty of jobs available among Melbourne's apparel manufacturers, I decided to try my luck by travelling into the city in search of gainful employment. This plan, a day or two after moving into our first home together, followed busy days moving our hand-held possessions and what we virtually stood up in, plus one additional change of clothes, all the clothing in our possession at the time. We then set about purchasing a set of bed sheets, crockery, cutlery, a couple of pots and pans, kettle, etc., and other necessary items with which to commence occupation. We also arranged for the company transporting our cabin trunk from its storage in Sydney, to now forward it on to our new address.

The next morning, while Mavis attended to buying food and other needed stuff from the shops along nearby Carlisle Street, with which to start our lives in Melbourne, I sallied forth on-board a city-bound bus into Melbourne's CBD, with the idea of exploring what the city had to offer regarding work.

I had noted a number of advertisements in *The Age* newspaper on the Saturday prior, all of which were seeking the services of cutters, tailors and machinists of various kinds. While none of these positions were of much interest to me, at least they went some way toward providing an indication as to company names and locations within the city, suggesting places where I should start my search.

On reached the city, I wandered around for a while to get myself oriented. This turned out to be simpler than I had imagined, with the city's main central streets set out in a square grid pattern. I found it relatively easy to orient myself, using the street map supplied by my uncle. Even then, the size of the Melbourne CBD was so much larger than anything I had experienced before, the centre of Leeds being relatively easy to fit into just a few blocks of the much larger central Melbourne shopping precinct.

Following Uncle Barney's more detailed advice, provided in the form of a scribbled diagram, I set about locating Flinders Lane, a narrow street which in those days formed the central focus of much of the then fashion apparel manufacturing industry in Melbourne.

Having located Flinders Lane, I started my job search by walking down that narrow, busy street, which by the time of my arrival was chock-a-block with people, vans, carts, clothes racks and other activities around the many small apparel related establishments that filled the lane. Nearly all were involved in the manufacture and distribution of all kinds of men's women's and children's clothing.

Most of the manufacturers I passed appeared to be small establishments, comprising what looked to be one or two owner-operated. The activities along that relatively narrow street also seemed to be organised very much along the lines of those I had left behind during my early years as a tailor's improver in the North Street district of Leeds, but on a much larger scale. None thus far however even looked to be of the size that would or could be interested in employing a designer/pattern-cutter on a full-time basis.

The further I ventured down the lane, the more it seemed that there were few manufacturing operations large enough to suit my needs located there. Disappointment was beginning to set in.

My search appeared to be developing into a non-productive first try. That is until on venturing further down Flinders Lane and closer to Swanston Street – Melbourne's major north/south central hub, where I finally arrived at a factory frontage that looked to be more substantial than those further up the street. On looking the building up and down from street level, it appeared to be a much larger operation than those surrounding it. The sign fixed on the building's facade announced the company's name as Keith Courtenay.

As luck would have it, I didn't get beyond this, my first inquiry, as following my approach and inquiry at the ground-floor office window,

I was pleasantly surprised. Following providing my name and asking the receptionist if the company had a vacancy for a qualified designer/pattern-cutter, I found myself being escorted up onto the first floor. There I was introduced to the factory manager, a Mr Fisher. I was then happily and even more surprised to learn that news apparently travelled very quickly among the widespread, but obviously close-knit Australian apparel manufacturing industry.

In spite of the distance between Sydney and Melbourne, it soon became clear that news of my arrival at the Ernest Hiller company and the manner of my departure was already known here in Melbourne. It also seems that the details of my loud and heated altercation with Ernest Hiller, followed by my abrupt departure from Sydney after such a short time, had also preceded me. During our conversation, I was happy to learn that there was a shortage of technically qualified designer/pattern-cutters across Australia's men's and women's wholesale apparel manufacturers, at the time mainly located in Melbourne and Sydney.

Following discussion regarding my qualifications, experience and expectations here in Australia, laced liberally with cups of tea and my first taste of 'Ginger Nut' biscuits, I was pleasantly surprised to be offered a starting position with the company as designer/pattern-cutter. The position offered and happily accepted, was on the basis of a three-month trial, during which I would be employed with a starting salary of £18 per week, these arrangements to be reviewed on completion of the trial period.

It was interesting to also learn that news of my clash with Ernest Hiller had shortly thereafter become widely known among Hiller's competition around Sydney. One or two Sydney-based apparel manufacturers had apparently expected me to remain in Sydney seeking another position. My demand for recompense from Hiller, along with our threat to sue for misrepresenting the position he had originally offered me, had shortly thereafter also spread to Melbourne.

I was left with the impression, thinking later about the offer I had received here in Melbourne, that the factory manager at the Keith Courtenay Company had decided to offer me employment before I got to call on another, perhaps rival apparel manufacturer? Hmm … chance had certainly popped up an interesting scenario?

"What a strange position to find oneself in" I mused, as excitedly I later exited the Keith Courtenay building, with a spring in my step, hardly believing my good luck. Unfortunately, in my excitement and desire to get back to Mavis with my news, I became disoriented, taking some time to relocate where I had left the bus back to Hotham Street. In my excitement at being successful at snaring a job at my first try, being unfamiliar with the layout of Melbourne's inner city I had seriously misread the city map my Uncle Barney had given me. I can only put it down to my excitement at securing a position so quickly that had left me confused, this also being my very first foray into the city of Melbourne.

After wandering around like a lost soul for a while, I at last managed to locate the right bus stop. On boarding the correct bus, I requested the bus driver to let me know when we arrived at the intersection of Carlisle and Hotham streets. On my arrival home at last, my good news had us both dancing for joy in celebration.

It had been a good day on several accounts. Mavis had stocked up the refrigerator with food and other goodies, plus a bottle of local wine that failed to last through the evening. My new position was a real plus and, also of importance, we two were alone at last in our own home for the first time in our married lives!

Life certainly seemed to be looking up. We had arrived in Melbourne but a few days since had found and moved into a comfortable little flat in St Kilda, and at my very first attempt I had managed to snare what I hoped would turn out to be a good position. The salary offered would enable us to pay our way, and having now settled in Melbourne would allow us to seek out and meet up again with friends, both old and new.

It didn't take too long for us to re-establish contact with Norma and Frank Brown, the Manchester couple we had met on the train to Tilbury, on the very first day of our journey out to Australia. Even more astounding was the speed with which we had been able to secure an apartment and that I was already looking forward to taking up my second position in Australia. I was still just 24 years old.

KEITH COURTENAY PTY LTD

Unlike most other apparel manufacturing and their associated textile supply companies that operated from various locations along Flinders Lane during the 1950s, 1960s and 1970s, the Keith Courtenay production plant operated over several levels at the one address between Swanston and Russell streets. Most of the other, mainly smaller apparel manufacturing establishments up and down that narrow and always busy lane had been established in what in earlier times had probably been either one or other of multi-storied residencies, shops, factories or warehouses.

The various large and small manufacturing organisations that operated in buildings along the Flinders Lane of the late 1950s covered the full spectrum of functions involving apparel manufacturing and marketing. Manufacturing and related activities operated between Queen Street in the east, to and a little beyond Russell Street to the west. These included warehousing and other connected operations of various kinds, most, if not all of which having something or other to do with something universally known across Melbourne as 'the rag trade'. The industry in later years even had its regular newspaper, titled *Ragtrader*.

Most of the smaller men's or women's apparel manufacturing operations along Flinders Lane during the 1950s and 1960s occupied one or perhaps two levels at any given address along the lane. Other manufacturers and suppliers of fabrics and trimmings were also located at the northern edge of the CBD, along Swanston Street, Carlton. A few of the manufacturing operations along Flinders Lane shared their building with other manufacturers, suppliers of fabrics, trimmings and other associated products – in other cases this included the offices of one or two manufacturers' agents.

Some of the apparel manufacturing businesses even had various parts of their activities located separately in different buildings along the Lane, requiring them to transport partly completed garments to and from one location to another. Thus, during a working day, a constant stream of handcarts, clothing racks full of part-completed garments of all kinds could be seen along the lane, all being pushed, pulled or carried manually.

During the late 1950s and 1960s, other parts of the inner-city area, away from Flinders Lane, also housed apparel manufacturers of varying sizes and areas of operation. These ranged from boys and children's wear, through to men's and women's fashion-wear, fabric and trimming merchants, knitters, garment finishers, dry cleaners and pressers, etc. The majority of these operations were to be found as far north as Carlton, Brunswick, Fitzroy and Coburg and as far south of the river Yarra as Prahran and South Yarra.

In addition to apparel manufacturing, Melbourne also housed an extensive range of spinning, knitting and weaving mills, most located in and around suburbs to the north and west of the city and nearby Geelong.

The nearby city of Geelong during the 1960s and for many years in the past had been the central hub for Australia's wool processing and export trade, with major wool-scouring, combing, top-making and spinning operations established there. Geelong also served to cater for the various needs of woolgrowers, wool traders and exporters operating across Australia's southern states. Geelong itself was home to some of Australia's leading worsted and woollen spinning, weaving and finishing mills.

As can be seen from this summary, both the textile and apparel manufacturing industries, at least throughout eastern Australia during the 1950s and 1960s, were both vigorous and widespread. While most manufacturing operations were located mainly in the major metropolitan centres, predominantly Melbourne and Sydney, there were also many country towns and regional centres in which spinning and weaving mills were established. Many of these smaller towns and rural centres also had their own, usually one owner knitting mills, a number of them producing high-quality knitwear. One or two local spinning mills specialised in the production of hand-knitting yarns.

Both major arms of the industry, apparel manufacturing and textile production had for many years formed a vital part of the established manufacturing, employment and social structures throughout

Australia's major cities and a number of inner-country-based rural centres.

Wool at the time continued to be the predominant fibre used by most, particularly in the manufacture of men's and women's outerwear. Wool was also Australia's then major export, and the country's major source of export income. To be discussed later in Part 8 and later, poorly thought-through industry policy-making led to the eventual collapse of the Australian wool industry in 1991.

Introduced by successive federal governments during the 1980s through to the early 2000s, reductions in import tariff protection for the textile and apparel industries eventually resulted in the all too rapid decline and ultimate near demise of local textile and apparel production across Australia.

A CHANGING INDUSTRY

Both the textile and apparel sectors of Australia's industrial mix found them having to adapt to massive changes during the two decades 1980–2000. During the period, rates of tariff protection for the textiles, clothing and footwear (TCF) sector declined from 85.5% to 25.6% and lower.

A Productivity Commission report published in 2003 noted:

> In recent years, competition from emerging low-wage production centres, slowing growth in consumer demand, large reductions in domestic assistance and increased concentration in retailing, have collectively placed new pressures on local TCF manufacturers. Many firms have left the sector, while others have rationalised, merged and pursued new sourcing strategies in order to survive. As a result, aggregate domestic TCF manufacturing activity has contracted and import penetration has risen sharply. Industry restructuring and rationalisation, in combination with a sharp rise in import penetration to more than 50% of the total TCF market, have resulted in contractions in overall TCF manufacturing output and employment ... The sector's aggregate value added fell by more than

30% in real terms between 1991–2001, while employment was approximately 35% lower.

Meanwhile back in 1959, Australia's still extensively based apparel, and textile manufacturing industries continued to operate profitably, with both sectors continuing to support high levels of full-time employment.

At the time, there were more jobs than people needed to fill them. Such was the state of the then Australian economy, where jobs were easy to come by and people managed to live reasonably well-paid, secure and fully occupied lives.

As for this young newcomer to Australia, the position and salary I had secured at Keith Courtenay enabled Mavis and me to settle into our comfortable little apartment and at last, begin to feel more at ease when considering our futures in Australia. Being in our own home at long last also served to diminish Mavis's desire to book passage on the next available ship back to Britain.

Jobs in those days were relatively easy to find in Melbourne, and in my case, my weekly starting salary was sufficient to enable us to establish ourselves with a reasonable amount of comfort, even allowing us the capacity to save some of my salary each week.

Within a few weeks of our arrival in Melbourne, Mavis successfully secured a permanent position, in her case in the administration offices of the then Caulfield Institute of Technology, a position that she held until a few weeks before the birth of our first child in August 1961.

FINDING MY FEET

During the month or so since commencing work with Keith Courtenay, future longer-term prospects there were looking to be somewhat limited.

I had very quickly found that although relatively comfortable as a workplace and being reasonably well paid, the manner in which the company operated did not appear to offer much in the way of personal development, at least beyond that of a barely functioning pattern-cutter. Here, much the same as I had found at the Ernest Hiller factory, there was a distinct lack of professionalism, particularly in the way the company's management and production system operated.

One aspect of this, particularly when it came to my area of operations, lacked any pretence of having a well-established formalised system of management and operations control. There was also little evidence of a formalised management structure operating across the factory, and in my field, there was a lack of any real interest in the development and implementation of product and processing specifications. There was also a lack of any interest on the part of the company's management toward any development plans, beyond the basic inflexible workflow system that had obviously been in use there for many years.

The importance, or rather lack thereof, when it came to the need to maintain a range of precise master patterns on the part of my employers, was similar to the attitudes I had found during my all too brief stay at the Ernest Hiller company.

Most of the master patterns used at Keith Courtenay had seen better days, most of them survivors from decades past. Having been altered and replaced many times, they now failed to represent a reliable and accurate sequence of sizes.

It also became evident, even after just a few weeks working for the company, that for such a long-established industry, there was no sign of any formal industry-wide technical training facilities having been established in either of Melbourne or Sydney. As a consequence, management and section leaders within the company appeared to have gained their knowledge of a technical nature by a process I think best described as slow osmosis. None I knew of held any form of recognised technical qualifications.

When discussing the issue of technical training with the company's management, they showed not even the slightest interest. None I got to speak to even felt any need for the establishment of technical training facilities, aimed at providing the company and industry in general with trained patternmakers and other well-trained technical and production management operatives.

For an Australian apparel manufacturing industry, as widespread as it was at the time, its leaders were less interested in providing their production staff with opportunities to advance themselves, being more interested in pushing as much production possible through their factories – at the lowest cost to them.

Such a policy, while understandable from their point of view at the time, also served to limit the interest of individual employers toward updating and incorporating modern methods of factory layout and management processes into their production plants, most of which it should be noted, were relatively small and dispersed.

The general attitude described here was in direct contrast to the range and scope of creative and technical design and production management training that had been available for years in the fields of apparel manufacture and textile production among leading companies in Britain and the United States. Even in Europe, not so many years following a devastating war, apparel manufacturing across the continent's major centres was already advancing rapidly when it came to technical training and the introduction of updated production systems and equipment.

Years of intensive study at the LCT had provided me with a much higher level of technical education – even experience, than that available to production staff thus far in Australia. That being the case, the two factories that I had worked in to date, fell well short of the level of technical and management standards under which I had been working, while receiving high-quality technical training.

While there were no recognised institutions in either Melbourne or Sydney specialising in the training of subjects like production management systems and design, there was one training centre that dealt specifically with the weaving and knitting industries. This excellent facility was based at the Melbourne College of Textiles, at its location in Cumberland Road, Pascoe Vale.

Historically, nearly every one of the larger Australian apparel manufacturing companies operating during the late 1950s and early 1960s had grown, mainly through acquisition or amalgamation.

Most of the original factory owners continued to operate their now growing organisations much in the same manner as they had when they were much smaller operations, operating in a style best described as 'hand-to-mouth'. The owners as their businesses grew, continued to remain in full control across every minor aspect of the growing company and its different areas of operation, this even as the company eventually grew to be much larger.

As their companies grew larger, owners found themselves having to employ organisers in the form of male or female section leaders (foremen and women). Eventually the need arrived when it became necessary to employ a staff co-ordinator, usually designated as the 'factory manager'. While staffing titles changed, the company continued to use the same workflow system and production methods that had worked successfully when it was still small. This usually meant the continuation of what was then best known and described as a simple 'bundle' system of production.

Once a company had expanded to become a much larger operation, continued use of the relatively simple bundle system tended to limit the flexibility and thus the flow of work along the factory's production line.

Throughout Australia little had changed over the years when it came to accepting forward indent orders from their retailer customers. Production management systems represented not much more than translating these orders into what were generally termed as 'cuttings', with the bundling of a number of garments together, as they passed through the various processes throughout the production phase.

It was not at the time thought to be necessary to upgrade and systemise materials purchasing, factory workflow, development of formal specifications and costing systems. Australia still remained a relative backwater when it came to technical training and systems development during the early years since my arrival. Overseas, the importance of technical training and improved production and management systems had been recognised for a number of years. Improvements to their internal systems were constantly being implemented in production plants across Britain, western Europe and the US.

In Australia, decisions on changes in the area of aesthetic and technical apparel design, pattern-making and the production of control templates and other key production aids, were usually made on an ad hoc basis. It was only later, as the industry began to consolidate into larger organisations during the late 1960s and 1970s, that company principals, who by then had begun to travel extensively overseas, began to realise the need for more expertise, accuracy and professionalism to be adopted in their manufacturing operations.

Pattern design eventually became more than just the representation of fashion and line. As the years progressed, company owners were forced to give more attention and recognition to the economic needs of their production plants. This also meant the need to take account, not only of the style of a garment – also the manner in which patterns were to be designed and arranged, so that the cutting of cloth and trimmings could be achieved as economically as possible.

As manufacturers grew and became more complex to manage, so their owners came to recognise the need to improve their management and control systems. In turn production became more efficient. The more innovative companies also began to incorporate more advanced features into pattern design, production systems and time management. All were aimed at improved economy efficiency and, as a result – increased profitability.

Increased profitability brought with it the opportunity for some forward-thinking companies, particularly those seeking to expand their influence across a broader front, to take over and absorb some of the still remaining smaller, less efficient manufacturing operations.

The Keith Courtenay company, along with other apparel factories located in the inner suburbs of Melbourne, had given little thought to improving its production system and style of management. Other than the introduction of improved sewing machines and other basic equipment, no attention was being devoted to the modernising of archaic and inflexible production systems. Neither was there felt a need for more critical thought being given to professional and further technical training for staff having the potential to move into management positions.

There was also a dire need to install improved lighting, consider the development of more efficient production layouts, along with seeking to upgrade and improve the state of master cloth and associated lining/trimming patterns and systems of manufacture.

At Keith Courtenay, most of the patterns still being used had been adjusted time and again by bits being trimmed off or stuck back on by various means, mostly in a less than efficient manner – so that the patterns currently in use had little resemblance to the originals.

On more than one occasion during my relatively short time with the company, individual section leaders would come to me and demand an alteration to a particular pattern be made, without even knowing how that alteration would affect the garment. While having to make ad hoc adjustments as demanded, the integrity of the patterns became disturbed and disjointed. Such changes often resulted in down-the-line production, fitting and, in some cases, styling problems.

Ultimately, by the time the industry had entered the 1970s and later into the 1980s, companies having a similar outlook to that of the Keith Courtenay Company, had either been taken over by larger, more forward-looking companies, or they gradually declined and gradually went out of business.

Following a month or so working with Keith Courtenay, I was also sensing that the future for me there was going to be limited. I resolved, therefore, to start actively looking around Melbourne in the hope of finding a more progressive company with which to work.

GETTING AROUND MELBOURNE BY RED RATTLER AND TRAM

While still working for Keith Courtenay, it didn't take long for me to become a part of what universally, affectionately and colourfully was known up and down Flinders Lane as – the 'shmatta[1] trade'.

My regular workday would commence with a ride into the city on one of the then infamous and relatively ancient 'Red Rattler' trains – mine from the nearby Carlisle Street station, but a five-minute walk from home. The train journey of around 25 minutes delivered both me, and thousands of other day workers into the venerable Flinders Street railway station. Melbourne's central railway station was located just a few minutes' walk across Swanston Street and up Flinders Lane to the Keith Courtenay factory.

Travelling into the city on one of Melbourne's Red Rattler trains was an experience that could be both uncomfortable and draughty.

This early type of Melbourne train, all painted a dusty shade of red, comprised carriages divided into single compartments, each compartment having a door at each end, across the carriage's width. Travellers, particularly during the morning or evening 'rush hour' could often find themselves being crushed together with other travelling companions.

Once wedged within a particular compartment and on their way to Flinders Street Station, passengers were unable to move from their compartment to another in a different part of a carriage, this type of train having no connecting corridor. Even worse, however, travelling on a Red Rattler during the colder, wet and wintry months became very uncomfortable, because the then ageing upper bodywork of each carriage along these by then rapidly ageing trains had been constructed mainly of timber.

Ancient even by the 1950s, the windows, nearly every door and even the general cabin structure of this type of train at the time had, after surviving many years of unstinting service, begun to 'shake, rattle and roll'. In some of the older versions the rattling sound as they travelled along, 'clickety-clacking' along the city's railway system, could almost feel as though the carriage in which you were travelling was well on its way to falling apart. Hence the 'Red Rattler' title for this kind of train had become universally applied by Melbourne's long-suffering travelling public.

At full speed, with every component of each carriage shaking and rattling – doors and window frames sometimes visibly flexing and moving around on some of the more ancient versions, would serve, depending on the speed of the train and the time of year, to release a blast of cold, often damp, rain-filled air into each compartment.

During the colder months, anyone seated next to a window or standing close to the door at either end of a compartment could expect to bear the brunt of a steady stream of cold air. The doors on these trains by now rarely closed without leaving one or two small gaps and, alongside their companion windows, would continue to rattle and creak, as the train clicked along on its merry way.

Melbourne's people-transporting system, comprising tramcars, buses and trains, was extensive in 1959. The city's trains today however, are much improved than those already old Red Rattlers, some 58 years ago.

The Melbourne tramcar network, in particular, is currently reputed to be the world's largest urban light rail network – with more than 250km of duplicated track. It is a system that has been operating continuously since 1884 when Melbourne's first public transport services began operations with the opening of a horse-drawn tram servicing the then outer northern suburb of Fairfield. This early service developed later into a cable driven system, similar to the famous cable system still to be found in San Francisco. Today's modern services are fully electrically driven.

Unlike Sydney's now long forgotten 'toast rack'-style trams, its narrower streets and less ordered city layout, Melbourne's inner city, with its well-planned wide streets and major boulevards, continued to retain and improve its tramway services. Today they cover most of the inner and even some of the outer fringes of the metropolitan area.

Melbourne's green and ochre painted W class electric driven trams entered into service in 1926. They continued to carry passengers around Melbourne for the next 40 years until updated and replaced by the more modern versions in service today.

Although relatively slow in terms of getting from place to place around a widespread metropolitan layout, Melbourne's tram services today continue to carry hundreds of thousands of passengers daily to and from the city and across most of its suburbs.

Notes

1. Schmatta – (Yiddish slang): clothing, textiles; pejorative – means rags worn by a person, old and tattered clothing.

A WORKING DAY IN MELBOURNE

A working day at most apparel, textile and other production plants across Melbourne during the late 1950s usually commenced at 8am. Work hours went through to a lunchtime break, usually at 1pm, the normal working day finishing at 5pm through Monday to Friday. This added up to a 40-hour working week. There was also what was known locally as a 'smoko' break during the mid-morning and afternoon. Smoko usually comprised a short ten-minute break that allowed sufficient time in which to swill down a cup of tea, munch on a bun or sandwich, and smoke a cigarette.

Smoking was not permitted anywhere in the Keith Courtenay factory but was allowed within the toilets. You can imagine the availability of clear, breathable air (or rather the lack of it) that would be left inside the windowless toilet facilities in this ageing factory, by the time the morning or afternoon smoko break was over. After my first visit to one of the factory's toilets, and failing in an endeavour to hold my breath until safely outside after one such smoko break, I decided to avoid as many future visits as possible, until well after the usually toxic cloud of tobacco smoke and other not very pleasant odours had cleared.

The factory machine room at Keith Courtenay, like many others at the time, was set out with parallel lines of sewing machines. Each of these lines was powered by an electric motor located at one end of a double line of up to 20 machines. Each separate machine had its own separate workspace, each set up in a row on each side of a central shaft, with each sewing machine powered by pulleys running from it. As can be imagined, this kind of setup was inflexible as well as being very noisy, particularly with every line of sewing machines going full tilt.

The factory workrooms were relatively dark, the only useful lighting, apart from two relatively small windows set into a sidewall, was provided by banks of fluorescent light tubes suspended above each double row of machines.

The cutting room was somewhat quieter, as was my working area, itself partitioned off from the second floor cutting room.

The owners of this and most other of the era's apparel factories were yet to learn of the psychological and medical need to supply ample natural light for their operatives to work under. It was to be some years yet before factory owners began to understand that the very nature of fluorescent tube lighting, made it a less than satisfactory means of illuminating work spaces, particularly where intricate sewing and similar functions were being carried out.

Having made it to the end of a day's work, many of the predominantly male workers down Flinders Lane, augmented by other male inner-city workers and professional, would usually stop off at one or other of the local pubs close by for what was generally termed as a 'wet'. I soon came to understand the need for a beer, or two or more, that many among the city's male working population felt, prior to them catching public transport home each evening for dinner with the family.

During the 1950s an after-work 'wet', as practiced almost exclusively by most Melbourne beer drinkers, bore not the slightest resemblance to anything I had ever experienced back in Leeds. The 'art' of drinking in Melbourne I soon found, had been elevated to a level well beyond just the mere partaking of an after-work beer, along with a chat with one's workmates…

MELBOURNE'S 'SIX O'CLOCK SWILL'

Those familiar with the layout of Melbourne's CBD would also be familiar with Melbourne's most famous, and in those days beloved central 'watering hole' (drinking venue). This was an old established pub known simply to all as 'Young & Jackson's'.

This famous inner-city pub was the best known of Melbourne's city-based and inner suburban drinking establishments; it also boasted a reputation, both interstate and international. Young & Jacksons had graced the city of Melbourne since opening in 1861 at its location on the northeast corner of the intersection of Swanston and Flinders streets. The pub's location remains in the same spot to this day, conveniently and strategically positioned directly opposite the equally venerable Flinders Street railway station.

Anyone entering the Melbourne CBD from Flinders Street railway station today, and having the intention of proceeding into the city centre down Swanston Street, will find them needing to cross over Flinders Street from the station and pass the Young and Jackson's hotel frontage and its ever-present 'crown' of illuminated advertising above the building on their way. The history of this famous hotel's site reaches back in time almost to the beginning of European settlement in then- fledgling Melbourne.

An early Melbourne pioneer and later businessman, John Batman[1] originally purchased the hotel site at Melbourne's first sale of Crown land, in 1837. At the time, he built a home on the site for his children, which later became a schoolhouse in 1839. Warehouses were erected after the schoolhouse was razed in 1853.

The Princes Bridge Hotel opened on the site on July 1st 1861 and was renamed Young & Jackson after the two Irish diggers who took it over in 1875, Henry Young and Thomas Jackson. The hotel still retains the names of its founders and has become well-known throughout Australia, as well to well-travelled drinkers across the world. To this day this famous drinking establishment is still known to all simply as Young & Jacksons.

It was to this now historic establishment that at the ending of every working day, many of the city's male population, including more than a few from the Keith Courtenay factory, would attend for their daily injection of alcohol. My first invitation to partake of what at the time was loosely described as 'a wet' came on the Friday evening that ended my first week working for the company.

Not being much of a beer drinker, the thought of downing a glass of shandy before boarding the train home that evening had appealed. It was also my first introduction to Young & Jackson's famous painting of a naked young lady, famously known as Chloe, then hanging in its pride of place on the wall of the hotel's main bar.

Chloe's full-length nude image had been immortalised by French artist Jules Lefebvre in 1875, the painting having first been purchased by a Dr Thomas Fitzgerald of Lonsdale Street. Following its hanging in the National Gallery of Victoria for three weeks in 1883, this at the time risqué depiction of the naked, young Chloe had to be withdrawn from view, due it seems to the uproar it created, especially by the then so-called 'Presbyterian Assembly', Melbourne.

The then owners of Young & Jacksons bought the painting for a reputed £800 in 1908, then hung it in the main bar where it graced the hotel from that time on.

The picture of young Chloe suffered a glancing blow a long time after being hung in a prominent position in the main bar. This unprovoked assault was reported to have occurred in 1943 when an overly inebriated and angry American serviceman was alleged to have thrown a glass of beer at her. The image of Chloe survived, prevailed and continued to preside in all her naked glory, on the wall of that venerable pub.

By five-thirty each weekday afternoon, following the time when most of the local working population 'knocked-off' from their daily labours across the city, Young & Jackson's would become crowded with working men of all descriptions, all drawn from every level of Melbourne society.

The Hotel's clientele included Queen's Counsels, perhaps even judges, solicitors and others from among the legal brotherhood. Also regularly in attendance were smartly dressed shop assistants, factory workers, bank employees and men clad in rough working clothes, all having just emerged from one or other of the banks, law courts, legal chambers, shops, factories and building sites around the inner CBD. All, in one way or another, could lay claim to have completed what was often referred to at the time as a day of 'hard yakka' (hard work). Now they were thirsty and in dire need of their daily wet.

Drinking Melbourne-style in 1959, at least to a newcomer like me, was very much like a kind of sport. It also became apparent that the status of being capable of drinking large quantities of strong, locally brewed beer, counted toward a 'bloke' (fellow or man) being able to make his claim to being a 'genuine Aussie'. This was a standard and status recognised among the Australian male fraternity as desirable in its achievement, at least it was among the city's regular drinkers.

The practice of copious beer drinking among men only in any of Melbourne's bars of the 1950s could also be likened to an exclusive gathering of the city's male brotherhood.

The scene during the late afternoon, on any day of the working week in Young & Jacksons, was an education, particularly to any newcomer like me, who had yet to see anything coming close to the drinking habits of Melbourne's hardened drinkers of strong, locally brewed beer. It often proved to be a deafening concatenation of kindred souls at that, once the pub's all male clientele got down to the serious business of downing as much cold beer possible, to be achieved in the shortest possible time.

If trying to carry on a conversation with a drinking mate just sitting across the table from you, or while breasting up to the bar, such was the throb of ultra-loud conversations bouncing off the walls of the main bar, that the conversation had to be shouted to rise above the echoing din that permeated throughout the public bar. At such times, a normal level of conversation became almost impossible to carry on, unless you were able to either lip-read or shout louder than other drinkers standing around a nearby, beer-soaked table.

By the time my new friends and I had successfully wedged ourselves around a corner table near the main bar at Young & Jacksons in preparation for my first visit to this holy of drinking holies, the place was already awash with brotherly love. Everyone present seemed intent on giving concentrated attention to one another's drinking needs. The drinking was generally carried on amid loud discussion around such deep and meaningful subjects as "the footy" (Australian rules football), or "what was running" referring to the local "gee-gees" (horse races), or "the bloody government" (self-explanatory) – plus anything else along similar lines.

Whether a Queen's Counsel, banker, tailor, cutter, retailer or plumber – be he a manager or just a lowly cleaner – there they all stood, cheek by jowl, everyone seemingly capable of non-stop drinking from extra-large glasses of locally sourced amber fluid, brewed in nearby Carlton. Powerful stuff it was too – served icy cold!

Like Mavis and I had found during our stay in Guildford, the local pub, particularly the main bar, was then regarded as being the sole and exclusive domain of the Australian male. Being so, it was perhaps reasonable to assume that other local pubs throughout the city and suburbs would also be regarded as a male retreat from the missus back home, or female work companions and girlfriends left behind recently, in and around the city or local workplace. The local pub, when it came down to basics, was a place where men could get together and feel safely locked-away within the security of an alcohol-lubricated sanctuary, well away from the influence of the women in their lives.

My first impressions of the scene on entering Young & Jacksons for the first time, was one of a milling group of trilby and similarly hatted gents, alongside overalls and manual workers wearing caps, all 'supping' on 'pots' or 'schooners' of Melbourne Bitter beer. Everyone in that bar seemed to be drinking with such intensity that it gave the impression that there was to be no tomorrow.

What was also amazing to watch was the speed with which the multiple barmen (including at least one female), were capable of speedily filling a multitude of rapidly emptied glasses, all at the same time, the beer being delivered by way of long, flexible hoses. At the delivery end of each hose, was a petrol bowser type of nozzle, through which beer was being ejected along and into the lines of glasses regularly presented along the pub's bar. The bar was covered in what very quickly had become a beer-soaked strip of towelling.

Talk about a quick and efficient delivery system! Nothing that I had ever seen before could even come close!

My first glass of the stuff that my new colleagues were downing with such gusto, seemingly without any discernible ill effects, was very strong. Too strong for me I had decided, after making an attempt to down a tentative mouthful. In contrast to my new-found friends, even at their urging and accompanying comments along the lines of… "Get some real beer down yer Pommie gob!" I found it impossible even to attempt to keep up with the voracious appetites of these lads. I did make sure though that I 'shouted' (bought) a round of beers for my companions when my turn came around.

It got down to me trying to keep myself in the background, as I sipped slowly at my smaller, potent pot of Carlton brewed lager – into which I had asked the astonished but co-operative barman to surreptitiously add a small glass full of diluting lemonade!

What an experience! The time slipped by rapidly, while the babble of voices around the bar got to reach an ear-deafening crescendo. The noise had increasing noticeably to an even higher pitch than when we had first arrived. I on the other hand was looking forward to an opportunity to slip away while I was still capable of walking steadily upright and in a reasonably straight line. I was hoping for a break in the proceedings that would allow me to escape across Flinders Street to the railway station and my Red Rattler train ride home to St Kilda.

It should be noted that I have never been a prodigious beer drinker, at best capable only of downing a couple of lemonade-dominated shandies without much in the way of visible ill effects. In contrast, the drinking skills exhibited by the lads back there in Young & Jacksons could only be described as of Olympic proportions, such was the number of and speed with which schooners of beer were constantly disappearing down their throats.

Nearing the critical point when I should be leaving to catch my train home, the drinking scene changed suddenly and in a most dramatic fashion...

It all started with a booming voice that emanated from behind the bar, the bar manager shouting in a manner and volume fit to raise the dead, in a voice that seemed to soar to at least ten decibels higher than the already high level of conversation. Anyone standing a couple of hundred yards away, including even a near deaf man would have found it impossible to ignore the cry of: "Last drink orders gentlemen please!"

Last drinks being called at 6pm? This sounded somewhat premature? I, of course, was used to the pubs in Britain having opening hours stretching into the night-time until closing at 10pm, when last drinks would then be called. This timing was followed by 10 or 15 minutes, during which the pub's customers were allowed to gradually down their last drinks and leave for home.

Here in Melbourne, things were very different. Following the shouted announcement from the head bartender, the scene changed suddenly, with drinkers making a concerted rush to the bar and ordering replacement beers – literally lines of glasses of beer were being ordered. When filled, they were quickly returned to the surrounding tables until it seemed that every man present, less me of course, had at least three or four large glasses of beer placed in a line in front of them!

The scene was bizarre… It was a virtual mob scene, one thankfully without any sign of violence I might add, with men from every corner of the room crowding the bar with intent. All were seeking to order enough drinks to keep them and their mates going for at least a further 30 minutes longer – all drinking at a somewhat slower pace than they had been drinking at before last drinks being called!

That day was my first introduction to Melbourne's archaic drinking laws. The phrase '6 o'clock swill' had been coined many years earlier, used to describe the drinking laws that continued to apply even beyond the 1950s.

That then law had appeared during the 1914–1918 war, with the introduction of new liquor licensing laws in 1916. The new law was aimed at reducing the consumption of alcohol, thus assisting to lower then levels of drunkenness. The law was introduced as a means of forcing public bars to close at 6pm, just leaving an hour in which anyone wishing to drink a beer or two could do so following the end of work, an hour earlier at 5pm.

That law instead created a huge crush at the bar, when "Last drinks gentlemen please" was called a couple of minutes prior to the legal time of 6pm, thus causing still thirsty drinkers to rush the bar and order a stock of beer for themselves and their fellow drinkers, before the taps were turned off at 6pm. The resulting noise, the crush of bodies, and slops, as the beer was spilled everywhere during the melee that followed the barman's call, led observers to describe the scene thus created as a 'pig swill', the term 'six o'clock swill' sticking for evermore.

Having downed their personal line of beers, usually well after 6pm, most of the by then 'well-oiled' drinkers would start to bid farewell to the fellow drinkers, leaving the hallowed sanctuary of the public bar to wend their beery way home to their 'sheilas' (girlfriends), wives and families. Most by that time were already looking forward to their usual evening meal of one meat, two veg and gravy, accompanied perhaps by a further glass or two of 'amber fluid?'

During the post 1939–1945 war years, the phenomenon in most Melbourne pubs must surely have provided any new visitor to the city with a strange spectacle, as men in business suits and hats, together with workmen in overalls and caps jostled with each other, demanding to be served. This was a sight that later would surely have been the scene of amusement to any European visitors who happened to be in Melbourne during the 1956 Olympic Games.

The 6pm Australian drinking ritual continued to be a male- only affair. Women were still being excluded from public bars much later even than 1959. It seems also that this form of excessive drinking in a male-only environment had earlier become a neat way of defining the term 'masculinity' across the Australian male population. It was also a kind of ritual that to my eyes, then a new arrival to Australia, that appeared to be used by men in general as a way of defining someone as being a real man, a good or 'bonza bloke' or even a 'dinky-di' Aussie mate.

Could you keep up with your mates when it came to the downing of multiple beers? The capacity to do so seemed to define the Australian male as one who could be relied upon to meet his 'shout' (buy a round of drinks), while at the same time downing his own row of beers in concert with the rest of his male mates.

This example of what was often regarded as a declaration of 'mateship' seems also to have extended into other areas of male companionship. Perhaps this was also a major contributor to the oft-touted and iconic image of something that over many years became known as a typical Aussie male – the 'Aussie larrikin' image so graphically interpreted by the comedian Barry Humphries in his later series of on-stage and film characters Bazza McKenzie and Sir Les Patterson.

Who could ever forget seeing the dissolute Sir Les for the very first time, as his creator and alter image, Humphries, presented him on-stage to an often aghast, unknowing, and unbelieving audience, in the form of Australia's beer spattered and unkempt cultural attaché?

Six o'clock closing and the irrational law that created it resulting in the daily rush to down as much beer as possible after the taps were turned off, existed in each of the other states. The practice lasted longest in Victoria where it was finally repealed during 1966.

Notes

1. **John Batman** (21 January 1801–6 May 1839) was an Australian grazier, entrepreneur and explorer. He settled in the north-east of the Van Diemen's Land Colony in the 1820s, and later as a leading member of the Port Phillip Association he led an expedition which explored the Port Phillip Bay area on the Australian mainland with a view to establishing a new settlement there. He is best known for his role in the founding of the settlement on the Yarra River which became the city of Melbourne.

THE AUSTRALIAN WAY OF LIFE – 1959-STYLE

While on the subject of categorising, the oft-referred-to phrase, 'the Australian way of life', became an often inaccurate but regularly celebrated description of life and living, offered by sociologists and native-born Australians as a uniquely Australian lifestyle. The phrase was often used to describe a somewhat restricted, but idealised style of suburban living.

The caption, if one was to be critical, has over the years served mainly to position Australian women, in what was seen to be their 'natural' place in society. While accepted as an important place, it was a position that invariably meant them being the one solely responsible for looking after the family home.

The then mainly sought-after style of housing during the burgeoning 1950s and 1960s, at least among the working class, was in the form of a three-bedroom timber or brick house, located on a quarter-acre block of land. The family setup became complete, once a Hills clothes hoist had been set up in the back garden. Following the Second World War, the change from austerity to growing prosperity throughout the country resulted in increased house sizes and sustained growth in home ownership.

Often characterised by what was known as the triple-fronted brick-veneer style of construction, houses tended to be larger than earlier, more comfortable and better designed for family living. Following the war, house designs also tended toward single storey structures, with interconnected living rooms, occasionally with a built-in garage. Mass produced windows also fostered a greater use of glass in this style of housing.

Historically, following the ending of the Second World War, there was an acute shortage of building materials and equipment. As the economy began to pick up and strengthen, there was a corresponding revival of domestic architecture, a trend that also mirrored a post-war baby boom and a massive increase in immigration.

Houses were now being built using a veneer of brick over a frame of green-sawn hardwood timbers. Most houses from the 1950s on were being designed and specified by building companies and not architects, one of the most universally known of these at the time being the A.V. Jennings Company.

The idealised style of what usually became known as a housewife, or 'the Missus' during the 1960s, found her squarely in the focus of advertisements aimed at the promotion of an expanding range of consumer goods. Mrs Housewife was usually depicted in newspaper advertisements and later on television, as she admired her new electric Hoover cleaner, new 'Keymatic' washing machine, new cookery book, and any other 'new' kind of domestic paraphernalia, at the time being spruiked by various producers of household appliances and a growing number of women's publications.

She (the 'Missus') cooked dinner in her new electric oven and was generally responsible for looking after all the domestic chores while nurturing the kids and any family animals. The man of the house, in contrast, would sally forth to earn a living, after being served with a prepared breakfast and then sent off to work with a lovingly prepared box or bag of white bread and Vegemite sandwiches plus a couple of assorted biscuits, by his dutiful, mainly housebound wife.

Once having borne one or two children, wives were rarely encouraged to seek to return to their earlier work or professions that had occupied them when single. In a number of professions and even in some public service situations, single girls could also look forward to the distinct possibility of them losing their job on getting married, presumably on the basis that once married she would soon thereafter become pregnant with her first child, thus seeing the end of a promising career.

Once married and now a mother, wives were from that time on expected to take on the role of general 'homebody', her days spent looking after the house and the welfare of her spouse and children. Few women returned to a job, even after their children had grown up and were either at university or working. The idealised kind of family household during the 1950s and 1960s was often then referred to as a 'nuclear' type family, comprising Dad, Mum and two children, ideally a boy and a girl.

BLOKES AND SHEILAS

In spite of the close relationship that still existed during the mid-20th century, between Australia and what in those days was often referred to as Mother England by many of the still diehard Australian born anglophiles, there also existed a degree of antipathy toward any recently arrived British immigrants. Such attitudes were regularly being directed at any newcomer that for one reason or another happened to find themselves on the wrong side of a 'dinky-di Aussie' (native- born Australian).

The term 'dinky-di' (a term rarely, if ever, heard today) even sounded rather quaint to my ears during my early days in Melbourne. This became a term that I quite quickly learned to mean 'a genuine Aussie' – someone born and bred, either in the suburbs, the 'bush' or the so-called 'outback'. The term was also used to describe a white Australian, as opposed to an Australian Aborigine, someone preferably able to trace his or her lineage back to a forebear transported from Britain or Ireland during Australia's early convict days.

Being able to trace one's lineage back to a convict forebear was proudly used by any dinky-di Aussie male or female able to prove such a claim. This they would regard as them being an even more genuine variety of Aussie 'Bloke' or 'Sheila' (girl or woman).

In another sense, having an ancient (very old that is in Australian terms) traceable convict family member was something approaching the Australian version of having a local form of collective royalty in the family. Anyone able to make such a provable claim was automatically seen as being a Proper Aussie – certainly not one of your Johnny-come-lately 'Pommies' or 'wog refos'.

Speaking for myself, another Johnny-come-lately boat person, paradoxically I cannot readily recall an occasion where I was ever made to feel like an unwanted outsider, even as a number of my former Pommie friends may well have. Maybe it was more to do with the way a British immigrant was able to deal with the need, and possess the capacity to blend into their new environment?

Australia was a completely different kind of country to Britain, having different mores, rules and ingrained values. Values and a way of doing things in no way similar to anything I had previously experienced in Britain, values that had become inherited from earlier colonial times. That being so, a Pommie migrant of 1959 vintage was therefore well advised to learn to tread lightly, if and when confronted by, or them having to deal with any among the more sensitive or aggressively defensive native-born Australians to be found among his or her new neighbours or workmates.

RED NED AND DEATH BY GARDEN SPRAY

Now that Mavis and I had settled into our own home at the back of 100 Hotham Street, St Kilda and both had full-time jobs, the weeks that followed began to open up a whole new window to the possibilities of achieving a potentially happy and productive lifestyle and successful future in our new country. Happily gone by now were Mavis's threats to catch the next ship back to England. She was already making friends at her new job and was also beginning to enjoy the fact that we were so close to St Kilda beach, the local shops and the easily accessible and extensive Melbourne CBD, its attractive shopping arcades and cafés.

The two other couples occupying the rest of the house in which we were living were helpful and friendly. The husband of the older couple, people that had already been resident there for some years, turned out to be uncontrolled, but an always friendly and relatively harmless alcoholic. Our alcoholic neighbour regularly created situations that resulted in scenes that would have fitted quite easily into the plot of a Mack Sennett 'Keystone Cops' movie. His long-suffering wife was constantly trying (usually unsuccessfully) to isolate and retrieve the regularly obtained bottles of Red Ned (cheap, usually nasty liquor) that her errant hubby had bought and stashed away all over the place. At times Mavis or I would come across on or two bottles, selectively hidden in the roof of our carport, or in a nearby hedge. At one stage, in exasperation, his wife tried to employ Mavis and me as occasional lookouts from our bedroom window, which overlooked the backyard and carports, requesting us to keep a watch out for her husband's latest hiding place for his secretive illicit purchases of cheap liquor.

Our kindly landlord at the time, Mr Grey, later succumbed to what appears to have been a case of self-poisoning. A heavy smoker, he apparently had managed to ingest what proved eventually to be a lethal amount of toxic garden spray, a deadly concoction that he used to make up to his own recipe. The poison that eventually led to his premature demise had been absorbed over a period, apparently leaching from his leaky handheld spray gun every time he drew on a non-stop cigarette, while tending to his beloved roses. Reminded me not to spray the roses when smoking, if and when I ever got to tend my own garden sometime in the future.

POUNDS, SHILLINGS AND PENCE

In 1959, the Australian pound and ten-shilling notes, shiny half-crowns, silver florins, shillings and sixpences, copper pennies, halfpennies and three-penny bits had continued to remain the then currency of the commonwealth. The system changed to a much easier to understand and calculate range of coinage when Australia decided in February 1966 to adopt the metric system. This move made calculations much easier to manage, although I must admit for some still unknown reason, to continuing to calculate using feet and inches when thinking about a person's height.

Settling into life in their new country was a very different situation facing nearly all of the many thousands of continental European migrants that were continuing to flood into Australia during the 1950s and 60s. Many older migrants had a deal of difficulty when trying to become reasonably proficient in the English language, them also having to learn to use pounds and ounces instead of kilos and grams. Many older continental immigrants never got to speak a reasonable level of English. As years passed few even found it necessary, as it didn't take long for members of the various immigrant communities to set up shops and other businesses, many now able to cater for fellow immigrant group members.

Local food, local dining habits and local customs were also very different from what most European migrants had been used to in their native lands. There was also the need to get used to the relatively laid-back laconic attitude that most immigrants tended to find when it came to dealing with Australians in general, Australian officialdom and its rules and regulations. One or two aspects of Australian life and living were also known to have caused a few occasional problems for even a few Pommie immigrants.

On the plus side, most native-born Australians I came across during the early weeks and months since our arrival in Melbourne, seemed to accept and get on reasonably well with most newcomers to their shores. Unfortunately, some immigrants' transition to life in their new country was made difficult at times, due to reactions from some of Australia's 'red neck' minority and their oft times hurtful taunts of 'dago' or 'bloody wop', when referring to Greeks, Italians and others from southern Europe and the Balkan countries. These continued to be names that would be thrown at anyone perceived to be looking reasonably close to an olive-skinned or darker complexioned southern European, particularly one who was also perhaps having difficulty communicating in English.

Those kinds of taunts and attitudes declined over ensuing years, as most of the earlier post-war European migrants began to assimilate. They gradually became familiar with Australia's laws, practices and the communities in which they had decided to settle. In some cases, not only did European immigrants find a way to blend successfully into the communities in which they settled, they eventually managed to become the medium through which significant changes began to occur to daily living in their community, town or city.

Eating habits were one area that began to change reasonably quickly. Native-born Australians slowly became more familiar with these in particular usually finding themselves better able to appreciate the variety of different eating experiences and styles of food that began to emerge as ethnic-style restaurants and cafés became established and spread across the country.

A good barometer of this kind of fundamental change was the rapidity with which the general Australian population eventually took to Italian-style coffee making.

The terms espresso, cappuccino and caffè latte gradually came to dominate the language of coffee drinking, until today nearly every Australian coffee drinker is well known to take a deal of pride, particularly when it comes to their claimed knowledge and appreciation of coffee, a now universally loved beverage.

Some of the earlier attitudes to foreign newcomers to Australia are reminiscent of similarly harsh and derogatory terms like 'slants', 'ragheads' and worse that continued to be directed toward later arrivals in Australia from South East Asia. Even later seekers of sanctuary, mainly Middle-Eastern, Afghan and Sri Lankan refugees continued to suffer similar kinds of taunts.

Being young and more adaptable, the children of non-English speaking immigrants in particular, usually found it much easier than their parents to learn English, and thus to meld more easily into their surroundings and make new, lasting friendships with their native-born street and school friends. Of course, the children of European and other foreign parents didn't have to worry too much about organising such things as a roof over their heads.

It was much different for their parents, having to seek out a means by which to earn a living wage, provide shelter for the family, beside which came the necessity of themselves also having to learn at least some English, not the easiest of languages to master. All this in addition to trying to adapt to the more relaxed form of their new country's way of living and inter-relationships.

THE ALUMINIUM PAN PATCHER

To divert just a little: In the late 1950s and early 1960s there were some notable categories of consumer goods that were regularly in short supply throughout Australia, some having been learned before our departure from Britain.

Goods in this category were mainly good quality general household items like finer wool blankets and goods designated as Manchester – the term used extensively across Australia to describe cotton goods. Good quality copper or stainless-steel pots and pans at the time of our arrival were also in short supply or not yet available.

I always used to think it strange in the case of wool blankets, that so few high-quality pure wool blankets were being produced or in demand in Australia, in spite of the fact that most of the world's fine wools at the time were being grown there. One or two of our Australian neighbours and friends would regularly comment on our British made beautifully soft, light and luxurious Merino wool 'Lan-Air-Cel' branded blankets.

To illustrate the shortage of quality cooking pots and pans on our arrival in 1959, I one day found myself observing the strange spectacle of my uncle hard at work in his garage, as he patched one or other of my auntie's aluminium pans that had apparently sprung a hole or two. The base of the pan in question was relatively thin and as a result had burned through in places following a great deal of use. When I got to know Uncle Barney better, even his son and daughter-in-law came to regard him as a 'stingy bugger' – a man not known to part with a penny without a fight!

In my uncle's case, it seems that the patching was done so that he could save money purchasing new, good quality pots and pans. Whatever, it was amusing to see Uncle Barney struggling to patch and repair a hole in one of my auntie's pans with a prefabricated screw-in aluminium patch, one of many differently shaped patches apparently designed for the purpose, which could be bought at one or other of the local hardware stores. It seems that other Australian husbands had similar problems.

SPAG BOG AND THE UNIVERSITA CAFÉ

My introduction to anything remotely foreign in the way of food since landing in Australia was via a cup of what some of the local Australians at the time referred to as 'wop coffee'. This turned out to be a distinctly Italian-style beverage (cappuccino or espresso) a delightful beverage that continued for some time to be described by that strange and decidedly pejorative term by my new-found Australian workmates. I also soon got to become closely acquainted with an Italian dish that bore the equally strange Australianised title of 'spag bog' (spaghetti bolognese), at least it was known as such by my same Australian friends. Now, this was a strange, new dish to me at the time, comprising pasta and meatballs, served up in a rich tomato sauce, the result proving to be both tasty, and very filling.

Spag bog was said to be traditional Italian 'tucker', or 'Itie' (Italian) style dinner fare, a plate of which I tasted and enjoyed for the first time at a small Italian family café in the inner suburb of Brunswick.

It was also some months following my arrival in Melbourne, when a couple of workmates and I wandered into the Universita Café in Lygon Street, in the then mainly Italian inhabited inner suburb of Carlton, for a dish of what my companions referred to as Itie tucker. In those days, the only Italian-style food that most native-born Australians would even try was a plate of spag bog or a dish of minestrone. How Melbourne's eating habits have changed over the years!

The present site of the Universita Café, still located at its address of 257 Lygon Street in Carlton, had, since 1931, housed a Mexican-style restaurant. In 1953, it was taken over by the Milani family, who changed both its name and menu to Italian. The restaurant was originally named, presumably as it wasn't very far from Melbourne University, usually attracting a large number of lunchtime students, in addition to local businesspeople and passing shoppers attracted perhaps to a cup of Itie coffee and an equally tasty brioche?

The establishment in the 1950s acted as both a café as well as an Italian social club, catering mainly to the culinary needs of the many young single male Italian migrants who then lived in one or other of the many rooming houses spread across the inner suburbs of Carlton, Fitzroy and Brunswick.

Giancarlo and Beverly Caprioli bought the Universita Café in 1978. At the time of writing it is still owned by the family, over subsequent years having become one of the enduring icons of Lygon Street, Carlton, in addition to being an ongoing source of traditionally prepared Italian food.

Every time I pass the Universita, drop in for a meal or just a caffè latte or lungo macchiato, just being there brings back memories of my early days in Melbourne and, my first introduction to Italian-style food and drink.

AUSTRALIAN RULES FOOTBALL

My earlier arrival in Australia had opened my eyes to a whole new way and style of life and work, including experiences already gained when it came to the Australian rag trade.

The practice of patching well-worn aluminium pans, a whole new world of food and coffee – and in particular the growing Italian influence when it came to food, wine and drinking was indeed a new experience for this Pommie immigrant. My early months living in Melbourne were also bringing home to me the fact that while Aussies spoke English, the country and its people were a unique brand. Native-born Australians still retained what I had already come to know as a form of 'colonial Britishness', their native-born state overlaid with a liberal layering of a kind of non-conforming larrikinism.

While still in the process of trying to absorb and accept the use of new-found descriptors like dinky-di, bonza, wog, spag, Pommie and others of that ilk, I was yet to experience a ball game that came so close to being a close competitor to any form of recognised religion. The sport which held the attention of the vast majority of the citizenry of Victoria in 1959, was one that could quite easily have been used to describe that unique result of 200 years of human evolution – the modern-day Australian male! Or was it the other way around – a ball game that could only have been designed by Australians?

The prevailing sport being played across Victoria during the 1950s was different to anything I had witnessed before in Britain. This was particularly so when it came to a game that the locals referred to as 'Footy'.

At first sight, this ball game appeared to be an adaptation of rugby union, but without the regular starts and stoppages that applied to both rugby codes, Union and League. Also different, the game was played on an extra-large oval arena, instead of the usual rugby or round football-style rectangular playing field.

At the time of my first introduction to what I came to know officially as Australian rules football, the game presented as a fast-moving spectacle, that in my innocence (locals would refer to it as ignorance) I described the sport in a letter back to my parents in Leeds as being a very physical kind of 'aerial ping-pong'! Small wonder you might say, as I had been brought up in Britain to Association Football, the round leather ball game as played in a rectangular stadium, and the biff, bash and run game of rugby league, as played with an oval leather ball just a little longer and rounder than an Australian rules football.

One Saturday afternoon a few weeks following my arrival in Melbourne, I was invited to attend one of the local Australian rules football matches, along with another recent immigrant and our host for the day, a friendly Australian workmate, one of the cutters from the Keith Courtenay factory. Our host promised to re-educate we ignorant Pommies, by providing us with the opportunity to gain a working understanding of what he enthusiastically described as the "only football code worth watching". What we got to see in fact turned out to be a ball game that was known proudly and simply by dinky-di Aussie locals as footy.

As with the term footy, I also was by that time becoming familiar with most Australians' propensity to foreshorten names or a title of something wherever they were able to do so, hence:

Good'arvo – as in good afternoon
cuppa – a cup of tea or coffee
g'day – good day
straya – Australia
biccy – biscuit

tinny – can (usually of strong Aussie beer)
postie – postman
Macca's – McDonald's fast food
the G – the Melbourne Cricket Ground or MCG
pokey – poker machine…

And so on across any words and phrases that could in some way or other be replaced with a much shorter version.

INTRODUCTION TO THE G

Our indoctrination that day was to be as observers of what our Australian guide termed delightedly as, "the footy match of the day". This match as it happened was being played at Melbourne's world-famous stadium, the stadium that just three years prior had been the venue for the 1956 Melbourne Olympic Games. It was to be my first of many attendances at both footy and cricket matches at that spectacular stadium. The stadium's official title was the Melbourne Cricket Ground (MCG), otherwise known to its local aficionados by its inevitably shortened title – simply as the G.

"Jesus, what a fantastic stadium," I well remember musing to myself as I, along with my two companions shelled out the then entrance fee of a few shillings at one of the turnstiles guarding the entrance to the equally famous (sometimes infamous) Bay 13 of the Great Southern Stand.

I must admit that even in 1959, the MCG was a sight to gladden the heart of any sports fan. It was something to admire in a football stadium, particularly as most of the football and rugby I had watched previously had been played at the pokey Headingly home ground of the Leeds Rugby League Football Club, or at the then scruffy Elland Road football ground, home of Leeds United football (soccer) club. Both those stadiums would have come close to fitting into the MCG and its surroundings.

The match on that day was between the Melbourne and South Melbourne football clubs, at that time both being among the leading clubs competing in the then Victorian Football League (VFL).

Once having gained entrance to the Southern Stand, we at last managed to find standing room on the terracing a few rows back from the boundary fence. The ground was crowded, as the match had been billed as a do-or-die clash between two of the league's leading teams of that season. Just a few of the names I remember from that period were Bobbie Skilton of South Melbourne and Ron Barassi, Bluey Adams and Brian Dixon, who played for the Melbourne Football Club, also known locally as the Demons.

I must admit that in spite of our companion's expert and continuous explanation as to what was going on during the first two 20-minute quarters of the match, all that I could see and understand in detail were the amazing ball handling and kicking skills with which the participants were able to accurately deliver the rugby shaped ball, not just for 10 or 20 yards – but up to 60 yards! Not only were the players able to kick such a long distance, but while doing so – every one of them could do it while on the run. Most of them also proved to be regularly able to hit their target on his chest or close enough nearby to enable him to mark (catch) the ball. Having caught the ball, a feat in itself as it was sometimes delivered to him spinning awkwardly, the recipient was then able to take his kick, in the form of a pass forward to another team player further up the extra-large ground and toward his opponent's goal.

If he happened to be within kicking distance of the goal area, and that could be anywhere within say 50 yards of the opposition goals, all he would usually need to do then was just to move back a few yards then take a running kick at goal.

Another aspect of the game that impressed me was the way in which all the players could run at full speed, while bouncing the oval shaped ball in such a manner as to enable it to bounce back and up into their hands, without them having to break stride – all this with them running at full pace! Players were limited when having to hand-pass the ball by the simple means of needing to hold it in one palm while whacking it with the opposite fist. I learned from our voluble tutor that this was the only legal way a player could hand-pass the ball to another team member. Unlike the kind of football I was used to, here also there were no offside or forward pass rules involved.

As to the goals, unlike rugby the goals for Australian rules football came in the form of four tall white poles, the outer two being much shorter than the two inner ones. The two inner poles formed the main goal and were worth six points, if the ball was kicked between them by the attacking side. If the ball missed the centre goal but went through either side of the centre poles but inside the outer poles, then this strangely was called as a 'behind' and counted as one point. This got very confusing to a long-time rugby league watcher, used to the much slower game with its constant stoppages for scrums, the play-the-ball variation and the battering-ram like qualities of a heavy forward pack, battling it out on a usually rain-soaked and often fog-shrouded ground in the north of England.

At each end of the massive oval on which the match was being played, stood a white-coated (very official and medical looking) so-called goal umpire. Both umpires were unnoticed for most of the time, standing stock-still and semi-invisible between the centre goalposts, each looking very official in his long white coat and white hat.

On a goal being kicked, the umpire standing at the goal in question would suddenly leap into vigorous action and, following an authoritative pointing downward of his two forefingers to indicate that a goal had been scored, he would then grab two white flags (previously kept rolled up and hidden from sight in a tube behind each of the inner posts) and, rushing back into the centre of the goals, he would wave the flags with a brisk flourish toward his opposite number, a similarly clad figure located in the far distance, at the other end of the ground.

A similar action, but involving the pointing of one finger and waving one flag only, would accompany the scoring of a 'behind'.

I'm not sure just why it was considered necessary to signal in this way to the distant figure in white, who also it seemed, felt it necessary to mirror the flag waving at the opposite end of the ground. Maybe it was designed to ensure that the other umpire was awake – the game being played and the goal having been scored so far away from him at the other end of that vast stadium?

I must say that I came away from my first VFL match that afternoon more than just a little confused, not at that time having gained much more than a vague grasp of the rules of the game. One thing I was sure of, it was a fast-flowing game that really got the crowds on the terraces and stands excited. So much so that at one stage of the match, proceedings degenerated into a near fist fight following what appeared to have been a rank left jab deliberately administered to a Melbourne player by an opposing player, just near our boundary. That blatant assault not only created a melee on the field of play, but also one in our vicinity amid the packed terraces in the Southern Stand, where a small group of umbrella wielding, ardent and mainly female supporters of the Melbourne club, commenced to lash out at nearby South Melbourne supporters with their team coloured umbrellas and loud tongues.

I didn't know which to watch first, the football which by then had resumed, or the elderly Melbourne ladies giving hell to a few of the more vocal of the opposing team's supporters, here in the MCG's Bay 13.

While suitably impressed with the speed and virility of the local game, I decided to take a look next time at what I had always regarded as an authentic and 'real' game of football – the one played with a round ball, which, strangely in Australia, people persisted in calling soccer.

AUSTRALIAN-STYLE SOCCER – A TOUCH OF WAR

I did try the local brand of what I had first heard referred to as wogball by most of the diehard native-born Australian male followers of Australian rules football. Wogball turned out to be the round ball version of the footballing genus that later became known across Australia more generally as soccer. Wogball it was in those days though, because it was being played predominantly by and in front of groups of European immigrants. So be it, here I was, about to witness my first game of wogball/soccer.

I got to see my first game of soccer, when a new friend and I decided to take in a match between two Melbourne-based teams. I can't recall the actual names of the teams that played that day, but it soon became obvious, even before the match had started, that the event could become a fiery exchange between two not very friendly ethnic groups. The two clubs involved that day, judging from their names and banners, were obviously from rival countries in or around the Balkans.

As soon as the match got started the referee's whistle heralded clashes, some of them violent, that began to erupt spasmodically both on the field of play and along the opposing terraces. This kind of behaviour continued intermittently throughout the whole of the first 90-minute-long half of the match during which the standard of the football being played could only be described using words similar to pedestrian, pathetic and uninteresting – lacking in the main a great deal of skill among most of those taking part.

Apart from the obviously rabid rivalry, the match started very early to descend more and more into a state of blatant fouling, coupled with regularly feigned injuries among the players of both teams.

Insults, angst, bottle and missile throwing by the chanting, ethnic flag waving rival gangs of fans on the terraces, accompanied what had already developed into a less than professional display of the skills of the sport. Not only this but on at least one occasion someone in the crowd lit a flare and threw it onto the field of play – an action that sent clouds of orange smoke billowing up over the whole ground, halting play until the smouldering missile could be removed.

As the clash continued, some among the home team fans seemed more intent on starting a fight with fans supporting the opposing team. Apart from the regular skirmishes, which eventually brought members of the local police force into the act, the standard of football was, to say the least abysmal. Comparing what we were witnessing here in Melbourne, against the speed and skills on show with division one English League (FA) football at the time, it was more like watching a couple of fifth division teams slogging it out through the mud of a sub-standard ground.

Not only that but the match as it progressed along its ponderous way, gave the impression that to all intents and purposes, it was more like a re-enactment of some unfinished middle European or Balkan war being played out in one of Melbourne's inner suburbs!

Halftime found my companion and I seeking a place on one or

other of the terraces, as far away from any potential conflict as possible. Eventually, having continued to watch the lack of skills on the part of both teams, in addition to the low standard, both of the football and refereeing, we decided to leave before the end of the match. Such a move was thought to be prudent on our part, mainly to avoid getting involved in what seemed to portend a running clash outside the ground, once the sub-standard spectacle inside had come to what promised to be a fiery close.

Following my first look at the local version of soccer, it seemed that, as there was no interest at the time in Victoria for the game of rugby league, in those day played exclusively in Queensland and New South Wales, there was little else in the way of winter sport worth watching. Rugby union didn't interest me, with its constant kicking for touch, stoppages, interminable scrums and lineouts, so it eventually became a case of watching Australian rules football (footy) or nothing.

As time went on, I gradually learned more about the rules of VFL football and, in my early days, living as I did in the suburb of St Kilda, with every other VFL team at the time being located and nurtured within in their local suburb – Melbourne playing in Melbourne, Carlton in Carlton, Footscray in Footscray, North Melbourne at North Melbourne etc. – I had to support the Saints, who then played their homes games at St Kilda junction.

In 1959, when compared to the amount of money being earned by the now Australian Football League (AFL) and its players, with income from TV rights and a vast amount of money coming into its coffers via product sponsorships, both the VFL and many of the local teams during the 1950s had relatively little, in terms of healthy finances. As a result, some home grounds in the late 1950s, particularly during wet winter weekends, could be very uncomfortable, with muddy terraces, smelly and nasty toilets and little if any cover when it rained. The MCG was the exception with its superb facilities and great visibility from all around the ground.

There were always a few of the local football grounds that fans tended to try to avoid during the 1950s and 1960s. Among these was the Footscray football ground, the club affectionately known by the locals as the Scraggers, who were kitted out in red, white and blue – very British! The old Brunswick oval was another ground you learned to avoid on wintry, rainy days – home of the then local Brunswick team. That ground and surrounding spectator banking in particular during most of the winter regularly became a morass of mud, a place also where the toilets usually managed to overflow. Another ground to be wary of was Victoria Park, an infamous venue suffering from a similar situation – the football ground that housed the Collingwood football club. This club also could claim another dimension to its infamy, it generally being disliked – almost hated it appeared at the time for reasons still obscure, by every other club supporter following the VFL code.

All in all, eventually I got to understand and appreciate the unique qualities and skills involved with Australian rules football. Aussie rules or footy – as I gradually got used to calling it, saw me eventually becoming a regular supporter of the Saints, only deciding to leave them as a supporter when I moved some years later to live in the inner northern suburb of Carlton.

In contrast to the VFL and its later national version of AFL, soccer in Australia today, although a vast improvement as a spectacle than the game that was being played and supported in the 1950s and 1960s, still has a way to go. Australian soccer, particularly the male variety – the Socceroos – still lacks the professional standards and financial capacity needed to compete with leading European, South American and some top Asian league soccer clubs.

Looking to the future, given a decade or so and like anything else toward which Australians turn their hearts and energy, particularly their almost universal love of sport, the day will come when the Socceroos will at last reach much closer to the top – if not to the pinnacle – of world football.

The Matildas, Australia's women's soccer team, are currently taking all before them; they are currently regarded as one of the world's leading teams.

Australian rules (AFL) football, on the other hand, having become a nationwide sporting code, has made one or two tentative efforts to extend its influence internationally. The game though, attractive that it is, is not expected to become a worldwide attraction. While an interesting, physical spectacle, it is not being played extensively on an international basis. No great loss to we Australian aficionados though when one comes to think a little deeper. After all, why should we even want to share our great game with the rest of the world?

Whatever, Aussie rules football will always be a reflection and a perfect example of the Australian attitude to life and sport in general. It will always remain an 80-minute-long spectacle of extreme, exciting athletic activity in ball handling, marking, kicking and running, all played out on an unusually large oval and in front of a correspondingly large vociferous crowd of supporters.

Long may Aussie Rules footy reign!

SUMMER'S COME, AND THE LIVING IS EASY

Inflation at the time of my arrival in Australia was relatively low – at least it seemed to be so to we new arrivals. Another big plus was the relatively friendly cost of living, which meant that it continued to be possible for a small family to live reasonably well at the time, even on one wage earner's weekly stipend.

Jobs were easy to come by across a variety of industries, the country having a reasonably broad-based economy. This was a situation that saw many working at more than one job, mainly as a means of supplementing the family's income for such pursuits as the acquisition of a holiday house nearer to the beach, or a camping holiday. Most Melbourne-based workers could afford to take their summer or Easter holidays either on one or other of the local beaches along the Mornington or Bellarine Peninsulas, or among the easily accessible local hills and Victorian Alps.

Also important, the cost of setting up a first home remained within reasonable reach of most young couple's ability to finance. Following a few years saving up for the initial 10% deposit they could apply to their bank for a long-term loan, usually available for around a 5% interest rate.

Among most of the population, the urge to save remained a powerful motivation. Most people at the time were more inclined to save to purchase whatever they needed for their house needs or family, as opposed to borrowing the necessary funds from their local bank.

The era of credit cards, offers of unlimited credit and the terrible consequences their introduction loaded onto to people who found it increasingly difficult to cope with the disciplines involved, were yet a number of years away into the future.

The main aim among most newly arrived migrants, Mavis and I included, was to save whatever we could toward the required 10% deposit on a house of our own.

As more houses sprouted up in the rapidly expanding outer suburbs, the kind of lifestyle to which even an ordinary Australian worker could aspire during the 1960s, was far in advance of what would have been possible for Mavis and me back in Britain. New subdivisions of brick-veneer houses, each with a front and back garden were then being built across Melbourne's rapidly growing outer suburbs. These newer suburbs were usually being sought and settled in by British migrants. Others preferred to rent, or perhaps buy, depending on their capacity to raise the 10% deposit required, closer in to the city and nearer to their work.

Wherever one chose to settle in Melbourne was a world apart from the streets of old, and in many cases uncomfortable, often unaffordable and inefficient housing stock that continued to dominate most working-class districts across Britain's north.

For Mavis and me, having insufficient funds saved for a deposit on a house, it would be a few years yet before we would be comfortably able to put down the required deposit on a newly built house of our own, with sufficient funds left over for furniture, other necessaries and a second car for Mavis to use. We decided, therefore, to continue to rent accommodation, at least until we were in a position to set up and furnish a home of our own, in which to bring up the family that we both were looking forward to creating.

Neither Mavis nor I possessed a driving licence. With locally available public transport close by, as was our nearest shopping precinct in Carlisle and Acland streets in nearby St Kilda, the need for a vehicle of our own was a little way down on our list of current priorities.

MENSWEAR DESIGNER

Some weeks had by now passed by during which, in spite of the fact that both Mavis and I were beginning to settle down and enjoy life in our new country, I continued to be on the lookout for a more challenging position.

My search eventually paid off after a number of weeks, during which I had consistently checked out every local newspaper for any sign of a potential opportunity. My search ended one Saturday morning with the sighting of an advertisement in *The Age* for a position that caught my interest and set my pulse running.

The advertisement in question sought the services of an experienced menswear designer – someone capable of establishing and running a modern design room in a young, forward-looking company. The company seeking such a rare animal, and the position they were advertising, which I believed was meant for me, was a Melbourne-based men's apparel manufacturer trading as Stafford-Ellinson.

Following careful research, I learned that the company was a new version of an older men's apparel manufacturer that had previously been trading as Ellinson Brothers. That company had recently been taken over by two relatively young brothers, Maurice and Simon Lubansky, who had established their headquarters at the company's production plant located at 473 Swanston Street, Carlton, close to that street's intersection with Grattan Street.

Here I was then at the tender age of 24, applying for a position which the advertisers had specified as requiring the services of an experienced designer.

Well, yes, I was young, and at my age relatively inexperienced, at least I was in the sense of years lived in comparison to someone twice my age. My experience had included two years working at my trade in the RAF. This had been followed by my role of assistant designer for a recognised leader in the men's outerwear field back in Leeds, I held the highest level of technical qualifications and was confident that I could do equally well as any older person that might also be applying for the position.

With the thought that little was to be gained by doing nothing, I applied for the position in a letter in which I did my best to whet the appetites of the brothers Lubansky.

My first interview was with Maurice, the elder and apparent leader of the enterprise, known to his friends as Maurie. The interview, as I recall it, could only be described as a grilling, two hours during which my prospective employer embarked upon a rapid-fire interrogation. I finally emerged, dazed and uncertain, caught the tram back into the city with my head spinning, but always with the feeling that the 'interview' had gone as well as I could have hoped.

After two anxious weeks, during which I kept wondering just how many others had applied for the job, I was eventually granted a further, much longer interview during which, following much haggling, I was pleasantly surprised to be offered the position, along with a starting weekly salary of £26 – a then reasonably good annual salary of £1,352.

With our rent at just £440 per year and Mavis's salary of a further £10 per week also coming into the equation, things were certainly looking on the up and up for two young newcomers from the old country.

I understood that my new employers were intent on taking their company up to becoming one of the industry's leaders and that taking on the position would represent a huge challenge. But, what the hell! I resolved to grab hold of the offered opportunity and give the job everything I had. What was there to lose?

Giving the required notice of my intended departure to my current employer didn't go down too well, but they seemed to accept my reasons for seeking another position. I am sure on looking back, that the curmudgeons running the factory were relieved to see the back of one or two obviously thought of as a young upstart Pommie intruder into their safe little world. Yes, I had often tried to meet and discuss the need to introduce some form of technical training, at least among those showing potential.

I had also tried to introduce a system of review relating to the condition of the company's master patterns, and other issues relating to costing and specifications. All my suggestions had come to nothing, leaving me at times feeling like an idiot for even trying to raise subjects that were seen by the management as having little interest to their concept of apparel production technology. Companies like theirs would very soon find themselves being left well behind.

I departed Keith Courtenay amicably, a couple of Fridays later, having first shouted a couple of rounds of drinks for my few new workplace friends at the six o'clock swill session at Young & Jacksons. I then meandered off once again on the local Red Rattler train from Flinders Street Station to Carlisle Street, St Kilda, feeling very good about the way things in Melbourne had panned out thus far.

The disappointments Mavis and I had experienced in Sydney and the uncomfortable train journey to Melbourne was fast receding into the dim, dark past…

7

A CHALLENGING NEW ROLE

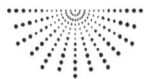

My new position at Stafford-Ellinson spanned nearly a decade. During that period, many things were in the process of changing across my newly adopted country, changes that paralleled others yet to emerge and affect the direction of both my business career and personal life.

The way, pace and the direction of life and living across Australia over the same period was changing in different ways. The growing number of European immigrants that continued to flow into the country becoming the medium through which changes in the way Australians would work and go about their lives would arrive.

Migrants, bringing with them different ideas, languages and customs were regularly arriving from many different countries. This movement of people eventually became the means by which time was involving itself in the changes that began occurring across the country. Australia was emerging from its pre-Second World War languor; people living there were now finding themselves facing a new challenge – the third major upheaval in their country's long history.

In the beginning, Australia's Aborigines had experienced what they had called their Dreamtime. This time though the changes that time was about to make, were arriving more in the way of it seeking to rearrange and add to the original colours on Terra Australis' first canvas. Time now was in the process of adding a new, more diverse and vibrant range of colours onto its already well-prepared canvas base.

Changes, some small and subtle at first, but expanding rapidly as each year passed, gradually resulted in the dynamic transformation of Australian society from what it had been during the earlier years of the 1950s, toward the truly multi-ethnic society that we know today.

Continuing migration of large numbers of people at the time was also creating stresses across parts of Australia's post Second World War society. Difficulties were also having to be faced by a then relatively small Australian population, finding itself needing to deal with such issues as the provision of more housing, infrastructure and everything else that a rapidly increasing population demanded. It was becoming necessary to cope with an increased need for medical and other necessary services, vital infrastructure that required more doctors, nurses and support staff. The rate of increase often made it difficult for the country to easily absorb and house all of those wishing to settle.

Immigration became the unrestrainable force responsible for powering these changes and the need to build more roads, install more and better communications and administration. As a result, life and living in what prior to the war years had been a relatively close and homogeneous society, now found every state, each capital city and many of the rural and decentralised centres across the commonwealth, being committed to a now irreversible process of renewal and expansion.

FIRST CAR

Before taking up my new role in late 1959, one of the first things needing consideration now that our combined income was starting to look healthy, was to equip ourselves with a set of wheels as soon as practicable. This was the first time in my life that I had found myself in the enviable financial position to be able to afford the cash with which to purchase a vehicle of our own. Our first car would, of necessity, be a relatively small, second-hand version – something that would enable Mavis and me to get around at the weekends, in addition to allowing me to travel in some sort of style, to and from my new position in Carlton.

Thankfully, it didn't take me too long to qualify for my Victorian driving licence. Earlier experience driving around the Cotswold Hills in our little group-owned MG roadster during my two years of national service in the RAF didn't do me any harm here either. So, with but a handful of formal driving lessons under the tutorship of the Royal Automobile Club of Victoria, it didn't take too long for

me to become certified as capable of being let loose by myself on the state's roads. Our first family car was to be a second-hand 1954 vintage, side valve Morris Minor.

STAFFORD-ELLINSON

My new role proved challenging. My new employers, Maurie and Simon, were a couple of virtual dynamos. Both were intent on turning their recent acquisition into the leading men's apparel manufacturing group in Australia. They managed to achieve just that over three decades later, following the takeover of two leading Sydney-based menswear brands – Anthony Squires and Ernest Hiller, the latter being the company that had brought me out to Australia.

The Lubansky brothers, together with their father, had commenced trading as a men's outerwear manufacturer with the acquisition of an even older company, C.A. Cohen & Co. in 1946. The family elders, like some others, had migrated to Australia from one of the Baltic States during the early years of the 20th century. Unlike my grandparents, their family's journey from under the oppressive hand of Czarist Russia had resulted in the Lubansky family elders crossing the world to settle in Melbourne.

The trading name Stafford Clothing Co. had been registered in

1948. In 1958 the family took over the already well-established company of Ellinson Brothers, changed the company name to Stafford-Ellinson, thus consolidating their manufacturing operations at 723 Swanston Street, Carlton, a block away from the Melbourne University campus.

The future for the young company, its dynamic owners and its newly appointed, much younger designer was ahead, well into the future. At the time of my joining, the company manufactured a range of men's and boys' outerwear at its plant in Swanston Street, Carlton.

The building was located on three levels at its then premises. It included a basement that was used mainly for fabric, lining and trimming storage. The first-floor level machine room was old, as was the whole building at the time. If it still existed today the local health authorities would most certainly condemn it as unfit for purpose. At the time, similar levels of working conditions applied to most other apparel manufacturing facilities across Melbourne, all leaving a great deal to be desired in terms of work safety, comfort and production efficiency.

The factory's two upper first and second floors housing the cutting room and garment production lacked any pretence of being an attractive or even an efficient work layout. Compared to similar production plants today, the Stafford-Ellinson plant in 1959 was only able to operate in its then form, due to the significantly lower level of health and welfare standards applying at the time. It fell far short if it was to be compared to a modern, one-level work layout that possessed airy, adequate natural lighting conditions for its operatives to work under.

The ground floor fronting onto Swanston Street comprised the two directors' offices, a general office, sales staff offices and a small showroom. At the rear was located the pressing and finishing room and a packing and dispatch room. Working conditions in the factory as implied earlier, were less than comfortable, particularly during the hot summer months, where temperatures in the final pressing room would often come close to unbearable.

During the warmer, usually hot summer months, steam and heat being generated by the bank of Hoffman steam pressing machines on the ground floor, tended by a team of perspiring male operatives, would gradually find its way up between the ageing, worn and loose fitting wooden flooring of the machine room above. This made working conditions among the mainly immigrant female machinists and other operatives on the production line uncomfortable, to say the least. Not what one could liken to 'sweatshop' conditions, but not very far above.

During hotter, more humid days, it often became necessary to provide those working in the pressing and machine rooms with containers of iced water, icy poles or even an occasional treat in the form of a short break and an ice cream. There existed little else to assist both pressers and machinists to cool down a little during the day.

It was to be some years before air conditioning was installed, but even then, the old building was totally inadequate, unable to support an efficient system of cooling in the summer or heating during the depths of winter. The best that could be provided in the summer was the later installation of a bank of large fans.

During the winter months, conditions among the lines of machinists working on the first floor were improved a little as a result of the steamy warmth that percolated up through the floor from the steam presses working below.

My design room was located on the second floor adjacent to the cutting room, where the manufacturing process commenced with the cutting out of fabric, linings and other trimmings. At least in that position, on the top level of the building, working conditions were a little cooler in the summer, but a lot colder during the sometimes near freezing, colder winter months.

The company in the early 1960s employed in the region of 250 production staff – not a large unit by British standards but relatively large locally.

Relationships between the factory workers and management operated in a usually amicable manner. The then union representative, one of the team of finishing pressers who regularly proclaimed his strong connections with the Australian Labor Party (ALP), was seen both by the management, and more than a few of his fellow workmates, as a rabble-rouser. He had been close to the former Australian Communist Party (ACP). The ACP in earlier times had claimed an extensive following in Australia and was regularly being attacked by the right-wing Liberal and Country party coalition government. The prime minister at the time, Robert Menzies, in 1950 even tried unsuccessfully to have the ACP banned in Australia.

Whichever political party the company branch union steward belonged to, he tended to raise the roof on some pretext or another from time to time. The mainly female staff members on the production floor, most of Italian or Greek origin, tended to ignore him and his occasional vociferous arguments and claims against the company's management.

Stop-work meetings with the staff often degenerated into a comical situation that sometimes led to amusing confrontations between the union steward and mainly immigrant female machine-room staff, the people he was supposed to be defending from the greedy bosses. The male cutting-room staff tended to be a little more militant. As a general comment though, good sense usually prevailed, with factory production rarely being disrupted for more than a couple of hours at any one time.

During the 1950s and 1960s, most Australian clothing factory operatives were members of their local branch of the Clothing and Allied Trade Union of Australia, a union that had been in existence since federation. Each state had its branches and locally based organisations, all of which were affiliated nationally with the Australian Labor Party.

A TRUE-BLUE AUSSIE BLOKE

On taking up my new position, I was to meet and work alongside an older man who, for eight years into the future would now find himself designated as assistant to the company's new, young Pommie immigrant designer.

Jack Dormer, the man with whom I was to spend the best part of a working decade, was a native-born Australian who, before being designated as my assistant had operated as the company's specials cutter.

Jack, since returning from the Second World War had been working for the company, with responsibility for cutting individual suit orders received from some of the company's retail clients, on behalf of one of their customers. At times, he would also become involved with measuring and performing the 'fitting' function with the directors' private clients, people for whom the directors, or the company's retail clients, wished to provide a more personalised tailoring service.

Such a role required the person carrying it out to be able to adjust a standard pattern template to the specific measurements and figure type of the customer involved, a skilled and often trying task. He was also required to carry out the 'try-on' function, at a point occurring at various stages of any one-off garment's production, being necessary to ensure that the finished garment fitted the customer correctly when finally finished and pressed.

This aspect of most wholesale apparel manufacturers at the time was a function that operated in parallel with the company's primary role of manufacturing and marketing a full range of standardised outerwear. The bulk of the factory's production of various garment types was destined for sale to their retailer clients, both intra-state and across the commonwealth. From there, garments previously indented[1] by the retailer were offered to the public. No local apparel production was being exported at the time.

In addition to their sales of ready-to-wear apparel, most of the company's major retail clients would also offer a more personalised service to any individual customer who wished to have his new outfit, usually a suit, made-to-measure. Such a service also attracted a higher cost, due to the extra amount of care and attention required during the cutting, manufacturing and fitting processes of individual garments.

In addition to his role as the company specials cutter, Jack had also been responsible, prior to my employment, for making any minor alterations to or replacing worn patterns being used by the cloth and trimming cutters. This function in the past had occurred using the usual practice of cutting bits off and sticking bits onto the original soft paper patterns, most of which had over the years had become so dog-eared that they too bore little resemblance to the originals.

Jack Dormer was a typically male Australian character of those times – a near perfect fit for the description, "a true-blue, dinky-di Aussie bloke".

Jack was a proud ex-RAAF (Royal Australian Air Force) member who, during the Second World War had spent most of his service time serving in various parts of New Guinea, often under fire and at times direct attack from the then Japanese invaders. A widower, since the war Jack had continued to live alone, residing as a long-term paying house guest at one of the local well-known and -attended hostelries, a pub known as Peter Poyntons.

The pub was a well-known and well-loved local watering hole, regularly frequented by local Carlton people and factory workers, at its convenient location on the corner of Drummond and Grattan streets, just a short minute or so walk from the Swanston Street factory.

Jack was what you could accurately describe as a typical Aussie male, one of the remaining few of his generation – a real dinky-di Aussie bloke from a fast disappearing era. He was also a typically laconic, seemingly laid-back – but often emerging as a strongly opinionated individual, then in his late 50s.

Working close by, Jack had the intensely annoying habit of making a disturbing, loud clicking sound, as he manipulated his full set of false teeth with his tongue. The clicking sound thus created would become augmented to a distracting degree whenever Jack became animated or agitated about something or other. The clicking would also become increasingly rapid when he was concentrating on the marking out and cutting out the cloth for a new suit order for a customer, particularly one with a difficult figuration that required a deal of intricate pattern manipulation. The disturbing sound of clicking teeth also became particularly active during the arguments that Jack would get himself involved with, in and around the various workplace discussions that would follow the weekend's local Australian rules footy matches.

Discussion on anything to do with the weekly VFL footy matches represented a regularly debated and discussed subject throughout each working week in and around the factory, with some sessions that could, and often did get to be quite heated and intense.

Jack was a dyed-in-the-wool follower of the local Carlton Football Club, along with his long-time and more elderly mate John Ridgway.

John Ridgway, too, was a well-known local Carlton identity, often to be seen walking around the local streets, accompanied by an ornate walking stick, as he occasionally stopped to shoot-the-breeze (chat) in one or other of the local pubs or cafés. John was a retired well-to-do local son of Carlton, who was also reputed to own at least half the commercial properties along nearby Lygon Street. He, along with his long-time mate Jack Dormer, were well-known followers of the Carlton footy team, attending every match, regardless of the weather, inclement or otherwise.

It was Jack who eventually introduced me to the Mighty Blue Baggers – the Carlton Football Club, the colourful description with which he used to fervently describe what he regarded as being: "The only VFL club worth supporting!"

Jack Dormer was now finding himself in the position of assistant to the company's new designer – a young, recently arrived, Pommie immigrant into the bargain!

I should add here that even though the term Pommie was often used by some native-born Australians in the form of a somewhat derogatory term when describing British immigrants, I had also learned that the term was not necessarily always used by them in a derogatory way when referring to a migrant from Britain. The term could often be used as part of a more benign, more 'gentle' kind of description of a reasonably close friend or work associate. It also could be used, and in some cases proffered, along with a variety of choice, typically Australian words (to be discussed later) as a term of friendship – but not quite one of endearment! The latter form of greeting I was pleased to learn, following the initial shock of hearing something similar being used to describe one or other of my fellow Pommie immigrants – in their cases in a derogatory way.

Jack didn't have much bad to say about the Brits, as he sometimes referred to my fellow British migrants, probably also me, when I was out of earshot. He always made it quite clear though, that he didn't like *'them'* very much. Them in this case meaning any and all recently arrived immigrants of any nationality! Jack Dormer also had little love, certainly little in the way of patience for what he often colourfully described as a "Flood of bloody dagos and wops coming into the country"! His sometimes description of bloody whingeing Poms was bad enough, but references to dagos and wops – his term for immigrant Italians, Greeks and Turks, and what he often described as the "smelly stuff they bring into the factory to eat", that in his view should be stopped!

References such as this and similar were usually delivered with a disturbing degree of vehemence – often accompanied by the ominous clicking of his false teeth, a sure sign of Jack's disapproval.

Jack Dormer, and more than a few other local native[2] Australians were possessed of a distinctly negative attitude toward any new immigrant that happened to cross their paths. In Jack's case, this included that which they brought with them to eat in the factory. In the case of all the Italian and Greek workers, lunch usually had more than its fair share of garlic and other combinations of powerful and pungent aromas surrounding its consumers as well as their workplaces following the daily lunchtime break.

Little did Jack and many others like him, who reacted to anything new that was often also seen to be a potential threat, accept or appreciate at the time that it was the energy, entrepreneurship and style of the new immigrants who were mainly responsible for propelling the country forward.

It was, in fact, these people, migrants all, plus those that arrived during the later boom in Asian migration following the ending of the Vietnam War in 1975, that ultimately served to force changes to the country's way of thinking, lifestyle and tastes. The latter particularly when it came to fashion, food and the constantly developing range of many other kinds of small businesses that were beginning to appear across Australia during the latter half of the 20th century.

Even the ranks of VFL footballers were at the time being gradually added to with sometimes difficult to pronounce foreign-sounding names like Demetriou, Bevilaqua, Silvagni, Kekovic, Barassi, Jesaulenko, Serafini – plus many others even more difficult to pronounce for some of the locals.

The waves of migrants arriving in Australia during the 1950s and 1960s was also serving to change the shopping, dressing, eating and drinking habits of a growing number among the population forever.

Many also from the ranks of foreign migrants, were becoming responsible for much of the ongoing development of new small, street corner milk bars and news agencies, plus at times a whole new variety of medium- sized businesses. Many also became responsible for the establishment of companies that eventually grew into large national and, in some cases, international organisations.

Immigration was changing the face of what, prior to the 1940s, had been a distant, somewhat torpid colonial outpost of the British Crown. Australia was also possessed of something that could fittingly be described as a distinct cultural cringe toward anything regarded as foreign. In this case, foreign meant anyone or anything not Australian, including New Zealand but excluding the Mother Country, Britain.

This so-called cringe often emerged in a form that tended to regard the world outside Australia, other than Britain, as a threat of some sort, requiring Australia and its native-born blokes and sheilas to be happier for the country to snuggle even closer to Mother England. Even when it came to Britain, Australia had, over many years, already become conditioned to a role within that relationship more related to that of a sometimes wayward or delinquent child.

Getting back to Jack Dormer. I am happy to say that once having understood a little more about his early years growing up in Australia and later service with the RAAF, it became much easier to make allowances for his attitude to what was happening to his Australia. It was difficult to easily accept his initial attitude toward so many of what he and many other Australians saw as being unwanted newcomers to their beloved Australia and the changes both Jack and others among his native Australian friends were finding themselves having to experience, along with a sometimes-disturbing level of angst.

Jack Dormer represented an Australia that over the space of but a decade or so was reluctantly finding itself having to undergo a host of changes from the kind of lives that he and many of his fellow native-born Australians had been used to before the Second World War. Those changes, as seen by Jack and others like him, were threatening to take his country far from the way of life and customs of his boyhood and growing years, spent mainly in and around Maitland NSW, between the 20th century's two major wars.

Jack's later years found him living alone and still occupying his one room on the upper floor of Peter Poynton's pub. In some ways his personal life, at least while I knew him, could be described as being lonely and sad. He had one daughter that I knew of who lived in Sydney, but while she had tried at times to maintain at least some contact with her father, he always, for reasons unknown to anyone outside his family, refused to maintain contact with her. As for the rest of Jack Dormer's family story, he never talked about it. He avoided any discussion, other perhaps than around the subject of "the bloody war", footy and his beloved Carlton Football Club.

Jack could be drawn out on occasion, telling many tales around the war that he had been a part of in New Guinea. He often recalled memories of vicious fights with the "bloody Japs", and battles across New Guinea that had raged to and fro across that island's northern shores, and along the now revered Kokoda Track.

Notes

1. Indented – This was a term used generally among the apparel trade to describe the arrangement whereby retailer clients would order stock to be delivered to their store/s, the stock paid for following an agreed period, usually 60 days from the date of delivery.

2. Native – A term that was then usually adopted and applied when referring to white, Australian-born citizens.

ANZAC DAY

Anzac Day was one day in the year that was looked forward to and cherished, both by Jack Dormer and many of his companion ex-Second World War diggers. Leaving aside opportunities to meet up with old mates, have a beer or three and perhaps a surreptitious game of 'two up' in the local park, the day would be followed by an afternoon at the local footy ground. I got to learn that Anzac Day had a very profound, emotional meaning to Jack Dormer and his ex-army and RAF mates, that at first I had failed to understand and fully appreciate.

To me and many others of my generation, the unsuccessful, often revered but patently disastrous assault on the heights of Gallipoli during the 1914–1918 war had over the years since, developed into an unrealistic legend that conflated the Gallipoli campaign with that of Australia's emergence as a fierce fighting and now modern nation. Anzac days since had become more and more closely linked with the war that had raged across Europe during the years 1914 to 1918. Politicians and others with a military axe to grind continued to embellish the role of Gallipoli, until that failed campaign eventually became regarded as if it had been a quasi-success. Even today, that totally disastrous campaign has come to be regarded by some as an occasion holding what they often term as a special place in the nation's proud military history.

To Jack Dormer and other older diggers that I got to meet and speak with over the years, Anzac Day had a very different meaning to them personally. In Jack's words, Anzac Day "has nothing to do with an over-glorified Gallipoli or some other bloody campaign on the Western Front in Europe". One day, over a beer or two in a local pub, Jack opened up and went on to explain that the term Anzac had everything to do with the one day in the year that enabled him, and many thousands of other returned servicemen and women, to meet up with old comrades who had survived wars in which Australians had been engaged. Anzac Day, according to Jack, provided, the opportunity to remember those of his many fighting mates, who failed to return home. "Anzac Day", he stated, "is not for the politicians and other hangers-on who like to glorify war, but for those who were sent to fight and die in wars started by other militant bastards, safe back home sitting on their arses in Canberra and London!"

Since that time, I have come to understand better, what that special day in April has, in fact, come to mean to most of Australia's ex-servicemen and women. Following Jack Dormer's heartfelt description of the emotional meaning of the day, I will always respect Anzac Day for what it truly represents to those of my fellow Australians who managed to emerge relatively unscathed from one or other of

Australia's wars: those who suffered and those also who continue to suffer.

These are the real heroes, fellow Australians who will continue to front up when the call comes for them to serve. Men and women who find themselves weeping for lost comrades in arms who, unlike them, failed to return home.

I refuse to support the often-blatant jingoism that seems to pervade the airways, TV and our newspapers every Anzac Day, and other, often over-the-top support for wars in which Australia continues to allow itself to become involved. Recent years have seen Australia involved in wars and campaigns that history has shown had little, if any, strategic value or long-term meaning to the country's security.

How many times now has Australia become involved in wars and fighting that had erupted on the tenuous basis of spurious, often dreamed up grounds? Australians, too often, have found themselves fighting on a tenuous basis, at the behest of a powerful and overly aggressive 'friend'.

Jack Dormer's later life, interests and activities, while I knew him, were mainly spent at his work, drinking with his football mates at the local pub, and his beloved Carlton Football Club, which he followed with religious fervour, until physically unable to do so.

Jack lived on and continued to work with the company long after I eventually had decided to leave, nearly a decade later. He continued to live at Peter Poynton's hotel until close to the time of his death in 1978.

BRITISH TO THE BOOT HEELS

You may well be wondering why I have spent so many words here referring to the man that was Jack Dormer. The best way I can answer that is by stating that to me, he served to describe that rare example of manhood known to many across the world at the time as a 'genuine Aussie bloke'.

Jack was an Australian of the old school, a man born in a country that during the decades prior to the Second World War, had fitted easily with the statement made famous as a result of Prime Minister

Robert Menzies' declaration that he and through him, all Australians were "British to the boot heels".

While not exactly British, at least in the sense stated by Menzies, while I knew him and many others like him, Jack always seemed to me to come closer to personifying that enduring kind of Chips Rafferty like movie character. Somewhat rough and ready on the outside and ready always for a fight if called upon to defend his way of life, Jack Dormer had a laconic, somewhat softer centre, particularly when it came to looking after someone he saw as being a mate. Jack was representative of many other Australian born men around the same age that I was able to meet and learn much from, during my early years in Australia.

These were men, citizens of an earlier, sparsely populated country many thousands of miles away from Europe, whose fathers and uncles had lived through, fought and many of them had died alongside their mates during the 1914–1918 conflict – often wrongly referred to as the 'Great' War. Many others, like Jack, had served in theatres of war on both sides of the world during the 1939–1945 conflict, and later in Korea. Many Australians had volunteered for service in the RAF, with some flying bombing missions over Germany, others fighting with distinction in the skies over early 1940s England during the Battle of Britain.

When one comes to think further about Australia's contemporary history, it seems to have always been bound up in one military action after another, usually, wars and other military campaigns that in reality had little to do with the country's safety or future. Nearly all had more to do with the military interests of one or other of Australia's earlier and current 'Allies'. The Second World War was perhaps the one exception, but even then, mainly due to the threat that Japan presented, and got so close to achieving.

To me as a newcomer, many older Australian born men met and worked with during my early days in Australia had a similar outlook on life to Jack Dormer.

As things began to change following the ending of the Second World War and the then massive waves of migrating Europeans and others into the country, many older Australians were less than happy to be then experiencing what was happening to their country and earlier way of life. Their unhappiness was then being expressed in terms of their opposition to then rapid changes and pressures being applied to their earlier way of living.

Jack, like so many others of his generation, was always happy to reflect upon and often seem to yearn for an Australia that was now rapidly disappearing into a now shadowy past.

He would often talk and express pride at having lived through or been closely related to some of the older perceptions of glory from Australia's past. Strangely, these also included the massive defeat and losses the then famed Anzac soldiers had suffered at the hands of the Turkish army, on the heights of the Gallipoli peninsula in 1915. That campaign as I understood it, could only be described as a poorly planned, badly executed and dismally led assault against a determined, well dug in enemy, by an army of relatively innocent heroes being led by a pathetic, inadequate group of British generals.

It is strange to think today that such a disastrous event as the brief landing on Gallipoli could eventually get to be regarded as a proud military moment. It is even stranger to hear some of the more imaginative (in my view misguided) modern Australian leaders regularly rabbit on about Gallipoli, as if what occurred there had turned it into a place where Australia's identity as a nation was forged.

To me, that which a young, totally inexperienced and minimally trained group of Australian soldiers managed to achieve in the actual defence of Australia during the Second World War is far more worthy of such a salute. It was in New Guinea that Australians bravely fought off a hardened, determined and aggressive Japanese enemy along the muddy and treacherous slopes and dense jungles along the Kokoda Trail.

Their desperate campaign and sacrifices left the disastrous Gallipoli episode well in its wake as a military campaign worthy of its place, and an occasion upon which to base a claim such as that to which the Gallipoli debacle has become linked.

Men like Jack Dormer were fiercely proud of what they would often project as their independence. Theirs was an attitude often accompanied by fixed views, particularly when it came to their slow acceptance of strangers, some of whom they had been fighting a bitter battle against in some war theatre or other until quite recently. Add to this, a calculated or measured indifference toward authority and a mistrust of politicians, both federal and state, including some of the laws they had been responsible for introducing.

One could often also detect a real fear that their blessed country was in danger of being overrun by strangers – strange people who had brought with them strange customs and equally strange eating habits. This attitude sometimes created a reaction, as they sought to resist what had become an onslaught of the inevitable. Such feelings as these were usually expressed vehemently and with more than just a little venom.

For the preceding descriptions of Jack Dormer and other men I met during my early years living in Australia, they need to be read as enduring impressions gained by a then 24-year-old British immigrant. At the time, I was still a very young man trying to settle into a new life in an Australia, which although very British in so many of its ways, was very different to the home from which I had so recently left behind on the other side of the world.

It was sometimes also disconcerting when in conversation with a group of older Australians, on being assailed with what seemed to be their almost overpowering desire for a return to an Australia, now long gone.

Many Australians that I came in contact with during my early years in the country saw themselves as independent individuals – dinky-di or native Aussies being terms that many I met during my early months in the country, liked to apply to themselves. This at times defensive mainly male self-description was often expressed in places like the local pub, on the terraces of a local footy ground and the local Returned Servicemen's League (RSL) club. Such attitudes would also be expressed on any other convenient occasion, where men were to be found, safely closeted among their male mates and shielded from the women in their lives.

It is also interesting here to describe occasions when, on being invited to a birthday or Christmas party, or even some other kind of friendly gathering – indeed, any excuse for a group of people to get together, have a drink, to chat and have a barbeque, etc. It was at one or other of such a gathering that a visitor would inevitably find that the hosts and their guests quickly, and strangely become divided. One group comprising the men and boys would form at one end of the room or garden, the other, comprising the women and girls, forming at the opposite end.

The men on these occasions would usually be heard talking about the footy, politics and possibly other women, while the women in their lives usually confined themselves to discussing things of the heart, the kids, home – and perhaps at times the foibles of their men?

On such occasions, I usually tried to sneak off toward the women's group, where the company, as well as the tenor of conversation and selection of food and drink, usually proved far more attractive to listen to and eat among, and of course the women and girls were usually far more pleasing to look at.

SPORT AND THE AUSTRALIAN MALE

To Jack Dormer and nearly every other male Victorian having a similar taste in sport, VFL and to a lesser extent VFA Football, (the VFA variety being a more localised, suburban football league) could well be described, as close to being a kind of religion. In some respects, the then weekly footy matches attracted more adherents than the various religious denominations.

Football, in fact, was more often than not taken much more seriously than anything the various religious organisations and churches could exert in the form of real influence. The one possible exclusion to this was among the more welded-on adherents to the Roman Catholic Church, headed up in Melbourne by the assertive and influential archbishop Daniel Mannix.

Discussion between and including many of the male and, even among many female factory, shop and office workers, would follow a regular weekly pattern of expert analysis. Discussion on footy would often rate even higher than complaints relating to the level of wages that the stingy bosses were begrudgingly paying to their hard-working workers.

When it came to the subject of football, very detailed and expert commentary would flow back and forth among the cutters and pressers working in the various apparel factories across Melbourne. A similar situation was also known to apply in most other business and factory location throughout the state.

Discussion on the forthcoming weekend's footy matches would usually start on the Thursday morning before the next weekend's series of VFL matches, in those days the games always played on a Saturday afternoon.

Each Thursday morning's newspapers, like today, would publish the expected makeup of the various teams playing on the following Saturday. Having absorbed this information, animated discussion and comment on the teams and their chances would commence during the morning smoko and lunch breaks. Friday would see discussion in and around footy heating up considerably, with various sweeps and betting trends the main information being clinically dissected. Saturday would see the various matches played at various grounds around the inner metropolitan area.

Sunday, being the day nominated for rest and recuperation and a day when most were not at work, would be spent with those supporters whose teams had been victorious resting happily with their world. The losers, in contrast, would in all probability be gnashing their teeth and complaining bitterly. Comments here would usually include the visual or mental capacities (or lack thereof) of the umpires officiating in their particular match.

"Blind bloody white maggots" was one of the phrases regularly used to describe the sport's umpires. This rather disparaging description often being heard when any discussion regarding their visual or mental incapacity came under animated dissection and discussion. The games' umpires were rarely spoken of in glowing terms.

It has always seemed to me that in the case of the average working Australian male – even today, one ever-present subject to be discussed on most days in and around his workplace during the winter footy season, would be of sport.

In Victoria, that means Australian rules football throughout the winter months, now also being played on Friday evening and Sunday.

These days though, most cities and towns around the country will also include a rapidly growing appetite for the round football game, being played mainly during the summer and autumn. Since the establishment of a rugby league team in Melbourne (Melbourne Storm), interest therein that football code has shown a dramatic increase, to the point recently where the possibility of a second rugby league team is sometimes being talked of.

These days, perhaps with the exception of an 'Ashes' series between Australia and England every four years, when interest often rises to fever pitch in a concerted desire to: "Give the Poms a good hiding", the sport of Test cricket takes over the interest of many throughout the summer months.

The latest cricket innovation of 20/20 cricket (20 overs per side) has taken a strong hold on an almost sport-consumed Australia these days, to the loss of the earlier introduced One Day cricket (50 overs per side), also known as World Series Cricket. The latter form of the game was an innovation introduced in 1977 by the then media mogul Kerry Packer.

In Queensland and New South Wales during the winter months, the sport of rugby league (some have been known to refer to it as thugby), and to a lesser extent, rugby union still dominates the sports scene, although both Australian rules and soccer appear to be gaining ground as each year progresses.

The recent establishment of a women's AFL football league is a positive step forward along what had in the past been a difficult road ahead for female lovers of the sport, who until the commencement of the AFL Women's (AFLW) league in 2017, found their access to the sport limited to that of a spectator.

Not only has AFL football for women entered the mainstream of contact sports in Australia. The country these days can also be proud of two other sports codes in which women's teams have reached the pinnacle of world-class, often achieving far higher results than their Australian male counterparts. Examples of recent women's team achievements include field hockey, soccer, women competing successfully also in international rowing, swimming and skiing. The rugby union also has a national women's team that has achieved more successes since its inception a couple of years ago than their male counterparts have enjoyed over the past decade!

Whichever is the sport of preference in whichever state throughout the Commonwealth of Australia one happens to live or be visiting, sport of some kind or other usually remains king, leaving the various religions way behind both in the number and enthusiasm of its players, followers and adherents.

Back in 1959, the main discussion taking place at most workplaces across Melbourne during the winter season, perhaps only to be displaced by some world-shattering news affecting the nation, was that of a sport. One notably different occasion that served even to link politics with the sport of swimming, was the disappearance in December 1967 of one of Australia's serving prime ministers, Harold Holt, following his ill-advised and poorly timed decision to go for a training swim from the Cheviot back beach near Sorrento in Victoria.

Other than news like war or that similar to the preceding, Monday morning discussions in most factories and offices across the state of Victoria during the 1950s and 60s would range across every aspect of every VFL match that had been played, won or lost on the previous Saturday. It became a virtual resurrection of every move, goal and the inevitable claims of wrong decisions made by the regularly blamed "bloody white maggot" of an umpire that had officiated.

This white maggot attitude was limited to opinions on the part of those whose team had lost, supporters of the winners would usually remain relatively sanguine, neutral and happy with the result.

The term white maggot incidentally, was universal and continues to be used. This decidedly unfriendly phrase still can be heard at times along today's football terraces, even though umpires nowadays usually appear garbed in a variety of colours. Umpires in the days of yore were dressed exclusively in an all-white strip – hence the title.

Once the Monday 'rake-over-the-coals' in detail of the games played on the previous Saturday had been dissected by all and sundry, Tuesday and Wednesday would see a relative calming down among the various opinions and dissections of play from the weekend prior, as everyone awaited the coming announcements detailing the team makeups for the following weekend's matches.

Following the ending of each football season, interest would change over to interstate Sheffield Shield and the international season of Test cricket. Everyone looked forward to the so-called ashes cricket series contests between Australia and England. These matches occurred in Australia every four years, the other years in between being played in England. I didn't miss many of the Boxing Day tests played on the MCG during my employment with Stafford-Ellinson.

A MEMORABLE TEST MATCH

One memorable day's Test cricket that Jack Dormer and I attended was as part of the record crowd of 90,800 that turned up on February 11th 1961 at the MCG. The massive crowd that day attended to witness the second day of the fifth Test match between Australia and the West Indies.

That Test was the last in that year's five-Test series – a memorable one in many ways that had included a tied Test in Brisbane. The games preceding the Melbourne Test had the series on 'level pegging'. Australia managed to snatch a win in Melbourne, at the end of what has been regarded since as the most entertaining and tight sporting contest between two teams of equal talent. The series ended with a motorcade through Melbourne, in part to salute the West Indies team, led by Frank Worrell.

It was a memorable day. The attendance record in 1961 stood, until surpassed by an astonishing 91,092 spectators who attended on the first day of the 4th Cricket Test held on Boxing Day 2013. This match was also against the hated foe – England, in Melbourne. That year's Test series was won convincingly, five tests to nil (a whitewash) by Australia.

ALL THE WAY WITH LBJ

For a short period, Jack Dormer temporarily moved his lodgings from Carlton to a small flat in Inkerman Street, St Kilda, not far from Hotham Street, where I was then living. I couldn't fathom the reason for his move at the time, but was aware that from time to time, he and his landlord, Peter Poynton, would have a kind of 'lover's spat' – a falling out over something or other that Jack would keep bottled up inside him.

And so, in my not very reliable Morris Minor, I would arrange to pick him up in the mornings on my way into work.

On one particular day, I had arranged to give Jack a lift home that evening following work. On emerging from the factory, which fronted onto Swanston Street in Carlton, crowds were already gathering, many of those present having the intention to demonstrate against the motorcade of a visiting US president – Lyndon Baines Johnson (LBJ).

From the noise and number of police that was beginning to line the expected route of LBJ's motorcade into the city that evening, it was clear that not too many among the gathered crowd were there in support of the American president. Rather, given the rapid decline throughout Australia of support for the then Vietnam War, the scene, as we emerged onto the backstreet where I usually parked my car, looked to be poised for a situation whereby many among the gathering crowd were looking to giving LBJ the 'Aussie razz', with catcalls and signs on sticks.

Motioning to Jack to get a move on so that we could get onto Swanston Street and away south through the city well before the arrival of LBJs motorcade, we hurried to my car. I was determined to get well on our way home before the expected motorcade due down Swanston Street, blocked off our route through the city. My aim for a quick getaway didn't go according to plan. As we entered Swanston Street after emerging from where I usually parked the car in the backstreet next to the factory, too late I was horrified to find that I had blundered directly into the motorcade, a few vehicles behind LBJ's black limousine and squads of gun-toting bodyguards.

By the time a patrolling policeman got to us, I was too far out into the street for him to turn me back. This found me slowly driving behind the line of big, black limousines all bristling with G-men, local Australian police, etc. There was my little green Morris Minor trundling along, with its escort of outriding motorcycles on each side, one of the cops shouting at me to keep in line and "Get the hell out of there as soon as I give you the sign to go!"

Jack Dormer was nearly beside himself in his agitation as our situation unfolded. His false teeth were clicking wildly as he muttered: "Fuck this Gerry, we'll bloody well find ourselves both fronting up to the beak (magistrate) in the bloody courthouse tomorrow for this lark!"

All I could do at the time was to keep my eyes on the police car in front of me and be ready for when the cop on the motorbike alongside gave me the word to swerve out of the line of traffic, whenever that would be. That moment didn't arrive until we had proceeded down Swanston Street and the motorcade became held up, due to a commotion further into the city proper, just before we reached Lonsdale Street, to the north of the city centre.

"Quick!" rasped the by now irate cop on the bike next to me, "Get this shitheap out of here and turn down that street on your right!" With that he shouted to a cop on the corner of Lonsdale Street, to make a way through the crowd for us to get through. Heart in mouth and in full expectation of becoming arrested by the cop on the bike and, with Jack Dormer, false teeth clicking furiously while mouthing all manner of not too nice thoughts on the subject of the "bloody Yanks again trying to take over the bloody country" sitting beside me, I gunned the not very powerful eight horse-power engine down a near-deserted Lonsdale Street. Turning into Elizabeth Street I hightailed it toward Flinders Street west and safety, through South Melbourne and directly home – not before dropping a sweating, smoking and very unhappy Jack Dormer, false teeth still a-clicking, as he wandered off toward his flat.

All the next day I fully expected to receive a call from the cops, who surely would have noted my car's registration number? But all turned out quiet and with nothing to suggest that they had decided to take my inadvertent injection into LBJ's motorcade any further. I suppose they had many other things on their minds that day, with some folks throwing red paint on LBJ's car and all manner of protests erupting as he passed through the city on his way to the haven of his Melbourne hosts, somewhere in the South Yarra area.

So ended my involuntary 'all the way with LBJ' brush with history. When I eventually made later inquiries, no one from the press it seems had taken a photo or two of the little green Morris Minor that got itself caught up in the LBJ motorcade that day – very disappointing.

FIRST NEW HOME

1965 was the year that saw my little family, which now included our two young sons, Andrew Simon (1961) and Philip Nathan (1963), moving into our newly built three-bedroom house of brick veneer over green hardwood timber frame, at 190 Centre Dandenong Road, Cheltenham, in Melbourne's then rapidly expanding southern suburbs.

Our new home, set on a quarter-acre block of land, complete with its Hills clothes hoist concreted into the centre of the back garden, was proudly acquired for the then princely sum of £12,750. Our then 30-year £10,000 bank mortgage commitment was entered into at an interest rate of 5%.

WHERE'S YOUR BLOODY HAT?

Having by now settled down into my new position at Stafford-Ellinson, it had earlier become necessary to review the fit and appearance of the various styles of apparel being produced by the company.

It had also become necessary to review every existing set of master patterns to ensure that their use would at the same time allow the most economical use of fabric and linings. New styling changes and fitting improvements also needed to be decided.

The main staple of the menswear trade during the late 1950s and 1960s was the two or three-piece lounge suit combination, a style of business suit worn universally by men working in a bank, office, or other 'white collar' position.

One of my first forays into one of the company's retail clients' store was to meet with the team of menswear buyers at the then Myer

Emporium (later the Myer Group), on the fourth floor of their headquarters store in Bourke Street Melbourne. This, my first visit, turned out to be a valuable learning experience for me in more ways than one, serving to highlight one seemingly important aspect of my role of which I had not previously been aware.

Australia during the 1950s and 60s was a country in which the wearing by nearly every business male in the population of the ubiquitous trilby, or similar style of formal business headgear was considered to be a necessity. Not having been used to wearing one myself during business hours, it came as a bit of a shock when on entry into the Myer store in Bourke Street for the first time, I was gently reproached by the head menswear buyer, Ken Michington, for arriving without a hat! Being reasonably fast on my feet, a necessary skill gained during my earlier life in the RAF, I managed to blurt out that I had been in such a hurry in my desire to meet with Ken and his staff that I had unfortunately forgotten to don my personal lid.

My apology was accepted along with a few laughs, but that didn't stop my boss Maurie, a couple of days later, from admonishing me for not wearing a hat when attending a meeting at one or other of the Melbourne CBD's retailers. "It is," he stated, "important that you don't forget your hat when attending any meeting with our customers. It is mandatory to buy and wear one whenever you represent the Stafford-Ellinson brand!"

Returning home that evening, resplendent in a newly purchased piece of headgear, resulted in a peal of laughter from my wife who offered the opinion "Now you really look like one of the Aussie male mob!" Yes, a hat during the 1960s was considered in the trade to be a required accessory – almost as important it seems as not forgetting to pull on one's trousers in the morning!

As the years passed into the later 1960s, most of the earlier more conservative dress codes were gradually becoming consigned to the pages of history. The need to wear a hat became less and less, until today it is no longer regarded as an important element in every man's daily attire. The later 1970s saw some rapid changes in the way men chose to dress for business.

Some of the more radical styles like the wearing of shorts or some form of relaxed/casual jacket continued to remain unacceptable when it came to men's business attire. Trilby-style hats, long-sleeved shirts, long trousers and conservatively coloured neckties apart, life in the late 1960s eventually merged into the early 1970s, with me also becoming established in my role as the company's designer.

Not only was I by then at last able to settle into my position, but by that time the various men's apparel manufacturing principals, particularly in Melbourne, were beginning to feel a growing need to provide professionally run technical training for some of their employees.

Organised technical training facilities for the apparel manufacturing industry throughout Australia at the time were virtually non-existent. In Melbourne however, there began early moves, particularly among a few of the more forward-looking manufacturers, for some form of technical training programme to be established, particularly in the areas of men's pattern design, cutting and tailoring.

SHOWTIME AND NEW CHALLENGES!

In the Australian apparel manufacturing industry of the 1960s and 1970s, there were two well-defined periods of the year when the pressure, both on design and production teams became almost unbearable. These occurred a few months before the spring/summer and autumn/winter showings, when decisions on an upcoming season's designs became necessary, fabrics selected and bought, styling reviewed, then sample garments produced and made ready for the forthcoming season's showings to retail clients.

All this feverish activity had to be completed in time to allow the sales team to make their biannual sales pitches to the various retailer buyers across the country, each client subsequently placing firm indent orders for the following season.

The manufacturing and retail sectors of the Australian apparel industry then worked almost exclusively by what were termed as retailer indent orders. Retailer clients would order and subsequently pay for all products ordered (indented) by them. Few, if any at that stage operated on the basis of some form of on-consignment deal. This was a process whereby the manufacturer was obliged to place stock in the retailer's store, to be credited later as sales were made from that stock.

Each seasonal process followed a fixed timetable, commencing with each apparel manufacturer working up ranges for the new season, following which competing manufacturers' new garment and fabric ranges were presented to retail buyers. The various buyers, in turn, would be expected to commit themselves, by putting down firm orders for future staged delivery into their stores.

It should also be noted that without exception, store buyers and floor selling staff during the 1960s, were expected to be familiar with every aspect of the products they were responsible for buying and selling.

In the men's and women's apparel trade, buyers and their staff needed to know their fabrics, understand how garments were made, and what level of work went into a tailored garment. They were also expected to have an up-to-date understanding of fashion trends and how to translate these into the buying and subsequent successful merchandising of the product ranges they were planning to indent on behalf of their store.

In contrast, and from observations during visits to apparel retailers in Melbourne today, it is all too rare to find a salesperson on the floor of any one of the major retailers or department stores who are in possession of the level of detailed product knowledge that in years past was required of someone employed in that role.

Another aspect of retailing today that differs considerably from apparel retailing in the 1960s, 1970s and 1980s, is the conduct of seasonal sales. During that period, end-of-season sales was limited to the tail end of a selling season, the remnants of whatever parts of a retailer's apparel range had yet to be sold, then being offered, at heavily discounted prices, during an end-of-season sale.

Today, in contrast, when it comes to the concept of a sale, most retailers are known to demand that their suppliers provide them with a range or two of specially priced apparel items throughout the year. These usually are offered to the public as sale items, intended to be offered for sale at any time of the year, as decided mainly by the retailer involved. These days, the meaning of an end-of-season clearance sale has in fact become meaningless.

TECHNICAL TRAINING

A proposal relating to the establishment of some form of technical training was raised at a meeting of Melbourne-based principals of major Victoria-based apparel manufacturing companies. The upshot of these discussions eventually resulted in me being approached by the Victorian chapter of the Australian Clothing Manufacturers Association (ACMA), and invited to set up and organise a Melbourne-based training programme.

I agreed to set up an after-hours course, which in its initial stages was to be established at the Melbourne College of Textiles (MCT) premises, then located in Cumberland Road, Pascoe Vale. Stafford-Ellinson and the Sackville group, another local menswear manufacturer, also located in nearby Carlton and at least three other manufacturers agreed to provide students, in addition to covering the cost of setting up the training facilities, their student's tuition and my expenses.

MCGREGOR

At work, my design workload, in addition to setting up and running the proposed technical training programme, continued to increase, with the company securing the Australian rights to manufacture and distribute men's leisure and sports apparel products under the then world-renowned and prestigious top US men's sportswear brand McGregor-Doniger.

Macgregor branded sportswear in the US and throughout Europe at the time was considered to be the most technically advanced, stylish casual apparel being produced and marketed.

From purely a technical standpoint, the design, structure and fit of McGregor garments had been researched and developed to such an extent over preceding years, that very little handwork was required during their production. The fit of McGregor sports and casual jackets, casual tops and sports pants, bearing in mind the lighter-weight construction they enjoyed when compared to the way Australian produced so- called 'tailored' garments were being constructed at the time, was demonstrably superior to anything we had been able to achieve to date.

Additional to the more relaxed form of apparel being marketed under the brand, McGregor's technical staff in the US had achieved phenomenal results, being able to produce garments using lighter-weight interlinings, in addition to adopting methods of construction that enabled them to produce jackets, sports tops and similar types of garments that were softer, lighter and more comfortable in wear, and superior for travelling with. The Americans, having the world's largest local retail market to work with, had explored and perfected a system of mass production that enabled them to produce lighter-weight garments capable of fitting a standard figure as well as any hand-tailored garment.

As a result, McGregor's US factories were able to reduce the number of production elements throughout the manufacture of apparel of all descriptions, enabling the cost of production to be significantly reduced. US wholesale clothing manufacture was well in advance of anything that Australian manufacturers were then capable of achieving.

Whatever we learned from McGregor design criteria and manufacturing techniques was also adapted wherever possible, to our standard Stafford-Ellinson production. At the time, locally based manufacturing expertise and our limitations regarding operator experience, when added to the factory's much smaller and less efficient workflow system and equipment, limited the level to which mass production systems and equipment used in the US could be readily adapted directly in Australia. Gradually, the more advanced methods of production learned from our new US partner were adapted to the company's local production. This required the retraining of some workers in various areas of the Carlton production plant.

The McGregor range of sportswear was immense. Here in Australia, with a much smaller and widely distributed population and much lower sales quantities, it became necessary to limit the range of garments being offered to style classifications able to be profitably promoted to a more limited Australian market.

All this was exciting but often frustrating stuff. For me at least, the addition of our new sportswear range offered the opportunity to develop my skills to the point where I had become involved across a range of garments that had more than tripled in size and scope.

While the company had grown larger and more diversified, with the principals now travelling overseas in search of new production trends both in Europe and the USA, they gave little thought to providing their designer with a similar opportunity to become up-to-date with technical and design developments overseas.

The company in the meantime had expanded in size to include the taking over some smaller, less efficient companies and the opening of a new trouser manufacturing plant in the Victorian regional city of Bendigo, two hours north of Melbourne. This new production facility required a constant toing and froing between Bendigo and the main plant in Carlton.

TIME FOR A CHANGE

As the 1970s approached, I was beginning to sense that I was approaching the time where I needed to look toward expanding my horizons, preferably on the marketing side of the industry. Unfortunately, my employers were happier to keep me in my present position as they both tended to brush off my regularly voiced interest in moving over to a more customer related role on the marketing side of the company's growing operations.

The Stafford-Ellinson brand had expanded rapidly over the years. It now included the Macgregor sports range and one or two other additional, internationally known brands and a small range of newly created house brands.

As 1969 rolled around, I was coming close to having spent nearly a decade with the now expanded Stafford Group. My personal life had become more comfortable, and the manner in which my family was able to live and my wife and me able to afford to provide both our sons with a good standard of education at Mentone

Grammar School, now had become relatively easy to manage and finance.

My business life, on the other hand, was stalling. I was gradually getting to the point where I was starting, instinctively, to examine whatever other options were open to me elsewhere, preferably in a more demanding role, one more connected with product marketing.

Over the years I had continued to keep myself interested and abreast of developments across both the wool textile and much broader apparel and synthetic textile fibre industries. I had thus been able, despite the restrictions of my current position, to gain a more rounded range of knowledge, experience and perhaps more importantly, a number of contacts across a broader range of industries, still related in some way to apparel manufacturing.

I also began to research information and background on some possible options, and was able to gain a great deal of information and contacts through meetings with client buyers across the Melbourne-based retail trade. I was also able to arrange valuable contacts among local and international fibre and textile manufacturing and marketing organisations.

In anticipation of a possible change in career direction, I continued to establish direct contact with other organisations, including the Australian Wool Board and ICI/Fibremakers, the latter being the manufacturer and marketer of polyester fibres in Australia. I also had over past years established contact with other international textile fibre and yarn suppliers and textile research groups – all this with the aim of keeping myself up-to-date with developments across the then rapidly expanding textile world.

I recall a saying first heard of in another world far, far away in a past life back in Leeds. It went along the lines of "Everything comes to them what waits and watches" (sounds better if spoken in a deep Yorkshire accent – but I guess you will get the picture). I'm not sure where this sliver of wisdom came from, but in my case, it seemed the only real and positive option open to me at the time.

And so I decided to wait a while and, like Wilkins Micawber, that ever-optimistic gentleman who featured so strikingly in Charles Dickens's book titled "David Copperfield", I too patiently waited for 'something to come up'.

OPPORTUNITY KNOCKS

The gods must have been smiling down on me once again, now having embarked on my search for a more challenging role.

One Saturday morning following a few months of waiting, Mr Micawber style, something did eventually come up…

Melbourne's *The Age* newspaper one Saturday morning contained the advertisement that once again served to create a series of changes, both to my professional and private life.

The Australian Wool Board (AWB), the statutory organisation originally set up in 1936 by the federal government, having responsibility for the promotion and other activities in support of Australia's wool, were seeking the services of a menswear product manager for its re-formed product marketing division.

The advertisement in *The Age* described the position as AWB requiring a senior executive possessing extensive experience across all levels of the Australian menswear industry, capable of representing Australian wool to Australia's textile and apparel manufacturing and retail markets. The position was described as encompassing product promotion and development of merchandising plans in support of wool, across all levels of the menswear trade.

Just what the doctor ordered, was my first thought, when my wife shoved the advertisement in front of my nose over my bowl of half-eaten cornflakes, with the comment: "Go for it!" And go for it I did.

I did know quite a lot already about the Australian wool industry, having studied the fibre. I also possessed a good working understanding of all the stages of wool processing, wool textile production, and design, and the various wool types involved, acquired during my earlier years of study at LCT in Leeds.

My application provided my background, qualifications and experience. I also described my activities in technical training at the Melbourne College of Textiles, including a reference from the head of that organisation. My Associateship (ACI) of the London-based Clothing Institute, being the sole Australian resident to hold that position wouldn't do any harm either. Also included in my application I supplied comments designed to illustrate my understanding of current discussions at federal government level on the subject of a proposed reserve price scheme for wool, also early discussions around the possible future acquisition of the Australian wool clip by AWB or an associated organisation.

I was already familiar with the International Wool Secretariat and its international research and promotional role, which operated parallel to the Australian Wool Board.

In addition to my application, I included my considered thinking on problems I saw to be facing Australian wool, together with a short discussion on the kind and range of activities thought appropriate to wool's ongoing support and marketing to consumers. Alongside this I included my views on the pros and cons of continuing to promote pure new wool products as opposed to opening up the board's policy thinking to include blends of wool with other fibres, both synthetic and natural.

The question of blending wool with other fibres was known to be a contentious subject in Australian wool circles.

DO I REALLY WANT TO DO THIS?

Once having mailed my application to Wool House, I reflected on what it may be like to become an employee of an organisation regarded by many decision-makers involved with the Australian textile and apparel manufacturing industries, as a less than effective group of people.

AWB Activities and expertise concerning the growing of wool and the launching of fashion parades and advertising aside, there were a number of other issues of concern to me at the time. My immediate concerns were in the areas of textile and apparel manufacturing and promotion, when added to perceptions of the organisation's limited value to Australia's textile and apparel manufacturers. These were but a few of the issues of the day, considered by most industry managers with whom I came in contact from time to time, to be in urgent need of improvement and change.

It was the general view among many Australian textile producers during the 1960s that AWB had not to date shown itself to be in the same league when it came to competing with the tactics successfully being employed in support of polyester, nylon and, then to a lesser extent, acrylic fibres. One case in point was the organisation's then strict adherence to its still current pure new wool policy, a policy that had been in operation since the mid-1930s, that was seen by nearly all involved with wool-based textile manufacturing to be in urgent need of change.

The fibre marketing business had changed considerably since AWB's policy on pure new wool had been introduced.

Another area of contention concerned AWB policy that continued to present wool via a solely generic promotional format, that concentrating solely on the promotion of pure new wool products via the Woolmark.

My own contacts over past years with the self-styled but always distant group of 'fashion experts' based at AWB's headquarters at 360 Bourke Street, Melbourne, had left me and other members of the local wool textile manufacturing and men's and women's apparel industries puzzled as to just what value they offered the industry. The generally expressed view here was that the only real value AWB provided was via the organisation's seemingly unlimited capacity to shell out large wads of promotional money from its seemingly bottomless bag of co-operative advertising funds.

What AWB staff seemed to regard as 'services' to the local textile and apparel manufacturing industries, other than co-operative advertising, were considered by most apparel company directors and managers to be less than helpful.

Trade visitors to Wool House in Melbourne were usually allowed only a 'look-and-no-touch' view of the latest textile and fashion trends, the regular useful information that was being received by AWB from their various overseas sources, Europe in the main. Most trade visitors to Wool House were also required to apply for a viewing, then conducted across the luxurious pile carpets of AWB's fashion office – all the time watched hawklike by one or other of the fashion office manager, Nan Brunner, and her assistants. Such treatment presumably was to deter anyone from secretly trying to snip off a bit from a fabric swatch or a colour card, as a reference to take away to his or her mill or apparel factory?

"They make you feel like you are a young child on its first visit to Santa's Grotto," was one comment a leading industry colleague once pointedly offered to me, following his visit all the way from his mill in Sydney, after him being told that he would not be allowed to take a sample or two from AWB's projected design trends for the following season.

While interesting to observe visually, the kind of services then being offered by AWB in this technically important area for every textile mill, was for all practical purposes a 'non-service' to his and most other textile and apparel manufacturers who, like myself on more than one occasion, was denied even the opportunity of a viewing!

It was also disappointing to find that AWBs fashion 'experts' hadn't thought it necessary to leave their plush offices in Bourke Street, Melbourne, to take their fashion services direct to mills, apparel manufacturers and retailers across the country.

Favourites of Nan Sanders (then director of AWB's marketing division) were known to receive invitations to long lunches, either at a catered affair at Wool House, or a restaurant nearby. These were known to follow a private preview of AWB's biannual colour and design service information. A similar kind of service was rarely if ever provided to nearly all the other run-of-the-mill textile operations across the country.

It was unfortunate, particularly during what proved to be a critical period for the Australian wool industry, that not one of the staff employed within AWB's then marketing division, possessed any previous working experience involved directly with or within the textile and apparel manufacturing industries. Nor did any of AWB's so-called marketing staff seem to consider it necessary to visit or establish close contact with textile mills and apparel production plants located outside Melbourne or Sydney.

Even in Melbourne and Sydney, company visits were known to be limited to one or two of the director's chosen few, her visits being conducted, according to reports, in the style of royalty attending a state occasion.

AWB's liaison staff nominally responsible for promoting the use of wool by local manufacturers, operated with a distinctly hands-off approach when it came to what they usually referred to as 'the trade'.

AWB was very efficient at putting on superbly staged fashion shows and entertaining lavishly. An invitation to one or other of AWB's promotional functions was keenly sought after, seen to be a good feed and drinking opportunity. Usually, these functions, mainly attended by fashion magazine, newspaper, PR company executives and other VIP types, offered little more than a preview of AWB's corporate advertising themes for the coming season, at the time being developed by one or other of Australia's leading advertising agencies.

When it eventually came to the position AWB offered, I found myself facing a series of intensive interviews at Wool House conducted by Mick Hull, the retiring manager of the then Merchandising Department. During subsequent interviews, I learned that Hull's objective in inviting applications from outside the organisation was to attract an experienced, practical and technically proficient applicant. A person, he stated, who could demonstrate the capacity and drive with which to make drastically needed changes to AWB's current product marketing and merchandising operations.

Hull's description of the position did serve to allay a number of my earlier concerns. I was also to learn that the appointee to the menswear position would be expected to take over responsibility for a broad range of AWB product marketing activities. His or her responsibilities would include the provision of colour and design services, the use of a travel budget, responsibility for the allocation of co-operative advertising funds and a budget intended for product development projects. It was also interesting to learn that within AWB there had been a somewhat belated acceptance of the need to attract more commercially and technically experienced staff to wool's cause.

I was eventually appointed to the position, along with the assurance, received during an interview with the managing director of AWB, Bert Overell, that my appointment was in the expectation of a number of major changes that he stated were going to be made to the way that AWB went about its business. It was also stated by Mr Overell that my input to discussions related to these changes would be both required and welcomed, at both senior management and board level.

One of the provisos on taking up the role of menswear product manager with the AWB was that I agree to relinquish my training role at the MCT. I was provided with a couple of months during which to pass over my responsibilities to my then assistant.

8
AUSTRALIAN WOOL

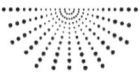

THE INDUSTRY THAT NEARLY DIED

The farming of sheep and the industry of woolgrowing dates back to the first years of European settlement in Australia. For much of Australia's early history, the growing of wool emerged as the industry that would continue to carry the country upon its woolly back.

Forming what amounts to a book within a book, the following Parts 8, 9 and 10 provide a unique view of the Australian wool industry during the 30-year period 1960–1990. It is a history that was witnessed first-hand by a middle ranking manager, who, from 1970 to 1978 worked for the then Australian Wool Board and its later incarnation – the Australian Wool Corporation (AWC), a critical period that preceded the industry's collapse in 1991.

Much has been written about the Australian wool industry. In the main, these writings have taken the form of general commentary or rural and government reports – inevitably to the accompaniment of reams of statistics relating to sales, wool prices, political events and the personalities that controlled them.

Some writings have been critical, particularly when commenting on Australian government and the various decisions of industry leaders', a number of the latter that resulted in the industry's premature collapse, just before the turn of the 21st century.

Issues and controversy had over the years become an inseparable feature of an industry that for more than 150 years had been a key element responsible for Australia's growth and ongoing prosperity.

During what has been described as the industry's heyday, particularly the late 1940s and early 1950s, the farming of sheep and the profitable sales of wool seemed destined to continue upward into the distant future. Unfortunately, those halcyon days were destined instead to come to a premature close, a situation that has sometimes been described as near death.

Most articles, official reports, statistics and books written on the subject since, have tended to concentrate mainly on the industry's political and economic machinations, alongside issues related to its continued support to Australia's economic well-being.

Historically, since its beginnings during the latter years of the 18th century, the growing of wool and later, Australia's own expanding textile and apparel manufacturing industries, had served to employ a large cross-section of Australia's working population.

Alongside the growing of wool, the production of textiles and apparel became important contributors to Australia's economy. Both industries in one form or another continued to thrive even among some of the provincial towns that had grown to eventually become established centres of the population, across and in some cases well beyond the hinterland surrounding Australia's major city-based populations.

A DIFFERENT HISTORICAL VIEWPOINT

What follows is a little different to the usual historical accounts and commentaries that have discussed and sometimes critiqued wool politics and those individuals leading the industry, throughout a history that has included a significant number of periodic ups and downs.

The following pages, covering just three decades of wool's recent history, includes discussion of the period 1950–1990, 40 years that were the prelude to a crisis. The ultimate paragraph of this story arrived in the form of a financial jolt of mammoth proportions, followed by wool's rapid decline from its historical position as a major force in the world of textile fibre marketing.

Parts 8, 9 and 10 are not directly related to the actual growing of wool. Nor is it intended to provide commentary on the sometimes brutish and often ill-conceived machinations and politicking of those responsible for the woolgrowing industry's overall direction and related legislation, other than how those decisions affected the operations of the AWB and its later re-incarnation as AWC.

Instead, the following chapters will present a unique view of the industry – a personal account that describes the inside workings of both organisations, at the time critical to Australian wool's future. It is a record of events covering eight years, as directly experienced by a middle-level manager, involved in the front-line fight between wool and synthetic fibres. It is a sorry but candid history that covers events directly experienced and recorded by the writer.

Later, in 1974, I was charged with the task of increasing sales of Australian wool across North America. The objective behind the setting up of an AWC office in New York had been to increase the consumption of Australian wool in North America, a previously important market for wool, at the time in rapid decline.

With AWC at the time holding a growing stock of wool in its Australian warehouses, the AWC board had decided, following discussion with a number of US-based wool processors and the International Wool Secretariat, to provide the US market with a direct supply of Australian fine wools, at stable prices unaffected by price fluctuations in the Australian auction system. Sales were to be conducted directly to US wool processors, with technical assistance provided down the textile and apparel manufacturing pipeline, through AWC's office in New York. Orders for wool would be delivered directly to its US clients, from a store at the Port of Charleston, South Carolina.

Looking back a few years prior to AWC's entry into the US, the events and decisions that ultimately resulted in the market collapse suffered by Australian wool in 1991 had their origin much earlier.

While some observers have continued to link the collapse of the wool industry in 1991 directly to the failure of the AWC's then reserve price scheme, introduced in 1974 – a number of other market-related issues were involved:

- First of these was the industry's decision to virtually ignore and fail to react early enough to the rapid emergence of synthetic fibres, mainly polyester, nylon and later acrylics, during the decade following the ending of the Second World War. This failure alone denied at least a decade and a half of tactical advantage to the industry – too much time during which it abdicated much of the influence previously held with primary processors and later stages of the textile/apparel and non-apparel product pipeline.
- The failure of those leading the industry to respond to the emergence of synthetic fibre production trends early enough despite appeals from processors and users of Australian wool, ultimately resulted in the demand for apparel wools worldwide being reduced considerably more (and far quicker) than should have been the case.
- The Australian government's decision to reduce the level of import tariffs on textiles and apparel, while allowing increased import quotas of textile, apparel and footwear didn't help. These changes, introduced over too short a period and with little thought to future consequences relating to local employment and prices, caused the collapse of textile and apparel manufacturing across Australia. Irrespective of whether or not they were using wool, it could also be argued that the loss of a once widespread and productive wool textile manufacturing industry across Australia paralleled similar losses that were occurring across the Western world.

The narrative that follows will inevitably contrast in a number of ways with other more official Australian government and woolgrowing industry oriented views of AWC's activities, successes and failures. While these views and opinions are important, it is also important that the detailed story of what was occurring deep within the management structure of AWB and later, AWC, during a critical period of both organisations' reign, be also recorded. Only then can a complete picture of the self-inflicted downward trajectory of Australian wool be more accurately portrayed.

It is with this object in mind that the following sections of this book are offered…

WOOL MARKETING AND PROMOTION

For over 150 years, the production and sale of raw (greasy) wool had been the industry underpinning the ongoing viability and growth of Australia's economy. Commencing during the mid-1930s, three new organisations, predominantly funded by Australia's woolgrowers were established. Each, in turn, was charged with responsibility for the promotion of Australian wool. The Wool Bureau, established in 1953, was followed by the Australian Wool Board in 1963, the latter becoming the pivotal organisation responsible for the support and promotion of Australian wool.

AUSTRALIAN WOOL BOARD

This became the organisation responsible for the promotion of Australian wool. AWB existed in its first phase between May 1936 and January 1945, in its second phase between June 1945 and April 1963, and in its third and final phase, between May 1963 and December 1972.

In 1973 AWB morphed into the Australian Wool Corporation (AWC), an organisation that brought together the AWB and Australian Wool Commission, the latter an organisation primarily concerned with the quality control, auction liaison and presentation of raw wool to users worldwide.

The functions of each of AWB's earlier stages varied, with its most recent incarnation, AWC, having the broadest powers. These included the promotion of wool and wool products in Australia and other countries, the capacity to inquire into, and from time to time report upon the methods of marketing wool and any other matters connected with wool. Other, unspecified, functions could also be conferred on the board of AWC by the Australian government, or as approved by the minister for primary industries from time to time.

The board's activities were funded by a levy on woolgrowers, first instituted in 1936, to enable the financing of AWB's ongoing wool promotional activities. This levy was later supplemented by additional funding from the Australian government.

The objectives of AWB and later AWC:

- Joint international promotion of wool products through the International Wool Secretariat. Funding for IWS to be provided in partnership with the wool boards of New Zealand, South Africa and Uruguay. Other responsibilities included the provision of testing services for wool and wool products.
- Provision of advice to government on wool research activities by government bodies relating to the needs of the wool industry, and oversight of all aspects of wool marketing but without executive powers over marketing.

THE INTERNATIONAL WOOL SECRETARIAT

The International Wool Secretariat (IWS) was established in 1937 to counter the then rapidly expanding production and use of synthetic fibres. The organisation introduced a promotional policy that restricted its worldwide network of offices, including those of AWC, to the support of products containing 100% pure new wool.

IWS was also responsible for the review of research being carried out by independent bodies, including the Wool Industries Research Association (WIRA), based in Ilkley, England.

The organisation, headquartered in London, was financed by levies on wool grown in Australia, New Zealand, South Africa and Uruguay, of which Australia provided by far the largest share of the funds provided to IWS.

At the time of IWS's establishment, there had been a leap in the production of synthetic (non-natural) fibres such as rayon (later polyester nylon and acrylic), acetate rayon fibres originally being used in some products, in particular as a substitute for silk.

Germany alone produced 9,200 tons of these artificial (synthetic) fibres in 1934, 19,600 tons in 1935 and 45,000 tons in 1936. It was anticipated at the time, that the production for 1937 would be 90,000 tons. Production increased dramatically following the ending of the Second World War.

The IWS came under the control of two Australians, Sir William Gunn (1914–2003) as chairman. Gunn was also chairman of AWB. Sir William Vines (1916–2011) operated as IWS's managing director.

A certification mark used on pure new wool products that met a specified standard of quality was introduced in August 1964. The design of this mark was selected following a 1963 competition won by a Milanese designer, Francesco Saroglia.

The objectives of IWS:

- To position and maintain wool at the pinnacle of the textile market.
- To ensure that products bearing the Woolmark label were made from pure new wool and manufactured to the highest standards.

The Woolmark logo was a success when introduced. It eventually ranked with two other universally recognised logos regarding consumer recognition and understanding: a large scallop shell and a three-pointed-star.

Within these two organisations resided the main players charged with the making of decisions and the setting of policies and activities in defence of wool across the world's textile fibre markets, including the development of products containing wool, and their subsequent promotion to the world's consumers.

IWS promotional policy recognised wool solely in a generic sense, covering products ranging across apparel, non-apparel products, carpets etc., that later were to be identified by the Woolmark. It was not intended to include the specific promotion of Australian, New Zealand, Uruguayan, South African or any other individual company sourced or branded products manufactured from pure new wool, or dominant blends of wool with other fibres.

With IWS activities continuing to be directed solely in support of pure new wool as a basic, generic fibre, similar for promotional purposes to that of cotton, the continuance of this policy beyond the late 1940s, served to severely restrict AWC's capacity to defend the position of Australian wool in what had developed into an increasingly competitive textile fibre marketplace.

The continuation of IWS's pure new wool policy, regardless of rapidly changing circumstances in the worldwide apparel fibre marketplace, would later become an issue of some importance to the success or otherwise to the international marketing of products containing Australian wool in pure form, and blended products containing wool.

As more synthetic fibre dominated products began to gain market share across the world's apparel markets, this trend resulted in a corresponding decline in Australian wool's share of textile fibres being consumed, even as overall demand was increasing. This trend resulted in Australian wool facing direct competition from other wools, a proportion of which was being sourced from other IWS member countries.

With funds and promotional activities continuing to be directed solely toward the generic promotion of pure new wool from whatever source, the identity of products containing Australian wool was soon to become lost among every other kind of wool-containing product.

Australian wools also began to come under increased attack on the basis of price. The use of branding or other form of recognisable image that made it easier for end-product marketers to promote other wool products to consumers assisted that trend. Alternative products included but were not limited to those containing wool that had originated in New Zealand, South Africa, Uruguay, South America, the US and various parts of Europe.

As the world entered the late 1960s and early 1970s, the former halcyon days during which wool products had benefited from being promoted as 100% pure new wool, along with the imprimatur of the Woolmark, had lost its capacity to hold sway in an increasingly competitive fibre marketing environment. A more creative way by which to promote the cause of Australian wool had by then become critical.

For all practical purposes, continuing reliance on the Woolmark and a label stating that a product contained pure new wool had run its course.

A growing number of Australian designers and manufacturers of higher fashion, general (everyday) apparel and knitwear, were already recognising the need to differentiate their products containing Australian wool, by the use – not only of the Woolmark, but some other additional and clearly definable brand identity. As a result, some of the more innovative among them began moving toward the identification and promotion of wool-containing products by the use of a brand, or some other form of identification, story or brand, often coupled to a recognisable Australian theme.

Two such Australians, one a spinner and marketer of wool and wool blended hand-knitting yarns, the other a women's fashion designer, earlier had recognised the need to change the way in which wool-containing apparel and related products were then being promoted. There were other Australian-based manufacturers and marketers thinking along similar lines at the time.

The then New Zealand Wool Board was already seeking to differentiate its country's wool products, mainly carpets, by identifying them as being made from New Zealand wools, in addition to using the Woolmark. They were also working toward the branded identification of other New Zealand sourced wool products, using their country of origin as part of the product's story – in spite of then IWS policy.

Australia at the time was providing an estimated 60%+ of total funds being used by the IWS organisation worldwide.

As the mid-1960s arrived, being nearly 30 years since AWB/IWS's original pure new wool policy had been established in the mid-1930s, changes in the state and direction of the worldwide market for apparel fibres required that IWS's pure wool policy be reviewed. The expanding use of synthetic fibres was a clear indication that a different kind of support for Australian wools was required.

From the 1970s onward, each of the world's producers of wool was beginning to find them competing with woolgrowers in other countries. Each had to fight more for their share of the decreasing market gap that was opening up between wool and competing synthetic fibres, as the latter began to gain market share. As the predominant producer of fine apparel wools and thus the major contributor by far to IWS funding, this factor alone should have triggered a total review of promotional and other activities then being devoted in support of Australian grown wool.

The original policy of generic wool promotion and advertising of pure new wool, as laid down in 1937, was itself long overdue for review, even before the arrival of the 1960s. Apart from New Zealand, a producer then of mainly coarser wool types, Australia's ongoing needs were rapidly becoming one of looking to the need to maintain its share of the worldwide market for apparel fibres which, while growing, Australian wool's share was failing to keep pace with an increasing variety of improving and cheaper synthetic fibres.

Some other important changes were occurring at the time. These were mainly in the form of increased consumer preference for lighter-weight fabrications, different kinds of more interesting fabric structures and more relaxed garment styling. Changes in fashion, office and other working environments and an increasing rate of travel among consumers, in particular, were by their very nature driving these and other related changes to the kinds of textiles required.

POLITICS AND POLICIES

How Australia's longer-term wool interests would begin to clash with IWS's activities, the main thrust of which continued to be directed solely in support of generic pure new wool and the Woolmark, will be discussed in more detail later.

During later chapters, occasional references to some of the political and overall policy issues involved will also be discussed. When highlighting some of the issues that arose, comments will be limited specifically to outcomes that resulted from Australian government and wool industry decisions and activities, as I experienced them directly. AWB/AWC board decisions directly affected my role and others of a small group working within both organisations trying, usually with minimal success, to defend wool in the Australian marketplace.

My promotion in 1974 to a position on the international stage, based in New York, involved me directly with the later implications of AWC board and other senior management decisions. It will later be shown that for the want of more realistic and reasoned strategies and tactics, poor decisions in key areas of marketing policy and a lack of co-operation from the IWS, resulted in a tragic outcome for Australian wool, at a time when it should have been possible to hold onto a continuing competitive position in the international market for apparel and non-apparel fibres.

A CONTINUING TREND DOWNWARD

It was mainly over the decade following the Second World War, more so since the early 1960s, that the Australian wool industry ultimately began to succumb even more markedly than had already commenced, with the entry of synthetic fibres, in the years before and following the end of that war. The years immediately following 1945 saw the production, marketing and promotion of polyester and to a lesser extent nylon, acrylic and advanced forms of viscose fibres, continue to represent a rapid and increasing threat to the continued use of fine Australian wools in apparel and non-apparel products.

Jumping forward a few years, the first and second decades of the 21st century have continued to witness a continuing downward trend for wool, with a few occasional variations in the price of wool occurring at auction. This trend has continued to extend further and deeper despite feeble, at times desperate, and as things turned out – belated and sporadic attempts to halt Australian wool's decline.

The charge downward toward the self-made abyss, to which the wool industry was galloping between 1960 and 1990, came about mainly as a result of blind adherence on the part of the industry's leadership to policies that in earlier, perhaps more stable times, were seen to be operating satisfactorily. Their inability to listen to the views of many of the industry's long-term supporters, and qualified internal staff working among the wool processing industry, later became a form of self-delusion on the parts of those who should have known better.

Unfortunately, the industry's leadership continued to barge ahead, their eyes focused mainly on industry politics and their ears listening mainly to a coterie of ill-advised advisers and often-theoretical agri-economists. Opportunities as a result were lost, leaving the industry incapable of moving in tune with the many subtle changes that were occurring in the marketplace. The lack of any form of educated analysis and planning based firmly on the realities facing Australian wool in the world's marketplace for fibres, led later to poorly thought-through policies. Whatever policies were pursued, were being implemented on the basis of a political whim, or what I think best described as ill-researched, 'ego driven fantasy'.

Another important factor working against any real long- term success being able to be achieved on behalf of the Australian wool industry was the industry leadership's continuing ability to lock then Australian federal government ministers into the decision that resulted in the adoption of an ill- considered price-fixing reserve price scheme. This scheme was conceived and promoted by people having little or no direct commercial experience with, or regard for, the commercial marketing and subsequent use and application of textile fibres, other perhaps than past experience with the auction system for wool. Nor did later AWC policy involving the marketing of Australian wool, possess a clear enough understanding and appreciation of the many differences that existed between the production, processing and use of wool fibre, particularly when comparing wool fibres to the production, processing and marketing of competing synthetic fibres.

As pointed out by Charles Massy in his book "Breaking the Sheep's Back",[1] the AWC board and senior management's lack of the necessary practical experience with the sale, processing and marketing of down-stream wool and wool-containing products, meant that its handling and early processing needs were misunderstood. The production of wool and its early processing was different in many ways to the processes governing the production and use of synthetic fibres. As such they needed to be thought of differently, with tactics used for their support in the marketplace, being designed accordingly.

There are a wide range of different types and diameters of fine wools, all being the result of different environments and conditions under which they grow. These are wool specific factors that determine quality and downstream technical processing parameters – including the characteristics, feel and appearance of the finished wool or wool-containing product. This presents a situation wherein it is practically impossible to market and supply a standardised wool fibre in the same way the manufacturers of polyester, acrylics and nylon are capable of achieving.

Apart from issues of a technical nature, one dream of many woolgrowers was the concept of an adjustable, 'stabilised floor price' for wool. Favourably adjusted, that is, to the perceived needs of some poorly informed woolgrowers, ill-informed federal politicians and more than a few so-called agri-economists, the latter having a less than useful understanding of the day-to-day realities of the textile fibre market.

This eventually became an issue, in that local wool industry and federal politics became the main factors influencing what should have been decisions made mainly on the basis of commercial, technical, market and processing considerations.

The disaster that eventually overtook the industry during the early 1990s was brought about ultimately as a result of the continuation of corrosive politics, incompetence and self-centred posturing by those who for over a quarter of a century had become the inbred leadership of AWB/AWC and IWS.

Each of these key organisations was being led at the time by two industry dominant personalities, Sir William Gunn and Sir William Vines. AWC was headed later by Alf Maiden and later still by Arthur Beggs and David Asimus. Dr John McPhee later took over the management of IWS.

In Australia, both AWB and later AWC had the responsibility of directing the industry's marketing strategies and tactics in support of wool. The leaders and senior management of both organisations unfortunately, failed to even concede that there was a need for current policies and activities in the marketplace to be periodically reviewed and, if necessary, recalibrated or changed. Change was seen mainly through the prism of their dreams to control the price of Australian produced wool via a reserve price scheme, and their long-held hoped-for control of the Australian wool clip.

AWC's board and senior managers, Malcolm Vawser, Maurice Pell and Lionel Ward, were at the forefront of a campaign to gain total control of the sale and marketing of the total Australian wool clip (acquisition).

The proposed acquisition scheme was an impractical dream. Impractical for some sound reasons, a number of which were highlighted in the book "Breaking the Sheep's Back" (referred to earlier), also to be discussed in a later chapter.

The point to be made here is that neither AWC nor IWS nor their respective leaderships and senior management possessed the management skills, technical/commercial expertise, or had actively sought to employ staff with the range of experience and skills required to carry out such a difficult task – at all levels of the textile and apparel industries.

Notes

1. See "Breaking the Sheep's Back" by Charles Massy, ISBN 978-0-7022-3885-7 (pbk).

THE WOOL RESERVE PRICE SCHEME

Alongside the usual politically induced chaos, wool, the most valued and universally desired fibre of them all, suffered from the disastrous introduction and handling of an ill-conceived and ill-fated Wool Reserve Price Scheme (RP scheme).

The RP scheme was expected to operate alongside the then auction system, purportedly designed to stabilise the price of wool. Built up around a median grade 21-micron Merino wool type, it was introduced to second-guess, bypass and exert control over the then tried, tested and accepted system of wool sales via public auction.

Unfortunately for the wool growing industry, management of the RP scheme only succeeded in eventually pushing the price for wool upward, until it had increased to a level beyond which international trade in the fibre could be sustained.

This required AWC to continue to buy in and store vast quantities of wool – all this at costs that in turn required ever-increasing borrowings. It got to the point when raw wool could no longer compete with the price, rapidly improving quality and lowering cost of production for directly competitive synthetic fibres, more of which was continuing to be produced, marketed and promoted in staple form.

Continuation of the RP scheme ultimately resulted in the crash of the international market for wool – an event that assisted in adding the final chapter of errors to wool's future as a major earner of Australia's foreign income. It also served to permanently damage Australian wool's status and virtually killed off its position as a major player in the apparel fibre market.

Whether those still currently involved with the growing of wool can, or are even interested in trying to regain some if not all its former glory, remains to be seen.

AUSTRALIA'S WOOL TEXTILE INDUSTRY

Moving a little away from wool, Australia, up to and including the mid-1970s, possessed a virile, highly skilled, profitable and creative wool processing, weaving and knitting industry. Most of the manufacturing organisations involved were located in and around Sydney and Melbourne, with a few others established in the other state capitals. Other manufacturers of varying sizes were located in a variety of decentralised rural and provincial centres.

All had been able, over many years, to employ many thousands of local workers. There existed near fully employed populations in and around many regional towns, where a local spinning, weaving or a knitting mill had been established. These were viable and innovative industries that for many years had served their local communities well by providing training and jobs, in turn boosting and maintaining local economies. Some of these communities were to be found in locations some distance away even from inland regional centres. At times, some of the larger decentralised communities managed to encourage and support a range of opportunities for local designers and manufacturers of high-quality wool apparel and decorative textiles to flourish.

BREAKING THE SHEEP'S BACK

I wish here to acknowledge the comprehensive description and commentary contained in "Breaking the Sheep's Back" by its author Charles Massy (see earlier note). A successful woolgrower himself and past member of a number of wool industry organisations, Massy wrote in great detail, charting the decline and fall of the Australian wool industry. His book is highly recommended reading.

Published in 2011, "Breaking the Sheep's Back", researched as it was over a number of years, dealt with the industry's near demise, mainly from the perspective of the major personalities involved and from an overall policy standpoint.

In his book, Massy describes year upon year of poorly thought-through, badly designed, implemented and often improperly promoted policies. He is even more critical when it comes to the way in which these polices were developed, promoted and hammered through successive federal governments by those situated at the pinnacle of then Country Party and wool industry politics.

With Massy's book dealing comprehensively with the intrigues and manoeuvrings among those running the industry, you may well be questioning why there exists the need to delve any further, below the surface so to speak, by undertaking a parallel examination of the internal workings of the AWB and AWC?

To understand the unmitigated disaster that overtook an industry that could and should have been capable of continuing to be a significant part of Australia's industrial mix, it is also important to gain an understanding of those same events as they unfolded 'under the surface' and 'front line' of wool's fight against competing synthetic fibres. What follows is such an account, reflecting the personal experiences of the writer.

The manner of the industry's collapse in 1993 and the activities that preceded it have more than just a few lessons of relevance for Australia, and what is left of its manufacturing industries – both today and into the future.

PULLING THE WOOL AND SINISTER MIDDLEMEN

The late 1950s had seen a major shift in the way the worldwide market for textile fibres was developing. Commercial interests behind the production and marketing of competing synthetic fibres were extending and refining their strategic thinking, product development, marketing and promotional activities. Those charged with the stewardship of Australian wool's fortunes were, by the very nature of their actions, more intent on maintaining the status quo, as well as their personal control of both the woolgrowing industry and the organisations running it. In other words, in spite of every indication to the contrary in the marketplace, the wool industry's leadership continued to apply policies and activities that served only to take the industry backwards.

From a political standpoint, then wool industry leaders like Sir William Gunn, IWS's Sir William Vines and colleagues in the then Country Party, as recorded in "Breaking the Sheep's Back", continued to 'pull the wool' over successive federal government ministers. Massy's book records just how both these men and others with a political axe to grind set about controlling wool industry and government thinking.

During that period, a number of organisations and individuals specialising in the sale and use of wool, nearly all who continued to have a long-term hands-on and financial commitment to wool and its ongoing fortunes, were continually finding themselves operating in a kind of vacuum. More than a few among the wool industry's leadership looked on many of those individuals as the enemy or sinister middlemen.

Most wool users and downstream textile and apparel manufacturers had every reason in the world to see fine Australian wools continue to prosper and hold a significant position in the world's apparel fibre market. They were also prepared to offer their expertise and assistance where necessary, toward ensuring wool's continuing success. Unfortunately, events found them having to lessen their dependence on or even abandon their earlier commitment to wool, in some cases entirely, to enable them to defend their capacity to survive commercially.

The wool textile and apparel industry during the period 1960 to 1990, continued to do business, but whereas in the past, their production had included wool as a dominant component of their fabric and apparel ranges, as time wore on most found themselves having to use it less and less out of commercial necessity.

HARD AT WORK UNDER THE SURFACE

Charles Massy's book offers a description of wool politics and other woolgrowing events that could be described as having occurred on and above the surface of a pond – an analogy referred to briefly earlier.

I and others like me, working directly with and among wool combers, spinners, textile and apparel manufacturers and retailers across Australia and later in the US, found ourselves operating at and below the surface of our imagined pond. There we worked directly with, in and among processors, manufacturers and consumers of wool and wool-containing textiles and apparel.

As a manager operating within the AWC organisation, or as described above, under the surface of our imagined pond, the account that follows was experienced from a position lower down on the wool industry totem pole. At the pinnacle of that pole were the industry's leaders, where they jousted with each other, supposed middlemen and other imagined foes, while neglecting the industry's real enemy, synthetic fibres – and later, competing wools.

Following my original position of menswear product manager, based in Melbourne, I was later posted to New York, where I worked as AWC's international marketing manager. In that role, I was authorised to work directly with textile and apparel manufacturers across North America. The US operation had been made possible following the establishment of AWC held Australian stocks of appropriate wool types, specifically earmarked for sale directly to textile fibre processors across the US.

As my term operating within the US marketplace continued, however, I could only watch on from afar, as the slowly disintegrating wool circus played on in Australia and London.

Personal experiences gained during my period working in the US served forcefully to plot the path toward the disaster that even by the mid and late 1970s was beginning to loom ominously over the horizon.

A MARKETING PLAN FOR WOOL

In addition to issues surrounding or affected by the proposed RP Scheme, the AWB board in 1973 continued its lobbying of the then federal government, led by the then prime minister, Gough Whitlam, around a plan proposing the introduction of a new marketing direction. Its nominated authors were senior managers based at Wool House Melbourne, my then boss among them.

Titled "An Integrated Marketing Plan for Australian Wool", the plan had been developed around the proposition that AWC would be granted full acquisition powers over the total Australian wool clip. The plan presented by AWC's senior management, called for what they referred to as 'experts' – in other words employees of AWC, who were to be empowered to select and target key players in the international wool trade with the supply of raw and part processed Australian wool.

Charles Massy in discussing this scheme made a number of points in relation to it in his book:

> Critical elements unique to the wool industry were conveniently dismissed or discounted: the diversity of growers and their different fibres; complex issues surrounding the conversion of the more difficult wool fibre; the rich diversity of players and relationships in the wool value chain; the variety of skills and depths of merchant capital involved; and the imagination and flair of such elements as creative Italian family operations, British artisan cloth makers or skilled Japanese spinners and weavers. At stake then, were some major practical, philosophical and strategic issues unique to the wool industry.

This industry was vastly different to the man-made fibre industry, to which a different business model applied. Yet this (the proposed wool acquisition scheme) was the template that (Bill) Vines and (William) Gunn, (leaders of both the International Wool Secretariat (IWS) and AWC) had adopted, and which was copied by the report's authors, (in-house economist Lionel Ward and Maurice Pell, ex ICI Fibre Makers).

My appointment in 1970 as product manager, later merchandising manager and later still, international marketing manager, formed perhaps the most eventful, also the most frustrating period of my working life.

In my then newly created position as AWB's Australian-based menswear product manager in 1970, I occupied a reasonably senior place within the organisation, a couple of levels below the AWB boardroom.

From there and later in the United States, I found myself in a unique position. I now became directly involved with events that were brewing inside the storm that was gathering pace. These events eventually developed into the disaster that a few years later proceeded to blow the industry apart.

While from a practical standpoint I was able to exert some influence in the area of end-product marketing activities on behalf of wool within Australia during my early role, this changed, despite clear statements made to me at the time of my appointment.

At no time while working in Melbourne, and later during my tenure in New York, was I, or others operating at what I will here refer to as 'the coal face', allowed to provide input into critical discussions being held at senior management and board level. Being locked out of these discussions made it impossible to become involved in decision-making – in particular on subjects and issues that had direct implications for our clearly defined areas of past experience and current responsibility.

The ultimate collapse of what at the time was a major source of Australia's export income, came about as a result of events and issues well recognised and commented on outside the woolgrowing industry at the time, some of which bear repeating:

- A lack of forward-looking leadership over, within and among woolgrowers, their organisations and the governing Country and Liberal parties then in power. This was central to events that resulted in the industry's later collapse.
- A gulf had opened over the years, between the long-term interests of Australian woolgrowers and the IWS, its policies and activities. Unlike the wool industry's needs as perceived during the mid to late 1930s, by the time the early 1960s came around, IWS's activities on behalf of Australia's woolgrowers, at least in its then form, responsibilities and activities, represented much reduced value.
- A continuing lack of capable and forward-looking commercial wool textile and apparel manufacturing industry expertise, understanding and judgment at the senior levels of AWB/AWC and IWS. The emphasis on employing and promoting mainly from within also contributed to the weakening of all three organisations' value to the woolgrowing industry and companies and others committed to and directly involved with the manufacture of wool-based textiles.

Early warnings on the direction that the senior management of AWC was taking raw wool marketing and pricing policy was being ignored by wool industry leaders and federal government ministers. Such attitudes continued, despite warnings and advice provided by some of the more commercially aware woolgrowers. To these need to be added wool buyers, early wool processors, spinners, weavers, knitters and some leading apparel manufacturers.

Traditional supporters and long-term users of wool were often treated as if they were the enemy! In reality, most, understandably, were becoming increasingly concerned that what was being proposed and later hammered through and implemented in the case of AWC's proposed RP Scheme, would only serve to damage the industry. It was believed that the scheme as proposed would cause financial chaos and serve to collapse worldwide demand for Australian wool. Later events proved this view to be correct.

Should the Australian government agree to giving AWC management the power to acquire, set prices and market the total Australian wool clip, was also considered by most of wool's major customers and users to be counterproductive. In addition to being impractical, few at AWC were sufficiently qualified, bearing in mind the necessary level of 'hands-on' commercial experience then available within the organisation. Added to this was the fact that the processes involved and the nature of wool fibre production was different to synthetic fibre production. As such, considerations regarding the best ways to combat growing competition from synthetic fibres needed also to take the many differences between the various wool types and between wool and synthetics into careful and detailed consideration.

Submissions and pleas being made by many of Australia's major buyers, processors and users of fine wools, called on AWC to face up to the need to change its attitude toward its long-term customers and users of wool. AWC was also requested to abandon, or at the very least re-think the scope of its RP Scheme.

At the time AWC merchandising division staff were also requesting changes to past practices. These ranged across policies allowing the blending of wool with other fibres, consideration for more carefully targeted technical developments, changes in the way financial support and end-product promotion were being targeted, plus the vital need to work continually toward improving the objective measurement and presentation of raw and part processed Australian wools to the world.

WORKING FOR AUSTRALIAN WOOL – 1970–1978

I was the first and, I believe, only AWB manager at the time, or since, to be recruited from the Australian textile and apparel manufacturing industries.

My appointment had apparently followed earlier discussion within the AWB, around the need to boost the level of technical and apparel marketing industry expertise available to the organisation and its soon to be remodelled product marketing division.

Moving into the AWB's headquarters at 360 Bourke Street, Melbourne, proved to be a whole world away from my previous employment as head designer for one of Australia's then leading menswear apparel manufacturers. It also meant moving into an office environment, where I was provided with the services of a personal assistant/secretary. I now found myself working alongside a group of technical officers, public relations people – and a cohort of overpaid, under-worked and over-inflated self-styled 'fashion experts'.

It didn't take too long to get used to the much slower pace at which the AWB had been running – mainly as a promotional/PR operation, one that over past years had tended to operate in relative isolation from most of Australia's textile and apparel manufacturers.

Early briefings from AWB's technical division staff followed my appointment. These covered various projects, one involving the development of a process that they claimed would render sports trousers or jeans manufactured from pure wool worsted woven fabrics – 'machine washable'. Thus, it was stated, "We should now be able to capture a major portion of the men's sports trouser market as a result of this development." More will be said about this project later.

A great deal of technical work and other resources had been committed to the machine washable project, in concert with the Commonwealth Scientific Industrial Research Organisation (CSIRO) wool research division, based in Geelong.

I spent time among staff of the then Australian Wool Commission and Australian Wool Testing Authority. My main interest here was to absorb the latest information on new technologies aimed of improving the testing, objective measurement, preparation and presentation of raw wool fibre to the world's markets.

A SURFEIT OF MARKET RESEARCH

Following my appointment, I was almost snowed under with reams of market research, together with a virtual mountain of other statistics and reports relating to my area of operations. AWB in those days had a well-staffed market research department, operating under its manager Michael Cooley.

AWB's market research presented an overly optimistic picture of wool's position and the fibre's potential to be increased in the Australian men's outerwear market. I had already been able to source a range of qualitative and quantitative research, including views and opinions provided from some operating in the textile and apparel manufacturing, locally and internationally.

I was familiar with much of the internal material being supplied by AWB, also figures and projections regarded as being closer to the actual position of wool, including actual usage and projections, as provided to the Melbourne College of Textiles by Australia's leading manufacturers of wool-based textiles. All were projecting a gradual decline in wool's share of Australia's and the world's market for apparel fibres.

Interestingly, both AWB and IWS forecasts at the time of my arrival at AWB projected some slight increases in wool consumption in one or two end uses related to the menswear industry. These were forecasts that tended to be overly optimistic when compared to more realistic market information and empirical data and observations, sourced from within both local and international textile and apparel industries.

Significantly, the projected decline in the use of wool as perceived from sources other than AWB and IWS was based on both organisations' continuing policy to limit their promotion and technical support to 100% pure new wool woven and knitted products. That in effect meant no technical or financial support for products manufactured from a blending of wool with other fibres.

On arriving at AWB, I learned that I would be expected to achieve the maintenance of wool consumption at least to then-current levels within Australia. This came in the form of a plan that was handed to me on my arrival at 360 Bourke Street, together with the statement that I would be expected to achieve the projected level of wool consumption in all end uses under my management. I, however, reserved the right to review this plan, following my own evaluation of the local market – this after I had been able to undertake a comprehensive series of discussions and in-depth consultations with the Australian textile and apparel manufacturing industry.

These were early days, and although I was in disagreement with some of AWB's internally produced research, and in particular, AWB's policy rejecting the blending of wool with other fibres, I hoped later to have some involvement with discussions aimed at reviewing this policy.

AWB's refusal to adopt a blend policy, one at least that recognised the realities of what was happening in the marketplace, had allowed competing synthetic fibre interests to undermine wool's image and market position. Thus, it was hoped that later discussion would result in the establishment of a more practical policy regarding blends – at the very least across men's apparel, my specific area of responsibility.

Visits to every major wool textile mill, spinner, knitter and apparel manufacturer across Australia were undertaken, prior to formulating a plan of attack. This aspect completed, planning was then focused on the development and, where considered necessary, the incorporation of any adjustments needing to be made to the original plan. The original plan, I later learned had been prepared by AWB's market research department, in isolation.

Parallel to becoming involved with an effective range of merchandising activities along the textile pipeline was also the possibility of being able to work alongside researchers at CSIRO, leading textile manufacturers and AWB's technical division, toward the conceptual development of wool-rich wool/polyester and wool/other natural fibre blended knitted and woven fabrics. All were products suitable for use in men's suits, trousers, jackets, knitwear and casual wear, designed specifically to compete more effectively with synthetic fibres.

One of the initial objectives here was to arrive at relatively lighter-weight fabrications, if possible to be introduced across Australia during the next spring/summer period.

INTERNATIONAL WOOL FASHION OFFICE – (IWMO)

IWS had earlier established offices in a number of the world's strategic textile manufacturing and consumption centres. Locations included

London, New York, Dusseldorf, Milan, Tokyo and Paris. IWS also had two technical development facilities – the main one based in Ilkley (UK) another in Delft (Holland) – both of which I arranged to visit as part of a projected visit to Europe, once having settled down into my new position.

In spite of much of the rhetoric and enthusiastic spin that had been emanating from IWS, the organisation year upon year had failed significantly to show progress of any note in the maintenance of wool's worldwide share of its main end uses. IWS had been successful with its launch of its Woolmark brand, introduced in 1964.

Of some relevance to our Australian operations at the time, during which I was intent on improving AWB's services to local Australian mills and men's apparel manufacturers, was one of the IWS's highly regarded fashion offices.

There were two such offices, small specialist groups within IWS, dedicated to the sourcing and evaluation of fabrics and styling for men's and women's Woolmark-branded textiles and apparel.

IWS's men's fashion office (IWMO), was located in London, being headed up by Iain Campbell, a craggy-featured and hard-working Scotsman. Campbell and his staff in London were responsible for keeping AWB and other offices in the various donor countries to the IWS up-to-date with, and possibly ahead of, men's fashion and colour trends, particularly as they were emerging in Europe.

Little use had been made of material produced by IWMO by AWB's similarly styled 'fashion office' in Australia, other than using the information they had been receiving on a regular basis from IWMO in London, mainly in a soft PR way with fashion magazines and occasional press releases. The way fashion, colour and technical design information had been used by AWB in the past, had been of little practical use to most Australian companies directly involved in textile and apparel manufacture.

On learning of such a valuable resource in London, I took over the service, not without a defensive fight from the then AWB fashion office incumbent, who in the past had neglected to use the information received from IWMO to any real effect. The information was then analysed with the object of developing a comprehensive colour and technically based yarn/textile design forecasting service directed to the specific needs of Australian textile mills, apparel manufacturers and retailers. When completed, visits were made to every major, and some not so major worsted/woollen spinning, weaving and knitting mills, located across each state of the commonwealth.

In addition to information being received from IWMO in London, contacts with a number of other independent overseas fashion colour and technical design sources, independent of IWMO, were also accessed.

This service, once established within the first two months on my appointment, rapidly developed into a resource in demand from every mill, apparel manufacturer, knitter and most retailers, all of whom were encouraged to consult before committing to their fabric and apparel ranges for a coming season.

Each spinning, knitting or weaving mill and apparel manufacturer, regardless of size or location, was invited to access our new technical, colour and design service well in advance of each selling season. Each company was provided with briefings and an analysis of forecasted fashion and colour trends. Of even more importance, advice on technical trends backed up by in-mill consultations and technical assistance where needed was also provided during face-to-face meetings in their mill, factory or retail store.

In this way, we were able to begin to form the basis of a timely and valuable resource that dealt with the full spectrum of fabric and garment design, colour trends, yarn and fabric structures. The service, while designed specifically for textile and apparel manufacturers, was shortly thereafter taken up by fashion writers and the local trade press as their preferred fashion and colour authority. The service became known and regularly used and publicised extensively across the textile and apparel manufacturing, and retail sectors, twice annually, well in advance of any decision-making for a future retail season.

One example of the level of services provided to the Australian industry, was one aimed at winter 1973. This took the form of a comprehensive fabric colour and design palette, featuring colours and textures selected from a range of five famous Australian Painters. The release of the 1973 colour and design service was launched at Victoria's National Gallery, sponsored by the then director of the gallery, Eric Westbrook.

The colour, design and technical service, following its launch during 1970 was updated, twice annually, well in advance of each selling season. It proved to be a much valued, practical and relatively simple way through which to exert more positive influence in support of the manufacture and sale of pure wool and wool-rich blended textiles and apparel.

It was also interesting to learn later that the service was even being taken up by most of Australia's leading women's apparel manufacturers, a comforting endorsement that we were on the right track – in that department at least.

These activities though were but a small start along the long, hard road that would become necessary for wool to travel toward the objective of improving its competitive position. The colour and design service at least proved to be a first step in the right direction.

TAKING THE INITIATIVE

As AWB's menswear activities became established and recognised across all sectors of the menswear apparel industry across Australia, other initiatives were introduced. Among these was a decision taken to change the way in which AWB co-operative promotional funds were used.

Considerable levels of advertising money had in the past been handed out to selected apparel manufacturers and major retailers, in what was supposed to be support for advertising their pure new wool garment ranges. What had previously occurred in practice, however, was a situation where funds would be allocated (literally given), mainly to a few of AWB's senior hierarchy's' preferred apparel manufacturers and retailers. This without any guarantee that the funds provided would even be used in support of the manufacture's pure new wool range.

In practice, funds provided to them were used by the recipients to supplement the use of their own funds, mainly in the promotion of their own corporate image and not necessarily wool's.

Previous to changing the system, wool promotional funds were all too often dissipated across a participating manufacturers' range, usually to no practical value, as far as the promotion of pure new wool (its only intended purpose) was concerned. Apparel manufacturers on the receiving end of most of AWB's largesse at the time, my former employer included, were provided with co-operative advertising funds, irrespective of whether or not they were being used to encourage the company's continued use of wool.

Too often, the most that the co-operative advertising liaison staff at AWB were able to achieve for the funds expended, was the nominal addition of a Woolmark logo in one corner of the apparel manufacturer's or retailer's corporate or co-operatively funded press advertisements.

From 1971 onwards, co-operative advertising funds were to be allocated solely on the basis of a manufacturer or retailer's proven level of commitment to pure wool fabrics, as defined by their projected buying patterns when compared to previous years. This policy was aimed at supporting pure new wool yarns and fabrics sourced from either of local and overseas weaving and knitting mills.

Accepting that this process was a long way yet from being the most effective method of influencing and 'locking-in' an individual apparel manufacturer's commitment to wool, it did, however, prove to be reasonably efficient. At the same time, it improved our capacity to gain better intelligence on each organisation's ordering patterns of fabrics from local and overseas weaving and knitting mills. In the case of retailers, this included their commitment to local manufacturers' apparel ranges, who themselves were also committed to the programme. Once again, as with the colour and design programme, controlling, wherever possible the use of AWC's co-operative advertising funds, was seen as a start along the road to a more positive strategy in support of wool.

Another important aspect regarding the strategic use of co-operative advertising funds was to be able to link the use of these, with whatever corporate advertising was being carried out by AWB, for each passing season.

The very nature of AWBs position as the promotional arm of the Australian wool industry still placed it at a distinct disadvantage to competitive synthetic fibre manufacturers. They, of course, could link any promotional funds, directly to actual purchases from them and their mill clients of fibre, yarns and fabrications they wished to promote.

SYNTHETIC FIBRES VERSUS PURE NEW WOOL

Pure new wool worsted or woollen spun woven, and knitted fabrics and knitwear had for many years formed the promotional bastion of wool, a unique and preferred fibre, particularly suited to and extensively used in the production of men's and women's outerwear.

Before and during the Second World War, synthetic fibres, mainly a range of cotton and silk competitive viscose and acetate rayon types, had not been able to match wool's quality, comfort and handling characteristics, particularly in end uses like men's woven woollen and worsted fabrics and knitwear.

Following the earlier discovery and ongoing development of filament nylon and polyester fibres, improvements with the handle and processing characteristics of these fibres improved rapidly. The quality of synthetic fibres continued to improve, particularly following research and development programmes designed to enable continuous polyester filaments to be successfully produced and marketed in what became known as 'cut staple' or 'staple' form.

This development soon began to see polyester fibre, mainly in staple form, being blended with wool, cotton and other fibres then spun into yarns. In yarn form, they were able to offer improved characteristics to those of the natural fibre with which they were being blended. On being blended with wool, they were able to produce yarns capable of producing similar, but lighter than equivalent pure wool yarns spun from mid-micron range wools. Staple[1] polyester for example, enabled the yarn spinner to produce finer yarns, offering a greater level of crease resistance in the finished fabric, while at the same time retaining acceptable handling characteristics.

Thus, major producers of synthetic fibres were gradually able to develop their offerings to a point where it became a far-reaching marketing tactic to specify and promote polyester dominant yarns blended with wool. Resultant fabrics possessed handling and wear characteristics acceptably similar to those of 100% wool, but lighter in weight and, most importantly, they could be produced at lower cost.

The use of improved types of polyester in blends with wool later encouraged producers of polyester fibres, based mainly in the USA and Europe, to expand their production, thus reducing the unit cost of resultant yarns and fabrications.

The 1960s saw some spinners and fabric manufacturers being encouraged to include blended yarns, mainly composed of 55% staple polyester with 45% wool in their ranges. Thus they were then able to reduce both the use of wool and the cost of these yarns, when compared to the cost of producing a 100% wool yarn.

During this period, no countering action was being considered or any discussion allowed by AWB. Nor would those leading the industry and responsible for directing its promotional activities, accept the fact that in a broad range of end products there were a number of proven advantages to be gained by blending. Reductions in cost and improvements with handle and wear could have been enhanced, to the advantage of wool, by the use of yarns built upon a dominant blending of wool with a much lesser component of staple polyester.

The main question here became: What blend level should the manufacturers of woven and knitted fabrics adopt?

Strong financial support aimed at spinners and weavers by the producers of synthetic fibres, allowed them to set up and establish a blend of 45% wool with 55% spun polyester as the benchmark blend in medium to lighter-weight fabrications. Later advances and improvements, particularly in the physical and handling characteristics of polyester fibres in staple form, gradually began to improve the acceptance of polyester by the textile industry.

The continued lack of interest and head-in-the-sand denial on the part of those directing policy at AWB and IWS, provided further, unopposed opportunities for the producers of wholly synthetic and blended synthetic-rich/wool-poor blends to set a barely acceptable blend level. Once having achieved general acceptance of that blend level, allowed the producers of synthetic fibres to cut deeper and deeper into what had until then been the exclusive realm of pure new wool. The opportunity was therefore lost for a wool dominant blend to be set as the industry standard!

Strong promotional programmes, aggressively funded by the major producers of synthetic fibres, provided the basis from which they were then able to push the increased use of a dominant synthetic blend, at a blend level that eventually became the standard blend accepted by the worldwide apparel industry. This trend firmed, once retailers and consumers became sold on the value and acceptable handling qualities of apparel manufactured from synthetic-rich blended fabrics.

Consumer attitudes were changing, as more and more apparel manufacturers, working alongside local synthetic fibre producers and their client mills were encouraged to move over to using the then competitively priced woven and knitted 100% polyester and polyester rich 55/45 blended fabrications. The benchmark 55/45 blend level continued to be aggressively promoted in Australia by ICI/Fibremakers, the major Australian-based producer of synthetic fibres.

Continuous filament polyester fibre production had come a long way from its early development and release in Britain during 1941. During the early stages of the fibre's development it had already become well-known following the ending of the Second World War. The post-war years saw the fibre being bought and preferred extensively by consumers, usually in the form of Terylene-branded curtains, tablecloths and similar kinds of domestic textiles, all of which were relatively cheap, washable and available in a range of colours.[2]

Fabrics woven or knitted from polyester thread or yarn are today used extensively in apparel and home furnishings, shirts and pants, jackets and hats, bed sheets, blankets and upholstered furniture. Other non-apparel related products like computer mouse mats, industrial polyester fibres, yarns and ropes are also used in car tyre reinforcements, fabrics for conveyor belts, safety belts, coated fabrics and plastic reinforcements with high energy-absorption.

Notes

1. Staple length is a property of staple fibre, a term referring to the average length of a group of fibres of any composition. Staple length

depends on the origin of the fibres. Natural fibres (such as cotton or wool) have a range of lengths in each sample, so the staple length is an average. For synthetic fibres that have been cut to a certain length, the staple length is the same for every fibre in the group. Staple length is an important criterion for spinning fibre, as shorter fibres are more difficult to spin than longer ones, so staple length varies from short to longer length fibres, short fibres also resulting in more hairy types of yarns.

2. Terylene was the first polyester fabric ever produced. It was patented in 1941 by its British inventors, John Rex Whinfield and James Dickson. Initially, it was kept secret and used to develop materials during the Second World War. After the war, fabrics developed from the fibre were first promoted for use in curtains by ICI/UK.

MAN-MADE SILK

To illustrate just how far polyester fibres have developed since their introduction nearly a century ago, in some cases, polyester-based yarns have been renamed to suggest their similarity or claimed superiority to various natural fibres. For example: China silk is a term used in the textiles industry to describe a specially processed 100% polyester yarn, spun to resemble the sheen and durability of insect-derived natural silk.

ICI in the UK (Fibremakers Australia), along with other international synthetic fibre producers DuPont in the US (Dacron) and Monsanto, proved successful in promoting their lighter weight and cheaper polyester-wool blends against pure wool, as a means of establishing a foothold in the apparel fibre market. Their persistent activity ultimately enabled them to gain market share and later market dominance, particularly in lighter-weight woven fabrics and apparel – all at the expense of pure new wool.

Subsequently, '55/45' blended fabrics became the Trojan horse used by ICI/Fibremakers that began the rapid slide downward in Australia's market share of pure new wool worsted and knitted textiles consumed by local men's and women's apparel manufacturers. This was a move that followed closely on similar situations in the US, and to a lesser extent across European markets.

The move toward lighter-weight 55/45 woven fabrics and 100% polyester knitted fabrics, which tended to crease less while at the same time produced adequately handling fabrics and garments, continued to grow in popularity over a relatively short period. This development made it even more difficult for AWB, its menswear operations in particular, to begin to compete effectively in the marketplace. This despite the millions of dollars being expended on pure new wool, Woolmark-branded advertising and promotion worldwide.

Despite the obvious trend to synthetic-rich blends, IWS, AWB and later AWC, continued to ignore what was happening in the real world. They instead continued to pour more and more financial resources into the generic promotion of pure new wool, Woolmark standard products. While this did a great deal for the recognition of the Woolmark, it did much less toward the longer-term future of wool.

Later years eventually saw the introduction of 100% polyester/viscose and other synthetic dominant fibre blends. As synthetic fibre technology advanced and improved finishing techniques were being applied to 100% synthetic fabrications, they too gradually improved, serving further to exclude wool in some of the more price sensitive segments of the world's apparel markets.

INTERESTING TIMES

It was totally incomprehensible to someone like me, arriving lately into the world of wool's oft-trumpeted duo of superior marketing expertise and authority in the form of AWB and IWS, to have to watch as synthetic fibres continued to launch attack after attack on wool, while the senior management of both AWB and IWS sat on their hands. At the time, all that was being allowed in the defence of wool was the continuation of an earlier, now outdated tactic promoting the Woolmark via extensive generic advertising in support of pure new wool.

What was worse, however, was that no countering strategies, other than to increase corporate-style Woolmark advertising, was even being contemplated by those heading up AWB and IWS. No amount of internal AWB discussion where alternative policies were being suggested, were even allowed to progress.

It was even more frustrating to have requests for the consideration of changes in promotional direction and a review of the pure wool policy turned down, time after time. At the same time, merchandising division staff were being told by AWB management that any attempt to introduce a change in attitude toward wool/synthetic yarn blends would be regarded as them being overly negative. Even the mention of blending was seen as bordering on sacrilege!

The request to include the promotion of specifically targeted wool-rich blends was a subject that IWS continued to reject out of hand. Not only this, but the knowledge that it was IWS deciding what strategies were to be followed in Australia itself seemed bizarre. Australia was a different kind of market with different weather conditions to those of Europe and other northern hemisphere markets. Having to continue to follow a now outdated course of action such as that being dictated by the IWS was like the tail wagging the dog. The situation bordered on the unreal!

Subsequent questions and requests to move away from the current pure wool policy, raised at internal AWB merchandising division meetings, were either ignored or put down as being unnecessarily negative.

Funding arrangements aside, anyone operating along the textile or apparel manufacturing pipeline, had for many years seen the direction in which the market was going. Unfortunately for Australian wool, the marketing 'gurus' having overall responsibility for policy, at board and senior management levels of AWB and IWS, failed even to accept what was occurring in the marketplace. Instead, they continued to claim that IWS research showed that AWB's promotional funds and activities should continue to be directed solely to the promotion of products complying with the Woolmark standard. And that meant pure new wool only – and, on a purely generic basis.

The issue of unilaterally raised prices for raw wool that escalated later as a result of the RP Scheme, when added to the continued refusal much earlier to allow and promote wool-rich blending of yarns, worked against the spraying of generic wool promotion around the world's textile and apparel markets by IWS.

These two elements of wool marketing, the RP Scheme and IWS's continuing opposition to a change in pure new wool policy, played their part in the eventual discounting of wool as a recognisable force in the apparel fibre market.

It is interesting to note here that even as early as the 1960s, most of the leading spinners and weavers of wool fabrics and their colleague Australian apparel manufacturers had warned of such a projected strong move toward wool poor polyester/wool blends by ICI Fibremakers, the local synthetic fibre producer. Unfortunately, those responsible for wool promotion, ensconced in their 'ivory towers' at Wool House in Melbourne and London, continued to discount these early warnings.

A growing number of local worsted mills, had for some time past been unsuccessfully requesting technical assistance from AWB to work alongside them in developing and promoting an 80% wool-rich blend with 20% staple polyester.

On this important point, I recall a function at AWB's head office in Bourke Street Melbourne, some three years before my arrival at Wool House, around 1966 or 1967.

I attended, representing the Melbourne College of Textiles. At some stage in the proceedings, the question of whether AWB would consider the development and subsequent promotion of wool-rich blended worsted spun fabrics in Australia, was put forward by attending representatives from the textile industry. The answer received from Nan Sanders, then AWB's head of marketing was along the lines, "There will be no promotion of anything other than pure new wool in Australia for the foreseeable future."

Most of the commercially savvy manufacturers who attended that session at Wool House left that day shaking their heads in disbelief.

In spite of AWB's pure-wool-only policy, one or two of the then major Australian worsted weaving mills were themselves already actively looking to produce a lighter-weight wool-rich/polyester-poor blend fabric, which included wool from the finer end of the wool spectrum (around 20/21 microns).

The superior qualities of blending 80% or even a minimum of 70% of these wools with 30% of staple polyester had been well known for some time to be able to produce superior handling, lighter-weight fabrics with a higher degree of crease resistance than an equivalent pure wool fabrication. With the promotion of wool-rich fabric blends not being countenanced by AWB, no technical assistance or promotional weight had been allowed in support of what could have proved a pivotal marketing initiative in defence of wool.

By the time I arrived on the scene at Wool House a few years later, AWB's policy was still dead-set against any technical developmental work being carried out in support of wool blends of any description.

On my arrival at Wool House, I decided to ignore the directive, and began working with a few leading local weaving mills, Yarra Falls, Foster Worsteds and others, toward the development of wool-rich blended fabrics and a range of specialty yarns.

The purchase of wool-rich blended yarns and fabrics for testing purposes were funded from my development budget – without previous approval from AWB's senior management.

AUSTRALIAN WOOL CORPORATION – 1973

January 1973 saw the change in name and expansion of some of the earlier functions of AWB into a new organisation. The new setup comprised a similar board, similar policies, but a new chairman in the form of A.C.B. (Alf) Maiden, a political appointment. Maiden, a career public servant, had previously occupied the position of permanent secretary to the Department of Primary Industry.

The 'new' AWC board comprised one or two new appointees in addition to the usual suspects – a bunch of woolgrower representatives, plus two new members, men who were supposed to bring to bear the latest in marketing expertise from outside the wool industry.

One of these marketing 'experts' was David Jones, son of Fletcher Jones, founder of the then well-known Australian clothing brand of the same name. The Fletcher Jones plant was based at Warrnambool in western Victoria. The other marketing expert was a gentleman not closely connected with wool, but with the Heinz Company of baked beans fame. Other members of the board were government appointments, including one or two agri-economists acting as advisers or something similar.

Fletcher Jones was an organisation that for decades had been a major supporter of pure new wool in all its apparel forms, being both a manufacturer and retailer of men's wear and women's wear.

David Jones was introduced to AWC staff as a 'leading expert' in the field of product marketing. Jones's title was one that few textile and apparel managers regarded as accurate, given the then declining position of the Fletcher Jones brand across Australian retailing.

Rural politics had once again come to the fore. Instead of building a new, perhaps non-statutory body – a reinvigorated, professionally staffed organisation capable of going to war with Fibremakers and the rest of the world's synthetic fibre producers – what had resulted differed little from the organisation that AWC had replaced.

The organisation had been given a new name but not much more when it came to providing the brains, experience and expertise required to meet the task of keeping the synthetic fibre industry at bay.

Not only that, but subsequent years served to demonstrate the statutory AWC board's incapacity, when it came to providing the kind of foresight, leadership and direction the Australian wool-growing industry so desperately needed, at so crucial a time in its long history.

AN INTEGRATED MARKETING PLAN

1973 also saw the release of AWC's proposal for an integrated marketing plan for wool. An ill-conceived creation, three of AWC's senior managers had been involved with its development. Pushed along by IWS's Bill Vines and the board's new product marketing expert, David Jones, the plan's central thrust was around the proposal that AWC be provided with powers over wool sales and marketing, in short, allowing AWC to act as Australian wool's virtual owner.

The key powers sought were the acquisition, marketing and sale of the total Australian wool clip. In so doing, AWC proposed to take on a role similar to that of a competing synthetic fibre manufacturer, operating in the world's textile fibre markets. AWC would operate as the nominal owner of all the wool fibre produced, in all its many known variations, across Australia.

I refer to the proposal here because located as I was, lower down on the AWC totem pole, I had a vital interest in understanding just how such a plan could operate in the real world. One of the principal authors of the plan was my immediate boss Maurice Pell, AWC's then merchandising group manager, himself earlier recruited from the local synthetic fibre producer – ICI/Fibremakers.

Pell and his colleague Lionel Ward, the latter AWC's then resident economist and sometime self-appointed oracle, were the two main senior staff contributors to the plan. As stated earlier, none among the rest of AWC's product marketing staff were allowed the opportunity to comment, critique or offer suggestions, prior to the plan's release, let alone allowed the possibility of discussing it and, if felt necessary, to voice any differing views. I can only surmise here that Pell may have had visions of turning AWC into a clone of ICI, the principal company behind the local Fibremakers organisation, presumably with him at its head.

I had previously expressed the view during internal divisional meetings, that the current makeup and staffing of AWC was incompatible with the proposal being developed – at least as I understood it. I, and others, had also expressed the view that AWC should be aiming at upgrading its current skill set, while concentrating on improving its effectiveness in the worldwide marketplace, alongside a policy that allowed the promotion of blends. That did not include trying to insert the organisation's current level of expertise and limited textile/apparel industry experience into the role of a commercial organisation that had manufactured (grown) and owned the product being marketed.

At the time, it was also clear that a continuing government and woolgrower squabble was going on at an even higher level up the totem pole, politically speaking, than where I was located. So other than sticking my two two-pennyworth in for what it was worth, it seemed there was little, similarly motivated colleagues at my level in the organisation or I could do to influence policy.

The proposal was also considered to potentially add further to wool's problems, while AWC was still trying to compete with synthetic fibre products, with both hands tied behind its back on the subject of blends.

Eventually, out of the blue things changed without much warning. Following a great deal of pressure being brought to bear on the board of IWS, particularly from members of the wool textile industry, supported perhaps as a result of the constant lobbying in support of a blend policy by AWC's merchandising division, those higher up the AWC/IWS totem pole finally relented. Even then the acceptance of a wool-rich blend was limited to worsted woven fabrics. They were at the very least, ten years too late!

With approval now received to design and promote wool-rich blended fabrics, we in Australia and more particularly, me in the men's wear field, made a fresh start toward the ongoing development and marketing of a range of lighter-weight wool-rich blended apparel to the Australian public.

Although too late to have any real effect on the longer-term direction of Australian wool's share in woven and knitted fabrics, we did at least have something with which to put up a reasonable rearguard action.

CELSIUS 30 – A NEW WOOLBLENDMARK CONCEPT

Thus, a new wool-rich blended fabric brand arrived onto the Australian market, albeit belatedly.

A new brand mark, the 'Woolblendmark', similar in style to the internationally recognisable Woolmark, was devised and registered for use in Australia. A new brand name to be used with fabrics that qualified as wool-rich (at least 70%), was devised. Its name: CELSIUS 30.

A minimum blend of 70% wool with up to 30% polyester, spun together in such a manner as to allow it to be used in the weaving and finishing of worsted woven or knitted fabrics became the minimum standard for fabrics to be included in Australia's new Woolblendmark programme. Fabrics that could comfortably be worn when the temperature reached and passed the 30°C level.

From a purely promotional point of view, it just so happened that about the same time as our efforts to promote a lighter-weight wool-rich blended fabric, Australia had made the decision to move from the old Fahrenheit scale for measuring temperature, from then on to be known as degrees Celsius.

The Australian Bureau of Meteorology had already moved over to recording and reporting temperatures in the new Celsius range on June 12th 1972, but it wasn't until September 1972 that the country also officially changed to the Celsius scale.

This timing was fortunate. Being September 1972, the change coincided with the proposed spring/summer release of Celsius 30 fabric and garment ranges to retailers and the Australian public.

The programme proved to be a relative, though belated success. Later research showed that the fall in wool consumption during the spring/summer season that year and the year that followed, had been slowed. More wool had been included in their ranges by Australian mills.

Unfortunately, in the long run, being empowered to promote wool-rich blends came much too late for AWC to compete effectively with the now well-established and increasing flow of man-made fibres into the men's outerwear market, an unfortunate situation in which wool's share continued on to trend downward – even as the consumption of total fibres in men's apparel steadily increased.

THE VICUÑA OF THE 1980S?

A senior manager working at the AWB around the time that I joined in 1970, Tony Lewis, once asserted during a group meeting that wool, in his view, when looking toward the coming of the second millennium, would, in his words, become "the vicuña of the 1980s".

As time passed, he was more or less proved partially correct. The share of wool as a percentage of total fibres was destined to continue downward, even as the world's consumption of apparel fibres kept moving in the opposite direction.

Development, improvement and extension of the qualities of synthetic fibres during the 1960s and 1970s were progressing rapidly, alongside their continuing aggressive promotion of 100% and synthetic-rich blends. The latter were mainly in the form of polyester/wool and acrylic/wool blends, along with some blending of polyester with later forms of viscose, cotton and other natural fibres in a variety of specialty yarns. Fabric manufacturers and knitters continued to switch to blends of various fibres, not necessarily containing very much wool.

Wool was increasingly being regarded as a more exclusive and expensive product as predicted by Lewis, gradually becoming more and more isolated regarding its market share. The cost of raw wool was also pushing wool-containing products further into the higher priced luxury end of apparel and textile products worldwide. The use of wool in some sections of the market was gradually becoming more restricted.

Wool was destined to become more closely associated in the minds of a growing number of consumers, to other, more exotic animal and natural fibres like vicuña, alpaca, silk, cashmere, and linen. Vicuña being a very rare fibre, being used only in the most luxurious fabrics and products, much like similarly rare fibres shorn from the currently popular alpaca – its wool used in jackets and expensive fashion scarves.

It should also be noted here that among younger consumers today, not having any previous experience wearing wool, pure wool garments are often seen as too expensive and available only as 'high fashion'. With growing preference for lower- priced garments, often being worn for a season or perhaps two, fashion, at least in pure wool form continues, at least in the minds of some younger consumers having less money to spend on their clothing, to be a niche product having little impact with them when selecting workday or 'going-out' apparel.

It is not implied here that there should be a direct comparison made between fine Australian apparel wools and the other more exotic, expensive and much less available and often more difficult to process natural fibres noted earlier. Those fibres are relatively rare, the only exception being cotton, which continues to be a short-staple apparel fibre that continues to be dominant across the world. Cotton is used extensively in fabrics, apparel and a whole range of other products that use its lower cost and unsurpassed range of universally known properties to advantage.

Price has its place in the worldwide production and manufacture of cotton goods, a universally used fibre grown and used in a wide variety of products manufactured mainly in lower-cost Third World countries.

Most textile and apparel manufacturers, particularly at the earlier stages of textile pipeline, during a critical few years during the 1960s, believed that the most effective way in which the ongoing use of wool could be most actively defended, was to critically assess where its economic and aesthetic benefits coincided. Only then when developing an optimum range of products – be they in pure new wool or a blending of wool with other fibres, including synthetics, would a more successful competitive position for wool be possible to maintain into the foreseeable future.

By designing apparel and other domestic and decorative products in this way was seen by most manufacturers as the only positive way to determining the optimum composition of the various yarns required. These could range from pure wool, through to mixtures with various fibres, determined by the qualities and cost parameters of the finished article. Thus, the final marketable article of clothing or other product and its potential sale price would be the determinants of the blend (if any) to be used and promoted.

The preceding was not a policy position acceptable to either AWC or IWS at the time, and in any event, even the decision to accept the limited blends described earlier didn't start early enough or go far enough once they were allowed – albeit with a great deal of reluctance.

AUSTRALIAN WOOL VERSUS COMPETING WOOLS

Another issue that began to emerge as the market shares for apparel fibres began to change was the need to review past relationships between woolgrowing nations, and how these were being affected. What also began to emerge was the thorny question whether policies set down in the mid-1930s following the establishment of IWS, were continuing to serve the needs of Australia's woolgrowers much later in the 20th century?

Whereas during the period 1936–1945, the notion of pure new wool in a generic sense, may well have been a reasonable strategy to adopt, the market situation during the later 1950s and into the 1960s had changed considerably. By the arrival of the late 1960s, it had become questionable, bearing in mind the increasing pressure on worldwide wool consumption generally, whether continuation of this policy continued to meet Australia's ongoing long-term interests.

New Zealand was already looking to differentiate its carpet production from other carpet wools by the use of a marketing programme featuring "Carpet wools of New Zealand".

Around the same time in Australia, a growing number of local designers and manufacturers of products using wool were also beginning to question the value of continuing to promote wool on a solely generic basis regardless of its source, using the Woolmark as its main identifier.

AWC had at the time been receiving requests from among some local textile manufacturers and designers to review the effectiveness of generic wool promotion. Similar thinking was also being expressed regarding IWS's policy that refused to allow the identification of a brand or source country to be included in its promotional activities.

When trying to open discussion on the subject within AWC however, such areas of discussion were actively discouraged. AWC and IWS, including their senior managements, were from a policy standpoint: 'Connected at the hip' – immovable and in lockstep.

Local Australian designers and manufacturers of wool products, from hand-knitting yarns through to men's and women's fashion apparel were then also seeing the need to differentiate products manufactured in Australia from Australia wools, from wool products being designed and sourced using wools from other producers. They saw an increasing need for AWC to take advantage of Australian wool's worldwide recognition as the premier apparel fibre, and use this to advance the cause of Australian sourced wool and wool-containing products. Such a move was known even then to be the subject of some discussion, in particular among a number of Australia's leading apparel manufacturers.

The concept around a theme of "Wools of Australia" or something in a similar vein was also being put forward, particularly as some Australian-based designers were already starting to design and export fashion and other textile-based products from Australia.

One local manufacturer, Fred James of Cleckheaton and later Wangaratta Woollen Mills, a spinner and producer of knitting wools, had already gone a step further by deciding to switch from relying solely on the Woolmark to a position promoting Cleckheaton products as "Australian Merino Wools". His view at the time being expressed from within the industry along the lines of: "It's about time AWC started to promote Australian made wool products, against competing wool and wool-containing products sourced from other woolgrowing countries!"

Australian women's fashion designer Norma Tullo had also recently emerged as one of a growing number of Australia's leading fashion designers. Between the years 1950 and 1980, Tullo, a delightfully innovative designer, was instrumental in raising the profile of the Australian wool industry by choosing to design using wool fabrics. In some cases, Tullo used fabrics, both printed and plain, made from Australian superfine quality wools.

Despite having no professional training, Norma Tullo began her fashion career in 1956 while employed as a legal secretary. In response to a gap in the youth market, unable to find the type of clothes she wanted to wear, Tullo started to produce her own designs to great commercial success.

She offered more youthful options that lacked artifice yet were stylish in design, manufactured locally, catering for the more relaxed Australian lifestyle. She is credited with having cracked the youth market wide open by fostering an environment that encouraged a new generation of Australian designers.

In the early 1970s, Tullo linked with the Wanganella (Boonoke NSW) producer of fine Merino wools to produce a collection of women's fashion apparel in Australia. Promoted under Tullo/Wanganella branding, it had also been hoped to promote the Tullo/Wanganella wool collection in Europe, in addition to Australia. Unfortunately, the project did not go ahead, due to its branding not conforming to IWS's generically oriented wool promotion policy.

The foregoing, together with menswear designers Mike Treloar, John Serafino and a number of other local women's fashion and knitwear brands, were also put forward as a possible vanguard of

Australian-designed and -produced wool fashion and other products, branded as such and promoted on the world's apparel markets.

As usual, AWC management saw the issues here as being impracticable and 'too hard to control'. Such attempts were set aside without even the possibility of any further discussion. Thus, any possibility of opening up new markets for Australian sourced wool fashion internationally had to be prematurely abandoned.

AND THE BAND PLAYED ON

Political wrangling and what can only be described as continuing refusal to accept what was happening in a rapidly changing marketplace, when coupled and augmented by the clash of personal ambitions among those occupying the leading positions at the head of Australia's woolgrowing, marketing and promotional organisations, served ultimately to deny the world's most desirable and prestigious fibre, a reasonable opportunity to compete more effectively.

As Charles Massy forcefully pointed out a number of times in his book, there had been many wool committed customers operating profitably across the textile world in Italy, France, Britain, the USA and Japan. All wanted to work alongside AWC and IWS in support of wool's future prospects. Customers and organisations like these should have been given more consideration and their views listened to with more interest and openness.

As the old saying goes, "Hindsight after an event is quite useless – unless of course it is learned from." Other words attributed I believe to Albert Einstein also have some relevance here: **"Insanity: Continuing to do the same thing and expecting different results."**

It had always been in the interests of the world's leading processors and manufacturers of fabrics and apparel, nearly all valued, long-time processors and users of Australian wools, to see Australian wool continue to be represented as a significant part of their fabric and apparel ranges.

As also pointed out by Massy, the hot political in-fighting that had been raging around AWB's ill-conceived RP Scheme, followed closely by its proposal to acquire and market the Australian wool clip, witnessed the final stanza of wool's decline and near demise.

By April 1990, AWC as a result of its reserve price scheme, found itself having to buy in well over 60% of the national clip being offered at auction. The raw wool marketing situation continued from there to go from bad to worse!

The RP Scheme presented a direct threat to the early processors and traditional buyers of wool, who had always been the industry's primary customers, providing nearly all the ongoing services from auction to the textile mill.

Anyone at the time wishing to open their eyes to the way the synthetic fibre industry had been developing, should have realised that moves to introduce and then harden up the ill-thought-through RP Scheme, and later trying to act in the marketplace as the virtual owner of Australia's wool production, could at the very best flounder along. Both arrangements offered not much more hope than a recipe for potential disaster!

Both programmes continued to be promoted by members of AWC's board and senior management, some agri-economists, a variety of political players within the Australian Country Party and others among the woolgrowing fraternity. A number of the preceding continued to view wool buyers and other operators along the wool textile manufacturing chain through jaundiced eyes, strangely and wrongly regarding them as being among 'the enemy'.

Just watching developments from the sidelines, with the politicking and power plays going on just above my head, it was felt prudent to keep as closely informed as possible about all that was going on around me. It was my responsibility to at least try to maintain wool's position wherever possible in the local men's apparel market.

My feelings at the time are best described as: "Why continue to knock your head against a brick wall and worry about something you have no control over?" It was a case of getting on with the job in hand and perhaps things may sort themselves out for the better?

They didn't, of course…

SUPERFINE MERINO WOOL

During 1973, AWC found itself for a period having to buy in most of the wools offered at auction as a result of a downturn in demand. I at the time began to research how best to achieve increased sales of that premium range of wool fibre known technically as superfine.

It seemed reasonable that wherever possible, AWC should try to reduce its growing stocks of superfine wools, at the time being accumulated at a higher rate than normal, even among AWC's increasing stocks across all wool types. The AWC owned stockpile, was threatening to swell beyond a million bales, a level it reached by the early 1990s!

To explain further, Australian wools coming under the classification as 'superfine' are very special. They have a much finer fibre diameter, less than 20 microns and usually closer to 17 microns, they also require more care in their production, and, they have a longer staple length than other grades of apparel wools.

Superfine designated wools produce soft, fine yarns and finished fabrics possessing superior handling characteristics. They are ideally suited to the manufacture of high-quality worsted woven and knitted fabrics, and apparel, across a broad range of structures and styles. Interestingly, this also includes the possibility of using superfine quality wools to produce lightweight next to the skin, thermally superior undergarments.

At the time, AWC was finding itself having to buy in higher quantities of superfine wools. It was during this period that it was proposed to take a few bales of superfine wools out of AWC's stocks, with a view to combing and cutting the staple lengths of a batch to see whether the resultant short-staple wools could be successfully spun on the cotton system and into yarns suitable for use in high-quality fashion knitwear?

The objective here was to research the possibility of developing a pure wool or dominant wool-blend yarn with fine Egyptian cotton or other premium natural fibres like cashmere, silk or even soft possum and similar other 'exotic' animal or vegetable fibres, all to be spun on the cotton system.[1]

I had already initiated a series of clandestine trials to see if the process was technically feasible. Results showed that while technically challenging, it was possible, resulting in some interesting and different yarns, suitable for the production of high-quality knitwear.

The question here, why not look to find some different outlets for overstocked superfine wools? At the time, there had been a continuing lack of demand for worsted spun fine men's suitings and women's apparel, scarves and other sundry low volume niche products.

The answer came quickly from on high – forget the inclusion of even a trial project onto AWCs development programme. AWC's senior management had high hopes of moving the growing pile of superfine wools out of its stores – a task that took years and millions of dollars more being poured down the drain in acquiring and storing the raw, greasy wool, for want perhaps of some creative thinking 'outside the square'.

The possibility of at least trying something different in a positive effort to explore the potential of developing a new outlet for AWC's overstocked superfine wools, died without a whimper.

A deal of research had already been carried out both in the US and Europe on the possibilities of combing, staple cutting and spinning wool on the cotton system. The process had shown some interesting results.

Notes

1. Comparison of the spinning systems of wool and cotton – see references section.

PIE IN THE SKY – MACHINE WASHABLE WOOL

The Celsius 30 project described earlier had been a positive move. It had linked a technical development, in the form of a new blend, to a specific product offering a distinct product advantage to consumers. The product was then supported with a positive marketing programme involving the textile and apparel industries, and later the consuming public.

A number of technical research projects had been injected into the

CSIRO (Commonwealth Scientific Industrial Research Organisation) pipeline from time to time over the years. Unfortunately, very little in the way of objective research or merchandising expertise appears to have been applied before going ahead with at least one such project.

The so-designated "Machine Washable Programme" briefly referred to earlier, had involved a great deal of funding and technical work on the parts of both CSIRO and AWB's technical division staff. Unfortunately, it ultimately proved to be of little benefit to wool's ongoing marketing strategy.

AWB's market research group had earlier come up with research that suggested the potential offered by providing worsted woven wool garments, mainly sports trousers, with machine washable characteristics to be, in their words, "a marketing winner". While such a product was considered to offer a technical advantage, the possibilities of actually achieving an acceptable and marketable result, bearing in mind the long recognised less desirable properties of wool when it came to laundering, left much to be desired.

This project did prove to be technically feasible, actually allowing men's pure wool worsted trousers to be laundered in a domestic washing machine. The major disadvantage of doing so, however, was the harsh chemical treatment required to render the item machine washable, not forgetting the increased cost involved.

Many years earlier, even as a young student at the LCT, our textile fibre studies had demonstrated that one major disadvantage of the wool fibre became apparent when trying to wash a made-up garment. The very nature of the wool fibre makes it difficult to chemically treat and modify to allow a wool garment to undergo any form of harsh laundering, other than perhaps via the gentler form of hand washing, as recommended for laundering wool knitwear and socks.

Machine-washing of untreated wool garments, on the other hand, was known to be well outside the practicality of doing so. This was due to their propensity to pill, the fabric to felt up alarmingly and become harsh to the touch, thus losing nearly all the wool fabric's original superior handling characteristics.

While it was possible to apply various forms of chemical treatments to a wool fabric to render it resistant to shrinkage and felting, such treatment tended to leave the finished fabric surface rough and uncomfortable in wear as well as being harsh to handle. In effect, the chemical treatment robbed the item of clothing of its most desirable characteristics.

Machine washable wool, in the form of trousers and one or two other men's and women's garments, while hopefully being promoted with a degree of enthusiasm, mainly on the part of CSIRO's technical boffins and those from AWB's technical division and public relations office during the early 1970s, proved disappointing. Despite the amount of effort and technical resources allocated to the project, the process required to render the finished product machine washable, offered little, if anything of advantage and value to potential consumers. In fact, the treatment served to drastically reduce the fabric's comfort and handle.

Pure Wool garments, particularly knitwear, appropriately spun and knitted from some of the finer of Australia's Merino wools, are known to be capable of being hand washed successfully, without any of the harsh chemically based treatments being necessary.

The concept of machine washable wool trousers was eventually dropped following zero interest being shown by manufacturers, retailers and consumer groups.

Only one company, Fletcher Jones, dabbled in the project for a short time on a trial basis, they dropped it soon after, due no doubt to a lack of consumer interest.

NATIONAL MERCHANDISING MANAGER

After three years as AWC's menswear product manager, and involvement with a number of marketing innovations in the menswear field, I was promoted to the position of national merchandising manager.

This role was very different to my former position, much broader than dealing solely with the menswear industry. It now encompassed all end uses in which wool was used. These included men's and women's apparel, children's wear and knitwear, carpets, upholstery fabrics, curtains and decorative textiles.

For the first time in my career to date I became responsible for directing the various product managers heading up these end uses, in addition to the co-ordination and control of the various colour, design and technical advisory services being provided to the Australian apparel and textile manufacturing industries.

At some stage shortly, there would also be the need to seek a replacement for myself in the now vacant menswear role.

My role now became one of managing, or more to the point motivating, co-ordinating and mentoring a group of individual product managers and associated support staff.

Increasing competition being faced by wool in the Australian marketplace also meant tightening up on the use of promotional funds and the manner in which they had been allocated via co-operative advertising, with selected manufacturers and retailers, across all end uses.

Corporate advertising and the generic promotion of wool resided outside the ambit of my authority as merchandising manager, being controlled by AWC's corporate advertising and PR department, who continued in turn to take direction from the AWC board.

A RAPIDLY CHANGING INDUSTRY – THE 1970S

During the 1970s, not many locally manufactured apparel or other wool products were being exported from Australia. One or two of the more successful women's wear designers were beginning to move away from the smaller Australian market, as they tried to develop a broader footprint for their designs and products overseas, mainly in the US and Europe.

Another significant change in the way the textile and apparel pipeline, in particular, was beginning to rearrange itself had already begun to appear. This trend included the projected move by the federal government toward the lowering of import tariff levels and changes to import quotas. These were changes from policies that previously had provided a high level of protection to the Australian textiles, clothing and footwear industries, protections that were now going to be rolled back.

Changes downward in import protection for local manufacturing became more widespread and deeper, with a number of the major manufacturers of apparel in particular, contemplating the gradual abandonment of their earlier role of manufacturing locally. Some of the more entrepreneurial were already looking to set themselves up as specialists and consultants in design, sourcing and marketing. As a result, more local production became outsourced to factories located overseas, in lower-cost countries. These at the time included but were not limited to P.R. China, India, Pakistan, Philippines, Malaysia and South Korea.

Specialist apparel retailers and major department stores were also starting to move away from their traditional role, solely as placers of indent orders for products sourced predominantly from local manufacturers. Some retailers had already begun taking on a more entrepreneurial role. This in effect meant them taking over of services previously provided by local apparel manufacturers and suppliers of imported products.

Recognising the opportunities now being presented by the soon to be lowered import tariffs, a growing number of retailers began setting up their own in-house buying arrangements, recruiting and training appropriate staff. This change in policy was aimed at controlling the cost of what they were buying, from where and how they were buying products, all with greater emphasis on them operating as the main determinant. Retailers thus took greater control over product, price, sourcing and branding, the latter eventually seeing the introduction of retailer house brands, which soon became part of retailer sourced product offerings to the Australian consumer.

In short, the retail sector of the apparel trade, from its position at the peak of the product distribution network next only to the consuming public, began taking over the lead in the product supply chain. In most cases this change in their role saw them becoming the principal decision maker. House brands also started to make their appearance on the shelves and racks of major department stores.

Major department stores like the Myer Emporium, David Jones and others, began to identify and seek to control their own supply pipelines, arranging in a number of cases for the manufacture of their own house-branded merchandise, in addition to continuing to stock brands being sourced from local and overseas manufacturers. Thus, most were aiming where possible to cut out the 'middle man', allowing retailers to retain a more significant share of the subsequent profits now able to be gained.

Incidental to this activity on the part of retailers and some manufacturers, now being able to import apparel of all kinds at a much lower cost than was possible previously, did not result in them passing on any savings in cost to their customers, resulting from the lowering of import tariffs. Instead, the end result of the subsequent overly rapid reduction of tariffs had little effect on retail prices.

What did occur arrived in a form directly opposite to that forecast by the then Australian government's economists and party members. Advice that went along the line, "The lowering of import tariffs will provide much lower retail prices to Australian consumers of imported TCF products."

The lowering of tariffs instead resulted in the closing down of a growing number of local manufacturers, the eventual loss of the majority of Australia's textile and apparel manufacturing industry, and the subsequent loss of many thousands of jobs across the country.

Most, if not all the savings gained as a result of becoming able to source products from lower-cost locations across Asia, India, and Korea were being retained by those taking advantage of lowered import tariffs and the changed quota regime being introduced by the government.

As time progressed into the 1970s and 1980s, individual chain store specialty groups like Country Road,[1] Sportsgirl, Sportscraft, Witchery, Just Jeans and a host of others, began developing into nationally recognised brands in their own right. These so-called 'specialty stores' began sourcing apparel products from suppliers overseas, having these manufactured to their own specifications and design criteria. In a few cases they continued sourcing products from a drastically reducing number of local manufacturers, even this gradually reduced until today, where most apparel products are being sourced from factories located in low cost, Third World countries.

The signs announcing that the pipeline for apparel products was already in the process of change, had become apparent even before my role at AWC had changed. Alongside these changes, the challenge for those of us involved with defending wool's position in Australia was also in need of review.

It had become even more apparent that there was a need to adjust AWC's operations to the way in which changes in decision-making were starting to occur along the local textile and apparel marketing pipeline. At the time, the AWC board and senior management, engrossed in their desire to control the Australian wool clip via the integrated marketing proposal, and wool industry pressure to keep wool's reserve price as high as possible, paid little attention to the need to react, in tune with what was happening along the textile/apparel pipeline.

As market conditions were changing, there also existed the need for AWC to consider how policy development and staffing policy needed to be always capable of moving according to changing industry needs. What was now occurring added emphasis to the need to be constantly reviewing current tactics, activities in the marketplace and staff training.

In view of the rapid rate of change in the way the local industry was beginning to operate, I had proposed to fill the position left vacant by my promotion to that of national merchandising manager with a replacement possessing extensive outside commercial experience – directly from either a textile or apparel manufacturing background. Despite the submission of a detailed job specification, and extensive supporting analysis, intended to be used for the appointment of a fully qualified replacement and any future appointments to the division's merchandising staff, a junior staff member who lacked any prior experience with textiles, apparel manufacture or retailing was appointed. The reason provided, without even allowing any further discussion: "It is current policy to promote from within."

The move into my new role presented some issues other than the foregoing. What in past years had been 'normal' circumstances and relationships along the textile and apparel pipeline were changing rapidly. It was already a situation that demanded the retraining, or possible redeployment of some staff in key areas, and the introduction of needed changes to the manner in which AWC was making important decisions and approaching the task of defending wool's declining influence across Australia.

Trying to co-ordinate and effect the required changes to wool supporting strategies, in the face of a changing marketplace was one thing, but how to redirect our product merchandising operations toward a more professional approach, was quite another. The now overriding question needing to be faced, in spite of the AWC board and senior management's apparent reticence, was to review and where necessary to re-organise, in a form better suited to meet those changes.

Notes

1. Country Road was founded in 1974 by Stephen Bennett initially as a shirt label. It grew to become Australia's first lifestyle brand. By 1980, the company was selling women's apparel and had product in department stores as well as in 10 Country Road stores. Other specialty brands developed along similar lines.

EXECUTIVE SCHOOL

My transition to the role of national merchandising manager had been assisted by my earlier enrolment at the Australian Administrative Staff College (ASC). The college was an elite executive training facility, at the time based in a stately residence located on the southern shore of Port Phillip Bay at Mount Eliza, a small township on the Mornington Peninsula, some 60km southeast of the Melbourne CBD.

The residential course at ASC was designed to provide expertise in general management. It provided management training for staff across a wide diversity of Australian industries and major commercial organisations. The course I attended was directed toward equipping management staff with the range of skills needed, in a rapidly changing business environment. Among the activities undertaken at ASC were research and development studies aimed at the preparation and implementation of business and marketing plans.

The course I attended during the early 1970s included a group of middle managers, a broad and diverse grouping brought together from a wide variety of industries and different states across Australia. A major part of our studies involved being allocated into a series of smaller groupings. Each group was set specific areas of study around the general question: "How is increased globalisation expected to affect Australia's manufacturing industries?"

One of the tasks given to the study group to which I was allocated, was to examine how the Australian textile, clothing and footwear industries would be effected, as a result of the federal government's recent and projected tariff cuts and changes in import quotas? How these changes were expected to affect employees also formed an important part of the group's considerations. The parameters of our study area included changes in the value of the A$ and any other factors the group considered relevant.

The overriding issue of all the various studies at the time was the increased trend toward the globalisation of worldwide commerce. Each group was required, in addition to discussing their particular areas of inquiry, to present their thinking as to how the industries under study should react to changing worldwide circumstances.

My group, the members of which, apart from myself, were from a wide range of industries, concluded that local TCF industries would continue to face increasing competition, mainly from low cost, Third World countries. A number of these countries were actively setting themselves up to offer 'First World'[1] companies and individual entrepreneurs, the opportunity to source competitively priced production facilities. This move alone was expected to drastically reduce employment opportunities for Australian workers across all three TCF industry groupings.

Local Australian manufacturers were seen as needing to adopt a more entrepreneurial approach to their previous roles. Of necessity, this would mean companies and individuals being forced to change their role in the product supply pipeline from one purely as a manufacturer, to a role somewhere between manufacturing and operating as an importer, co-ordinator, facilitator or distributor. In part and where appropriate, this was seen to provide an opportunity for local manufacturers to use their already extensive expertise in setting up their own or partnership arrangements with lower-cost manufacturing operations overseas.

At the same time, fewer jobs were expected to result in the industries under review, should the federal government continue to reduce tariff levels beyond their current levels.

Questions relating to the increased threat posed to Australian grown wool by other wool producing countries as wool's worldwide market share decreased was considered to be in need of urgent discussion by the local Australian authorities.

Australian wool and the woolgrowing industry, at the time regularly featuring on news bulletins and in newspaper articles, was also expected by the Mount Eliza group to find itself increasingly in direct competition with wool and wool products being supplied from and on behalf of other, competitive grower countries.

Australia, the world's major supplier of wool was seen to be more vulnerable than other woolgrowing countries. Thus, there was a need for discussion to take place and positive support provided behind the branding and promotion of products specifically manufactured from Australian wools, in Australia and elsewhere across the world that offered the opportunity to do so. The other elephant in the room was seen as increased levels of wool substitution by synthetic fibres.

On returning to my day job, and later appointment as national merchandising manager, the month spent at ASC, in particular finding myself among a broad range of industry managers, all providing inputs based on their personal experiences gained across a variety of industries, occurred at a most useful time.

These were industries that included mining, banking, steel fabrication, engineering, retail, accounting etc. The timing of this opportunity to engage with managers from across Australia representing a wide variety of other industries proved extremely valuable, serving to emphasise even further the urgent need for changes to be implemented across both the AWC and IWS – if Australian wool was to become better equipped at defending its market position against the continuing threat of synthetic fibres.

My detailed report and recommendations to senior management

on my return to AWC probably ended up in some dusty drawer, filing cabinet – or perhaps a conveniently located wastepaper basket?

Notes

1. First World countries: The concept of the 'First World' originated during the 'Cold War' and included countries that were generally aligned with or on friendly terms with the United States (including all NATO countries). They were generally identified as non-theocratic democracies with primarily market-based economies. While there is no current consensus on an exact definition of the term, in modern usage, "First World country" generally implies a relatively wealthy, stable and functional non-theocratic democracy with a reasonably well-educated population, or just any developed country.

A FLOCK OF SHEEP

When it came to those growing the wool across Australia, at least those that I had the opportunity of meeting or listening to at various wool forums and meetings, most seemed to accept without too much in the way of educated questioning, the way their industry continued to be managed. They appeared to amble along like the fabulous four-legged wool factories they were so expert at breeding, farming and shearing. While expert in producing the world's premier fibre, most appeared unable to see much further ahead when it came to their industry's future. Not much further that is – than the amount of their next wool cheque. Most consistently failed to recognise what was already beginning to rear its ugly head just around the corner.

With few exceptions, woolgrowers, certainly during the period of my tenure with AWB/AWC, tended to follow those leading them. A few isolated egg-throwing and similar-style rowdy complaints issued from time to time, most of them aimed at the towering figure of Bill (Sir William) Gunn.

Like a flock of their sheep, Australia's woolgrowers had over the years become adept at hearing the mainly good news – at least as it was being delivered by a slick IWS/AWC spin machine. As individuals, a considerable proportion of Australia's woolgrowers appeared to lack even the basic understanding of what was facing wool out there in the worldwide fibre marketplace.

While prices for their wool kept moving in an upward direction, as a group they seemed happy to rely on the regularly provided assurances emanating from IWS and AWC as to the prospects they could expect for their continuing efforts and financial investment in the industry.

The AWC board and senior management, in particular their much-touted marketing experts David Jones and the gentleman from Heinz baked beans, continued to favour the IWS's approach to the generic promotion of pure new wool and the Woolmark, which, in effect, meant providing continuing financial support for pure new wool products. The continued refusal to even consider the need for some changes to be made, meant that most of AWC's development and promotional funds continued to be directed toward even more grandiose advertising and public relations campaigns.

While these may well have continued to win advertising awards each year for the ever enthusiastic and exceedingly well-paid advertising agencies involved, this strategy lacked the ability to change what was occurring in the textile market.

AWC's then agency, Leo Burnet, and others over the years continued to rake in lots of woolgrower and Australian government money in their enthusiastic, very professional and dedicated efforts to win more and more advertising awards. I suppose this could be seen as a form of success as far as creative advertising went, but it added very little more than a flash-in-the-pan as far as changing wool's fortunes across Australia and the worldwide marketplace.

9

APPOINTMENT TO NEW YORK

The AWC board continued in its quest to establish its credentials in a role similar to that of a competitive synthetic fibre producer. The authors of the board's Integrated Marketing Plan also had their hearts set on dealing as such in the not-too-distant future.

The opportunity to do so, when it arrived, soon became known among some of the more inquisitive keepers of our ears to the ground, most of whom were, like me, working under the surface of our imagined pond, a level or so down from the AWC boardroom.

A few of the more entrepreneurial wool textile processors operating in the US market had already initiated discussion on the subject of Australian wool. No doubt the Americans had noted that stocks of wool were building up in Australia, prompting interest in the possibilities such a situation offered. Among those companies showing interest were: Burlington Industries, JP Stevens and Wellman Combing, supported by a number of smaller US mills, combers and spinners.

The American processors had come to the view, that value could be added to their US operations, if they could encourage AWC to establish a permanent stock of appropriate wools in the US. Their object here was to gain direct access to a regular supply of Australian wool at stable prices, preferably lower than those regularly fluctuating at public auction in Australia. Wellman combing was known to be suffering from reduced orders for wool processing, due to the continuing turndown in demand for wool generally throughout the US.

AWC management was enthusiastic, particularly as the US was a major apparel fibre market in which wool consumption was declining faster even than in Europe. The situation in the US presented just the opportunity the AWC board was seeking to enable it to prove that such a project could achieve the goal of providing a direct and regular supply of wool, together with supporting merchandising assistance, to overseas wool processors.

Perhaps it was a coincidence that some months earlier I had visited the US at the latter end of an overseas visit to the textile and apparel industries in Europe and the UK? During my visit to the US, in addition to visits to the IWS office in New York, I visited the JP Stevens Company, one of the US's major users of wool. JP Stevens, along with Burlington Industries, were the two dominant textile producers in the US, processing wool from greasy stage through to finished fabric. Both used US and Australian wools. I had also sought introductions to an independent top-maker based in New England and a worsted spinner in South Carolina.

At the meeting with JP Stevens, they offered the comment that there could be a potential opportunity to expand the consumption of Australian wools in the US – if wool could be sourced in the US, with guaranteed continuity, direct supply and stable pricing.

As part of my subsequent report on returning to Melbourne, it was suggested that in view of the general decline in the consumption of Australian wool in the US, that attention could perhaps be directed toward the better servicing of the wool processing sector of the US textile industry. This could be achieved by channelling appropriate types of AWC's then excessive wool stocks directly into that market?

I was unaware of what, if anything would result from my comments. It was interesting to later learn that plans were underway to set up a stock of appropriate grades of wool in the US.

Whether the notes in my earlier visit report had had any effect on the decision, I never got to know. Later, as planning for the stocking of wools in the US progressed, I was approached by Malcolm Vawser,

AWC's general manager, and offered the opportunity to open an AWC sales office in North America. The proposed office was to be established in New York, adjacent to IWS's US headquarters. I was also given to understand that full IWS co-operation and assistance, wherever required, would be provided to AWC's efforts in the US.

In deciding to accept the appointment, I did so in the knowledge that the project could well become undone at some time in the not-too-distant future, should AWC's desire to become the sole owner and seller of Australian wool be rejected by the Australian government.

On the plus side, the offer did represent an opportunity to move on to a much larger market, and in a very different, and challenging role, one well suited to my earlier years of training and professional experience since.

SOME CONSEQUENCES

Having to move over to the United States to carry out this new assignment meant leaving both my sons behind in Melbourne, where they would need to become weekday boarders at Mentone Grammar School, their current day school. The option did exist for me to move them both over to a suitable school in the US, once I had become established in my new home in New York.

In Melbourne, my personal life had recently become complicated. I had already found myself in the position of having to board both my boys at their local school occasionally. Boarding my boys during times when I was required to travel interstate had become a necessity, following my earlier separation from my wife of 14 years, a year or so earlier. Our parting left both boys living with me.

My marriage breakdown had placed me under a great deal of mental and emotional stress. At the time, I was also very sensitive to ensuring that my boys, then aged 12 and 10, were affected as little as possible from their parents' separation. At work, I also had to carry on operating as effectively as possible, in what had developed into a demanding role.

The stress and disorientation that had resulted from the ending of my first marriage was bad enough, but it became much worse when added to the constant pressure I was experiencing at work. The need to carry out my responsibilities, while at the same time having also to provide a safe, loving and nurturing environment at home for two young boys, at times got to be overpowering.

The pressure over past months just trying to cope with my domestic responsibilities, while having also to deal with managing staff, running meetings and dealing with the day-to-day issues that were part of my management role, would often leave me unable to sleep for nights on end. With pressure building up on both accounts, I found myself beginning to lose the capacity to cope, a load that on more than one occasion brought me close to suffering an emotional breakdown.

The issues I found myself having to face resulted in me seeking counselling and medical attention to assist me to maintain balance. My life during this period had become a sometimes almost impossible and barely bearable pattern of daily existence.

The offer of an overseas appointment, when it came, presented the opportunity to move away from Melbourne for a period. It would also mean me having to arrange for both my boys to be enrolled as permanent weekday boarders at their school. Such an arrangement was originally intended to be temporary, at least until I could make other suitable school arrangements for schooling and their possible move to live with me in New York. For their part, AWC management had agreed to assist in arranging regular visits to me the US during their school holidays for both boys, should my ultimate decision be for them to remain in Australia.

While also scheduled to return to Melbourne at least once each year to report in person to AWC management, this arrangement seemed in the circumstances to at least allow me some space in which to readjust – the circuit breaker I desperately needed at the time.

Whatever the reasons at the time that culminated in my acceptance of the US role, I continued to question the wisdom in accepting the move over to the US, which could also mean leaving both my young sons behind. Both boys would be able to spend weekends with their mother in addition to spending some time also with both sets of grandparents, who lived not far from their school. Such arrangements, of course, were less than ideal for two young boys, whose parents had parted and whose young lives were being further disrupted, their father now thinking to leave them to move to another country.

Looking back to that period, I was at the time desperately in need of finding some balance in my life, which was beginning to spiral downward, possibly toward some form of eventual breakdown.

While recognising the need to add as little disruption as possible into the lives of my sons, the opportunity to move over to the US at least promised to allow me a period, during which to get my life back onto equilibrium, emotionally. This was important as I was fast arriving at the point where the stress was sometimes becoming unbearable, as I continued trying to cope with the pressure of my work, while at the same time trying to fulfil my parental responsibilities.

I was at the time finding myself betwixt two rocks. While on the one hand there existed the possibility that the US operation offered an interesting challenge and the kind of opportunity for which my whole working life and experience to date had been equipping me. On the other hand, I was also concerned as to the possible consequences of leaving my sons behind, even if it were only for a few years.

I finally decided that I would take up the opportunity being offered by AWC, but would also initially research the possibility (and advisability) of arranging for both Simon and Philip to accompany me to the US. If it was considered practicable, and in the boys' best interests, I planned to enrol them in a similar quality school to that which they were currently attending in Melbourne. I had been advised by one or two people familiar with the US education system as to the standards of schools in the US and the availability of good schools within the city of New York. I was also thinking that a few years living in another country would perhaps provide my sons with a much broader experience of life.

Following my subsequent arrival in the US, I immediately began to make inquiries with some US schools that were said to be able to offer education and facilities close to or perhaps higher than the same level they were enjoying at Mentone Grammar School in Melbourne. That plan though was soon abandoned when it became apparent that, for reasons related to some social and other issues that had emerged during my inquiries and visits to some of the top schools around New York, such a plan was not considered to be in the best interests of my boys.

Once I had actually moved over to New York and was living and working there, it also became clear that to find a school that could provide the level of education required, as close as possible to the standard of their school in Melbourne, would still mean Simon and Philip becoming enrolled in a school a little distant from where I was based.

It was finally decided, following discussion and agreement with my estranged wife, that moving Simon and Philip over to a school in the US would not provide the best answer for their ongoing well-being. At least in Melbourne, both boys would be among their long-time friends and schoolmates. They would also be close to their mother, grandparents on both sides and other family members. Perhaps most important, they would continue to be living in a familiar and safe environment.

The arrangement seemed the best of all options, much better than trying to settle both boys as part-time boarders, in a strange school, in a strange country, while still needing to live some distance away from their father for much of their time as boarders at a US school.

AUSTRALIAN CITIZEN

Before my departure to New York, I had one other piece of personal business to attend to.

It was now 15 years since my arrival in Australia. At times during the ensuing years, I had given thought to fulfil my relationship with the country for which as a boy I had developed such an undiminished fascination, and in which I had now set down permanent roots, by applying for Australian citizenship.

While from time to time I had thought to do so, something or other at the time always seemed to get in the way.

During a recent visit to Europe however, particularly as I was travelling as the representative of an Australian statutory organisation, the need to do something more positive grew stronger. I could no longer regard myself as being a true representative of my adopted country, without at least a more formal commitment on my part.

Now with the prospect of representing AWC in the US, that need became urgent. I felt that I could not contemplate a situation where I would be representing Australia in the US, still officially a citizen of the UK, a country that to me over the years had, for all practical purposes, become a foreign country.

I was in truth no longer an Englishman, although I still retained a clearly identifiable Yorkshire accent. For some years now I had become a proud Australian, a relative newcomer perhaps, but in both mind and soul there existed no other country than Australia that for me was home.

CERTIFICATE OF AUSTRALIAN CITIZENSHIP

Emotionally, even though not officially Australian I had, in fact, become a citizen in mind and outlook. Although I could never claim to be a genuine dinky-di Aussie, my future life and that of my children and any of my future grandchildren would always be bound to my now adopted country – Australia.

March 7th 1975 dawned one of the proudest days of my life as I took the oath of allegiance to my new country, now officially becoming a proud new Australian.

NEW YORK AND THE GODFATHER

My arrival in New York during early April 1975 followed the shipment of a range of selected wools from AWC's Australian stocks to a storage facility in the port city of Charleston, South Carolina. A shipping agent had been appointed in Charleston, banking arrangements arranged in New York.

US delivered prices for AWC stocked wools were set at a level below the then-current prices being achieved at auction. It was intended to keep these at the same level throughout a given season into the future. What such a season was in fact to represent was as yet to be determined.

One glaring issue here was that while auction prices in Australia could fluctuate over a much shorter period, how would the proposed US arrangement work over the longer term – given that AWC did not, in a true commercial sense at least, own the wool being stored in the US? The purpose of setting US pricing in this way had been justified by Melbourne on the basis that AWC was doing so in an attempt to defend the declining use of Australian wool in the US.

Looking at the arrangement from a different angle however, it was clear that the wool being offered in the US was being discounted and offered, more in the form of what retailers and others would normally regard as a 'loss leader'. An attractive price being set on a selected product range, to attract more trade to other, more profitably priced stock offerings. Perhaps even more important it meant the setting up by AWC of a two-tier sales system for wool – public auction in Australia as against direct sales at a 'stabilised' price in the US. More will be discussed on this and similar issues in a later chapter.

On my arrival in New York, I took up temporary residence in a small but comfortable hotel – the Sheraton Russell, conveniently located uptown, at the intersection of Park Avenue with 40th Street. Following a couple of lonely weeks hunting for a more permanent residence, I eventually took a lease on apartment 31G (31st floor) in a relatively new residential block located at the intersection of 33rd Street and 3rd Avenue, in local New York City vernacular – pronounced locally in a form sounding more like "toity toid and toid".

The apartment was well placed, being in the Midtown section of Manhattan, just two blocks east of 5th Avenue, its shops, the Australian consulate and within walking distance of my office building at the intersection of 40th Street and Lexington Avenue.

Typically for the city of New York, my apartment was located adjacent to streets that contained what were referred to locally as 'walk-up' apartments and flats, the adjoining 33rd and 32nd streets being two such locations. Both these streets were lined on both sides with these familiar older-style New York apartment buildings – each having two, three or more stories, but nothing in the way of elevator access to the upper floors, hence the term 'walk-up'. This kind of accommodation housed a large cross section of Manhattan's working population, particularly in those areas having a preponderance of lower-cost apartments, further downtown.

One example of the level of New York society that inhabited some of the walk-ups very close to my very comfortable upmarket apartment building was the family of the cleaning lady I later managed to locate and employ. She and her husband – also a cleaner at the nearby Bellevue Hospital Centre on New York's 1st Avenue, lived in the basement of one of these walk-up tenancies, with their two children. Both earned just enough to live and pay the rent on what was in effect a cellar containing two rooms plus a bathroom/toilet.

Many of the local streets, further downtown on the East Side of New York featured similar apartments, the cheaper being virtually a basement, with others more comfortable and accordingly more expensive to rent, located higher up in the building. All this, next to my spacious 1½ bedroom, two bathrooms 'bachelor pad', 31 floors up with its balcony overlooking Manhattan's 3rd Avenue and across town to New York's Midtown and West Side.

This was a sought-after position. My apartment had an unimpeded view directly across Midtown, a couple of blocks west to the Empire State Building and beyond that toward the Hudson River and New Jersey in the distance. The location proved a very acceptable and convenient one in which to be living while resident in what continues to be the most exciting city in the world.

5th Avenue, together with its big stores and expensive boutiques, the famous Rockefeller Center and a very conveniently placed Australian Consulate, and Qantas's offices were located just a couple of blocks west.

An early meeting at IWS's New York office introduced me to its manager, Felix Colangelo. Felix immediately gave one the impression of being a smooth, controlling character. Here was a manager, I learned later, who ran his little kingdom very much in the Godfather style, controlling every aspect, large or small among his staff. It very soon got to the stage, following moving into AWC's new office suite, one floor above those of IWS's, that it also became necessary to change the locks on the outside door. Changing locks was found to be necessary to stop Felix from snooping through my office when AWC's office suite was unoccupied in the evening.

On one such venture, very early on in my tenure, Felix was caught in the act by my then temporary secretary – an occasion which found her needing to return to the office to pick up some personal stuff she had inadvertently left behind on leaving for the day. On entering, she stumbled on Felix snooping around in my office, in my absence and without permission. On another occasion, the same Felix was reported as having tried to gain entry into my filing cabinet. This called for a new lock on my office door and AWC's suite entrance, as well as me taking the precaution of moving some of the more confidential of my files to my apartment each evening after work.

Not an encouraging beginning for AWC's New York operations, but one that gradually became even more difficult as time passed.

SETTING UP OFFICE IN NEW YORK

During the 1970s, the usual means of communication back to Australia from the US, apart from the usual 'snail mail', was either via the ordinary telephone or 'Telex' service. Telex was a system that sent and received messages printed on a paper strip. The days of the day-to-day use of computers, email and mobile phones were still a long way ahead into the future.

While on the subject of new technology, one significant new piece of equipment purchased during the setting up of AWC's offices in New York was in the form of a Texas Instruments 'pocket' calculator, a relatively new development at the time.

While the calculator could carry out some functions, it could more accurately be described as relatively basic when compared to a cheap modern-day pocket-sized calculator that can be bought anywhere for a few dollars. It was also a little large to be carried in one's pocket.

When I say relatively new invention, the latest Texas Instruments 'pocket' calculator purchased in New York in the mid-1970s was miles more capable than the Sinclair 'Oxford' calculator I had purchased in London a couple of years earlier, during one of my early overseas visits.

That then British made Sinclair brand calculator was one of the first commercially available so-called pocket calculators to become available commercially. It, unfortunately, was a little too large to carry in one's pocket, and could only carry out some very basic calculations, while costing in the region of £300!

Ridiculous to spend that much on such an instrument, but it was after all one of the first so-called pocket calculators anyone at Wool House had seen, when I brought it back to Melbourne. The Sinclair unit unfortunately gave up the ghost a few weeks following my return to Melbourne and had to be sent back to the Sinclair organisation in London to be repaired.

Following the appointment of my personal assistant/secretary, Kathleen Gallagher, New York-bred lass of Irish extraction. I also needed to appoint an experienced locally based salesperson capable of handling the day-to-day functions of raw wool and eventually our sales of wool tops.[1] My search proved difficult at first, as surprisingly there were few available people around in the US wool trade possessing the range of expertise, contacts and presentation skills desired.

I was eventually successful in locating the man I was seeking, but he was employed and living in Canada, where he was working for a local wool merchant based in Montreal.

Roy Lockwood hailed from 'Bronte' country, near Bradford, the world-renowned wool capital of Yorkshire. While Roy was currently working in Canada, he proved knowledgeable when it came to his familiarity with the companies and most of the personalities and wool processors then operating in the US and Canada.

I first interviewed Roy in one of the most unlikely places in which one could have expected to undertake such an interview – in a discotheque, surrounded by loud music and gyrating bodies, located in a basement, among the streets and alleyways of the city of Montreal. We did meet later in my hotel room before later offering Roy the position, which required him to move from Canada to New York City.

With Roy's appointment, the AWC's New York office was now fully staffed, up and running, ready to do business with combers, spinners, worsted and woollen mills throughout the US, Canada and later Mexico.

Notes

1. The wool *top*-making process follows scouring and carding. It prepares the *wool* for the worsted spinning process, at which the *wool* is formed into a yarn. Tops are combed into a rope-like form ensuring the *wool* fibres are thoroughly blended to form a homogenous mixture, and that all fibres lie parallel to each other.

LIFESTYLE MANHATTAN

New York is an amazing city, unlike anywhere else in the known world. The island of Manhattan is a place where everything and anything is possible, where people live, work and play in close proximity to each other. Residents live in a variety of tall, sky scraping buildings or streetscapes lined with 'Brownstone' residences or 'walk-up' apartment buildings.

The 1970s, during the four years of my life there, could also be more than a little dangerous, particularly if an unwitting visitor happened to wander into the wrong neighbourhood or if white, they tried to visit a jazz or other club, far uptown in Haarlem – without a coloured friend to vouch for them. All in all, New York City and its local boroughs of Queens, the Bronx, Brooklyn and further out to the east on Long Island, was capable of offering any visitor a wide variety of lifestyles from which to choose. The city was a compact, but broad, interesting palette from which to choose, offering a range of options not known to exist in any similarly sized city in the then known world.

As for me, the island of Manhattan and its Midtown neighbourhood became my preferred choice of a place at which to settle, reasonably close to my work base on Lexington Avenue.

Once settled into my apartment and having established the office and recruited my staff of two, it wasn't long before I was able to slip into a daily work routine. This time though, my work also had me undertaking a great deal of travel, both by road and air, to establish and maintain contact with the various levels of textile and apparel manufacturing organisations spread throughout the US.

It was but a short five-minute walk that would take me from my apartment on 3rd Avenue in the Murray Hill district of Manhattan Island to my office on the fourth floor at 360 Lexington Avenue.

Living on Manhattan Island was very convenient. Everyday shopping close to my apartment was easy, with a number of small to medium-sized local markets, bars, cafés, restaurants and shops of all kinds situated within easy walking distance. Most of New York's department stores were also close by, just a block or so west to 5th Avenue with Bloomingdale's famous department store a short bus ride uptown. If deciding to dine Chinese-style it was but a bus or subway ride south to the tip of Manhattan, with the theatre district and Broadway, well within walking distance on the West Side.

Being known as an 'Aussie expat', or as designated officially by the US immigration service – a 'Non-Resident Alien' and living among so many other expatriate workers on Manhattan during the 1970s, meant regular invites to gatherings, both formal and informal. These were regularly organised by staff employed by the United Nations (UN), the various overseas banking, as well as other representative organisations, including Australia's banks, the then Australian Meat and Livestock Corporation, Qantas Airways, the Australian Consulate, not forgetting Australia's offices in the United Nations building.

It didn't take very long for a newcomer to meet up with and become familiar with colleagues from across many other nations, in addition to Australia and our near neighbour New Zealand, not forgetting a large group of Pommie (British) United Nations and various bank and diplomatic service staffers.

Regular meetings of expat Aussies would regularly get together for late afternoon tea, coffee and 'bikkies' (biscuits), or a 'Victoria Bitter' 'Tooheys' or 'XXXX' beer or two at the Australian Consulate at its plush offices in the Rockefeller Center on 5th Avenue. Qantas too had offices on 5th Avenue, where expat Aussies would be welcome to visit and view film of the previous weekends sporting clashes of the VFL or New South Wales rugby league matches – gatherings such as these were always well lubricated with a selection of Australian beer and wine!

These meetings with staff at the consulate and other Australian organisations proved very useful, particularly when it came to picking up information on various policies of interest to an expat Australian, particularly how policies and other rules operated in US government departments, particularly those relevant to my own activities.

During the late spring and during the summer months, I spent most of my weekends on Long Island's Great South Bay, at the Narrasketuck Yacht Club in Amityville. There I crewed and raced regularly on a 'Lightning' design three-man racing dinghy owned by a new friend Frank Marinaccio. Frank's champion sailboat was quaintly named Cookie Monster.

Life in New York, once having got myself settled into an apartment and offices, proved both interesting and full, regardless of the passing seasons. But – I was always counting the days and weeks as I looked forward to welcoming my boys Simon and Philip on their visits to the US during their school holidays. Both were growing quickly. Not being able to see them both on a more regular, day-to-day basis often had me fearing that I was in danger of missing out on too many of their growing years.

New York City was like no other major city that I had visited during my work with AWC. It was a city that never ceased or slowed down for anything or anyone, regardless of the season or time – day or night, rain or shine. The city offered everything. From the heights of culture to the depths of depravity, New York had it all!

INTRODUCTION TO TAR BEACH

As summer approached, a warm sunny day would regularly see many residents across Manhattan Island taking a sun lounge up onto what was known by New Yorkers as 'Tar Beach'.

While a New York-style Tar Beach was nothing like a real beach by the sea, it was a unique New York way of finding a comfortable place in the sun, whenever it appeared. For all practical purposes, Tar Beach referred to the usually flat, tarpaper-clad rooftop of most of the taller apartment buildings in which permanent and visiting residents such as I had chosen to live.

As the summer approached and the weather was getting warmer, many of the more financially able residents would have already planned to 'fly the coop' from the usually muggy and often stiflingly hot and sticky city. Most of the city's richer residents would spend some or all of the summer months in their Miami, South Carolina or elsewhere 'down south' apartments or beachside townhouses. Others might do the same using their property on Fire Island or one or other of the seaside resort towns further along Long Island's Atlantic coast toward Montauk Point.

Tar Beach for those of us left behind in the city was the closest one could get to a convenient sunbathing position within the city's limits. While nothing like a beach in a true sense, this was at least an acceptable alternative to trekking uptown to Central Park, or hiring a car and taking the long, often frustrating drive from Manhattan along the Southern State Parkway to the popular Jones Beach, located on the Atlantic lapping south shore of Long Island.

Unfortunately, driving out to the beaches on the south shore of Long Island usually ended up being a long, boring trek that few Manhattan residents would choose to venture on, particularly during high summer. This was due mainly to the heat and often banked-up and frustrating traffic jams that regularly came to a standstill with monotonous regularity along the Southern State Parkway – the major highway running parallel to the Atlantic coastline of Long Island.

As a close-by alternative that fell far short of lazing away stretched out on a soft sandy beach with the sea gently lapping at your bare toes, our own Tar Beach was really the only practical and close-by place one could access to try pulling in a few rays. The only other alternative close by was to venture uptown and spreading oneself out on a blanket or towel on the Sheep's Meadow in Central Park. A visit to one or other of the small parks around Midtown was not really a good idea, as doing so could result in a mugging attack or worse – even in broad daylight!

It was on one lazy, warm Saturday in the late spring, that found me sunbathing on my newly acquired aluminium sun lounge, on the roof of my flash apartment, that I got to be closely acquainted with a group of fellow residents, also intent on taking in the sun's rays. Of these, some of the more interesting to look at happened to be a number of New York's more expensive and exclusive 'working girls'. This was a work title that I was soon to become more familiar with, as one day early in my residency, having first got over the shock of seeing so many gorgeous bodies displayed before me, I innocently ventured to ask one of the girls what she did for a living? Her direct and candid reply to my query was illuminating!

The crop of working girls in my apartment building was certainly a group of attractive – no, more than that – enticingly sexy professional escorts. Most occupied apartments on mine and other upper floors of my building. A warm sunny day would always guarantee to attract a bevy of these delectable beauties out to grace Tar Beach, usually clad in the skimpiest bathing attire imaginable – attire that usually left little to the imagination. Disporting their lithe bodies was tantalising enough to distract any male in the vicinity who, like me, would usually contrive to appear to be pretending to read a book or the day's financial news.

It was too much to expect of a mere male in such a sexually stimulating situation to refrain from at least trying to gain an eyeful of the talent that lay temptingly before him. Few males rarely resisted a regular surreptitious glance, to gain a lascivious eyeful of the range of sexy gals laid bare or close to it, almost within touching distance.

During the summer months, even into the autumn, many of the girls, relaxing during the day before going about their business as escorts, and whatever else they got up to, could always be seen sunning themselves – just a level or so above my apartment. This was an attraction during the more summery days in New York that this lonely Aussie bachelor found difficult, often impossible to ignore. Even if it meant carrying an awkwardly folding lounge chair up the narrow staircase and onto my building's roof.

Sun bathing on the roof of my apartment block also served over time to provide a number of dates with one or two of the less professional, but still good to look at business lasses, also residing in my building.

THE NEW YORK DELI

Just across from my office on 40th Street I very soon found what was reputed to be one of the best delicatessens (deli) on New York's East Side. While there were also many other delicatessens across New York and in other cities across the US, there are none to compare with the New York version of the deli, particularly those located in the Brooklyn district, places which I would sometimes visit, as a sometime alternative to my local deli on Manhattan.

The 40th Street deli was a place where one could, and I often did, order a meal either in person or by phone. It could come in the form of pastrami on rye or one or any of a whole range of other mouth-watering combinations that the mind could conjure up. One of the biggest sandwiches that you could ever imagine was the locally well-known and oft-touted 'House Special' creation of this particular deli.

New York's delicatessens were renowned for the selection of bagels, cakes of all kinds and sandwiches of every description that the proprietors and staff could, and would make up to whatever combination their customers desired. The particular specialty at my local deli on 40th Street was the vast array of every kind of pickle you can imagine and many other homemade dressings that were also available to their lunchtime clientele. Each order would be hand delivered to one's office location, plus any form of beverage desired, be it beer, coffee, tea or whatever else took your fancy in soft drinks – all delivered in a big brown-paper bag – complete with a wad of white paper napkins.

Any newcomer to New York would soon find that just one regular size pastrami on rye sandwich, chicken soup or bagel combination of delectable deli inserts and a coffee (the Americans, unfortunately, made terrible coffee), would be sufficient to slake the hunger of any normal person. A deli-style lunch would usually last until well into the late evening, the time when most New Yorkers would then start thinking about stepping out for dinner.

Another delectable local specialty in New York was a wedge of genuine New York cheesecake.

Now you might feel tempted to comment here that cheesecakes are available at any pastry shop across most of the Western world – even beyond, but no! – There is nothing to compare with a large wedge of a genuine, and I stress the word genuine, particularly when discussing a New York-style cheesecake. Even more so, one baked in or around the traditional pastry shops of Brooklyn. There is nothing lighter and so melt-in-the-mouth perfect as a slice of cheesecake baked in New York. Believe me; I've tried them all!

When it comes to dining in New York, a visitor can still find whatever kind of food they desire, on any day of the week, and at a wide variety of restaurants, both small or large – expensive or tiny 'hole-in-the-wall' style family-run eating houses that offer food both delicious and inexpensive. My local favourite was a family-run Italian café a couple of minutes' walk from my apartment that seated but four tables. Here Mamma did all the cooking while Pappa chatted and looked after the wine, beer and regular clientele. No need to book here, just make sure a table was free then sit yourself down and accept what was on Mamma's menu for that day.

There was also a whole selection of cafés and small, family- run restaurants in the vicinity to choose from, should you decide to go for a sit-down lunch with a visiting US client or one or other of what became regular visitors from the textile, apparel manufacturing and retail trade in Australia.

Locally, at the intersection of 2nd Avenue and 32nd Street, a couple of hundred yards away from my apartment, I eventually found a comfortable bar with its unusual but cute name of Mumbles. This became a place where, at any time of the day or night, one could – and I often did – wander in for a beer or a coffee (I used to wish the Americans could make a cappuccino or caffè latte even close to the quality to be found at the Universita Cafe in Lygon Street, Carlton). Should you be looking for something a little more international – the chef there (a Chinaman with not much English) made the most delicious French Onion Soup that you could wish for, outside a top-class restaurant in Paris.

Following a busy day working in my office until late in the evening, and with just a call to my apartment to change into something a little more casual and take a shower, I would often wander down 32nd Street and into Mumbles for a relaxing meal and a beer – the perfect ending to what often had become a long working day.

Sometimes after a little after-office work in my apartment, I would 'hang out' at Mumbles or some other local bar, for a late-night snack, before eventually returning home and bed, close to or even well past midnight.

Sort of like living 'New York-style'...

DAVID COPPERFIELD

Not far down Lexington Avenue from my official office was a small pub run by two ex-Royal Navy sailors. The pub was well known to many working along the avenue, particularly those regularly in need of a beer or two, a coffee or a bite to eat. The pub's name: David Copperfield.

The two guys that owned and ran the pub had also managed to build a lucrative business importing and selling English sausages and Yorkshire made pork pies, which they regularly had flown in by air and both sold and served to their many and varied clientele. In the main David Copperfield's clients were expat Aussies, Kiwis and Brits, most who were either working for the United Nations or other nationally representative organisations.

The pub soon became my second office location in New York, as me and my sales assistant, Roy Lockwood, would stop off there during or following a working day. For the rest of the evening work was exchanged for a jug of ale, a pork pie complete with HP sauce, and a long debrief on the day's wool selling activities.

The pub's owners sometime earlier, had begun to sponsor a live concert every Saturday night. The concert took the form of a series of impromptu performances by a regular group of volunteer participants, along with an occasional 'blow-in' comedian. A regular and usually well-attended feature of the concert would regularly take place with the whole pub taking part in any singing and dancing until well past midnight. The most popular feature of David Copperfield-style entertainment would be a performance to end the evening's entertainment, with a professional rendition of Mel Brooks' hilarious comedy opera aria "Springtime for Hitler". By that time in the late evening the whole pub and its two owners, by that time everyone having become 'well-oiled' and eaten to excess, would join in the chorus with gusto.

Many a happy evening was spent relaxing at David Copperfield. I also later began to use the pub as a more private place in which to meet with clients. David Copperfield's back room proved valuable in this respect as a convenient meeting place, in addition to providing a welcome respite from having to run the gauntlet of snooping, interference and undermining from the IWS's New York manager.

A LOCAL STREET PARTY

An interesting and often entertaining feature of life in and around New York City was the regular sequence of events that were known locally as a street party. Manhattan was unique in this respect, with the weekend closure of a residential street somewhere on the island, with the prior agreement of the city's police and permission granted from the city's administration to close off the street to road traffic.

Residents along the street, plus other irregular traders, would organise entertainment and set up market stalls from which the street's residents and others were able to buy and sell prints, drawings, used clothing, flowers and pot plants. Some of the more adventurous would organise tables that offered different kinds of food. Still others, depending on the makeup of that street's residents, would specialise in the sale or barter of car parts, cameras or other kinds of bric-a-brac.

After settling into my new home, I just happened to spend one Sunday afternoon during which I wandered into a local street party a couple of blocks downtown. During my casual flit-around during which sampling the various styles of food and chatting with the locals running the various stalls and food tables, I eventually espied an interesting looking plant, also being offered for sale.

"Just what I need to brighten up my place" thought I, following which I sought to negotiate a price with the plant's seller, a gorgeous local lass, who in agreement with my caveat that I would purchase the plant if she agreed to my offer of dinner one evening, clinched the deal.

Bearing that tall and beautifully trimmed plant and its weighty glazed pot up to my apartment, I proudly set it up in the window next to my balcony, where it graced the room for many months. I did get to enjoy more than the one evening following that purchase with the local lass who had sold the plant to me, only to find out later that what I had bought was a near fully grown marijuana (pot) plant that was about to flower.

Of all the people who could have put me in the picture as to the true identity of my new plant, the person who later provided the information was non-other than a New York cop friend. We had met during an earlier investigation into a near assault of one of the secretaries from an adjoining office in my office building.

Joe, I later learned, was attached to the New York drug squad. On entering my apartment for the first time, he took one look at my prize plant and with a laugh asked: "Where did you get that magnificent pot plant?" He grudgingly accepted my dazed look and ignorance when it came to such stuff and again asked me where I had bought it?

To cut a long story short, I didn't get arrested, but it appears that the lass I had bought my prized plant from was one of a group living together in a nearby walk-up apartment. She and a few of her friends had been running a sideline growing, processing and selling 'pot' to some of the locals. They had been growing the stuff in a lean-to glasshouse on the roof of their building, and were apparently known to the local cops. They had been raided the week before I had wandered along to that particular street party and bought my plant.

JOE'S PET PYTHON

My new friend Joe, the New York drug cop, also proved to be an unusual character himself, in that he had a weird kind of preference when it came to his choice of pets.

Lobbing up to Joe's Upper West Side apartment for the first time on a Saturday evening, before going off to a jazz club downtown, I was sitting peacefully sipping on a beer on one of his lounge chairs, happily chatting away with the occasional sip of the amber fluid. Not many minutes following having settled myself into my chair and sipping on my beer, I sensed a slight movement in the corner of my eye. Turning to the source of the movement you can imagine my horror to find myself staring directly into the beady and compelling eyes of a long, plump, hungry looking snake. Too late I realised that the snake was sliding across the apartment floor toward me, seemingly intent on having me for dinner!

My instantly emitted horrified yelp, accompanied by what I am told was a leap that took me vertically from my then sitting position to what felt like four feet in the air, my can of Budweiser sent flying across the room.

As I returned to Earth and was about to make a desperate dash for the door, with my new friend nearly peeing himself with laughter, he coolly requested me: "Please, Gerry, don't move so quickly, it upsets Harry!" (The snake's name I learned later). It turns out that Harry at the time was a young royal python. Harry had been a pet since being a short, little pythonette (not sure if that's the term for a young python, but I'm sure you will get my meaning), and was tame, serving both as a pet as well as Joe's personal apartment 'guard snake'.

Harry, I learned was apparently happy to spend most of the time sleeping, curled up in his cushion lined orange box in Joe's bathroom. Joe used to feed his pet with chicken and other meat leftovers from a nearby deli, plus an occasional delicacy in the form of any rat or mouse he was able to trap in and around his and a few of his neighbours' old-style walk-up apartments.

Prior to any later visits I made to Joe's place, and to avoid disturbing Harry in his bathroom place of rest, I was always careful to make sure that I had been to the loo beforehand – just in case Harry the python decided to adjourn to his box for a nap.

I lost touch with Joe so never got to hear much more about his strange pet. At times, I found myself wondering what, if anything, had later happened to that very odd couple? I had visions of the snake, now perhaps fully grown, one day deciding to coil a few tight rings around his owner while he was asleep?

NEW YORK CITY CAN BE DANGEROUS!

New York for the unwary, like many other major cities during the 1970s, could prove to be a dangerous place to work in at times. The case of the secretary that was assaulted as she walked from her office to the office toilet, referred to earlier, serves to highlight the seedier and sometimes dangerous side of life in New York's residential and office precincts, during the time I was a resident.

The secretary in question had left her office to visit the company restroom. She had just opened the restroom door, conveniently located down the hall. As she opened the door, a man obviously waiting for the opportunity to have his vile way with her, approached and, grabbing her from behind tried to push her into the restroom. She was lucky in that she was able to fend him off, running from the doorway and screaming for help. Help did appear luckily for her, in the form of one of her male colleagues, who managed to grab her attacker who unfortunately for him pulled a knife, slashed at him and escaped down the staircase and out into the milling crowds along Lexington Avenue. All this incidentally occurred during business hours.

Following that incident, my secretary would always be accompanied to the doorway, whenever she needed to use the office restroom – it too located down the corridor from our offices.

Other cases of muggings, rapes and stabbings, which had occurred both in the vicinity of corporate offices as well as on the streets – in broad daylight as well as after dark, were well-known daily happenings during the New York of the 1970s.

Even walking down the street or across town you couldn't be too careful, particularly at night if out and about on your own. It was always wise to stick to walking down the main streets or avenues, if possible depending on traffic, choosing to walk down the centre of the street or avenue. I even had situations where members of the Australian apparel and textile industry and their wives, while visiting New York, would be reluctant to venture out from their hotel or our office building and onto the street, for fear of being assaulted. That was until they had been assured that provided they kept to the main streets and avenues, they should be in no danger, at least during daytime.

At night, it could be a different matter, with visitors advised to take a cab to and from a restaurant or Broadway show that they had decided to take in. If deciding to walk to and from their hotel, visitors were always instructed to keep to the main thoroughfares and crowded areas of the city.

As for myself, apart from a near mugging during my first couple of days in the city, I never found much to trouble me, as long as I kept aware of what was around me in the area around wherever I needed to walk.

"DEEP THROAT" – THE MOVIE AND ME

Perhaps you recall the movie? No? Well, it starred a raunchy lass known as Linda Lovelace, the principal actor in an equally raunchy, explicitly sexy show, in which she starred in what some would describe as a 'mouth-watering' role.

I got to see that movie, whether I wanted to or not, on too many occasions to count during my time working in New York. Not being interested in the slightest to see it, I nevertheless found myself a fairly regular attendee at the sleazy down-market movie theatre that was featuring it on nearby 42nd Street. I was at first taken aback, when among some of the company executives and other male business visitors from the Australian and US, Canadian and Mexican textile industry that visited my offices while I was resident in New York, some expressed an insatiable desire (or lascivious need?) to view that movie in particular. This found me regularly being 'required' to accompany one or other of my male visitors to yet another boring viewing.

I often used to wonder what was going on in the head of the regular ticket lady at the movie theatre, on seeing me once again turning up to see that particular movie. I was always accompanied by a local American or strangely accented Aussie male in tow, my companion looking sheepish, as he slunk into the theatre after me, his reluctant host. I'm not certain but quite sure that her thoughts on seeing me once again, went along the line: "What back again – that Aussie sure must be a sexually deprived son-of-a-bitch!"

I like to think that it wasn't true, of course, and after my first viewing of the movie it got to be boring – obviously not so for most of my bug-eyed guests! I used to wonder just what outlandish sexual demands my clients would be making on their wives or girlfriends, when they eventually returned to their obviously dull, sexually deprived lives, either back in their New York hotel, their North American cities or back home in Australia?

STRATEGIES AND TACTICS

Apart from numerous interesting interludes in and around New York outside working hours, every working week overflowed with the business of increasing the use of fine Australian wools by the North American textile trade.

To provide a better service to local spinners, it was soon decided to extend AWC services by offering to supply them with wool tops. It had been agreed, following discussion with Melbourne, that in addition to the sale of raw wool, we would convert some AWC raw wool stocks held in store at Charleston, holding a quantity for sale in the form of scoured and combed tops.

It was decided to carry the programme out in partnership with the Wellman Combing Company, one of the US's independent top-makers, holding stocks of processed tops at the Wellman plant in Johnsonville, South Carolina.

Once able to build a stock of selected wool tops, meetings were held with spinners and weavers, advising the regular availability of raw wool and now tops at a stable price, prices being set at a level designed to encourage them to purchase Australian wools.

Initially, I received heavy criticism from one or two of the other local top-makers who wished to be included in AWC's top-making programme. The main criticism here being that AWC was trying to pick favourites with whom to commission our top-making activities, to the exclusion of other top-makers who were understandably keen to join in. Another complaint was that AWC was now placing itself in direct competition with other wool processors in the US – these being mills also committed to purchasing wool, but happened to be doing so via the auction system in Australia.

One complaint, in particular, came from the US branch of one of Europe's major wool-buying and -processing companies, Prouvost Lefebvre, whose US manager, Philipe Berthet, registered his principals' strong objections to what AWC was proposing to do in the US. Berthet's complaint was to be expected and understandable, going by the strong opposition that AWC and the Australian government were already known to be receiving from wool processors throughout Europe, the United Kingdom and Japan, following AWC's recently announced US programme, and its already announced desire to gain acquisition of the Australian wool clip.

AWC's aspirations toward control over the marketing of Australia's wool clip didn't help, as most of the then-current users of Australian wools were being led to believe that what we were doing in the US was to be the forerunner of what was yet to come internationally.

Prouvost Lefebvre later agreed to become one of our customers for raw wool sourced from US stocks. Eventually, along with Burlington Industries and JP Stevens they became one of our main US clients for raw, greasy wool. They and others had been encouraged to work with AWC, as the raw wool prices we were quoting in the US were lower than those currently available on the regular auction market in Australia.

Setting prices for US stocks significantly lower than those applying at the time at auction in Australia, made wools being offered in the US much more attractive to local buyers in a number of ways. Not the least of these was the easy and on-time access to deliveries into their stores closer to the time they required feedstock to meet their production of yarn and fabrics.

We had already negotiated a competitive price for the processing of AWC tops with the Wellman Company, who had also agreed, as part of the deal, to hold stocks of processed tops on their premises at no extra cost.

The argument here, at least from AWC's perspective, was that we were acting in defence of what had been a neglected and rapidly declining market for Australian wool in North America, in spite of IWS's efforts there over the years.

The main problem here though went much deeper, in that

Australia's other major wool customers, outside North America, were continuing to express their deep concerns at the prospect of AWC gaining full acquisition powers over of the Australian wool clip in the not-too-distant future. Some also suspected that if the US operation proved successful, the programme would later be extended to other markets, a situation that some saw as potentially undermining their wool-buying operations in Australia. This was a weak argument. The US market was relatively easy to isolate from other world markets and AWC management had stated that it was intending to keep its operations in North America contained there.

How AWC proposed going about the sale of wool to customers worldwide, once and if the acquisition proposal occurred, at prices and against selling policies that were still to be developed and announced, was as yet vague. Thus, the international trade continued to watch the US operation with understandable concern and continued scepticism.

As things stood, in New York I continued to receive phone calls from some of Europe's wool processors, requesting that we also supply wool to them from Charleston at the same prices we were selling in the US. This expected turn of events, understandably got to a point where the only possible course to take was to pass any such enquiries and any complaints on to Melbourne and let them deal with the growing political implications.

So continued AWC's attempt to insert itself into the US marketplace. In that market we were, in fact, operating as if AWC was the owner of wool being shipped to and sold from its US-based wool stocks. The reality here of course was that AWC didn't actually 'own' the wool – at least in the true sense of the word.

Operating the way we were in the US had resulted in the setting up of two competing selling systems – direct sales at lower, fixed prices to customers in North America, against the auction system back in Australia, where prices moved according to regular fluctuations in supply and demand across the rest of the wool consuming world.

While wool prices in the US were attractive, the basis upon which they had been developed was unrealistic. It was obvious to all that price levels being set were unrepresentative of the true costs involved.

As things stood it was virtually impossible to apply an accurate costing method to the US operation, one at least that related to the true cost of wools being marketed to our US clientele. The other question arising here was: "What was to happen if (and when) AWC found itself unable to stock the specific wool types preferred by US buyers?"

It became well-nigh impossible to gain a clear understanding as to the actual costs of AWC's US activities, even as it had been stated that the US operation was an isolated programme in defence of strong competition from synthetic fibre producers. AWC's activities in the US, in particular the arbitrarily setting of prices, bore little resemblance to the actual costs being incurred on the project. The process had, in addition, created an understandable degree of confusion and unrelenting opposition, a situation that continued to grow and gain momentum.

Criticism continued to mount, even among a few of the deeper thinking Australian woolgrowers with whom I eventually was able to discuss AWC's US operations during my annual returns to Australia. Opposition continued to grow outside the woolgrowing fraternity and among some of the industry's regular customers in Europe, the UK and Japan.

Most international wool traders and others, in some way or another having an interest and concern regarding the future health and direction of wool marketing, were also expressing growing concern at the direction in which AWC intended to take the industry. Their concern was based on their view of the future consequences to themselves, their long-term financial investments in the industry, and their commitments to Australian wools already being bought, held or committed to by them. Their business interests and objectives were very different to those of the Australian woolgrowing industry and its representative, the statutory AWC, which they saw as proceeding blindly down a dangerous and unpredictable path. The recent introduction of AWC's RP Scheme wasn't helping either.

During a visit to the UK and Europe during 1976, I received a number of objections along the line, "What you are doing in the US is serving to disrupt the whole of the world market." It was, of course, explained that the intention was to confine AWC activities within North America. Ultimately it was begrudgingly accepted by some that there was little real opposition, at this stage at least, provided AWC limited its wool marketing activities to within North America. Others continued to be sceptical, still believing that AWC would seek eventually to expand the US programme.

In Bradford, I was requested to meet with local wool brokers and processors who, although they recognised that I was not one of the senior managers or board members of AWC, demanded that I convey back to Australia their strong views and opposition to the thinking and intended direction in which AWC was apparently planning to go. In particular, a great deal of concern was continually being expressed regarding AWC's Reserve Price activities.

In the circumstances, there was no other option other than to continue to carry on with my part of the programme, servicing the wool trade in the US as professionally and as transparently as circumstances allowed.

Unfortunately, also, working in the shadows, supported it was later learned by his colleagues at IWS London, the IWS manager in New York was beavering away and, for reasons unknown to me at the time, seeking to white-ant (undermine) AWC's US operations wherever he could. I learned of this relatively early during our activities in New York from some of my US clients, who found it strange to be hearing what they termed as 'strong criticism' of AWC and our activities in the US, from the IWS's New York management – people working for an organisation funded mainly by Australia and its woolgrowers!

With the stream of criticism from the international wool using fraternity, and IWS 'white-anting' going on against the AWC's US operation, the latter emanating from our alleged 'associates' in IWS's New York office, it rapidly became apparent that IWS was also seeing AWC's US-based activities as a direct threat.

In their case, the establishment of an AWC office in New York began to emerge at the heart of a claim that AWC's US project was infringing on what IWS, at least its US manager, regarded as his exclusive territory? I could only assume here that Colangelo, IWS's New York manager, regarded AWC, his organisation's main source of funding, to be some kind of opposition?

The inference here, as explained by more than one friendly senior executive in the US textile trade, was that IWS New York regarded AWC's New York operation, managed as it was by an Australian manager who had been professionally involved with textile and apparel manufacturing and retailing in Australia, was transgressing the previously agreed relationship between IWS and AWC. This was in reference to the original relationship set down for the AWB and IWS, under totally different market circumstances, during 1937 – close on 40 years in the past!

This was a strange, unfounded and unrealistic claim being made by IWS's New York manager. At no time since the establishment of an AWC office in New York had he or his staff, despite regular requests for assistance or information, offered or attempted to provide support to AWC's US wool project – a project with the sole aim of increasing the consumption of Australian wool across the US!

AWC management, via Malcolm Vawser, had been very clear that this was the aim of the US project. I was also given to understand, prior to my departure from Melbourne, that this policy had been cleared and agreed to by IWS's senior management in London.

Despite the various political manoeuvrings going on around the US operation, it had come to a point where, as I had little or no power to change whatever events may eventuate there was a job to be done. The best route to take in the circumstances was to stay as far away as possible from any politicking and continue, within the specific guidelines provided, to work toward the success of the project. Wherever possible, every attempt would continue to be made to work in co-operation with IWS's New York's staff.

There was one other important point to be made here, and that related to the fact that despite the activities of IWS's North American office, the consumption of wool throughout the US had been and was continuing to fall-away rapidly. One would have thought that the added presence of AWC in the US should have been welcomed and embraced? It was unfortunate that instead of co-operation, what had been received thus far was criticism and attempts to undermine AWC's activities.

SUPERFINE WOOL KNITWEAR

We did achieve success with at least two projects. Each offered lessons and pointers toward other, potential future opportunities. A number of hard lessons were also being learned, particularly when it came to researching and implementing different ways and means of increasing the consumption of Australian wool, not only within the US but internationally. One of these had of necessity been placed on hold during my period as menswear product manager back in Australia.

The earlier proposed trial project had been with the aim of testing the possibility of combing, then cutting the staple length of tops produced from some of AWC's then heavily overstocked superfine wools, then spinning and knitting the result into various styles of high fashion knitwear. The original idea behind this project had been to cut some of these wools, then spin them on the cotton, instead of the usual longer staple 'worsted' system.

Now having both the authority and opportunity to instigate product development projects, it was arranged to take a quantity of superfine quality wool tops currently stored in Johnsonville, and cut them – arranging for the now short-staple wools to be spun on the cotton system.

Some of the trial tops were blended with silk, others with animal hair – the result knitted into a small number of stylishly designed fashion tops.

When a small number of sample knitted tops were produced, costed and shown to a select group of known buyers at Bloomingdales (one of New York's leading fashion retailers) and a couple of fashion boutiques on and around 5th Avenue, the trial knitwear was greeted with interest. The finished samples handled particularly well, in one or two cases producing an even more luxurious handling end product, at least equal to cashmere.

The first batch of sample garments and fabric samples proved acceptable to the retail buyers approached, the expected wholesale price (costed on a conservative basis) also seen to have merchandising potential. The knitwear had been temporarily labelled 'Australian Superfine', the intention being, should the project prove to be a commercial possibility, to research and register an appropriate brand name under which to market the knitwear in the US.

Two things happened as a result of this preliminary trial. Felix Colangelo of the IWS's New York office virtually blew his 'top' (excuse the unintended 'top' pun), with both he and presumably his colleagues in London howling that AWC had encroached on their territory.

Their objection was puerile. The project was a technical trial, in which the IWS's New York office had shown absolutely no interest when I tried to discuss it while requesting assistance from Colangelo and his menswear product manager before proceeding. In any event, it would have been up to IWS to decide whether or not to promote the end product – if and when it eventually proved commercially viable.

Back in Melbourne, there were the expected mutterings once again regarding the 'sacrilege' of cutting long stapled wools. Nobody seemed to be interested in the fact that AWC possessed a few thousand bales of the long staple stuff, wools that the trade wasn't interested in buying.

Stocks of these wools were continuing to be bought-in by AWC, alongside the rest of its continually growing stock of other wool types, all eating-their-heads-off in storage costs and interest charges. Along with the 'cut-superfine' trial, it was also planned to look into the possibility of manufacturing and marketing a range of full staple superfine and other fine wool blended knitted products as a designer item.

Bloomingdales and one or two New York fashion boutiques had expressed interest to proceed further with the project, also expressing interest in participating in styling and colour development. The project, later costed, showed that it could have returned a profit to AWC (calculated on the basis of an 'at best' estimate of cost inputs at the time) from the superfine wools involved, should the project be eventually given the go-ahead.

Should the project eventually prove successful, potential orders from some of the US's leading men's and women's fashion retailers for the proposed superfine product were being talked of in terms of on the basis of a hundred dozen per style. Unlike retailers in Melbourne or Sydney, where individual retail outlets were more likely to order 50 or so units per style over a limited size range, US retail orders could, at some time in the future, increase to at least ten times that number.

It should be remembered here that the much larger US population and its apparel markets, just considering New York, Washington, San Francisco and Los Angeles alone, was and remains today, many times the size of Australia's retail market for apparel products!

The project, unfortunately, suffered its inevitable demise, due mainly to the undermining politics involved and the childish and overly jealous guarding of supposed rights by the IWS, and its US manager.

Ultimately, reaction to the project and issues of a similar nature that had occurred since the opening of AWC's New York office, led me to the inevitable conclusion that there were just too many differences between what the IWS was doing – and the long-term interests Australia's woolgrowers. In the US, IWS and its staff showed little, if any interest, other perhaps than maintaining their well-paid positions, while protecting what the IWS office manager apparently saw as AWC attempts to usurp his authority. At no time was even the slightest interest shown in any efforts toward closer co-operation – the object of AWC operating in the US being solely to restore, wherever possible, Australian wool's declining fortunes.

Colangelo had demonstrated almost from the first day of AWC's entry into the US, that he was motivated more to defending what he saw as his personal fiefdom, than any genuine interest in the longer-term future of wool.

Interest in Australian wool was non-existent during any of the New York office's so-called 'merchandising' meetings that I attended, usually at my request. My remit on the other hand, as had been stated in Melbourne, was to expand the consumption of Australian wool by local US mills, apparel manufacturers and, where appropriate, retailers.

SUPERFINE UNIFORMS AND OTHER STUFF

Finding the prospect of being able to work in concert with supposed colleagues in IWS's US office a distant dream, it became necessary to change tack with a view to seeking out other potential options in support of Australian wool sales, in addition to those of raw wool and wool tops.

During a private meeting with Burlington Industries' managers in New York, one such project was discussed, which could, if successful, result in the sale of a quantity of superfine Australian wools, at the time overstocked in Australia.

The US was known to be a large donor of foreign aid to the kingdom of Saudi Arabia. During an earlier visit to Washington, the then thorny subject of the level of import duty being charged on Australian wool was being discussed. During negotiations between Australian government, AWC officials and the US department of trade, it was learned through one or two unofficial 'friends' – contacts operating on and along the Washington Beltway (diplomatic) grapevine – that the Saudis had indicated interest in the US supplying uniforms, in addition to other goods and military equipment, as part of their next issue of US aid to the Saudi kingdom. What was interesting to me, was the mention that uniforms could form part of the US's future aid programme.

On returning to New York and following discussion with executives of Burlington Industries, it was agreed that the use of a worsted fabric, spun and woven using 100% Australian superfine wools, could prove a practical proposition, the resultant yarn and finished fabric being designed to meet the specific needs of a desert climate.

A fully integrated weaver of textiles (raw wool to finished fabric), Burlington Industries bought and processed wool on its own account, both locally produced and imported. Burlington usually had their ear to the ground when it came to government contracts. Thus, they regularly managed to find themselves on the 'inside lane' when in the running for a project like the projected supply of uniforms and other textile related goods to the Saudi kingdom.

The Saudi-Arabian climate, although it can be very hot during the day, on many nights during the year the temperature is known to drop to near or even below zero on a regular basis. By developing a tightly spun 100% superfine wool yarn, it was considered feasible to produce a superior performing fabric capable of providing the Saudi army with uniforms that would look and perform well across the full range of temperatures expected to be encountered year-round in the desert or in near desert conditions. That decided, Burlington arranged for sample fabrics to be made up and submitted as part of their bid for the project. It was agreed, following private discussions on the project, that Burlington would include the exclusive use of Australian superfine quality wools, sourced from AWC stocks in Charleston.

Once awarded, with Burlington Industries appointed as supplier of the fabrics and co-ordinator of the programme, stocks of appropriate superfine wools were shipped to Charleston, South Carolina in quantities sufficient to cover the project.

The Saudi uniform project proved a success. It contributed toward the use of more of Australia's stocks of superfine wools – at a time when AWC was buying in and holding more stocks of raw wools than it and the Australian government would have wished. A further point to be made here is that through paying close attention to the search for alternative ways through which to open up a new, to date untapped area of potential additional future wool sales, we had been able to achieve sales of wool that hitherto would have been unknown to us.

A potentially valuable spin-off from this programme, had there been closer co-operation from IWS New York, could have emerged in the form of some form of promotional project featuring the fact that wool had a role to play, even in a harsh climate like that of Saudi Arabia. Unfortunately, even here IWS showed absolutely no interest when the idea was submitted later.

It is also interesting but disquieting to note here that until the Saudi superfine project became known to IWS New York, neither Colangelo, or any of his product merchandising staff had thought to cultivate links among the leading operators in the US textile industry and relevant US authorities, through which it had been possible to instigate the Australian superfine/Saudi uniform project. I was instead criticised by IWS's US manager for having the temerity to involve myself with officers of the US's various trade departments and other potentially useful agencies in and around Washington!

This project and the strategy of keeping as many potential 'irons in the fire' as possible, had proved an important element when it came to the opening of potential channels to the massive US government and apparel marketplace. The effort involved proved conclusively that by maintaining a finger-on-the-pulse by the employment of intelligence and the cultivation of a wide variety US government and other key contacts, the possibility existed through which to define and develop similar projects, even in Australia? If coupled with an active policy of continuous product innovation, similar projects of all kinds, in support of Australian wool, could offer future success, not only in North America but elsewhere across the world.

As further proof of this project, I retained the first two loom bobbins of the superfine wool yarns spun and used for the Saudi army uniform project. They still provide a talking point for any curious visitor to my home. They are also a reminder of at least one project, that in spite of IWS New York's stalling tactics had proved positive and a pointer toward other marketing possibilities in the future.

This relatively confined project, even though it served to diminish the wool stocks being held by AWC by a comparatively small amount, proved that by taking a more expansive and entrepreneurial approach to product development and merchandising, was the direction AWC needed to take, if it was to have any chance of retaining Australian wool's share of the textile fibre market.

Thinking 'outside the square' both in Australia but more particularly among other of wool's leading overseas textile and apparel markets would certainly have resulted in more positive results being achieved on behalf of Australian woolgrowers during the 1970s and later. The primary requirement here though was the political will to make the changes needed – unfortunately that was a quality sadly absent at the time.

Note: It is important to state here that such an approach did not as its first or later option, require AWC to acquire and be in complete control of the entire Australian wool clip.

It would have been possible, had AWC chosen to review, remodel and re-calibrate its activities toward meeting the growing challenges facing Australian wool worldwide, to open up a whole new range of marketing opportunities to exploit on behalf of Australian wool.

Experience in the US had also provided clear proof that Australia's relationship with IWS needed to be reconsidered, in line with

Australian wool's ongoing needs and expected future challenges. By the arrival of the 1970s, the market for textile fibres had changed completely from that wool had faced during the period 1937–1950.

While the Woolmark was undoubtedly universally recognised, what was becoming even more important at that time was the then need to develop and promote a broad range of products, some, where considered to be necessary, carrying additional, unique branding. Perhaps also, the direction in which the production of Australian wool needed to move into the future, was to research if it was possible to move future production toward the finer end of the micron spectrum? Only time would prove the practicality of such a move. Technical factors like locality, breeding, climate and time would become involved – even if such a move proved both possible and practical.

The US project had pointed to the fact that to be successful with any future projects, whether technical or marketing, would require that local and international product development and product merchandising functions become directly linked.

Unfortunately, by that time, it had become clear that while both AWC and IWS were supposed to be working along parallel lines, from a purely Australian standpoint both managements' structure, staffing and policy development had become too inflexible. In their then-current form, neither were capable of developing and carrying out the strategies and tactical disciplines necessary.

Front-line operational managers of IWS in particular, following nearly 40 years of operations, had become locked into a hierarchy that lacked the vision, expertise and flexibility required to meet the challenges that were then being thrown up to wool.

Australian wool's need at the time was for an organisation more related to the active promotion internationally of its wool and end products containing Australian wool. The time then was right for an upgraded form of the then AWC/IWS entities to be merged and controlled from Australia. Preferably, the structure of such an organisation needed be set up in a manner different to the then statutory format. Politics, together with the diverse interests, personalities and egos at play at the time being what they were – a radical change along the lines suggested, was never going to be possible.

PURE WOOL BLANKETS

Anyone who has slept under the soft comfort and warmth provided by a 100% Merino wool blanket, will attest to its qualities. Particularly when trying to generate some overnight warmth in the midst of a cold and snowy winter's night, anywhere such conditions exist.

On moving to New York, as my first autumn turned too quickly into a cold, wet winter, I went in search across New York for a wool blanket for my bed. Not wishing to live in the overheated atmosphere that one always seems to find when entering any building in a city like New York, I switched off any devices that I found pumping heated air into my bedroom. Even in New York during the cold winters there while I was resident, my bedroom window always stayed open, the usually cloying heating turned off – hence the need, on the arrival of winter, for a bulky pure wool blanket or two.

Unfortunately, my inquiry with the product manager responsible for non-apparel products at IWS New York, followed by a subsequent search across New York could only turn up acrylic or brushed and lofted cotton blankets, neither of which suited my needs. And besides, how could I, the North American representative of the Australian wool industry, in all conscience even think to purchase blankets made from synthetic fibres or brushed cotton?

At the time, I found it strange that IWS New York hadn't even looked to locate and promote wool blankets, well before commencement of a usually cold North American winter.

On my return to Australia the following January, I sallied forth among the local mills were known to manufacture some of the most desirable wool blankets to be had anywhere in the world. Among them were Laconia, Onkaparinga and North Western Woollen Mills, plus one or two lesser-known brands. All were suppliers of pure wool blankets to the local retail market. While in Australia, I had Laconia make me up a half-dozen blankets, with the object of using them to research whether it would be possible to whet the appetites of one or two upmarket US bedding retailers?

The blanket samples I took back with me to New York were in a variety of bright colours and cubic patterns, among them, a beautiful

Berber-look blanket, a design that contained various subdued colours similar to those favoured by the Berber tribes of North Africa. Other samples were finished in a variety of different colours and modern designs. Samples were later shown to a select few of the US's leading home-wares stores, at first only in New York and Boston, with the result that even though they were more expensive to land in the US than the cost of acrylic or brushed cotton blankets, they were considered to be a saleable item. The Macy's store in New York, for example, showed interest, to the extent that they were prepared to indent a quantity – provided that a continuing supply, including a range in lighter weights, similar to the British made Lan-Air-Cel style of blanket, could be guaranteed from the mills in Australia.

The IWS office's product manager with responsibility for the promotion of wool non-apparel products was approached with a request for some promotional support with a selection of New York retailers, should they decide to purchase a quantity of Australian made pure new wool blankets. I was told in no uncertain terms that they were not authorised to spend IWS money on specific Australian wool products. "It would conflict with our other generic wool commitments and other donor countries to the IWS." The US office would not use any of its promotional funds to support the promotion of Australian made wool blankets!

IWS funds? The answer was the same even when pointed out that New Zealand made wool carpets were being promoted as such by IWS New York, with clear reference to the wool being from New Zealand!

With around 60% of IWS operating funds being provided by Australia – was there something not quite right here? Even when again pointed out that there had been no discernible US promotion of pure wool blankets, the attitude remained negative.

I also found that on passing the good news of the interest shown in New York and Boston to the mills back in Melbourne, I could not find one in a position to supply the quantities mentioned by interested US retailers.

Oh, what the hell! Were my feelings at the result of what could and should have become a handy niche export market for what in reality were some beautiful examples of Australian wool products?

I retained one of my own Berber-look blankets on my later return to Melbourne. These days though, I use a lighter-weight silk filled doona on my bed in the summer, and a heavier, wool filled doona during the cooler winter months. No blankets needed these days. Indeed, a sign of the times and changing consumer preferences. At the very least, wool today continues to be present and valued, both for its comfort and warmth as a doona filler by many Australian consumers of bedding products.

OTHER PRODUCT ISSUES

The amount of interest shown by retailers for some innovative styles of blankets in one of the largest consumer markets in the world was encouraging. When added to the proposed short-staple superfine wool sweater project, and other areas offering similar potential in the US marketplace, the interest shown at the time served to confirm that maintaining an ongoing and profitable position for Australian wools was eminently possible.

At the time there already existed sufficient evidence to suggest that with a well-thought-through co-ordinated approach, using people skilled in the art of textile/apparel design, merchandising and innovation, it would have been possible, without the need for AWC to act like it was one of its competitor fibre producers, to maintain a profitable position in an increasingly competitive world market.

The possibility existed to use Australia's international image much earlier, when looking to promote wool-containing products, locally, internationally and for export.

On this very point, four decades later and during a recent visit to New Zealand, I was able to discuss a current project in support of locally designed and manufactured superfine wool sweaters and similar products. These were being marketed under a specific New Zealand brand: Avoca 100% Pure New Zealand made "Merinosilk".

One range of products was composed of a blending of 20% possum fur, 10% silk with 70% sustainable superfine 17-micron Merino wool. I'm not sure what the sustainable part of the New Zealand programme referred to – I would have thought that all wool was a sustainable product, growing as it did on the back of a sheep? It is however, a good example of creative marketing – also a reminder of a knitwear programme that had been denied years before by then restrictive AWB and IWS policies!

New Zealand companies in particular, have for a number of years, continued to lead the field when it comes to the creative development and inclusion of what they constantly promote as "Wools of New Zealand", in carpets and apparel, now promoting Merino wool in products aggressively marketed along with a New Zealand flavour, both locally and internationally.

Another example of innovative product marketing is Auckland-based Icebreaker Ltd. This company offers Merino wool apparel as a part of its extensive range, designed for both winter and summer outdoor wear, under a series of brands. These include a 75% Merino wool/25% polyester 'Merino loft' ½ zip hoodie, a 'Merino Loft' shirt comprising a 100% polyester body and 100% Merino wool lining, also a flannel shirt in 100% Merino wool. Icebreaker also offer summer apparel manufactured from what they call 'Cool-Lite', a blend of Merino wool with Tencel (a 'natural' eucalypt-based wood fibre).

The earlier examples of Cleckheaton, Tullo, and the unsuccessful attempts to redirect AWC operations in the US toward a more innovative product development approach 30-odd years ago, had pointed the way along a track similar to the way NZ wool interests were also seeking to move, in spite of their then IWS connections. During the 1970s, New Zealand wool's marketing activities were mainly behind wool carpets and a variety of mainly coarser knitted wool sweaters.

The point to be made here regarding the preceding activities is that they are but a few of the possibilities that were then available, well before the turn of the 21st century, had Australian wool's leadership at the time kept their eyes on the ball. By the time Australia's wool-growing industry had entered the early 1970s, the need had already arrived for major changes to be made in the way both AWC and IWS were operating.

Unfortunately, it bears repeating once again, that by that time it had become clear that it would not be possible to change what had become etched into the woolly heads that ran the AWC boardroom, IWS in London and grower politics in Melbourne and Canberra.

SECOND TIME AROUND

On a more positive and decidedly happier note, alongside my work in the US, and in spite of continuing issues with 'friends' at the IWS on the increase, I was at least able to look forward to occasions when my two boys were able to visit me during their school holidays. In between times, to follow my love of sailing I had purchased a 26-foot sloop rigged yacht and become an active member of the Narrasketuck Yacht Club, on nearby Long Island's Great South Bay.

My yacht, appropriately named Kookaburra, was the instrument that enabled me to escape on nearly every weekend, during the late spring to fall season, from a usually crowded and always full week of travel and sales related discussions – and the crowded city of New York.

The city during the hot summer months could, and often did get to be an almost unbearably hot and humid canyon of steaming buildings and streets, from which those who were able to do so would seek to escape. At least over the weekends from spring into autumn, the township of Amityville and my yacht Kookaburra was where I would make for to hang out and sail, mainly within Long Island's Great South Bay.

It happened that during the July 4th holiday period of 1976, and racing as crew at the Babylon Yacht Club, that while lazing one morning on the deck of a friend's yacht on-board which I was staying that weekend, I happened to glimpse an attractive girl sitting on a yacht parked across the other side of the dock, alongside which we were also berthed.

The sight of that girl created the strangest feelings and emotions in me, feelings that exploded upon my being and sent my pulse racing.

The experience was strange, my heart beating like a drum as I found that I could not take my eyes away from her. Eventually she saw me staring at her and even smiled back, which prompted a fierce desire to meet her, despite the fact that she was obviously spoken for. You can imagine what that did to my blood pressure, and interest in yacht racing that day?!

My friends were amused, one even daring me to go across the dock to 'chat her up' – "if I was man enough", bearing in mind that she was probably spoken for. Another of my friends even laid down a $50 bet that I couldn't get a date with her… Now that was a challenge, boyfriend or not, on which I was prepared to take my chances.

At the time, I couldn't even believe what was happening to me. My usual attitude toward attractive women, while understandably having a keen interest, was one usually of casual indifference, other perhaps than the welcome opportunity for a night or two on the town and whatever else eventuated. Here on the dockside at Babylon Yacht Club she was something different, and strangely – I knew it. But how was I going to make my approach?

My chance came at last on the day before the end of the weekend regatta, when I just happened to meet up with the girl of my dreams at the club's swimming pool. She was there teaching some of the youngsters how to swim.

I still recall my first line, admittedly a rather lame one that went along the lines of, "Hi, I just wanted to apologise for staring at you." She just smiled the kind of smile that melted me, leaving this usually articulate lad feeling more like a gibbering idiot! Time went by on wings as we chatted, the kids in the pool getting less of her attention, and me hoping that her boyfriend wouldn't show up! He didn't and as we continued to chat, we also watched a beautiful setting sun as it began to drop toward the horizon to the southwest. "It will be just rising at home in Melbourne" I mused, voicing the regular feelings of nostalgia that I often used to get while living in the US, watching the sun go down and to know it would also be rising over my Melbourne home down under.

I should add here that I had an earlier evening experience following a sunset when cruising on a yacht in the Caribbean with some friends. One evening during a cruise near the British Virgin Islands, the Southern Cross just happened to lift itself above the southern horizon, leaving me with tears in my eyes as my thoughts drifted back to my two sons and home back in Australia, under those very same stars.

Similarly, I often used to feel homesick, even at the sighting of the Flying Kangaroo emblem on the tail of a passing Qantas aircraft, at one or other of the airports I happened to be passing through in the US or Europe.

Getting back to me and the girl of my dreams... "So, you are from Australia?" said the beautiful she. "Yes," said I, but then, unfortunately, and before I had even a chance to talk more, she had to leave abruptly... It seems the boyfriend had cottoned on to the fact that a lad from down under was trying to chat up his girlfriend.

I learned later, through a girlfriend of hers, that Kathie was attending the Babylon Regatta along with her then-boyfriend, who was described as being 'not very amused' at a stranger, a foreigner at that, trying to cut into what hitherto he had come to regard as his exclusive love interest.

To cut a long story short, in the dying hours of the final day of the regatta, I managed once again to meet up with Kathie and was overjoyed to secure her phone number, happily learning also that she was living and working in New York City! Wow thought I, at least I have some a chance of making an impression – never mind the thought of winning my friend's $50 bet.

Kathy and I later met up in New York. Following a few months dating, and later sailing together, she said yes to my proposal of marriage. We married in New York on October 14th 1977.

THE COCKROACHES OF NEW YORK

At this point, and not intending to divert far from life and my work in New York and the US just to discuss those omnipresent insect residents of that fair city, I must relate one incident involving the usually elusive and long-lived, omnipresent cockroach.

The cockroach is an interesting species of insect, with a history that goes back to prehistoric times. It was inevitable that the many temporary and long-time human residents of New York City, and other locations throughout the world, would at one time or another find themselves having to live alongside the modern incarnation of that enduring, often disliked, universally detested insect.

Anyone who has lived in New York will surely attest to the presence all over the city, in addition to the biggest rats to be seen anywhere, of hordes of cockroaches. The cockroach being an insect that nature had designed to perfection continues to thrive, is so well designed that individuals and families of them have proved themselves capable of gaining entrance anywhere their desire takes them.

Even living as I was at the time in my luxurious and relatively new apartment on the 31st floor above 3rd Avenue, the local cockroach clan had managed to penetrate even up to my apartment, distant that it was from street level. That pesky little insect became an affliction among the building's residents, who continued to devise ways and means of ridding themselves of their unwanted presence.

On the 31st floor, even, it became regularly necessary at around three-monthly intervals to release a couple of insecticide filled 'bombs' into my apartment. This kind of action was necessary to drive any resident cockroaches temporarily from sight. The task on a regular basis usually served only to drive the current mob of cockroaches now resident in and around my apartment, back to another neighbouring apartment on my floor or elsewhere. Anywhere, as far away as possible from me!

It became a constant battle the whole time I was resident in New York – every couple of months trying to drive the enemy out of my apartment and into someone else's. It didn't seem to matter where they were shooed off to, as long as those pesky marauding insects went somewhere else in the apartment block! It was like a game of tennis, each resident trying to volley their crop of unwanted insects to some other apartment by means of a couple of insect bombs let loose in their apartment – driving them away, anywhere, as far from them as possible.

Kathie had recently decided to move into an old brownstone walk-up apartment, somewhere uptown in the region of 70th Street. Inviting me to inspect her new home, we first met for dinner then wandered, hand in hand to her new address. On opening the door, I was shocked to hear the sound of crackling, crunching and skittering, as we tried to enter the main room, to find on switching on the light that the sounds had been made by the scurrying about of thousands of cockroaches, some having been crushed underfoot as we tried to make our entrance!

My skin was creeping with the thought of Kathie sleeping that night among this lot, but she, stoic New Yorker that she was, had the instant answer to the problem. Said she, "No problem, we'll just go down to the local hardware store or supermarket and buy a few bombs – that'll get rid of them quick smart." That we did but I, the gentleman that I was in those days, insisted on her not venturing into the apartment until every one of the horrible little beasts had been either killed dead, or driven into her next-door neighbour's apartment!

Of course, she had to spend that night as my house guest, having now given up her old apartment … not a bad ploy on my part. We eventually rolled up the next evening to vacuum up what was left of the invasive critters, before allowing Kathie to take up residence.

While the work side of my life continued as if borne along on a speeding switchback, my eventual marriage to Kathie created a much more relaxed person within my skin. I continued to anguish over my continued separation from my two sons. Simon, the eldest, had earlier expressed his opposition when I got both him and Philip together to break the news of my intention to remarry.

My continued absence from both the boys continued to haunt my innermost thoughts the longer I remained isolated from them. I was also missing watching of them growing up, a situation which, on the occasions we were together, had me fearing of eventually growing too far apart from their fast-developing young lives.

MORE POLITICS AND IWS BASTARDRY[1]

Personal stuff aside, my work in the US went on apace. AWC activities across North America were progressing to expectations and had later expanded to include supplying raw wool and tops to spinning mills in Mexico and one in Canada, necessitating the making of regular visits to new clients.

While sales of wool were progressing, relations with 'colleagues' in

IWS's New York office were going in the opposite direction. IWS's New York manager, continued with his undermining tactics. I later learned of him reporting a discussion in which he and I had chatted, in a very general way over a coffee, around the merits, possibilities or otherwise of eventually combining AWC's New York operations with those of the IWS. It seemed logical that eventual closer collaboration on projects of interest to Australian wool would prove of benefit, both to Australia's wool growing industry, and the consumption of wool generally within the US.

Colangelo, falsely reported this informal discussion as if I had agreed that the AWC's US operations should be included under the IWS umbrella and subjected to IWS oversight. This was a ludicrous suggestion, given the lack of co-operation being provided by IWS management and him in particular. The reaction to this on my arrival back in Melbourne for my annual briefing that year was not one supported by the AWC board. It was noted by one or two members of AWC's senior management, that such a merging may eventually become possible at some time into the future, the result of AWC being granted control over the sale and international marketing of the Australian wool clip.

The more time passed, the more it became obvious that my time heading up AWC operations in New York was going to be limited. This despite assurances to the contrary received from Malcolm Vawser, AWC's then joint general manager.

What was getting lost amid all the IWS hand-wringing, together with the pressure and regular disruptive activities being applied by IWS New York, was that while concerning themselves with peripheral organisational issues relating to the perceived interests of IWS in North America, it was the interests of Australia and Australian woolgrowers who, above all were the ones financing the AWC and most of the IWS's operations and staff.

The interests of Australian woolgrowers were being ignored in the process. As a result, Australia continued to lose out on the potential of increased sales of Australian wool and wool products across North America.

As each merchandising season passed by, so the position of

Australian wool was becoming more difficult. It was also becoming clear that over the longer term, a growing number of internationally based wool traders and many operating within the international textile manufacturing industry, were planning to reduce their dependence on wool. They were not prepared to continue to allow their futures, as one British long-time wool textile manufacturer forcefully expressed it, "To be pissed up against a wall by a bunch of rank amateurs and charlatans in Melbourne!"

As the mid-1970s arrived, the Australian woolgrowing industry continued to be led along by the nose, by the inseparable twins – AWC and IWS. The leadership and senior management of both organisations continued to demonstrate an increasingly dangerous incapacity to recognise the need for a change in the direction of their policies and activities. No one it seemed, was capable of opening their eyes to what was actually happening across the world's apparel fibre markets, the growing dominance of synthetic fibre marketing and sales in particular.

Support for the policies originally set for the US operation before my departure from Melbourne in 1974 was constantly being eroded, as AWC management failed to live up to and back up their original assertion that "Complete co-operation would be forthcoming from the IWS office in New York." This ultimately served to severely restrict the project's capacity to achieve and consolidate increased sales of Australian wool across the North American market.

The longer I remained working in the US, it had become clear that any chance of being able to break through the web of intrigue, jealousy and what had clearly become a case of sheer incompetence and lack of commitment, had been a delusion. It had become obvious that there had been no clearly laid down agreement between Melbourne and London regarding how the US arrangements were to work in practice. Such an omission only served to further underline the haste with which Melbourne had come to the decision in the first place.

As time progressed, I had already decided that there was no place or future for me in the kind of organisation AWC had become.

The world was changing rapidly, and for Australian wool it had become a case of having to exist in a worldwide market for textile fibres that was so different to the heyday, high wool prices and strategic thinking based on the 1950s. It was now a world, just 20 years on, in which wool was no longer dominant, regardless of the reams of AWC and IWS projections that continued to spin inaccurate stories of potential gains in market share.

Reality, in the form of the objective discussion and subsequent implementation of decisions guiding the direction of technical development, product development and innovation, wool promotion, merchandising and marketing tactics, was being studiously ignored, as the egos and political ambitions of those leading both organisations continued to dominate. As a consequence, the Australian woolgrowing industry continued to fumble and stumble along its inevitable way toward the market collapse that finally arrived in 1991.

It had also become clear, even at my level of the AWC hierarchy, that what was being perpetrated in the name of wool marketing could only result in the eventual "breaking of the sheep's back" – coincidentally, the aptly selected title of Charles Massy's book.

During September 1977, I was advised in a telephone call from AWC's marketing division general manager, Malcolm Vawser, that I was to be replaced at the end of the year by a manager (Bill Saunders) who was being reassigned from AWC's raw wool operations. The US operation was to be scaled down.

Notes

1. Bastardry: Here defined as unpleasant, aggressive and disruptive behaviour.

TO DREAM THE IMPOSSIBLE DREAM

During the last remaining weeks of my work in New York, my wife Kathie, acutely aware as she was of the years of frustration, angst and bloody-minded incompetence that had followed the establishment of AWC's office in New York, took my arm one evening, having earlier booked seats at a Broadway performance of "Man of La Mancha", the adaptation of Miguel de Cervantes' 17th-century novel "Don Quixote".

New York's Broadway was featuring the well-known story that told of a crazy old knight who, accompanied by his faithful servant, rode onward, constantly tilting at windmills, but never able to achieve a desired outcome. In particular, the title song of the stage show, "The Impossible Dream", struck deeply into my innermost soul and emotions that night.

The music and words of that song hit hard at what had become a very emotional being, suffering from constantly felt regrets at not being allowed, but actively prevented from achieving that which had been mandated as my role and objectives in the US. A great deal of time, treasure and potential opportunities had been squandered in the process.

The music affected me, to the extent that I found myself unable to stem tears, as I related and emotionally reacted to the song and its message to dream the impossible dream! That evening at the theatre was perhaps one of the most poignant and vulnerable moments of my life.

AND SO… LIKE THE LITTLE TRAMP

Charlie Chaplin's Little Tramp of the silent movie era, another of my film heroes, was an unforgettable character. His attitude to life has regularly spurred me on through some of the more difficult periods of my own life's journey.

Charlie's usually unkempt little character, twirling his cane, had appealed to me due to his enduring capacity, always in the face of seemingly overwhelming odds, to never allow himself to be put down for very long. I, therefore, decided that the time had arrived for me to pick myself up, brush off the dust and dirt kicked up both by IWS, and AWC management back in Melbourne. I also decided that the time had now arrived for me to stop tilting at any windmills in the vicinity and, along with my new wife, to fly off into the western sunset, back my Australian home under the Southern Cross.

Kathie and I spent a delightful week-long delayed honeymoon on the exotic French Tahitian island of Moorea on the way back to my home and two fast-growing sons.

At least following my arrival back in Australia, following a short period of R&R, during which we would need to find ourselves a place in which to live, I once again was looking forward to meeting up with a possible new and hopefully different and interesting turning point in my business life. I had come to the decision to leave wool and the AWC behind me at the earliest opportunity.

Once back in Australia, I was now a long way from what turned out to be another freezing cold winter in New York. I was also looking forward to seeing and spending much more valuable time with my two beloved sons over weekends spent down at our small house at Balnarring Beach, where Kathie, I and the boys spent the summer holidays hanging out and sailing on Westernport Bay.

10

RETURN TO MELBOURNE – 1978

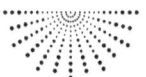

Having first arranged for an Australian permanent resident's visa for Kathie while we were still in New York, we flew out of a cold and storm beset Kennedy Airport during January 1978. Following a sublime, week-long delayed honeymoon we arrived back to a hot and steamy Melbourne. I was happy to be returning as I would now and into the future be closer to Simon and Philip, now living with their mother.

Following a short period living in a rented apartment in Marne Street South Yarra, we moved to my small beachside house in Balnarring, a small bayside township located on the Westernport shore of the Mornington Peninsula. From there Kathie and I commuted to work in the city. I was now based at AWC's new offices on Royal Parade Parkville, just north of the Melbourne CBD. Kathie had found it relatively easy to secure a position with an advertising agency, also located in Melbourne's CBD.

Before returning to Melbourne, I had decided that, regardless of whichever position was offered, I would look to move away from wool and the AWC.

It was a sad time for me. All my industry training and experience, before joining AWB had prepared me for the role I had taken up eight years before. My experiences over recent years, however, instead of being provided with honest, open support and responsible leadership, AWB and those in senior management to whom I had pledged loyalty, had failed to demonstrate the level of competent leadership and integrity I and others had expected in return. I could no longer remain working for an organisation and senior management for whom I had lost any respect.

The future for wool was looking bleak. There seemed little chance of any change in direction even being discussed within the organisation. That being the case, there appeared little value in hanging around and waiting for "something new to come up".

AUSTRALIA'S TEXTILE AND APPAREL INDUSTRIES – 1978–2000

Change had made its inevitable mark across the textile and apparel manufacturing industries since my departure to New York four years earlier. For many of the smaller companies involved in the local production of textiles and apparel, the lowering of tariffs on imported products that were soon to arrive, all too quickly for most, had already begun to have an impact.[1] Eventually, this led to the virtual dismemberment of what had for many years been a vibrant, innovative, skilful and important socially supportive sector of the Australian economy.

Both industries had been responsible for the employment of a large cross section of Australia's working population in every capital city. Perhaps as important, the opportunities provided involved populations spread among many of Australia's inland towns and townships. Falling tariff protection started to bite in the 1980s, eventually resulting in the shedding of employees from many of the population centres within and near which, some form of textile processing or apparel manufacturing had become an important part of the local employment scene.

Some of the more entrepreneurial, more forward-looking companies and individual employers were already beginning to organise themselves, moving at least some part of their commercial activities offshore. Other local companies found themselves being taken over by larger entities. Others that continued to struggle on regardless of the changing business environment tended to 'die on the vine'.

An increasing number of regional centres that in the past had relied upon their local spinning and knitting mills, or other textile related industry for an important part of their income, were already feeling the long hard, cold fingers of decline threatening to take a choke hold on their communities.

Rural farming populations were also feeling the winds of change, as woolgrowing entered a period of decline. Fond but unrealistic hopes held among most woolgrowers for continued expansion of the wool side of their individual operations also began to falter. Little did they realise at the time that in less than a decade, all the exaggerated IWS and AWC forecasts of continuing growth and prosperity would come to naught. IWS projections based on overly optimistic research had ignored or downplayed realistic market analysis and intelligence. It would take a decade yet before woolgrowers' hopes would collapse in a heap following years of poor decision-making and incompetent industry leadership.

Some apparel manufacturers with a weather eye to the future were already acting in defence of their businesses. Most even then were planning to reduce their reliance on local manufacturing in expectation of achieving the higher profits expected to result from lower import tariffs and increased import quotas.

Along with increased importation of apparel that soon began to flow into Australian retailers from lower-cost countries, some of the more entrepreneurial manufacturers were already seeking to follow their retailer clients overseas. In some cases, this saw them seeking to co-operate with factories located in lower-cost countries like China, the South East and East Asian region, and the Indian subcontinent.

It is interesting today, to look back over the past 20 or so years and make a comparison between the current government-facilitated demise of Australia's vehicle manufacturing industry, and its neglect of a number of other Australian industries with potential for growth, with that of the then advancing demise of the best part of Australia's TCF industries during the 1980s.

The level of jobs lost to Australia during that earlier period of enforced adjustment, before and following the early years of a new century, occurred at an even higher rate than currently being experienced across the vehicle manufacturing industry; following the closing down of Ford's, General Motors' (GM) and Toyota's vehicle manufacturing activities:

From over a reported 400,000 employed during and up to the late 1970s and early 1980s, local TCF industries still surviving today are estimated to employ less than 7.5% of that number – less than 30,000 employees!

In addition to this drastic readjustment and the induced demise of the three TCF industries and the massive losses in jobs that followed, needs also to be added the loss of billions of Australian dollars that resulted from the collapse of the wool industry in 1991. Massive financial losses were occurring even before 1991, as a result of AWC activities since its creation in 1973.

It is important here to reflect on the fact that financial costs to the Australian economy, and the opportunities lost as a consequence of years during which the wool industry's fortunes were being presided over by AWC and the various woolgrower councils, leaves the current problems being experienced as a result of the loss of GM, Ford and Toyota in the shade. While this is so, it also begs the question as to what advantage has been gained, following decades that have seen the loss of the major part of Australia's manufacturing and industrial research base,[2] prior to and since the turn of the 21st century?

Notes

1. Until trade liberalisation in the mid 1980s, Australia had a large textile industry. This decline continued through the first decade of the 21st century. Since the 1980s, tariffs had steadily been reduced; in early 2010, tariffs were reduced from 17.5 percent to 10 percent on clothing, and 7.5–10% to 5% for footwear and other textiles. As of 2010, most textiles manufacturing, even by Australian companies, was being performed in China: Source Wikipedia 9/01/2017.

2. Losses to Australia's industrial base are known to include: textiles,

apparel and footwear manufacturing, steelmaking, general engineering, shipping, ship-building and more. Add to this list activities resulting from Australian based industrial research and development that also were being lost to overseas countries and locations, including: development and marketing of computers and related systems, space related systems and services, solar-sourced power/other systems and storage, aeronautics.

WOOL HOUSE – PARKVILLE

In my absence overseas, AWC had moved its head office from 360 Bourke Street, in central Melbourne, to a new building on Royal Parade, Parkville – on the inner city's eastern perimeter. The location was bounded on one side by the Carlton Football Club's home ground, while a couple of hundred metres away to the building's rear was located the Melbourne Zoo.

The zoo seemed a very appropriate location to now find myself working near. On reflection, during some of my more reflective moments since, the years I had spent representing AWC in New York could reasonably be described as being thrown into the midst of a pack of not very friendly animals. Some had been wild, most certainly self-serving, with others having habits and instincts not so very far removed from the inhabitants of the Melbourne Zoo.

I returned to Australia in January 1978 to a nominal role, one in which I was requested, very politely by the general manager, Malcolm Vawser, to 'soldier on', while at the same time expected to report to a former technical division officer who now occupied my former position of national merchandising manager.

The current holder was an individual who some years earlier I had declined to consider for the role of a junior product manager. My reasoning at the time had been that he had no previous technical or commercial experience with either the textile and apparel industries, or retailing. In the circumstances, I resolved to keep to myself as much as possible, as did he. This resulted in a kind of unstated mutual pact aimed at avoiding any contact that may end in a clash.

Space thus created allowed me a great deal of freedom and flexibility to move around the local industry.

THE TIMES THEY ARE A-CHANGIN'

As noted earlier, the competitive situation facing Australian wool that I had left behind in 1974, had changed dramatically. Competition from synthetic fibres had continued to gain ground against wool, increasing their dominance over woven and knitted apparel.

It was difficult to find much that had changed from the organisation I had left earlier, at least any visible creative changes that were now being applied in defence of wool in the Australian market.

Morale among AWC's product managers was low. Apart from the merchandising manager's position, most of the group's staff remained much the same as four years prior, all going through similar hoops, at least in terms of the scope of their activities.

Despite the worsening position of wool, the level of promotional funds being poured into AWC's generic corporate and co-operative support programmes behind the Woolmark had increased.

Products manufactured from pure new wool continued to be in less demand than during its earlier heyday. In spite of this continuing trend, managements of a number of textile manufacturers I was able to meet with at the time, continued to hold the view that demand for wool could be improved – provided a more realistic approach to its positioning could be generated and maintained. Wool's competitive position however, continued to decline.

Even during recent times following the industry's collapse during the mid-1990s, the possibility of rebuilding demand and market presence for Australian apparel wools, at least partway toward what is was at the height of wool sales and consumption during the 1960s, remains questionable.

Even following the establishment of the latest organisation to be charged with research and promotion on behalf of Australian wool, I have yet to see evidence of a serious attempt aimed at recovering at least some of the ground lost following the events of the 1990s.

This view persists, confirmed in later conversations initiated with various employees of Australian Wool Innovation (AWI), whose current website, together with utterances and activities of its current leadership, offers little to inspire. Take for example AWI's description of the organisation's role:

> AWI is a not-for-profit company that invests in R&D and marketing to increase the long-term profitability of Australian woolgrowers. Based in Sydney, we have offices in key markets around the world to help us increase the global demand and market access for Australian wool.

Apart from presenting as a warm 'motherhood' statement, even the list of what the organisation refers to as 'Marketing Highlights', while high-sounding and colourful, AWI's current listing, in my view fails to begin to address the main issues facing the wool industry. Nor do they offer much different to AWC/IWS pronouncements from the past, or highlight new initiatives offering potential growth opportunities for Australian wool across the world's markets.

IS THERE A FUTURE FOR WOOL PROMOTION?

Accepting that Australian wool continues to be engaged in a bitter battle for market share in apparel, decorative textiles and home products, (blankets, doona fillers, furnishings, etc.), there has never been any doubt in my mind, that there could still be a brighter future for wool. The question, of course, is how to go about achieving this?

One possibility that could see some improvements from what has gone before, would be to abandon the organisation's role as a statutory corporation, once again being run by a woolgrower who appears to be running the organisation much in the way of an earlier chairman, Sir William Gunn. As reported recently by *The Australian* newspaper:

> The head of Australia's wool industry has apologised for covertly viewing a focus group of stud merino breeders behind a one-way mirror as well as swearing like a shearer at an ABC reporter.
>
> Australian Wool Innovation chairman Wal Merriman, who has

been accused of being "punch drunk on his own power", delivered the twin apologies today in a Senate estimates hearing in Canberra.

During the hearing, the industry body was attacked over allegations it bullies woolgrowers and publicly shames them. The inquiry also heard that one of the nation's oldest industries, which is steeped in cultural and historic importance, is wracked by "warring tribes" who have different views on how to breed sheep.

The question here: "When will Australia's woolgrowers learn?"

It would be useful to pause here for a short time and take another look at what has gone before. It shouldn't take much in terms of effort when trying to analyse what mistakes were made and where opportunities were lost as a result. To do so should do little harm, provided of course that mistakes made earlier are not repeated, but carefully studied and learned from – so, let's start from there…

It has always been clear to anyone possessing even the modicum of technical and marketing expertise, that once synthetic fibres had made their strong entrance onto the world's markets, Australian fine wools should never have been allowed to continue to be promoted solely and completely on the basis of an amorphous and narrowly based, inflexible generic campaign. A promotional programme hung mainly on the hook of the universally recognised Woolmark.

The continuation of this policy, without some changes, also later served to limit the possibility of distinguishing Australian sourced wool and wool-containing products from competitive wools.

Even allowing that the Woolmark itself was, and presumably still remains a recognisable emblem, much more needed to occur, in terms of branding and a more innovative and creative tactical approach being applied on a number of fronts.

It had become clear even as far back as the late 1960s, a position that became much clearer while working in the United States, that there was no future trying to compete with synthetic fibres, particularly on the basis of price.

Continued reliance on generic promotion, even with the assistance of the Woolmark and warm 'fluffy' references to fashion, events that focused primarily on the 'luxury' of wool, had reached its limitations. The time for continuing to rely on the same policies had passed. As the 1970s and 1980s opened, Australia needed to 'think and act outside the square' in terms of how Australian wool was to be presented, firstly to the people involved with buying and processing it, closely followed by the world's consumers.

To explain why I believe this:

Once synthetic fibres had made their presence felt across the world's apparel markets to the extent they had, continuing to follow the same policies that had worked previously, but expecting to see different results was never going to be successful. Such activity was and is – as a dinky-di Aussie would more than likely say: "Just plain bloody stupid!"

Neither was the IWS arrangement that had lumped Australia together with New Zealand, South Africa and Uruguay, going to be capable of providing the amount of creative and concentrated thrust necessary through which to defend Australia's share of a declining world market for wool, from whatever source.

Australia, as the world's major grower and supplier of apparel wools needed a different promotional strategy, that could be adapted more strongly toward the promotion of products made from or containing Australian wool.

The adoption of a changed strategy did not necessarily mean limiting any future development and promotional activities to wool-containing products made in Australia. On the contrary, what was needed here was to include well-designed products containing wool, processed and manufactured wherever a particular product was best suited to be produced, be it in Australia or any First or Third World country that provided the best facilities and cost structure. Thus it would be possible to determine the wool type required, at what blend level – not ruling out pure new wool in the product mix.

The late 1960s and 1970s, should have seen the introduction of a policy promoting products manufactured from Australian wools, both in pure form, or where appropriate, wools blended with other fibres, synthetic, natural and exotic.

While cost was and remains of importance, one or two Australians at the time, referred to earlier, had already pointed to the potential promotional way ahead. They proved later that with the right approach and appropriately targeted and nurtured promotional support, success was possible across a broad range of wool-containing products.

The need here was and continues in two key areas:

- To defend the use of Australian wool in every possible end use that the fibre could be adapted and designed for, in both apparel and non-apparel products. This means precise research, innovative product development, followed by the promotion of Australian wool, in pure, cut, blended or whatever other form is seen to be necessary to the desired end product. For example, if that means cutting superfine wool-staple – then so be it!
- To seek out, research and develop new markets and other innovative possibilities (refer here to the Saudi uniform project discussed earlier) for Australian wool and products manufactured from it. Then go about the task of promoting them and their value to end consumers, wherever, whenever and however deemed appropriate.

Where possible and practical, the promotion of pure Australian wool should be maintained, but only where the finished product allows it to command the price required. Allow also for the blending of wool with other natural, synthetic, animal or any other kind of exotic fibres. Should other fibres need to be included – blending, in that case, to be determined and promoted, according to the desired qualities and sales story of the product being marketed. Refer here to current New Zealand projects, briefly discussed earlier. They are considered to represent simple, but effective niche marketing.

One or two other marketing projects in Australia and the US, also described earlier, had proved that wool could compete successfully, without the need for considerable extra financial support from the federal government, or acquisition by AWC of the Australian wool clip.

Any possibility of any part of the foregoing even being considered by the AWC board and wool industry leadership at the time proved, like in the story of "Man of La Mancha", to have the same chance of succeeding as the old knight had enjoyed, as mounted on his charger he constantly jousted unsuccessfully at imaginary windmills.

It was long past the time for a major shakeup and reconsideration of the future direction of Australia's woolgrowing industry – and the fibre it produced. Had such open discussion, consideration and planning been able to take place, a different style of organisation possessing more professional, innovative and flexible policies related to the long-term needs of the Australian wool industry could have been developed and established, well prior to the industry's eventual collapse in 1993.

IF ONLY?

How many times have we personally mouthed or heard the lament, "if only", as it was rung out of us following a real or perceived failure to achieve something we had set our heart on? Perhaps the same could be said of the cry of inconsolable members of a football team, having suffered yet another defeat at the hands of a rival team? If only we had played better? If only I had run just a couple of seconds faster, in the case of a runner? If only I had driven my car more carefully, and – closer to the subject being discussed – if only the wool industry had been better organised and led?

The history of Australian wool is long. Even now, most people with whom I have spoken continue to value wool as a highly desirable apparel fibre. Wool has always retained a reputation as the provider of comfort, pleasure – even safety to a wearer, regardless of the environment. Despite the trend toward what has relatively recently become known as a 'throwaway' society, a well-designed fine wool dress, skirt, pantsuit, man's suit, jacket or item of knitwear continues to be valued. Wool continues to be a product most consumers will aspire to owning at some time during their lives.

There remains a future for wool. What happens from here on from an Australian point of view however, rests with those currently charged with its marketing and promotion. It is they, who in concert with what's left of the world's committed wool textile processors and manufacturers who will ultimately determine the future of the world's most valued fibre.

WHY WAIT UNTIL NOW?

It had occurred to me at this point that you might well wish to ask why I didn't put pen to paper in 1979, following my departure from the AWC? The answer to that is simple:

At the time, all I wanted to do was to put as much space as possible between the Australian wool industry and myself. I no longer wished to be involved with what had become a dysfunctional industry and an organisation led by incompetent, ego driven empire builders. Unfortunately, at the time the industry's leaders were being backed by a succession of federal governments, whose ministers were finding the industry's problems too difficult or too distracting for them to spend the time trying to understand. The constant pressure being placed on government by wool industry leaders didn't help.

While having prepared notes on my tenure with AWB and AWC, together with ideas and possibilities that had emerged from experiences gained, I had lost both the interest and motivation to continue butting my head up against a brick wall!

It was only with the writing of this book that the period of my involvement with the Australian wool industry needed to be included. Wool, textiles and apparel had consumed a large part of my private and business life.

THROUGH THE REAR-VIEW MIRROR

Looking back as objectively as I can against the backdrop of what was happening to the wool industry while I was part of it, time has confirmed that the five-year period 1974–1978 could have been a turning point. Instead, it became, however, a period during which the industry's leaders became exposed as "emperors with no clothes".

Both of the organisations that the 'Emperors' and their supporters continued to support and promote proved totally inadequate when it came to meeting the needs of an industry under attack. While originally the title International Wool Secretariat was a good fit for the level of activities it was expected to carry out as a 'secretariat' in 1937, namely:

> Officials or office entrusted with administrative duties, maintaining records, and overseeing or performing secretarial duties, especially for an international organization.
> (Source: Dictionary.com)

The organisation's later activities fell tragically short of the role necessary for wool's survival as a major textile fibre during the 1960s and beyond.

It eventually, but belatedly, became clear that the then Labor government could no longer support the unrealistic ideas and calcifying politics that in the past had cost Australian woolgrowers and the public purse well in excess of $12 billion!

I will repeat that figure: **12 billion Australian dollars!**

Few among the Australian public were even aware at the time of this conservative estimate of AWC's losses – losses as detailed on page 382 in "Breaking the Sheep's Back":

> Even without allowing for any indirect and opportunity costs or wasted billions (that had been poured) into the IWS marketing efforts during the Corporation's (AWC) life, if this $1 billion (referring here to estimated losses resulting from AWC's management of the RPS) is then added to the conservative $6.6 billion Wool Corporation or associated losses, plus the $1.5 billion (and up to $3 billion) global stock write-downs, then a conservative estimate of $9 billion makes this the biggest corporate disaster in Australian history in terms of losses generated by a single corporate or statutory business entity. The nearest was the HIH Insurance Group's $5.3 billion loss in 2001. In today's real purchasing terms the

Corporation's and associated losses would easily exceed $12 billion. But a full costing could dwarf this.

AUSTRALIAN WOOL INNOVATION

The latest edition of a wool promotion entity in the form of Australian Wool Innovation (AWI) and something known as the 'Woolmark Company', have taken over the industry's reins. Both emerged from the mess that followed the collapse of AWC's reserve price scheme during the early 1990s, and the subsequent dismantling of AWC and IWS.

The wool industry is now reduced to less than a third of its size during the heyday of the late 1940s and 1950s. The organisation's title incidentally doesn't fill me with much in the way of enthusiasm, nor do its press releases and statements of intent appear to offer much in the way of hope regarding Australian wool's future possibilities.

As a barometer often used to gauge its success in terms of growing demand, wool prices continue to fluctuate, much as they had over past years. It's worth referring here back to the 1950s, at the height of the Korean War. During that period, the price of greasy Australian Merino wool reached a high of around $37/kg (in 2003 prices). Compare this with mid-2002 when wool's price had declined to around $3.20/kg. (Source: 2003 ABS yearbook).

The 2003 yearbook of the Australian Bureau of Statistics (ABS) also noted:

> It was during the 1990s that the Australian wool industry came to fully realise that wool is merely one of a number of fibres which apparel makers can choose to use in their garments, and that demand for wool (relies) significantly on the relative prices of substitute fibres, particularly the high quality but cheap synthetic fibres being produced today.

Tell me about it! The ABS statement in 2003 was already clearly apparent to most of Australia's and the world's textile industry managers, well before the arrival of 1970 – at least 33 years before the desk jockeys at ABS felt the need to offer the comment!

Whether the current AWI, the Woolmark Company and any other entity engaged in chancing its arm at the game of promoting Australian wool, will eventually prove to be any more successful than their predecessors, is something we are yet to witness.

If by chance someone possessing the foresight and energy does happen to appear sometime in the future, I sincerely hope that whoever they happen to be, they possess the good sense to learn something from the past.

The eight years during which I was employed by AWB and AWC, were years during which internal and external politicking and utter pig-headedness continued to rule everything connected with the growing, sale and marketing of Australian wools. This was to the detriment, not only of the Australian wool industry but also the Australian economy.

During meetings between Australia and the US, Australia at the time negotiating a hoped-for reduction in the US$0.255/lb US import tariff then being imposed on imported greasy wools, Australia continued to come out second best. During a lunch in Washington late in 1977, a member of the US team pulled me aside and, with a firm, comforting hand on my shoulder, proceeded to describe the Australian team that the Americans had been negotiating with in the following terms:

"I'm sorry to have to tell you this Gerry, but negotiating with your Aussie colleagues was like herding sheep to the slaughter – we didn't even need to give even an inch!"

It sure is a cruel world…

IS THERE A LIGHT AT THE END OF THE TUNNEL?

In contrast to the disappointing wool prices quoted earlier in the ABS 2003 yearbook report, a report in the Melbourne *Herald Sun* newspaper of July 2017, trumpeted the good news that:

Global demand for Australian wool has pushed prices skywards as the commodity bounces back from a 20-year lull in production." The report went on to state: "The strong demand and a limited market supply led the Eastern market indicator to rise 10% to 1507c/kg in the first half of 2017." Also noted, was that of the 341,000 tonnes of Australian wool produced during 2016/17, 75% went to a single buyer – PR China.

Discounting the flutters of joy and excitement at the news that must have arisen in the hearts of Australia's woolgrowers, reports such as this should be seen as also carrying with it a more sobering message.

It is to be hoped that this recent increase in wool sales will not encourage fond hopes for an eventual return to the happy days of the early 1950s? Rather it points up the fact that in spite of all the tribulations of the late 1990s and beyond, there remains an underlying demand for the world's most sublime fibre.

IN CONCLUSION

As for me, 1978 ended a near-decade that had commenced with exuberance, excitement and unbridled enthusiasm for the job ahead. As the years passed, my hopes turned gradually to disillusionment and later to frustration and a deep sadness.

Ultimately, any respect for the organisation to which I had originally arrived bright-eyed and bushy-tailed, finally turned into abiding disgust. In particular, as an Australian citizen I eventually found myself reacting to the way many millions of Australian dollars (my taxes among them) were being flushed down the IWS and AWC toilet, by people who should have known and done much better.

The market crash that arrived hammer-like during the early 1990s (1991–1993), put paid to AWC's ill-fated policy that had resulted in pushing the price of Australian wools up to a point beyond the level capable of being sustained by the world's textile market.

Following my return to Australia and Wool House in 1978, I found an organisation dominated, even more than when I had left it nearly five years earlier, by a management level thick with wall-to-wall market researchers, economists (agri- and otherwise, having little practical experience other than that of university and theory), assorted doctors (non-medical), academics and raw wool oriented sales administrators. All were scurrying around the AWC board and its members. Alas, the presence of even one entrepreneurial and well-credentialed textile and apparel savvy operator was notable by their continued absence.

Few of those that I was to meet, as they hovered, attended meetings and caucused around AWC's new headquarters, possessed little more than a peripheral understanding or a deep gut feel for what made the real world of textiles, apparel manufacture and retailing tick. Few, if any even seemed interested enough to get their hands slightly soiled by visiting and learning more about the actual workings of a textile mill or clothing factory. Perhaps they didn't see any need to?

And so AWC continued onward, hell-bent on pushing through high-sounding but unworkable policies and an overly high reserve pricing structure for wool, the result of which was to eventually cause AWC's house of cards to come crashing down in an expensive heap.

11

TRANSITIONS

The commencement of a new century saw my life continue to wend its way willy-nilly, without any assistance or command needed from me, as it made its way across a variety of work and business situations.

Following a near-decade trying to defend wool, I was destined to regularly find myself having to learn different skills, also needing to become familiar with and proficient in a few very different industries. My road ahead, although unknown at the time, required even more study and a need to obtain different qualifications, setting up the opportunity later to establish my own company in an industry a whole world away from my original qualifications and expertise.

In the midst of all this, I was also destined to encounter a frightening, near-death experience.

I had now arrived at the point in my life where I was in a reasonable financial position, and possessed of some time in which I could choose whatever line of work I now wished to pursue. I had also reached the point where I hoped to find the time to do something that to date had eluded me – my desire to write.

Before that dream could become a reality, however, life and the universe had already decided that I had a little way yet to go before that could happen. I still had a few more windmills at which to tilt my lance, Don Quixote-style before dismounting from my long-suffering steed to take up my pen ... or rather in this modern age, get to tap on the keys of my recently acquired laptop computer.

THE RAG TRADE – JUST ONE LAST TIME

Casting around for ideas as to what to do in the interim, until I could get myself organised sufficiently enough to be able to sit down and perhaps write something about my recent experiences with wool, a short-term opportunity offered itself in the form of an industry acquaintance in need of assistance…

Frieze Brothers Pty Ltd was one of those men's apparel manufacturers to which I referred earlier. A medium-sized company that had grown from its earlier roots a generation prior during the 1930s, a then small two-man tailoring workshop, established in Melbourne by immigrant brothers.

David Frieze, son of one of the founders, had succeeded in developing the then small organisation into one of Australia's smaller but at its peak, more successful producers and national distributors of men's fashion apparel. It was not a large company, but one that during the 1960s and early 1970s found itself universally recognised as a leader among Australia's younger menswear brands.

During the 1960s, the Frieze brand became associated with a local rock group that had taken on the Frieze name. Such was the widespread reputation that over the years had been built up by the Frieze brand.

By the time I agreed to join David Frieze, his company was struggling to survive. The position I agreed to take up following my departure from AWC I regarded as temporary, my intention being to provide myself with space within which to review where next to tilt my imagined lance.

I was well aware at the time that things had started to go astray for David and his company, mainly as the result of a lack of management foresight. Frieze's difficulties were not the result of lacking fashion foresight, but more to do with its principal's penchant for recognition and applause as a fashion leader. This tendency had led him to ignore the need to keep a close watch on costs, a fault that led to his company's deepening financial problem – unsold stock and resulting debt building at an alarming rate.

The cause of the company's debt had come about as a result of David's continued hesitancy when it came to the need to quit stocks of unsold garments and fabrics close to the end of a selling season. Instead, Frieze had continued to hoard an ever-increasing quantity of each, in the hope of selling or including them in a garment range at some unspecified date in the future. This practice over some years was now rebounding. The company had become overloaded with debt, due to the steady accumulation of a warehouse full to overflowing with unsold and broken size ranges of apparel and fabrics, all being weighed down with the cost of their original purchase and production. Unsold stock accumulating ever-increasing costs.

You might be tempted to suggest here, that the problems facing Frieze were not very far removed from those facing the wool industry?

This build-up of debt and the gradual loss of agreeable creditors ultimately resulted in the company's inability to continue trading.

During the few months I spent with Frieze Brothers, increasing debts began to rapidly outweigh any possibility of turning the company round to a profitable, or at the very least a break-even position. Its principal, in the meantime, continued to press on as if by doing so the company's problems would disappear. They didn't, and the company was eventually forced to close down.

My departure from Frieze Brothers some months prior to this served to finally sever my connection with the apparel industry, one that had spanned over 30 years.

Having decided to leave the industry I had earlier begun actively to cast-around in the search of a position, preferably in product management. Strange that it may seem, one such position did eventually appear – a role far removed from anything to do with wool, textiles and the manufacture of apparel.

VICTORIAN TIMBER PROMOTION COUNCIL, 1979–1981

Anyone might think that there is too vast a difference between wool, textiles, apparel and the timber industry, for anyone to consider moving from the former closely related industries, to the latter?

Well, yes, there are some significant differences between the products involved, mainly in the domain of each product's different physical characteristics and a much different range of possible end uses. In my case though, skills learned from my cabinetmaker father that had lain dormant for the best part of 40 years, actually came to the fore on sighting an advertisement on behalf of the Victorian Timber Promotion Council (TPC) seeking the services of a marketing manager.

The role being advertised was described as "Manager – Hardwood". The position, in support of Victorian sourced hardwood timbers, was their sale locally, interstate and possibly overseas. Timber, as it turned out, was a subject of which I had spent a great deal of time learning about, handling and using during my youth, which as a result had provided me with a reasonably broad knowledge of timbers and joinery. I had also managed to become the proud possessor of a wide range of practical woodworking skills.

My father, being a skilled cabinetmaker and joiner, had, from when I was a young boy, taught me much about the different kinds of timbers, their uses and the skills involved in working them. These were skills gained over a number of years during which I became interested to the point that I loved to handle and work with timber. I had regularly been co-opted to assist my dad, as he built furniture pieces to order in one of our two cellars, following his return from the Second World War.

Working with my dad, I had learned how to use and care for tools, how to make and fit all the various kinds of joints then being used, as well as many other woodworking skills. These were skills that eventually provided me with more than the average person's knowledge when it came to recognising and working with various timbers, timber veneers and other materials used by him as part of his everyday work.

I had also gained skills in the art of French Polishing, a handcrafted process used extensively during an earlier era to impart a deep mirror-like finish to a finished piece of timber furniture.

My application for the position advertised by TPC included details of my knowledge of the various species of timbers and their uses, in addition to my offering of capabilities when it came to development and implementation of innovative marketing projects. Even though wool and wood were vastly different regarding their structure and end uses, both were natural products that needed to be treated and marketed according to their individual uniqueness and aesthetic qualities.

My application must have impressed the people who interviewed and tested me, particularly on my knowledge of Victorian timbers. Thus, as TPC's hardwood manager, I was tasked with studying the makeup of the Victorian hardwood industry, and the later development of a programme aimed at the more profitable utilisation of Victorian hardwoods.

Rough sawn (green) structural hardwood at the time was a timber resource fighting for its earlier dominant position in an increasingly competitive fight with radiata pine plantation softwoods. There was also the question of the possibility of exporting Victorian sourced hardwood products, and if so – to where and in what form?

One of my first projects, undertaken in conjunction with Ian Kennedy, a senior researcher with the then Victorian Forestry Commission (VFC), was to undertake a study of the range and depth of the Victorian hardwood industry. Such a study was first needed to accurately analyse the industry's productive capacity.

The resulting survey, titled "Hardwood Sawmilling", was published in 1980.

Victorian sourced hardwoods at the time were used predominantly as house framing, mainly as rough sawn green (undried) structural timbers. A lesser proportion of sawn hardwoods were being kiln-dried, dressed and sold as fully stabilised structural timbers. A much smaller amount of kiln-dried Victorian hardwoods of various species were destined for use in furniture, flooring, panelling and other decorative, domestic end uses.

One issue that became apparent as a result of the 1980 hardwood survey was their increased potential to be dried, processed and used more as decorative items, furniture and flooring. Up to that time, most hardwoods were being sawn, straight from the felled tree and shipped off in bundles to be used to frame houses. Additional market research had also nominated other end uses with some potential – few of which were then being exploited to the extent possible.

While a small proportion of what was usually termed 'select' alpine or mountain ash species were being kiln-dried and prepared for use as stabilised structural timbers, smaller quantities of these and other timbers like blackwood, sassafras, red gum, beech and similar species were being used for furniture and panelling. In addition to some timbers being used as floor and wallboards, not much of the vast amounts of Victorian hardwoods being harvested at the time were being processed beyond the 'green-sawn' stage. These were structural products referred to by the building trade as 'Ordinary Building' (OB) structural timber.

As OB structural timbers, there was no reliable and recognisable system being used at the time to clearly identify green-sawn timbers that complied with Victorian building regulations and specifications governing the strength grading of different hardwood species. Producers of softwoods, many years earlier, had established their own RPAA quality mark, a grading system that was being used and promoted in support of fully dried and stabilised radiata pine structural timbers.

WORKING FOR VICTORIAN HARDWOOD

During the two years during which I worked with TPC, I was responsible for setting up a programme designed to identify hardwoods that met structural strength standards, bringing them more into accordance with already established Australian Standards. The system titled Australian Hardwood Quality Control (AHQC) was introduced during 1980. I see no evidence of the system remaining in existence today, perhaps because very little if any, green-sawn hardwood continues to be used as house framing.

In addition to quality control, a number of months were spent in an effort to encourage local sawmillers to sort out and isolate hardwoods better suited to furniture and other structural and decorative products and to dry these. Understandably, however, most of the smaller sawmills preferred to continue to cut and sell lots of green OB building timber, without any regard for its potential to be upgraded to higher value furniture or other potential end uses.

Most sawmillers ignored drying timbers known to be appropriate for use as furniture or other value-added end uses. This was understandable from the point of view of many of the smaller sawmilling operations that had much more financially to gain by cutting up their allocation of sawlogs into house framing lots, then selling the result directly to builders.

Historically there were easily obtained profits to be had by not investing in expensive drying equipment and storage facilities, the financial cost of the latter alone representing a major disincentive. To do so meant them having to become involved with a long period during which the timber needed to be dried, this being achieved by 'sticking-out' (stacking) sawn timbers in the open for some months, depending on the weather. This aspect of value adding to the raw, rough sawn timbers also required additional financing. Instead, most chose to stick to their age-old practice of felling, sawing and selling green OB structural timber directly to builders.

Even some of the larger sawmillers found it more rewarding financially to fell (cut down) trees, cut them up as quickly as possible, sending packs of framing timbers to their builder clients across the state, usually within a few days of harvesting the saw logs. In this way, they were able to turn over extremely good profits as a result of not having to pay for the saw logs until well after they had sold the results of them being cut and shipped. Thus, profits were assured – well before them having to pay FCV for the felled sawlogs!

Successive state governments of the day had no policy in place requiring such a valuable natural resource to be selectively used – according to its value-added potential.

Ultimately, it became an impossible task trying to change the attitudes of a lifetime on the part of most Victorian hardwood sawmillers.

The attitude toward drying and processing improved products has changed over the years, probably due to a more stringent policy of payment for saw logs, plus the later realisation, brought on as the use of kiln-dried radiata pine virtually took over from the use of green-sawn OB hardwood, in housing construction.

Another dimension to the reduced sale of green OB hardwood was the development of pre-constructed roof trusses and wall framing, all requiring a completely stabilised product as the basis for their construction. Development of metal framing components later resulted in less unstable OB hardwood being used in house framing.

Many hardwood sawmillers remaining in the industry were eventually forced to diversify and look to other end uses for their production, or found themselves operating in a rapidly shrinking market. Others were eventually taken over by larger, more forward-looking companies having sufficient financial backing to extend their operations to producing dried and stabilised products for structural, furniture and decorative uses.

THE STORY OF THE KATIWARD

The two years spent in the hardwood industry played a small part my next foray into a very different kind of work. Not work in terms of the need to earn a living from my efforts, but more to do with my desire to fulfil a long-time dream to sail across the world's oceans.

Over the years I had been able to build a small financial reserve, sufficient to provide the opportunity to opt out of what had become a daily grind. I had grown tired of working in an office environment, among people who, for the most part, appeared more intent to eke out their working years in the expectation of eventually receiving a golden handshake, then head into retirement. Once having arrived into their fifties, sixties and 'retired', retirees chose to spend whatever years were left to them, in either of three ways, always assuming they still had their health and were reasonably financial.

Some choose to run down what years are left to them by going the 'grey-nomad' route. This meant selling or renting their family home, then wandering around the countryside pulling a caravan, mingling along the way with a host of other grey-headed adventurers until having decided that they had had enough of the wandering 'gipsy-like' lifestyle.

Others tend to stay at home filling in the time left to them playing golf, tennis, lawn bowls, or gardening and 'smelling the roses'. This kind of person seems happy to spend their days pottering around the home, in between looking after and bouncing grandchildren on by now arthritic knees. Some act as substitute parents for grandchildren, while both the young children's parents struggled along in jobs, trying to earn enough money to enable them cope with heavy mortgage payments and child rearing costs.

Still others, decide to invest their time and whatever funds they have left, on becoming 'cruisers'. Their preference, if so inclined, is to travel on-board one or other of a growing fleet of 'luxury' liners. Usually this means them happily cramming themselves, like so many sardines, on bright, loud and flashy multi-decked luxury ships. They sail on-board large, usually white ships, 'floating pseudo-paradises', where they and thousands of other cruisers pay lots of money, just to wander around their seaborne playground, while paying fleeting visits to ports that begin to look the same after the first few days of the cruise have worn off.

None of the foregoing had been my idea of life among the August, September and later years of my time on Planet Earth. For me, having now reached the August/September stage, presented the opportunity to learn new skills, meet new people, as far away as possible from a supine, and to my mind depressing future of becoming a caravan pulling wanderer, or a relatively inactive couch potato, TV watcher, babysitter or starry-eyed cruiser.

My love of sailing, both in the US, where I had owned a 26-foot sloop, in addition to sailing and crewing on a variety of dinghies and large seagoing racing yachts, had continued back in Australia where I had built myself a racing dinghy. This small project started within me the desire to use the skills in woodworking I had learned many years earlier working alongside my dad as his young, enthusiastic assistant, to a more positive and enjoyable end.

I had read a great deal about the voyages of famous sailors – ranging from Magellan, Vasco de Gama and Captain Cook, my childhood hero, to Captain Joshua Slocum. The latter of these was a then retired American captain, who gained the reputation of being the first mariner to circumnavigate the world single-handed in a small wind-driven sailing ship.

The then retired Captain Slocum had taken ownership of the derelict hull of an old New England fishing boat that had been left to rot in a local field. He rebuilt it, renaming his little ship 'Spray', then over the years 1895–1898 had successfully sailed her single-handed, without any form of mechanical propulsion, around the world. His subsequent book "Sailing Alone around the World" was written following his journey, the first solo trans-global sea voyage.

While having no intentions of trying to emulate the amazingly skilled Captain Slocum, I did have a growing desire, like many others before me, to build and sail my own seagoing yacht. The skills and patience needed to build a 40-foot timber small ship however, are far removed from building a sixteen-foot plywood dinghy, but what the hell – if Joshua Slocum could do it, why not I?

I had grown tired of working day after day within a large corporate structure, often as a result feeling mired in a place that someone earlier had spoken and written about in a book titled "The Executive Jungle". After having spent so much of my business life within a working environment in which I had grown steadily less enamoured, even considering the satisfactory level of recompense I had been receiving for my efforts, the time had arrived where I felt in dire need to break out and into something completely different.

With my children now young adults and showing the capacity to run their own lives more or less successfully, the need to be earning money to educate, clothe and feed a young family had by now ceased to be my central need.

I had come to a point in my life when I needed much more than an executive type position, accompanied by a large company salary, company car and office, to stimulate and inspire me. Building and sailing a small ship I therefore decided was to be the theme of the next stage of my life.

So commenced a four-year period during which I drafted and lofted my little ship's lines, and specified and ordered the timbers and other equipment, wiring and materials that would enable me to build and sail a modern version of Joshua Slocum's little ship. This meant I would not be able to hold down any other permanent position. My wife Kathie, while she enjoyed sailing didn't share my enthusiasm to go sailing across an ocean. My decision to go ahead proved to be a major project, having huge physical and mental dimensions. It was also one that eventually took four years to complete, in the process unfortunately causing damage to my marriage.

I had much to be thankful for during the project, Kathie's support for one, without which I could never have succeeded in finishing the project.

To keep my hand in with some form of business project that would allow me to at least earn some income during the time my little ship was being built, I set up a small company, "Traditional Timber Boats". Working through this company I began to take on a few maintenance and repair jobs, working on other people's boats and yachts needing maintenance or repair – in addition to building my own.

At times boat work, outside that of my project, involved me with insurance repairs and other jobs, including undertaking fit-outs of other people's yachts, installing inlaid timber decking, re-planking and spar building. At one stage I had sufficient work on hand requiring me to employ casual workers to assist me.

I also took up a technical training skills course in welding and marine electrics, to gain the additional skills I would also need during the construction and fit-out phases of my little ship. This included learning the traditional arts of rope and wire splicing. I also learned how to 'parcel and serve' wire shrouds and other control lines, skills I was lucky enough to acquire from a retired tugboat operator in nearby Geelong.

My little ship was to be built old-style, with galvanised wire shrouds, traditionally parcelled and served. She was to be timber hulled, built up of strip-planked Tasmanian celery-top pine, and laminated select grade Oregon timber masts and spars, both main and mizzen. I later even learned to install the Perkins diesel engine and the various bits of the relatively simple electrics needed.

Eventually, my beautiful 40-foot, 8-ton displacement, gaff main and lugsail ketch rigged ship was finished, engine and tanks for water and diesel installed. I had earlier also designed and lofted out the sail plan and, along with a great deal of assistance from a fellow boating friend Mick Hubbard, and a couple of other sailing friends, built the ship's masts, spars, rigging and galvanised iron mast and hull fittings.

Following four years of intense work, the Katiward was finally finished, painted and ready for launching, along with the usual traditional bottle of champagne. Kathie named our little ship (an adaptation of her maiden surname). She, the ship that is, was formally launched in March 1986 at Hastings Marina, on Victoria's Westernport Bay.

I had the immense pleasure of sailing my little ship around Westernport and Port Phillip bays and was also able to take part in Australia's bicentenary celebrations in 1988, a year that celebrated the First Fleet's arrival in Sydney Cove 200 years earlier.

Along with a couple of friends on-board, Kathie and I sailed Katiward from Hastings in Westernport Bay, around the Bass Strait coast, past Cape Schanck and through the narrow, dangerous Port Phillip heads, and into Port Phillip Bay. Our entry into Port Phillip was timed to arrive at the same time some of the world's tall sailing ships that were also sailing to the Port of Melbourne as part of the Australian 1998 bicentenary celebrations.

THE END OF A DREAM

Over the years I have learned, sometimes to often-boyish disappointment, that life does not always run the way we humans plan, too often in the hope that our plans will turn out as we wish them to. In my case, the universe seems to have decreed that my beloved little ship and my plans for her were eventually to be curtailed.

Having a seaworthy ship which, after a couple of years sailing her on Westernport Bay and in the Bass Strait, had started to get me thinking in terms of: "Why not sail her up into the South Pacific, wander around the islands and perhaps beyond for a while?" With a question like that running through my head, my thinking began to return to the days of my boyhood, turning once again to then dreams of following in the footsteps of James Cook and sailing my little ship to and among the islands of the South Seas.

I had no enthusiasm to return to a jacket, tie, suit and the executive jungle, and even fewer intentions of ever getting involved again with either the wool industry or apparel manufacturing.

My youngest son Philip was keen to join me on a voyage north, as were my next-door neighbour's son and daughter, Garry and Julie, both of whom were around Philip's age. Unfortunately, Kathie had decided that she was not happy to leave her job, her horse and the house – just to go cruising.

I guess that by that time, Kathie had become more than a little uncomfortable with the thought of ocean sailing, as well as frustrated with a husband who had spent four years totally absorbed in his shipbuilding project, all the while spending less time with her and being more closely involved with some of her interests and deeper felt needs.

Whatever was going on in her mind at the time, I had committed myself to sail north and so was left with a dilemma – to leave or not to leave? I had the ship capable of sailing the oceans and now having sailed her in all weathers in local waters and the boisterous and dangerous Bass Strait, I was now positively itching to take her on a real ocean voyage.

I guess it was more in the way of a recurring dream for me, one experienced long ago, rarely very far away from the dreams of a small boy back in Leeds and later. I had always held the picture in my mind's eye, as I regularly read books on sailing and discovery, around the possibilities of sailing myself across the exotic South Seas, to the Pacific islands and coral atolls to Australia's north and east, much like the voyagers and discoverers of old. Of course, the islands of the South

Seas of the 1990s would be far less exotic than they had been in Cook's days, but surely it would be an interesting challenge to sail in and among them?

What a rotten decision to make. To leave my wife at home and sail off into the sunset for god only knows how long? I was always hoping that Kathie would change her mind – but that, unfortunately, stayed the same. I had the little ship, and following so many years involved with her building and subsequent sailing in local waters, I was locked heart and soul into a state of mind that kept telling me to try myself out for a few months sailing Katiward across an open ocean.

The fateful decision made, it was with more than a heavy heart that I made the fateful decision to sail away from Hastings, along with my crew of four, accompanied at least for the first part of the voyage by my close sailing and boatbuilding mate Mick Hubbard. Having to say goodbye to Kathie as she stood on the dock at Hastings, waving us goodbye had me close to tears and a heart heavy with regret and foreboding.

As we sailed across Westernport Bay from the Hastings channel, all that I could think of at the time was "What the hell am I doing sailing off into the sunset like this?" I was always hoping that Kathie would decide to join us later in the cruise – but something else inside kept telling me that I had made the wrong choice, which in all probability ultimately added just another element toward the later ending of my second marriage after 14 years together.

PORT MACQUARIE, NSW

Following a reasonably fair trip through the usually boisterous and often dangerous currents flowing through the Bass Strait, rounding the south-east corner of the New South Wales coast, and a couple of days in the port of Eden, we sailed up the coast and into the famed Sydney Harbour. There we stayed for a few days to rest and replenish the ship. Mick left us there to return to Hastings. We, the remaining four on-board then set off up the coast of New South Wales, eventually finding ourselves having to wait out a storm at sea in the partially exposed and very uncomfortable northern New South Wales fishing port of Coffs Harbour.

The following morning, March 8th 1988, following advice from the port-office at our next intended port of call at Port Macquarie, and advice that the bar into the port was calm and safe to cross, we set sail toward Port Macquarie.

On approaching the entrance to Port Macquarie harbour, all seemed calm as forecast. The sea in the area was flat, with just a few low waves visible over the bar area, just outside the harbour proper.

The situation changed dramatically, as we passed over the first bar and was about to cross what turned out to be a smaller, secondary bar just outside Port Macquarie harbour.

As Katiward was crossing the second bar, I was suddenly shocked to realise that something connected with the steering had failed. As a consequence, I had lost the ability to steer her clear of the waves that were breaking to the north of the harbour entrance!

My little ship veered abruptly to starboard, at which time Philip and Garry rushed below in a desperate attempt to get the emergency tiller rigged onto the top of the rudder shaft.

Unfortunately, by the time they had got themselves in place, Katiward, while turning to starboard was hit by a solid wave amidships, rolling her over onto her side. At that, both Philip and Gary managed to scramble back onto the sloping deck through the main cabin skylight. As Katiward was starting to roll even further over onto her side I shouted to all three, including Gary's sister Julie, to get off the ship and into the water – as another wave pushed my poor little ship further over, threatening to turn her turtle in the surf to the north of the harbour mouth. The voyage at that moment had turned into a desperate and dangerous situation.

Just as my three companions got clear of the ship it was hit with a large wave, following which I realised that she was going to roll over. I had just enough time to grab hold of the mizzen mast for support, in the vain hope that once through the surf, she should be able to right herself, allowing me sufficient time to at least get the emergency tiller onto the rudder stock and steer her away from any further danger.

But no, my beautiful little ship was rolled completely over onto her back by yet another wave well outside the channel into the port. The force of the rollover snapped off her mainmast as it hit the seabed, with me desperately clinging onto the mizzenmast with both hands!

Katiward continued to be pummelled by the surf, eventually turning turtle. This movement caused me, still hanging desperately onto the mizzenmast, to slide down the length of the mast, until my left hand got caught among the mizzen shrouds, just below the mast peak – some distance beneath the waves!

I was now deep under the water with my left hand caught in the mizzen shrouds. I could feel my body being waved from side to side like a flag in a boisterous breeze – a position that prevented me from releasing my hand from behind the point where the mizzenmast shrouds were looped over the mast.

"So, this is what death is like were my thoughts at the time?" I can still clearly remember exactly what was going on in my desperate mind at the time, as I wrenched and pulled at my left hand in an effort to free myself from the now bloody shrouds. Those shrouds were wires that I had lovingly spliced, parcelled and served, and now they had me trapped in a seemingly final embrace. I was in danger of drowning, if I couldn't get free!

I could see blood pouring from a gash in my wrist and remember thinking "Sharks can smell blood from miles away, O hell, please don't let them smell my blood!" I realised also that I was going to drown if I couldn't get my hand out from under the shrouds that were trapping it.

I don't recall what happened then but luckily for me, my upturned ship must have entered a pocket of calmer water between a series of waves. This slackening of the water surrounding me allowed me to at last wrench my hand free from the wire shrouds, blood pouring from my left wrist. Someone or something must have been watching over me, for with a mighty twist and a desperate tug, at last my hand came free – with me, lungs near-bursting and screaming for air, kicking for the surface.

How lucky could you be? I am convinced that had Katiward remained in the swirling, rough water much longer, I don't believe that I could have released my hand.

Just as I popped to the surface, I recall being hit in the face, full on by a wave which left me coughing, spluttering and gasping again for breath, scared stiff that I was going to drown, out here in the god-forsaken blood-streaked sea around my injured hand. "Serves me right for leaving Kathie, what a bloody fool you are!" ... This and a whole host of other desperate, stupid thoughts were whizzing through my mind in what seemed an eternity, but probably only lasted for a few seconds.

Just as I was desperately trying to clear my lungs of seawater, I felt a strong hand grab hold of the back of my tee shirt and heard my son Philip's voice shouting above the spray "Hold on, Dad, I've got you. Relax and I will hold your head above water!"

Winded, bleeding and scared, my lower back painful, I had thoughts that my son, our two friends and I were going to die.

In between breaking waves now having drifted to the north of the entrance to Port Macquarie harbour, all four of we shipwrecked mariners floated around for a while, Philip and I not far from our other two companions, all four breasting each wave as it came toward us, while holding an arm up into the air above the water in the hope that someone, anyone – had witnessed our plight. We were sure someone on shore must have seen the incident as we were so close – and called the local coastguard out on our behalf.

After some time treading water, the local volunteer coastguard came belting out toward us from the port and began, in between breaking waves, to haul us one by one into their rubber dinghy. From there it didn't take very long for them to cart three wringing wet crew and one ship's captain in deep shock, bleeding profusely and suffering a terrible pain in my lower back. The pain had probable been caused as I was being waved around under the water, trapped by my left hand at the top of the mizzen mast shrouds of my poor little ship. Katiward's broken hull and what was left of her mainmast had been washed to the north of Port Macquarie harbour. Her hull had been breached which left her wallowing in the surf. Her captain's heart and dreams of sailing the South Seas was broken, his back excruciatingly painful.

I don't remember too much between being hauled out of the water and being driven to Port Macquarie hospital where, in deep shock I was told that it would be sensible if I were to be kept there overnight under observation. My son Philip and our two companions, having lost most of their clothes, were booked into in a local motel. I don't recall much of the rest of that morning and afternoon in the hospital. I was in pain from my back and must have descended into a delirium, being later told that I cried intermittently and was calling out to Philip.

Later in the day, although with my lower back painful each time I moved, my left wrist having required a stitch or two and bandaged, I insisted on leaving the hospital to join Philip, Julie and Garry in their motel. That night was an absolute nightmare, I couldn't sleep and the pain in my back persisted.

The next morning, we accompanied the local police on an inspection of how much of my four years of blood, sweat and now copious tears was left of my little ship, following a nightlong pounding and being beached to the north of Port Macquarie harbour. I also had to report the loss of my ship to the insurance company, who quickly organised a local salvage company to recover the diesel engine and gather whatever else they could retrieve from the by now badly damaged hull.

What was left of Katiward's hull was systematically broken up by chainsaw – its rigging and other components being claimed by some of the local yacht chandlers and others – who were grabbing blocks, lines and whatever other deck equipment they could get their hands on. The sight of all this scavenging of what was left of my little ship sickened me, adding further to the depths of despair and grief I was experiencing on seeing her being ripped apart. It was just like watching a pack of ravenous wolves devouring my dream – cutting out and taking anything that they could salvage, with the agreement of the salvage company, and with me in the meantime deep down in the depths of despair and disbelief at the tragedy of my loss.

It was sickening, I was emotional, crying and wishing that I could be released from what had become a horrible real-life nightmare I was being forced to live through. All four of us had lost everything we had owned on the boat: cameras, money, clothes, tools … everything! At least we had escaped with our lives.

Just the thought that I could have lost my youngest son and my neighbours' two children kept turning my stomach upside down, the emotional waves beating over me to such an extent that that night in the motel with Philip, Julie and Gary, I kept having nightmares in which I was imagining Philip drowning, with me not being able to reach him. I kept waking up, after which I didn't dare to go to sleep for the rest of the night.

The images were so intense. It had been such a horrible and intense an experience that day that for weeks afterwards I would relive what had occurred – vividly and nearly every night, waking up time and again in a muck sweat and feeling like I was going to die under the waves back there, outside Port Macquarie. I later began to realise just how close I had been to drowning, held in the grip of my little ship, under the surface of the sea.

It was lucky for me I guess that I had always been very fit and capable of swimming underwater for nearly a full-length and more of a 50-metre pool. Otherwise I am sure that I would have been unable to hold onto my breath for as long as it took me to get free of the mizzen shrouds and kick up to the surface. And, what if Philip had not been close to where I finally bounced up out of the water? I didn't dare to think about that! He later said that he had been swimming around looking for me and it had seemed ages before I eventually breached, like a small whale just close by.

AFTERMATH OF A NEAR TRAGEDY

The salvage people managed to save most of our joint supply of cash from the wrecked main cabin as their local diver also managed to salvage Katiward's engine, radio and other equipment. Having now some money we were able to use the phone at least to call home and have funds transferred to the local bank, at least enough to pay the motel for the time spent in Port Macquarie and the bus trip back to Melbourne.

Having only my tee shirt and underpants still clinging to me following our rescue, the others similarly, we had kindly been provided with clothes by some of the local people and coastguard crew. We then decided, following a couple of days during which I had to complete police and insurance requirements, to take an interstate bus trip back to Melbourne. Our journey back to Melbourne took nearly two days via Sydney, eventually delivering me into the welcoming arms of a wife, who many hours later met me off the local bus in Mornington. Kathie was both caring while at the same time understandably angry at the antics of her stupid husband, still stiff with back pain and unusually subdued and reflective.

I eventually received the $100,000 insurance, reluctantly paid up by the insurance company. The company tried very hard, but unsuccessfully, to claim that I had deliberately wrecked Katiward to claim the insurance money! Would you believe? Real bastards they had been toward me, trying all the time to press me into accepting less than I had insured my little ship for, all the time trying to prove that it had been my fault that the steering quadrant had failed, the cause of the loss of steering.

It was eventually accepted from a report by the insurance company's technical assessor, that the quadrant's failure had been due to inaccurate machining of a keyway by the local engineer who had carried out the fitting of the steering quadrant to the top of the Katiward's rudderstock. The inaccurate machining had apparently allowed the steering quadrant casting to slowly work loose and eventually to fail completely, resulting in me losing steering control at a critical time, and too close to shore.

Whatever the cause, the loss of Katiward had been devastating, not forgetting that the failure of the quadrant could quite easily have caused my death, and that of my youngest son and two sailing friends. Regrets, I had more than just a few, but what could I do about that? My little ship was now gone.

That period over at last, at least I could get on with my life and try to move on … but to do what now was the question?

As for yachts and sailing, my recent too close a brush with death had left me with little desire to sail, at least until my back had improved. Nor did I feel like even looking at a yacht, or working anywhere near one, particularly while locals knowing me kept asking for information, stating their sadness at my loss, etc. Each time the loss of Katiward was mentioned in conversation or asked about by friends and even strangers, had me feeling a new wave of nausea and mental pain. It got to the stage that I tried wherever possible to avoid any mention of the death of my little ship.

I even tried, unsuccessfully, to blot the incident out of my mind. That was often possible during the day when my mind was occupied with other issues, but it was at night that vivid memories would return, often in overpowering detail, dominating my dreams. Nights like this usually resulted in me awakening in a sweat, my heart pounding.

Kathie would tell me she would often be awakened by my dreaming shouts for Philip and Julie to get off the boat! It was awful and often got to the stage where I tried to remain awake until later at night or into the early hours of the morning, in an attempt to get myself sufficiently tired, in the hope that I would sleep through the night, perhaps avoiding yet another bad dream.

That near-death experience had left me with a painful back that prevented me from returning to running, jogging or even trying to move or turn too quickly for some months following the accident. I learned much later that the injury to my back had probably caused changes to my stance, while trying to cope with the pain, a situation that over the years also affected my walking and running gait. Years later, I often wondered if what had occurred at Port Macquarie boating had caused the gradual wearing down of my left hip joint, a problem requiring me to undergo a total left hip replacement operation during my early seventies?

My nightmares kept on re-occurring for some months following the loss of Katiward. At times, even years later, I recall dreaming that I had managed to salvage her, only to awake to the real world and the realisation that that part of my life had gone forever.

At least my son our friends and I were alive. We may have lost clothes, equipment, cameras as well as me losing my beloved little ship but there was nothing I or anyone else could do to change that fact. It was a case of life goes on.

I was eventually able to accept the loss of my beautiful little ship. At least I had experienced the challenge and joy of being able to build and later, to sail her. All I could do now was to get myself physically and mentally back onto my feet, and get on with life… For the second time, to dust myself off and follow the example of Charlie Chaplin's Little Tramp. To stride down the road once again to see what life tomorrow had in store.

ROUND THE WORLD AND NEON

On receipt of the $100,000 insurance money following the loss of my little ship, it was decided to use some of the money to finance an overseas trip. At least this would be a small way in which I could try to repay Kathie for her support, patience and understanding and what she had had to put up with over the four years of Katiward's construction.

The trip we planned took Kathie and me over to the UK for a tour around the country, also visiting friends and relatives. From where we then flew on to New York where we stayed with Kathie's parents at the Ward family home at Port Jefferson – a famous old whaling town located near the north-eastern tip of Long Island.

Strange as it may seem, once again and for the fourth time, this visit to the US opened up yet another new change in my life and, a very different kind of opportunity to run with. This time, however, opportunity called out from an industry as far removed from that of apparel, textiles, wool or even Victorian hardwood, as it is possible to go.

I have often wondered since, why so many of the unplanned and undreamed-of diversions that changed my business life as a result also effected changes to my personal life. Those changes, when they arrived, managed to bring with them a major, often seemingly illogical change in direction. Twists and turns that from time to time served to re-route my life's thread. What superior force had prompted these abrupt changes, appearing as often as they did 'out of the blue', continues to remain a mystery.

Each unplanned change I found myself making, strangely and mysteriously occurred at a then pivotal point in my life. This thought has often led me to question whether there is truth in the view of some, that an all-powerful being or other of that ilk, is lurking around somewhere out there in the cosmos – perhaps watching over us? Such thoughts have often lead me also to wonder – but not too much and not for too long – before finding myself once again jumping into whatever life, and the universe had decided for me at the time.

I have over the years since concluded that wondering too much about "what It (life) is all about" and trying to find answers to questions around what fate and life occasionally conjures up for we humans, offers the distinct possibility of driving one crazy – to little or no advantage. That being the case, many years ago I decided to stop wondering about such stuff, to accept the inevitable, then try to concentrate my mind on getting on with whatever life has decided to throw my way.

It also goes to the question of why so many people I have met over the years struggle to resist change, particularly if that means them having to accept a change in direction from one occupation, job, industry or place of living, to something a little or a lot different to their original training or location. Others, on the other hand, seem to find change much easier to accept and cope with, some even experience a great deal of stimulation in the very act of changing, whether it be in the form of a personal relationship, a place of work, industry, a move to a different city or even perhaps a move to a new country?

I have come to the conclusion that the very act of throwing oneself into the ready acceptance of change can often prove good for the soul, and, an individual's state of mind. Living as we do today in this sometimes crazy, fast-changing and often dangerous world, it seems to me that the future demands of life, living as we do on this fast-changing planet, that people need to prepare themselves – just in case the need to make a change arrives at some time in our lives. The question here: "Are you sufficiently prepared to cope with change if and when it arrives and knocks on your door?"

Finding oneself faced with an opportunity to move from one industry, location, city or country to another, regardless of any differences between the former and situation ahead – could certainly pose a challenge, possibly even an opportunity, my next move being one such example.

So here I was once again, this time having recently lost my little ship and now on a round-the-world trip. While visiting the US, could I once again find myself on the cusp of a new challenge?

NEON AND COLD CATHODE

It was during our visit to the US and an unplanned off-the-cuff tour that had been arranged for Kathie and me to fill in a daylong visit to relatives in New Jersey, that I once again found myself entering a new phase of my business life.

Kathie and I found ourselves visiting a factory manufacturing components used by the neon/cold cathode industry. Having a few hours to spare, Kathie's uncle, the production manager with EGL, one of the world's leading manufacturers and suppliers of cold cathode[1] components, had invited us both for a tour of the plant, based in New Jersey. It was during our tour that I got to meet with Frank Cortese, the president of EGL and one of the industry's earlier pioneers.

A day or so following our visit to EGL I was approached and asked if I would have the time available on my return to Melbourne to carry out some basic market research for the company. The research as proposed was apparently needed to provide data that EGL could use to assess whether there existed any scope for the company to gain a share of the Australian market. If the research proved positive, the company planned to explore the possibility of gaining entry to the market. Neon sales in Australia at the time was dominated by a rival British neon/cold cathode component manufacturer, known to enjoy a virtual monopoly both there and in nearby New Zealand.

EGL, one of the world's two leading manufacturers and suppliers of products used by the neon/cold cathode signage and architectural lighting industries, had over the years been considering how to set up a branch in Australia. They had a problem in defining the best way of going about the project. So, here was me, once again blasting off into what – I didn't know?

EGL's problem sounded interesting, and having nothing in mind that was pressing me at the time, I agreed to assist on my return to Melbourne.

On returning home I set about researching the Australian neon and cold cathode lighting industry. I had also been requested to make recommendations to EGL on a workable course of action, should my research result in a positive conclusion.

My subsequent study of the Australian market for neon and its associated products proved positive, in that it did offer EGL the opportunity to gain a reasonable share of the market, provided they could set up to stock, distribute and promote EGL neon tubing and associated products, at a competitive price.

Notes

1. A *cold cathode* is a *cathode* that is not electrically heated by a filament. A *cathode* may be considered *cold* if it emits more electrons than can be supplied by thermionic emission alone. It is used in gas-discharge lamps, such as neon lamps, discharge tubes, and some types of vacuum tube. Neon lighting and signage is a popular form of cold cathode illumination.

JEFFERSON BAY NEON

Following receipt of my report and recommendations, I was offered the opportunity to set up an EGL distributorship across the Australian and New Zealand. Thinking things over, even though I had absolutely no understanding of the technicalities relating to high-voltage cold cathode lighting systems, it seemed that fate had knocked on my door once again – at just the right time for me to branch off into yet another, totally different industry, my fourth major change to date.

My plans to write it seems, would once again need to be delayed, just a little longer.

The neon signage and cold cathode architectural lighting industry was unrelated to any of my earlier training, or experience, but what the hell? I was a fast learner.

Neon and cold cathode lighting and signage production used highly specialised technology, equipment and intricate manufacturing processes. This was a task that first of all required me to undertake and get my head around an in-depth technical training course, provided by EGL. The course proved to be an intensive programme that covered the design, manufacture, installation and testing of high-voltage, low ampere cold cathode and similar types of lighting systems. Cold cathode systems at the time were being specified and used extensively in the US and many other markets worldwide, including domestic and architectural lighting and signage. Signage systems using handcrafted, gas-filled glass tubing were universally known throughout the world as neon.

The possibility of gaining market share against a well-entrenched opponent, and one who currently dominated the Australian market, presented a challenge. For someone who only recently had suffered a tragic bereavement (death of my little ship Katiward) and in the process had nearly succeeded in drowning himself, the challenge of taking up the cudgels on behalf of EGL seemed to pale into insignificance. Having also recently returned from a difficult and frustrating time trying to increase sales of Australian wool in the United States, I was now 'fully open' to any new possibility, difficult or otherwise – any new project through which to dust myself off, twirl my imagined Charlie Chaplin-style walking stick and strike out along the road to wherever!

Even though at the time I had no background or even a basic understanding of high-voltage cold cathode lighting systems, I did know something about colour and good design, as a result of my earlier training in textile design. That, I mused, should, at the very least, prove to be a good enough basis from which to make a start.

November 10th 1978 saw the registration of the Jefferson Bay Company Pty Ltd, a few months following my escape from the cruel sea. But as they say, whoever the ubiquitous 'they' happen to be? "Life goes on" and the death of my little ship, no matter how hard that had been for me to take at the time, was now in the past.

Before I could even launch myself into this new venture, it would be necessary to undertake a great deal of technical study to gain a firm grasp of the specialised technology involved, before attempting to approach sign and architectural lighting companies. I needed also to be at least as informed as those individuals and companies operating in the industry – otherwise, the project upon which I was about to launch myself would more than likely end in failure.

At EGL's headquarters and production plant based in Newark, New Jersey, I spent time learning all I could about the history of cold cathode, high-voltage transformer installation systems and testing, including low ampere lighting system specifying, their installation, wiring and associated componentry. I later attended an intensive technical course in Melbourne that provided me with a Victorian State approved 'N' licence. This licence, issued by the then Victorian State Electricity Commission, certified me as competent to design cold cathode installations and test/approve neon and cold cathode lighting installations throughout the state.

Now fully armed technically and having gained working familiarity with the equipment, testing and processes involved in the manufacture of neon tubing and signage, 1989 saw me venturing out for the very first time into the local market as the EGL Company's official Australian representative. Products including neon tubing, electrodes, high-voltage transformers, various gases, pumping and vacuum equipment were then offered to the local sign trade, in addition to a complete range of other associated signage testing equipment and accessories. Some of the insurance money received upon the death of my little ship provided the financial feedstock upon which Jefferson Bay Neon was launched.

All now in place, saw the commencement of business on behalf of EGL via the sale of sign and lighting componentry to sign and architectural lighting companies, both large and small, across every state in Australia. Some months later I commenced initial activities aimed at expanding the business into New Zealand via a local agent based in Auckland.

CONSULTANT – ARCHITECTURAL LIGHTING

The 1990s also witnessed the near demise of the Australian wool industry, a situation when it occurred in 1991 that found within me deep feelings of regret and sometimes anger. At times, the latter bubbled over, as I looked back over years of sheer incompetence and a lack of leadership among those responsible for bringing the Australian wool industry to its knees. While there was little, if anything that I could do now, the situation that had arrived as expected, left me feeling sad to now see all that I, and many others like me had worked for, now lying in a very expensive, tragic heap.

A new neon and cold cathode distribution company, Jefferson Bay Neon (JBN) had been born. It soon would grow and prosper to the point where my new company eventually succeeded in capturing an estimated 40% of the Australian neon sign componentry market. Hard work and the determination to succeed had achieved much, in spite of the later entry of other competitive suppliers that followed JBN/EGL into the local market.

In addition to supplying components, it was later decided to take advantage of my earlier training in textiles and apparel, calling on some of my textile colour and design skills and adapting them toward the design, specification and marketing of white and coloured cold cathode lighting systems to architectural and developer groups. This new branch of the business was developed and marketed separately to neon signage.

Later in my new career I was invited to write a series of technical articles for one of Australia's sign industry magazines. I was later invited to present a technical/creative information workshop to a broad grouping of architects, lighting designers and developers, at a major Southeast Asian architectural lighting convention in Singapore. My architectural lighting activities were added to later with a presentation and technical demonstration at a sign exhibition in Jakarta.

I also became involved with the establishment of a new professional association of companies involved with the design, manufacture and installation of illuminated signage – Neon and Illuminated Sign Association of Australia (NISA).

WHERE TO FROM HERE?

Having built up and expanded the signage and architectural lighting business to the point when it had become satisfyingly profitable, I was beginning, once again, to feel the need (rather the itch) for yet another change in direction. Change, it seems, was a state of mind that appealed to me.

Following a lean first year of trading since the establishment of JBN, during which time I had put in a lot of work, long hours and financial resources just to get the business off from ground zero, JBN had now started to blossom. The company's sales had expanded beyond its original role of servicing the neon signage industry, now offering additional services: specification writing and technical testing. The scope of services now being offered further enabled expansion of the neon/cold cathode componentry side of company sales. JBN was now achieving success well beyond my original expectations.

After four years trading and constant monitoring of the Australian sign and architectural industry, both were beginning to show clear signs that other lighting and sign systems, less prone to breakage and easier and safer to install, were being developed and improving rapidly. Some were being offered in the form of LEDs (light emitting diodes) and fibre optics.

The fragility of and specialised skills and cost required to produce, install and service glass neon tubing, was hastening the constant search for an alternative, by sign installers, designers and sign company owners. All were on the lookout for a more efficient lighting system, one that could replace the often breakage prone and costly to install and repair, neon. An increasing number of the newer systems being developed were proving more robust and economic, in terms of their cost, ease of installation, power usage and longevity.

One obvious downside to the use of neon signage and cold cathode lighting was the specialised hand skills involved with the manual manipulation of small diameter glass tubing into the various forms necessary, then attachment of electrodes to each end. Also included here were potential problems, particularly when dealing with the type of high-voltage transformers required for cold cathode. On the electrical side, these installations required close consideration of tube 'loading' – calculations requiring the careful balancing of tubing to transformer. The latter aspect alone, when added to the dangers inherent in 'stray capacitance'[1] and other potential fire safety issues, makes neon/cold cathode systems more vulnerable to fire and breakdown than other sign and lighting systems.

I had already received a few expressions of interest to buy the business – offers to which I was starting to give serious consideration.

Selling JBN while it was going well, would release me to look to other possibilities. It would also allow me perhaps to embark on a long-delayed career as a writer, something that continued to lurk in the back of my mind. Writing had always represented an interest, from the first time I had enjoyed learning a little of the gentle art of painting pictures with words as a student at Harehills Secondary Modern School, many years ago back in Leeds. Years spent bringing up children and pursuing a career had pushed my earlier desire to write, well into the background. During those years, particularly while working with AWC in Australia and the US, I had made notes on issues and my experiences, with the thought that sometime in the future I might find the time write about them.

I eventually decided that the timing was right to sell my interests in JBN. The sale was completed to one of my interstate agents, Russell Signs – an Adelaide-based sign company. Interestingly, following the sale of JBN, the purchasers wished me to continue to run the business under its original name, initially from Melbourne.

Thus, having now sold the business for a satisfactory price, I found myself still managing it – but without the financial responsibility involved as its owner. Not only that but the Adelaide buyer invited me to join their board of directors. This arrangement lasted for a few years, until the Adelaide management decided to take over the running of JBN from Adelaide.

I had been well recompensed financially for the years spent in the neon/cold cathode industry. My new situation and financial position now freed me from the need to take on a new business venture, whatever that proved to be, or to make a start on my long-delayed writing career.

The security gained as a result of the sale of Jefferson Bay Neon, provided space during which to look forward to the next stage of my business career. I didn't need to earn a living from writing, but if some recompense ensued, why not take a stab at doing something, that from my boyhood days had a loomed large as a career option that had interested, but to date eluded me?

I had never seen myself as a writer of fiction, although as a boy I had attempted to write short stories. As my life has progressed, changed and teetered along on its tortured, sometimes frustrating but always interesting path, writing about real-life situations, while expressing views based on my many and varied experiences, was perhaps the answer I was searching for?

On the more personal side of my life, with the failure of two reasonably long marriages, followed later by a long de-facto relationship, I cannot in all honesty claim to much in the way of success when it comes to relationships with the women in my life. I had at the very least managed to win the love of at least three beautiful, talented women. I also count myself lucky to have been able to experience the joy of becoming the father of four children, now grown up, having presented me with five grandchildren and, to date, three great-grandchildren.

Notes

1. Stray capacitance is unintended and unwanted capacitance in a circuit. Capacitance doesn't exist only within capacitors. In fact, any two surfaces at different electric potential, and that are close enough together to generate an electric field have capacitance, and thus act like a capacitor. Such effects are often present within circuits (for example between conductive runs or component leads), even though they are not intended. This unintended capacitance is referred to as stray capacitance, and it can result in a disruption of normal current flow within a circuit.

CONSUMER ADVOCATE – REAL ESTATE

Coincidental with departure from the neon and cold cathode industry and the ending of my marriage to Kathie, the universe once again seems to have decided on a different course for my life. Once again, I was destined to venture into another totally different set of experiences – this time a career involving the real estate industry.

My second wife Kathie and I had parted a few years earlier. During the first few years of my association with the third love story of my life, a long, often stormy de-facto relationship with Pierina, an artistic, vivacious multi-talented Australian born lady of Italian heritage, I became directly involved with a court case that set the scene for my entry into career number five.

My next acute change in direction followed the unsuccessful auction sale by Pierina and I of our earlier home, an extensively renovated heritage-listed terrace house located at 100 Carlton Street, in the desirable inner northern Melbourne suburb of Carlton.

Pierina and I had earlier bought the property, which for many years prior had been allowed to run down, being used by its previous owners as student accommodation. Over the years the property had been allowed to deteriorate, although the outer shell and roof of the house were still in good order. Following our purchase of the property it was gutted, following which, we commissioned an architect friend, Joe Toscano, who transformed the house into a modern, award-winning residence.

After years of residence along with Erica and Leon, Pierina's children, both of whom had bestowed on me the honour and joy of being adopted as their father figure, it was decided to sell the property following Pierina's and my decision to go our separate ways.

The sale programme of our property, an auction that took place in March 2002, was a disaster. It had been a sale for which at the very beginning, we had defined a specific minimum price to our selling agent-principal. The subsequent auction and the agent's unilateral decision to indulge in the questionable practice of 'underquoting' our property to potential buyers, led to a failed auction.

Dissatisfaction with the manner in which the agent had conducted our selling programme, and our subsequent refusal to pay for advertising developed by the agency, prompted us to take our complaint regarding his unauthorised underquoting and associated activities, to the Victorian Civil and Administrative Tribunal (VCAT).

During VCAT's hearing of our case, we successfully claimed that the agent-principal had deliberately misquoted (under-quoted) the minimum price that we had previously set for the sale of our home.

As a result of our case before VCAT, we learned that the agent involved had referred to his experience with us as having to deal with what he, very poetically, termed as "vendors from hell". The case proved to be one of the first to have been won by a property vendor against the real estate agency involved, on the basis of the agent deliberately and knowingly underquoting our price to potential purchasers. Our successful action was against the Melbourne-based Woodards Group.

The result of our dispute was later featured on Melbourne's Channel Nine, a local TV news station, it was also used as a case study in a book published a little later by Terry Ryder, a local writer on real estate matters. His book is titled "Real Estate without Agents".

The case, strange as it may seem, led on to the next stage of my business career. Yet another strange twist of fate in a business life that still appeared happy to continue to waltz along on its own merry, twisting and turning way, without any assistance or guidance from me!

Our real estate agency opponent later approached and invited me to a coffee and a chat at his offices in Carlton.

John Piccolo, the agency-principal, had apparently been thinking how he could establish a point of difference between his group of agencies, and his competition. During our conversation, he offered me a role with his group, which comprised a number of individually owned agencies. The position proposed was one of working alongside him in the suggested role of 'independent client advocate'.

The position, as he explained it, was to be one in which I was to be available to any client of the group who wished, as the result of them having a problem or dispute with one or other of the group's real estate sales or property management agents, to appeal and establish a claim against the group, or an individual agent operating within any one of the Woodards Group offices.

While not being even in the slightest interested in becoming involved with a real estate agency, it occurred to me that his proposal could be turned to something positive. Taking up his offer would enable me to gain valuable access to the inside workings of a real estate agency group, offering the later possibility of using the knowledge gained, for inclusion in a book. This coincidentally had been a subject that I had already decided to write about following our recent successful experience at the VCAT.

Accepting the offer to join the Woodards Group, it was agreed, that I would be authorised to act with full independence in the unique role of client advocate. Any of the group's clients wishing to raise an issue or register a complaint against any one of the group's offices, or any one individual sales agent or rental property manager operating from any Woodards branded office were to have direct access to the group's new client advocate.

Thus commenced a period of varied, often illuminating experiences during which I found myself having to deal with a wide variety of cases, many involving minor – or in one or two cases, serious – breaches of rules governing the sale or rental of real estate.

My new role continued for four years until I finally decided that the time had arrived to pull back from the day-to-day world of real estate – at least from continuing to be a salaried person, independent or otherwise!

The role I had occupied with the Woodards Group, a first I believe anywhere in Australia for a person to operate as a true client advocate from within an agency, and in a demonstrably independent capacity, had further delayed my growing desire to spend as many of my future years travelling – at the same time as trying to become a reasonably interesting writer.

The experiences and contacts gained during the four years of my involvement with the Woodards Group, had added to my already broad understanding of how the Victorian real estate industry operated. Involvement with agency operations from the inside, provided valuable first-hand data and day-to-day experiences that later resulted in my first book.[1]

Notes

1. Earlier books: See details listed at the beginning of this book.

AT LAST – PUBLISHED WRITER

Following the ending of my association with the Woodards Group, a couple of years earlier I finally reached a status generally spoken of these days as 'semi-retired'. Retirement, although a word that according to my trusty dictionary is described as, "to give up work", plays no part in my idea of how to spend one's later years. Retirement is not the status that I have in mind, or a description of my intended route from here on in.

Apart from using the diary notes I had amassed following my four-year career as client advocate in the real estate industry, and eight years working for Australian wool, I was now at the point where I could at last spend the time necessary to learn to become a reasonably interesting writer.

Poetry, apart from a couple of feeble attempts at trying to smooth over oft-strained relationships with the loves in my life, rarely proved successful, at least for me. I decided therefore to try my hand at writing non-fiction, primarily about subjects I either know something about from my own life's experiences, or situations related to the world and events that I feel deeply about. Maybe I could write something that some future descendant of mine may find to be of passing interest, sometime during the second decade of the 22nd century?

So, once again seeking to follow the example of my favourite silent movie character Charlie Chaplin: It's time to pick myself up, brush myself off, kick up my heels, take up my pen – and wander off down the road to find some further adventure…

What has followed to date has included a series of yearly travels across the world and four previous books – now five, if I am to include the one you have just read through and, I hope, enjoyed?

EPILOGUE

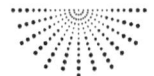

Question:

What have I learned from my years of successes, failures and more than a few disappointments, that all too often have accompanied me throughout this long and varied life? Have I learned anything of enduring value worthy of communication to the world at large? And, even if I have, will anyone be interested enough to listen?

When the time arrives for me to return whence I came a near lifetime ago, will I have left anything worthy of being passed on to the generations that follow?

NEARING THE TOP OF THE MOUNTAIN

An elderly tailor alongside whom I worked for a short while as a young 'improver', used to express the view that growing older could be likened to climbing a mountain. The theory here appeared to be that the higher one climbed, the further one would be capable of seeing and thus, he regularly liked to explain to his then young work companion, the wiser one should become. Note the word used here was 'should'.

Now nearing the summit of that mythical mountain of which my then mentor used to speak, I am not so sure about his theory. While one might well suggest that the getting of age should allow one to see further back in time, as to equating that with the gaining of wisdom – I think the jury is still out on that score?

Trying to look back, while endeavouring to objectively review a lifetime that is gradually nearing its final stanza, is one thing. Seeking to provide coherent answers to the question of what an individual gains in terms of wisdom as they progress through life is another.

To search one's past life is similar to trying to look backward in time through a telescope, as we search and scan the faraway reaches of the cosmos. The images to be found there are often at best distorted and indistinct, the distances so great as to be beyond most of our imaginations.

The same can also be said when trying to look back while endeavouring to draw objective conclusions as a result of the various experiences, beliefs and prejudices that have built up and eventually become the theme of one's life.

LOOKING BACK

Much water has flowed under the bridge since my own story began, and I continue to live through a period during which many momentous world events continue to occur. It is also true to say that technological changes that my generation has been lucky enough to experience, have been much broader than my parents witnessed during their relatively long lives.

The way we live today and the way in which we perceive changes and their effect on us as we carry on with our relatively short individual lives, often tends to get lost among a whole host of other invading issues. Changes such as these I have come to regard as 'background noise'.

Our lives, thankfully, are sometimes punctuated by a few small successes. At the very least, they can at times serve to wrap a warm glow around us for the usually short time that glow remains. These occasions may offer a false sense of security and encourage an overly high opinion of our self-importance.

Problems, real and imagined, may occasionally hurt us. They may also serve to stunt our growth and confidence in ourselves, depending on how we perceive and deal, both with them and other setbacks that all must face at some time during our journey through life. Issues like these however, can also provide the inspiration needed for us to get back on our feet, dust ourselves off and amble off into a different direction.

Let me digress a little here to describe what life was like for me as a boy growing up in faraway Yorkshire, the better part of a century ago. I have on occasions found it useful and at times educational just to try going through the exercise of wandering back in time, especially when trying to relate to how far I have come following growing up in a country during an era now slipping away into the pages of history.

Doing so may sometimes emerge as a relatively useless occupation, as well as being an exercise in futility? On the other hand, doing just that could also serve to provide a better understanding of how far our lives and experiences have taken us. A chance also perhaps to learn from past mistakes.

Looking back while comparing then with now, a time that found my generation growing up amid a devastating world war and the later threat of nuclear annihilation, we find ourselves living in a fast-moving, overcrowded, still dangerous world. In that world are a growing number of fellow planet dwellers, people trying to leave the lands of their birth – a struggle that finds them trying desperately to find a safer, happier place that will accept and allow them to settle. All they seek is to be free to live their lives in peace, and be safe from danger. Others among us, having better luck as a result of the accident of their time and country of birth, are casting their eyes beyond this world, looking outward toward space, seeking to explore distant planets, and galaxies.

Allow me to tell you a little more about my generation, as I wander back a few decades into the last century…

In contrast to today, the life experiences of a boy born during the 1930s are often considered to have been much narrower than one growing up today. Not necessarily so. In a purely physical sense, my boyhood during the 1930s and 1940s were not nearly as narrow as some might think.

As a boy, my pals and I were regularly able and confident to roam well beyond our homes. Interestingly, while doing so it was without fear of getting lost, being attacked or physically or sexually abused, as we went about exploring far and wide, bird nesting, fishing, collecting frogs, newts and sticklebacks (small fishes). We sometimes played 'hooky' from school and got involved with a range of activities that could be described as bordering on nefarious, even illegal – too many to now recall in detail.

We kids 'played out' a great deal, in and around our local streets, while our families and we intermingled much more. The intermingling was unavoidable for most of the time, a consequence of families having to live amid miles and miles of narrow streets, and little houses in which it was possible to listen into an argument, or the next-door neighbour's overloud radio set through thin dividing walls. Privacy in those days was at a premium and near impossible to achieve in Harehills.

Our school and the extensive web of streets and factory yards that surrounded us formed the virtual front garden in which we played. Most of the houses around where I grew up had little, in most cases nothing, that came anywhere close to a small garden attached to our small back-to-back homes. Our worldview was the local streets, a few churchyards here and there and the local cemetery, among which we kids played rounders[1] and other of our favourite games like cricket, hide-and-seek, kick-out-ball, whip'n top – and many others.

As kids, we were always in the process of innovating. Inventing new games to play and things to make, do and experiment with – things that we ourselves had to discover how to do, make and improvise, as our parents were unable to buy us expensive new toys. Our efforts even went as far as scavenging for the materials with which to build a billycart or snow-sled, for when the winter arrived.

In spite of the dangers to life that swirled around Leeds during six years of war, we managed to feel secure, at the same time receiving what perhaps could be described as a broad grounding in life and living, even as the war and its consequences raged around us, only ending a few months following my tenth birthday.

I was to have my first viewing of television on being invited one evening to a friend's house, his family financially able to afford one, early in the 1950s. Wrist radios were a fantasy of the future, as were computers, electronic notebooks, smart-phones, calculators and every other kind of electronic gadgetry that fills so much of a modern-day boy's world. Our first family telephone was a shared line with a next-door neighbour, also installed during the early 1950s, along with our first taste of the luxury of electrically heated water for our once weekly family bath night.

While aware that there was a war going on at the time, as a boy I was blissfully unaware of the real dangers the war represented, only fearing attack, usually during the regular, frightening nightly bombing raids on my home city during the early years of the 1940s.

Between the ages of 4 and 11, I attended an ordinary state school where I learned to read and write well, also gaining a good working understanding of mathematics. Between then and the age of 15, I received a firm grounding in the arts, basic science and the history of living things.

While once or twice teetering on the edge of juvenile delinquency, I learned to respect the law, and the friendly helmeted local policeman – a helpful man who patrolled his daily beat in and around my street.

Recalling also that in 1940s Britain – in addition to living under the threat of constant German air raids and the need to be evacuated from Leeds to the country village of Rufforth in North Yorkshire, we students still had to cope with learning to add, subtract, multiply and divide the tortured British currency of the day – pounds, shillings and pence.

We also had to cope with a long-outdated measurement system, in the form of miles, furlongs, yards, feet and inches, the latter that we learned to divide into halves, quarters, eights and often infuriating sixteenths, and more. There also existed acres, poles and perches. Add to this tons, hundredweights, stones, pounds and ounces. Each of these 'Imperial' systems of measurement required a different scale by which to calculate when making comparisons. All required us calculate and compare – without the assistance of a pocket calculator, laptop, computer or slide rule!

I left school at the age of 15, the product, not of a university, private school or college, but the British state school system. This was followed later by tertiary textile and apparel studies at the Leeds College of Technology.

By the time I left my local 'Secondary Modern' school, I was capable of reading any book written in English. I understood and could analyse its structure. I possessed a practical grasp of English grammar and could use, write and spell words correctly. I could also consider a piece of prose or poetry, prepare a reasonably intelligent essay and argument, compose a letter and put together a descriptive article, painting the required picture of what I wished to communicate, in reasonably clear English words.

As a result of my school years, I learned of the world's early explorers and thinkers, the histories of the British Isles and the ancient Greeks and Romans. I learned much about the history of the Arabs, Jews, and other ancient tribes who for many centuries were known to inhabit what we now refer to as the Middle East. I was also able to gain a firm grasp of the history and subsequent collapse of the Russian Czarist and Ottoman empires earlier in the 20th century. I learned about the discovery and development of the Americas, India and China. Add to these the history of Australia – at least that part of Australian history following the arrival of James Cook, during the latter end of the 18th century.

I grew into my teens having escaped injury resulting from German bombing. Unfortunately, however, I was to feel first-hand what it was like to be hunted, ridiculed, physically attacked, beaten up and left bleeding – just because my family were Jewish. As a boy, I experienced physical pain and anguish, as both were meted out, when they were able to corner me, by other boys who, from the safety of one or other of the local gangs, seemed to get a great kick out of beating up one small Jewish kid that they claimed had had some connection with the killing of their lord and saviour Jesus – also a Jewish guy it seems, who lived 2,000 years ago!

I accept the fact that the lives of children today are different in any number of ways to the way life was lived back in the 1940s. They, like I used to be, are the products of a modern world, their lives in tune with the needs today, its technical trappings, issues and education system.

Unfortunately, the children of today are growing up in a country and under an economy that over recent years, despite the claims of successive national governments, has proved unable to provide a working environment in which most young people have the later promise of a regular job following their emergence from university, private or state school. Working-class parents today struggle to provide their children with an education that will provide them with an equal opportunity to achieve later success in their lives.

Australia in 2017, a country with vast open living spaces, a range of natural resources the envy of a world, a healthy climate and sufficient food enough to feed much more than its present 24-plus million population, has failed to live up to the expectations of most of its citizens.

While their parents struggle to maintain a reasonable standard of living at a time where the national government is unable (or unwilling) to provide today's school-leavers with the promise of a permanent and reasonably well-paid job, the children of today's Australia have an even bleaker future to look forward to than I had on my arrival in Australia during 1959.

Notes

1. Rounders: A ball game similar to baseball, usually played with a tennis ball.

WHERE ARE WE NOW?

I could write more about how I feel about the world that now surrounds me, in particular, and perhaps more important, how I feel about Australia – the country to which I had the good sense to emigrate and make my home, so many years ago.

While searching for a reasonably accurate way in which to present my thoughts, I think it would assist, if I were to commence with a summary of two pieces of contemporary literature. Both serve to describe feelings and observations similar to my own, but perhaps expressed more succinctly than I am able to. Their authors express varied but strong views about Australia and the course the country now seems to be taking.

The first of these is an essay titled "What Happened to You Our Open, Welcoming Land?" It was published in the *Sydney Morning Herald* on January 26th 2014, its author essayist and writer Alex Miller. The book, titled "Australia's Second Chance", was published in 2015, its author George Megalogenis.

Both are Australians. In these and other of their writings, both have provided interesting and incisive descriptions of the way modern Australia has developed. Both are at times critical and question the way in which Australia is currently presenting itself to the world.

The Miller essay dealt mainly with the still current vexatious and divisive issue of immigration, in which he makes some incisive observations, among them: "The generous spirit towards new arrivals has grown cold and now we stand at a crossroads."

When I first read Miller's essay, it expressed much of that which I, also like him being a £10 immigrant British 'Pom', have come to feel as well as fear about my adopted country's future direction and its place in a smaller, closer and continually troubled world.

In his essay, Miller wrote about the many cultural changes that have occurred in Australia, changes that had been driven by generations of immigrants. Like Miller, I too often pride myself on being what he referred to himself as "an exemplary outsider".

Unlike Miller, I don't have much in the way of recall, of being referred to or having felt that I was being treated as an outsider by any of the native-born Australians among whom I lived and have worked for over 50 years. He does, however, make the prediction – that the Australia of tomorrow will not be the same as today, writing, "If we hang onto the same old verities, we end up talking to ourselves, and a few stodgy old mates just like ourselves, because everyone else has moved on." This is a telling statement, the truth of which continues to carry steadily increasing weight, as the country wanders on toward the third decade of a new but troubled century.

On the question of migration to Australia, Miller made the telling point in his essay that Australia is a wealthy country and that we have been lucky. He offered the thought that we Australians at times have been thoughtful and planned well enough to have experienced 20 years of consistent increase in the country's net wealth. This, he wrote, "makes us rich by any world standard". While accepting this, I would prefer to add in the words "Some Australians" here, as not many are enjoying the undoubted riches that have come the country's way over the past two decades. Such a trend bodes ill for the future of Australia, if allowed to continue for much longer.

It is true to assert that recent years have seen a widening gap opening up between the rich and comfortable in Australia, and those who continue to struggle to keep themselves, their families and their financial heads and lives 'above water'. The lot of the latter group today is tending to become even worse than it was in 2014 when Miller published his essay.

Miller went on to note that in years past, Australia had opened its borders to many thousands of Vietnamese and Cambodian people who were then seeking refuge from tyranny and an extended and bloody war in their countries, he also wrote:

> Although we were poorer in those days, we nevertheless seemed to have enough to share around. Or we thought we did. And no one today, looking at the cultural enrichment that followed from this act of neighbourly largesse, would suggest we were mistaken in making these people welcome among us back then; people who have, of course, since then become us.

Referring to the migration to Australia of Vietnamese in particular, Miller also offered the comment, "It was a good thing to do, and we did it well back then. We felt some responsibility for those people and their needs."

We Australians need to think a great deal more about this view, particularly when contrasting what a smaller number of Australians were able to achieve earlier, against the current government's harsh and devious attitude to refugees appealing to today's Australia for protection from fear and danger, and a place in which to settle peacefully.

Relating to Australia's current treatment of refugees, I also often ask myself: "Don't we Australians bear at least some responsibility to the many Iraqis, Afghans and Syrians, for the currently disastrous state of their countries?" We after all were and are still involved with bombing and other military activities in their countries, aggressive actions that have contributed in a direct way to their becoming refugees.

Miller's essay goes on to describe what had happened to an earlier Australia under Hawke, Keating and Fraser, a time when we accepted our responsibilities to those genuine refugees seeking sanctuary. I would add the suggestion that many of those displaced as a result of recent incursions into their countries in which Australia was involved have a valid claim to be granted sanctuary here.

Miller also referred in his essay to the lack of forward thinking that resulted in the decision taken by Australia's federal parliament, when Prime Minister Howard found it so easy to plunge Australia into the US's original and ill-thought-through assaults on Iraq and Afghanistan. I would go even further here and question why it remains within the sole power of the Australian prime minister of the day, to be able to decide, without a parliamentary vote, to commit the country to war – any war?

I, like Miller, believe that we, Australians in general, are still the generous people I came to know as a new 24-year-old migrant who arrived here in 1959.

Miller went on to make the further point, "Surely we will find the decency to deal with the problem of refugees arriving here by boat? Surely we can't go on deciding not who comes to Australia, but who goes to Manus Island? It is a Guantanamo solution and we all know it is immoral and deeply un-Australian in its meanness." The great irony here is that Afghans were some of the earliest successful settlers in this country.

Megalogenis' book travels a different path. This book provides a comprehensive analysis of Australia's development from the time that some regard as Britain's invasion of a then long-settled and peaceful Terra Australis, in 1788. A continent that at the time was regarded by Britain as 'terra nullius'.

Megalogenis also draws out and writes comprehensively and in great detail about the factors that have paved the way along which the country has developed and moved on from the beginnings of Western settlement, through to the present day.

While he regularly includes references to how the various tides of immigration have benefited the development of Australia, he also analyses in detail how different periods of more restrictive immigration and related government policies have created the reverse effect.

Megalogenis'[1] book discusses Australia's ongoing development in three parts: *The Rise*, *The Fall*, and *The Return*, each part plotting the course the country and its people have taken, up to what he refers to as, "the longest boom – Australia in the 20th century". He noted further:

> Our periods of strongest migration have been our most successful; our busts are distinguished by the closing of our doors, through policies of racial selection and import protection.

Megalogenis also noted that Australia's least productive and most divisive eras have been those in which migration was at its lowest ebb, in the early decades of convict settlement in the half-century-long stagnation of 'White Australia', from the 1880s until the end of the Second World War.

Migration is also the main theme here, the author making the further point that migration is the greatest compliment that can be paid to a nation. He comments further that for the second time in history, a significant share of skilled arrivals are choosing Australia over the United States.

Notes

1. "Australia's Second Chance – What Our History Tells Us about Our Future", Author: George Megalogenis, published by Penguin Books.

LOOKING TO THE FUTURE

At the time of my arrival in Australia in 1959, close ties remained between Britain and its one-time colony down under. Australia was still in the early stages of easing its way, tentatively at first, alongside a defined cultural cringe, as the country edged away toward an existence increasingly distant from the earlier overpowering influence of Britain.

For the greater part of the 20th century, Australia continued to exhibit a residual form of obsequiousness in its relationship with 'Mother England', a status I think best described as a form of 'colonial Britishness'.

During the 1950s and 1960s, most of the older generation of Australians that I was to meet, now having emerged from a period during which they were considered to be as British as we British-born newcomers, continued to regard the British flag, the Union Jack, as their own.

Former 1914–1918 and Second World War 'diggers' continued to talk of "fighting under our flag". In reality, the flag they were talking about was dominated by the flag of Britain – the 'Union Jack', even though the flag also included the stars of the Southern Cross, plus one other star – a kind of second thought, a design that stated clearly that the country flying it continued to be dominated by Britain.

For many years before the Second World War, Australia's national symbol had remained virtually the same as the flag that flew over a then distant British colonial outpost, over a century earlier. It is often pointed out by visitors that the current Australian flag, to all intents and purposes, is similar to that of neighbouring New Zealand, each often mistaken for the other by foreigners.

Both countries' citizens were at the time also considered to be British. Not so of course in the case of Australia's Aboriginal population.

Both countries' flags continue to remain a point of interesting discussion that has often created questions and prompted amused confusion in the minds of foreign visitors. Many continue to question whether Australia's flag continues to represent the country's continuing subservience to Britain in some way?

I would suspect that many among today's Australian citizens, like me, find it regrettable that nowhere on our flag is there a representation of Australia's true heritage, something more representative of the continent's history and character, whose origins go back much further in time than 1788. Surely the time has arrived for the nation to be thinking to adopt a design that more accurately represents a now modern, independent Australia? Take as just one such example, the national flag of Canada.

Australia has the longest continuous history of any country. We are also unique among the world's nations in that we have a history that over millennia has been richly recorded by its original inhabitants, via their detailed stories, songs and memories passed down from father to son and mother to daughter over millennia. Australia's ancient history has also been most colourfully represented in paintings, rock-art, and a uniquely designed flag that bears the colours: black, yellow and red.[1]

Notes

1. The symbolic meaning of the aboriginal flag colours: Black – represents the Aboriginal people of Australia. Yellow circle – represents the Sun, the giver of life and protector. Red – represents the red earth, the red ochre used in ceremonies and Aboriginal peoples' spiritual relation to the land.

AUSTRALIA'S FLAG

The design of Australia's current flag continues to be regarded by many across the world, as evidence of remaining Australian subservience to the British Crown. Others continue to question why Australia continues to link itself to a monarchy that no longer retains any real relevance to, or has a genuine interest in the country and its population. Britain no longer plays a significant role in Australia's future.

The country's current flag design is, in reality, an anachronistic statement, one that in a real sense continues to anchor Australia to a position of lesser importance and status to that of Britain, a statement that also implies subservience to that now foreign nation's head of state.

Our nation's flag, the nation's outward statement of self, should at the very least represent who we are today, not the different place Australia occupied in the world, in the dim, dark past. It surely needs also to have some reference to the country's history, not only from 1778 onward but also to include some form of recognition of our first Australians.

The history of Aboriginal Australia is a history that belongs to every Australian – whether white, black and every other colour in between, religion or ethnic background represented among Australia's now 24 million citizens. Our flag should proudly represent that history, describing a nation whose story has continued unbroken, almost since the beginning of time.

WHY NOT AN AUSTRALIAN HEAD OF STATE?

Australia, it sometimes needs to be pointed out to some of those among us, is no longer a colony. We are a country that by the year 2017 should have attained the maturity, pride and confidence to feel that we are now capable of appointing one of our own distinguished citizens as our head of state. Call the position what you like – president, governor general, boss-man, boss-woman, head-mate – or another title a majority of the population deems appropriate.

Some of those among us will continue to argue that there is no reason to change Australia's past relationship with Britain, or its inherited head of state from the current format – one in which we share, but rarely see or hear from, Britain's current queen.

Gracious and admired by many as Elizabeth II might well be, Megalogenis' book and a growing number of other writers have noted that the Australian is no longer the same country it was during the 18th and 19th centuries, or even during the earlier half of the 20th century.

Why then, I will continue to ask, do we continue to cringe from taking that final step needed to become a fully independent nation – independent in our own right? What is it that holds us back? What are we really afraid of? Are we so insecure that we continue to feel the need to cling to a relationship, now long gone?

Australia's interests, strategic and cultural, relate more today to our location in the world. The country is no longer a small, totally dependent European outpost, isolated amid Asian neighbours. We are a progressive, prosperous and strong trading nation. Our strategic interests are more related to our country's status and position on the edge of Southern Asia and the Pacific, than to the North Atlantic and Europe.

Our geography, not our history, will determine our future.

Reviewing a much shorter time span, the aspirations of the Australian people today are no longer the same as they were when I first arrived, a mere 60 years ago. Neither is the makeup of the population predominantly British as it was then, with most of its incoming migrants before 1939 having arrived from the United Kingdom and Ireland. Today's Australia is a truly multi-cultural, multi-ethnic, and multi-talented society, drawn from the four corners of the modern world.

We are a people having arrived from every continent, we practice many different religions, and we also have the use of many different tongues.

Why then, do we continue trying to avoid our true destiny?

AUSTRALIA'S CONSTITUTION – DOES IT NEED AN UPDATE?

The time has also arrived to give recognition to the original inhabitants of our country. Australia's constitution was created during the late 19th century, a long distant era. It was designed to meet totally different conditions and status, to those applying today.

There remains no good reason why Australians should feel bound to show allegiance to members of a foreign royal family, a group of people who no longer serve to advance the ongoing interests of the country. The close relationship once existing between Australians and the British royal family is but a remnant of a now long gone past, that gets dimmer by the day, destined soon to be lost in the mists of time and history.

There is another, important issue relating to some current internal arrangements, concerning the process involved with the taking of their oath of office, upon an Australian citizen becoming a new member of Australia's federal parliament. Currently, that process requires the member, on entering Parliament for the first time, to swear their allegiance in the form of:

"I ***** do swear that I will be faithful to Her Majesty Queen Elizabeth II, her heirs and successors, so help me God."

This now outdated oath of allegiance to the crowned head of what in reality is a foreign country. It is also an important issue in need of serious discussion, the question here:

Why is it considered necessary in 2017, for Australian citizens, native-born, naturalised or otherwise, to be required to swear allegiance to the head of state of a foreign government, before them being allowed to sit in the parliament of the country of which they are a sworn, committed and true citizen?

Learned lawyers and others with a mind to do so may well argue over the finer legal points involved with such issues as flag, Australia's current status, its head of state and constitution. The country, regardless of conventional arguments like "why change something if it is continuing to work satisfactorily", surely has arrived at the point in its history when its citizens now need to take the final step toward the creation of 21st-century Australia.

Are we happy to wander along, as described by author Allan Gyngell[1] in his recent book "A Fear of Abandonment": "An Australia that over its contemporary history has continued to live with the fear of being abandoned"?

A growing number of Australia's more forward-thinking citizens, authors and others concerned as to the direction of our country into the future, are continuing to stand up and raise these and similar questions.

Also worth noting on this subject is a recent article by Mark Kenny, the national affairs editor of *The Age* newspaper. In his article, Kenny made some comments and posed questions on the subject of Australia's current position in the world. The following statement, a part of his column published in *The Age* newspaper of August 30th 2017 stated:

> Australia is a nation scared to fully stake out its own flag. Scared to install an Australian as its head of state. Nervous even about bringing into the daylight a more complete account of its own creation.

Australia at this time needs to see some bold, forward-thinking national leadership on such issues. Positive leadership that serves to take its citizens toward a new, adult and more confident conversation that includes the important question: "Where does Australia go from here?"

Notes

1. "A Fear of Abandonment – Australia in the World since 1942", by Allan Gyngell, published by La Trobe University Press 2017.

AUSTRALIA'S RELATIONSHIPS

Looking first at the relationship that existed between Australia and Britain prior to the Second World War, the then mother and child bond that had applied between Britain and its earlier colony, the arrival of the 1940s witnessed the start of its irreversible breakdown.

Australia had by that time reached a crucial stage in its development. The 1940s was period that became etched into the souls of every one of its then 7 million citizens, as the rampaging Japanese Imperial Army threatened to invade their country. The realisation that changes in the country's relationship to Britain were required, was emphasised with even greater force as a result of just one, singularly disastrous and unnecessary loss of 15,000 Australian soldiers to the Japanese invaders, following the fall of Singapore to the Japanese on February 15th 1942.

That military disaster, including the loss of what Britain until then had regarded as an impregnable fortress, robbed Australia of a full division of its defenders. Australia's wartime leaders, only then began to realise that Britain, regardless of earlier words of its then prime minister, Winston Churchill, was unable to defend Australia.

Since the ending of the Second World War, the United States has taken over the mantle of Australia's closest strategic partner and defender. Even here over recent years, an increasing number of the country's citizens, many also concerned with the country's future direction, are questioning the manner in which Australia's more recent relationships with the United States have been developing.

Despite some of the more sycophantic utterings of senior members of successive Australian governments, Australia's military relationships with the US over past years have become close, perhaps too close, too unquestioning and some might say – more than a trifle too obsequious? The latter at least in the way federal government leaders have appeared only too happy to slavishly follow US foreign policy, and its government's apparent relish to involve itself and others among the more pliable of its allies, in a series of disastrous wars.

Who could ever forget the promise of the then US president, George Bush, in praising John Howard, then the Australian prime minister, and his description of Howard as, "a man of steel", following Howard's arbitrary and unilateral decision to commit Australia in full support of the US's invasion of Iraq on March 20th 2003?

The commitment of Australia to that war, unauthorised by the United Nations, was made without consideration of many overwhelmingly contrary reports to the US's assertion that Iraq's president, Saddam Hussein, was amassing weapons of mass destruction. Nor was Howard's decision to partner with the US subjected to the prior approval of or agreement from Australia's federal parliament.

Australia over recent years has followed the US into some very questionable military actions – actions that in every case have proved to be poorly judged, poorly managed, strategically tragic mistakes. The result most apparent here has been one of Australia being led into unnecessary wars, and the poorly thought-through consequences for the populations involved, and the regular, unnecessary loss of Australian lives, reputation and treasure.

Over recent history, it is difficult to find much of anything, with regard to long-lasting security and economic gain to Australia and the country's health, as a result of these military actions. Instead, the wars and other military activities with which Australia allowed itself to become involved, with a degree of hard to understand naiveté, has done more to add to subsequent, continuing terrorist threats to Australians, at home and abroad.

Some might argue that if Australia wishes the US to continue to provide Australia with its umbrella of military security as part of the alliance between the two countries should Australia ever become attacked – Australia should also expect to be required to pay what are often referred to as "Alliance dues".

The obvious question here: "From where can we reasonably expect such a direct attack on Australia to come in the near or middle future? Indonesia, the Philippines, P.R. China, New Guinea, South Korea, Japan, New Zealand or perhaps India – even North Korea? And if so – when and how would such a threat be expected to arrive?"

Does Australia need to keep itself tied to what in effect amounts to a relatively one-sided arrangement to defend, at best a vague comment of questionable value? Shouldn't we Australians, like other similarly sized democracies, be aiming to make alliances among nations of a similar outlook, while at the same time attending to our own preparations for the defence of our country – in the unlikely event of Australia being attacked in the foreseeable future?

Interestingly, it has been suggested recently that Australia is in more danger of being hit by a large, errant lump of celestial rock from outer space, than being attacked from across the seas surrounding us. Perhaps there is some sense in this? The question at least is something needing a far broader range of discussion than that currently apparent among our present national leadership.

Being a nation dependent on a flourishing trading environment suggests the need for Australia to be aiming more to becoming like other similar, prosperous and non-militarily inclined countries – a country confident in our own capabilities, all the while retaining an independent, middle-sized power outlook and attitude toward the world in which we live.

The importance of P.R. China as a major customer for Australia's exports of minerals, food products and services, plus that country's rapidly expanding economic and military importance across the Asian region, requires careful monitoring and an even more careful and thoughtfully crafted style of diplomacy.

China's threat to the US's earlier hegemony in the Pacific and East Asia is growing. This trend alone suggests that Australia should in the future, at the very least be looking to adopt a more independent, less acquiescent position, when dealing with our North American friends, in particular their recently elected president.

Recent revelations of Chinese activities involving the buying up and control of Australian agricultural land, the recent purchase of the Port of Darwin by Chinese interests, a number of other Australian companies, and major rural properties need to be carefully monitored and controlled. Add to this the amount of financial largesse being splashed around by Chinese businessmen. The object here seems to be one of exerting influence over Australian government and local business leaders? Any kind of activity having the potential to damage Australia's worldwide and home-based interests needs to be controlled and defended against with firm resolution.

Australia in the future should, at the very least, seek to stake out for itself a more delicately balanced, more carefully defined and developed position in the world, particularly when dealing with our long-time friend, the United States, and a China that has become the first among Australia's major customers.

Surely, we are a country having the confidence, inner strength and financial capacity to be capable of operating and making decisions based on our own long-term interests – independent of any current world-dominating power, or political grouping?

To follow such an independent line requires a high level of inspired leadership and a correspondingly high level of flexible and influential diplomacy. Judging from performances over recent years, few of our national leaders to date have shown either the strength, or the independent and creative capacity that such a role requires.

There is a need for Australia to adopt a role that truly represents the aspirations and identity of a people, no longer 'British-to-the-bootstraps,' as claimed by an Australian prime minister in an earlier age – Sir Robert Menzies. Australia is approaching the third decade of the 21st century. Surely the country has reached the stage where it should by now be capable of demonstrating independence, self-confidence and an outward-looking foreign policy – fearing none, powerful enough both in mind and arm, to assert its strength and protect its citizens, while at the same time striding out along its chosen path into the future.

I also look forward to the time when we Australians can show genuine pride in not just 200 years of history but our over 50,000+-year-long heritage.

Hopefully the nation will eventually attain maturity and reconciliation, as evidenced by the inclusion of a strong representation of Australia's Aboriginal culture and colours, alongside the stars of the Southern Cross. Only then will our original Australians feel included in our nation's statement of self. We need to project these powerful symbols as part of the design of a new Australian flag – both elements set above a much smaller rendition of the Union Jack, on the flag of a newly established Republic of Australia.

I look forward to that day in hope, pride and anticipation.

AND FINALLY…

Something that continues to eat into my soul also needs to be stated:

As I write here, the Australian Human Rights Commission reports that over 1,000 human beings (including children) remain in detention on tropical islands to Australia's north. Many of these unfortunate people have, over a number of years, been subjected to inhuman treatment. All attempted to arrive and settle in Australia by the use of 'people smugglers'. According to the United Nations, they are people who conform to the classification 'refugee'. As such, they are entitled to receive humane treatment and succour.

They have done no wrong. They tried to come to Australia leaving life threatening situations in the countries of their birth, much in the same way as my grandparents did when they pleaded for asylum in Britain at the turn of the 20th century.

Alex Miller, in his essay described earlier, made an eloquent plea for Australia to show compassion to those adults and children remaining in detention on Manus and Nauru. I wish here to echo his thoughts and go further to request the Australian government to allow those remaining in Australian sponsored detention to now settle in Australia – less, of course, those who perhaps will be taken up by the US as part of the earlier agreement between the Australian prime minister, Malcolm Turnbull, and the US president, Barack Obama.

As things stand today, the majority of Australians will continue to support the government's strong stance on people trying to arrive on Australia's shores via unauthorised small boats and people smugglers. Both sides of politics are in total agreement with the need to continue to enforce strong border protection.

While recent prime ministers past and present have declared a policy of 'none shall pass', surely it is within the power of the Australian government, its conscience and humanity, to end the suffering of the few remaining long-term detainees currently held on Manus and Nauru. Haven't they suffered enough?

We now have the power to ensure that no further unauthorised incursions into Australia's waters will be tolerated. The government already has turned back a number of such attempts, so there is no convincing reason to suggest that we cannot in all humanity declare a cessation of detention, at least for those genuine refugees among the human beings still being held. Those refugees remaining should be allowed to enter Australia on the basis of their agreement to conform to Australia's laws, values and customs.

Such a move would not weaken Australia's position in the world one iota, nor would it be seen as a weakness on Australia's part and an opportunity for a new rush of unauthorised boats trying to make their way to Australia's shores. That possibility is now well within the capability of Australia's Border Force to close off and maintain it so into the future.

The people now in detention have suffered enough. Now is the time for Australia to show that it is not afraid to make a change, when such a change in response to a humanitarian need is warranted. Why can't we for once show the rest of the world that Australians can and often do, change their minds, where the health and danger of fellow human beings demand such a change be made?

Let them come to live in safety and peace, along with the other over 60% of the population, also relative newcomers for the most part, who were immigrants or are the children of earlier immigrants.

The one real certainty regarding the future today is that life will continue, regardless, unless and until our little planet has the bad luck one of these days, to find itself in the way of a very large out of control chunk of space rock, sometime in the not-too-distant future. Not too soon I hope?

That being the case, I plan to continue exploring further what my one among many millions of lives can continue to offer to the world.

Who knows what new opportunities will present themselves over the years still left to me? Maybe I will continue to be blessed with the strength, capability and opportunity to experience new things? Perhaps I will continue to travel, experience and photograph new places? Perhaps also I might even attempt to master a new language, or even commence writing yet another book?

Above all, I will seek peace, wisdom, patience and understanding, with the offer of love and friendship to all I continue to meet along life's way…

Gerry Dubbin
Hastings, Victoria, Australia

REFERENCES

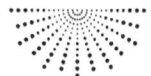

1. AUSTRALIAN HISTORY – WHERE TO FROM HERE?

George Megalogenis, referred to earlier in this book – the author of "Australia's Second Chance", asks perhaps the most important question confronting the country today – how do we maintain our winning streak?

Following what Megalogenis' book describes with the words, "Our future is in our foundation," "Australia's Second Chance" goes back to 1788, the first contact between locals and migrants, to provide a unique and fascinating view of some of the critical events of Australia's past, right through to the present day.

"Australia's Second Chance" includes newly available economic data and fresh interviews with former leaders (including the last major interview with Malcolm Fraser). George Megalogenis crunches the numbers and weaves Australia's history into a compelling thesis, brilliantly chronicling our dialogue with the world and bringing fresh insight into the urgent question of who we are, and what we can become.

2. CAPTAIN JAMES COOK

Captain Cook's Journal. First Voyage around the world in H.M. Bark Endeavour 1768–1771 – Project Gutenberg Australia. *gutenberg.net.au/ebooks/e00043.html*

This is a literal transcription of Cook's original journal. The publication, available as an iBook, is recommended reading for anyone interested in obtaining details of one of the world's most famous voyages of discovery and surveying.

3. THE GWEAGAL PEOPLE

The Gweagal (also spelt Gwiyagal) is a clan of the Tharawal (or Dharawal) tribe of Indigenous Australians, who are traditional custodians of the southern geographic areas of Sydney, New South Wales, Australia. The Gweagal lived on the southern shores of Botany Bay (Kurnell Peninsula).

en.wikipedia.org/wiki/Gweagal

4. THE AUSTRALIAN WOOL INDUSTRY

Many books, newspaper and journal reports, TV and radio broadcasts, speeches and other analyses have been produced over many years, on different aspects of this industry, once critical to the economic well-being of Australia. Following are a small selection of contemporary writings and reports that the reader may find of interest.

4.1 Technical

"Wool Processing on the Cotton System: A Comparison Between Cut-Top Wool and Six-Month Shorn Wool in a Blend with Polyester", by Christopher J. Lupton. First published February 1st 1980.
journals.sagepub.com/doi/abs/10.1177/004051758005000212

Abstract:

Fiber blends composed of cut-top wool/polyester and short-shorn wool/polyester in the ratio of 60:40 were processed on the short-staple system of spinning into 49.2 mg/m (12/1 N_o) and 98.4 mg/m (6/1 N_o) yarns. Subsequently, apparel and home-furnishing fabrics were woven and their physical properties were measured. Generally, fabrics containing cut-top wool exhibited higher grab strengths than their short-shorn wool counterparts. Conversely, resistance to flex abrasion tended to be better in the case of the fabrics composed of short-shorn wool/polyester. Other fabric properties including tear strength, shrinkage due to home launderings, and appearance after home launderings were very similar.

4.2 Wool Industry

The Australian newspaper – July 30th 2011. "How Wool Was Pulled over Investors' Eyes." www.theaustralian.com.au/news/inquirer/how-wool-was-pulled-over-investors-eyes/news-story/cab8089aa5329c15b3181cbea4bb6bb8

This article was a then-current description of the disaster that befell a once great industry. The article records how, over earlier years, that the seeds of what was to come in the early 1990s were planted well before the 1980s and involved corruption at the highest levels of the country.

A later report titled "How an Industry Got Fleeced" was essentially a report together with the newspaper's comments, on Charles Massy's book "Breaking the Sheep's Back". Both make interesting and illuminating reading.

ABC Rural. "60 Years of the Country Hour – The Rise and Fall of the Wool Industry." by Georgia Bateman, dated March 28th 2006 (also discussed in a later audio report in 2014).

Bateman referred back to 1973, when Sir William Gunn, the then chairman of the Australian Wool Corporation stated: "the wool industry is broke with prices at rock bottom". This was when the now infamous Reserve Floor Price Scheme was introduced as a disaster relief mechanism. The broadcast went on to discuss issues relating to the eventual collapse of the RPS scheme.

Farm Weekly (Western Australia). A special feature of this rural newspaper published on July 21st 2011 titled "Wool on the Move", a report following 20 years since AWC's reserve price scheme was abolished.

This review covered a number of issues facing the wool industry. These titled "Wool's Tough Climb", "Fleeced", "Why Not $20? – AWI Boss Raises the Wool Price Bar", "Wool's Chequered Past" and "The Major Players Look Back". The feature also includes comments and articles from a variety of industry people in which they provide their view of both the past and some thoughts into the future.

The feature was comprehensive in its coverage, providing a summary after the event and a selection of opinions of where things went wrong. It ends with a page: "On the Record", in which it cites comments that had been made from time to time, across a wide range of wool industry executives, growers and others.

Mercardo Blog. "Australian Wool Industry – Is it All Doom and Gloom?" posted by Robert Herrman –December 10th 2015.

This industry-oriented blog provided a number of opinions on the blogger's views relating to various issues, mainly those facing woolgrowers. Headings discussed in the blog relate to: Prices (but wool prices are not low). Is it all too hard? Rest easy – It's not all doom and gloom, and Where is the innovation?

The foregoing are but a small selection of many other publications and other information, much of which continue to discuss and define the woolgrowing industry and those who have been appointed in the hope of improving the standing and profitability of the industry.

www.ingramcontent.com/pod-product-compliance
Lightning Source LLC
Chambersburg PA
CBHW022226010526
44113CB00033B/484